Wordsworth's Bardic Vocation, 1787–1842

On the 1st edition of *Wordsworth's Bardic Vocation*

'[This] erudite exposition, profligate with its ideas ... succeeds as few others have done in apprehending Wordsworth's career holistically, incorporating all its diversities and apparent inconsistencies into a unified vision. It justifies fully the notion proposed by Hughes and Heaney that he was England's last national poet. '
—Duncan Wu, *Review of English Studies*

'A remarkable account of Wordsworth's long writing life, with something fresh and often provocative to say about its many extraordinary poetic achievements, both famous and forgotten. It is difficult to imagine a better explicator of this most complex of modern poets: Gravil is scholarly and humane, sharp-eyed and good-humoured.'
—Seamus Perry, Balliol College, Oxford

'This outstandingly original book reveals in fascinating detail how William Wordsworth—prophet of nature, remembrancer of his kind—attuned his poetry to the bardic voices of the ancient world. Embracing the full diversity of Wordsworth's career.... the Wordsworth that emerges is freshly situated in his own cultural milieu and times, and speaks to us with renewed vitality.'
—Nicholas Roe, University of St Andrews

'Richard Gravil's richly rewarding monograph is ... one of the most important publications on Wordsworth in recent years'
—Matthew Scott, *Yearbook of English Studies*

'Engaged and refreshingly direct ... this is criticism which discusses craft and concept with equal facility and insight.'
—Damian Walford Davies, *Romanticism*

Also by Richard Gravil

Wordsworth: The Prelude, a Casebook
edited with W J Harvey (1972)

Swift: Gulliver's Travels, a Casebook (1974)

Coleridge's Imagination: Essays for Pete Laver
edited with Lucy Newlyn and Nicholas Roe (1985)

The Coleridge Connection: Essays for Thomas McFarland,
edited with Molly Lefebure (1990)

Romantic Dialogues: Anglo-American Continuities, 1776–1862 (2000)

Master Narratives: Tellers and Telling in the English Novel. Essays for Bill Ruddick (2001)

Wordsworth and Helen Maria Williams; or, the Perils of Sensibility (2010)

The Oxford Handbook of William Wordsworth
edited with Daniel Robinson (2015)

Wordsworth's Bardic Vocation, 1787–1842

Richard Gravil

2nd edition, revised and enlarged

$\mathcal{HEB}$ ☼ Humanities-Ebooks

Cover image Frontispiece: *The Bard* (1774) by Thomas Jones of Pencerrig,
© Amgueddfa Genedlaethol Cymru
National Museum of Wales, Cardiff

First published by Palgrave-Macmillan in 2003.
Second revised edition published in 2015 by Humanities-Ebooks, LLP
Tirril Hall, Tirril, Penrith CA10 2JE.

This book is available in Kindle format from Amazon, as an ePub from Google, in paperback from Lulu.com, and to libraries (in PDF) from EBSCO and Ebrary

The PDF is available to individuals exclusively from
http://www.humanities-ebooks.co.uk.

ISBN 978-1-84760-344-9 PDF
ISBN 978-1-84760-345-6 Paperback
ISBN 978-1-84760-346-3 Kindle
ISBN 978-1-84760-347-0 ePub

For
Richard Wordsworth
1919–1993

If there is a cry on the hill,
Is it not Urien that terrifies?
If there is cry in the valley,
Is it not Urien that pierces?
If there is a cry in the mountain,
Is it not Urien that conquers?

—*The Book of Taliesin*

The three primary and indispensible requisites of POETIC GENIUS *are, an* EYE THAT CAN SEE NATURE, *a* HEART THAT CAN FEEL NATURE, *and a* RESOLUTION THAT DARES FOLLOW NATURE.

—Iolo Morganwg, *Poems Lyrics and Pastoral*

A bard is to be commensurate with a people…. His spirit responds to the country's spirit … he incarnates its geography and natural life and rivers and lakes…. To him enter the essences of real things and past and present events….

—Walt Whitman, *'Preface' to Leaves of Grass*

Contents

PART 4

WORDSWORTH AND KINDLINESS

EPILOGUE

Preface and Acknowledgements

I am most grateful to Brigitte Shull of Palgrave in New York for the opportunity to revise this work, first published by Palgrave-Macmillan in 2003.

The great temptation in revising this book was to expand it enormously, restoring chapters reluctantly omitted from the first edition (including three chapters on *The Prelude*), and splicing in all I have done, or half done, since *Wordsworth's Bardic Vocation* first appeared. On the whole I have resisted that temptation. The best of those omitted chapters, '"Some other Being"; Wordsworth in *The Prelude*' (*YWES*, 1989) has in any case already re-appeared in Stephen Gill's Oxford casebook on *The Prelude* (2006) and has been complemented in my *Wordsworth and Helen Maria Williams; or, the Perils of Sensibility* (2010).

I have, however, enlarged the treatment of some poems where it appears from responses (or non-responses) to the first edition that I had left matters implicit that needed to be made explicit. Here and there, while placing the notes and references where they belong, I have also taken the opportunity to respond to critical debate in the years since the book first appeared. Also, where it seemed appropriate I have changed textual references to what is now the closest approximation we have to a standard, complete reading edition of Wordsworth, namely Jared Curtis's three-volume paperback edition of *The Poems of William Wordsworth: Collected Readig Texts from the Cornell Wordsworth* (Humanities-Ebooks, 2009) with its electronic *Addendum*. The major change is the inclusion, as an epilogue, of one of numerous recent attempts to understand the *Ode: Intimations of Immortality*.

As stated in the 2003 edition, my specific debts are, I hope, fully acknowledged, but to Hugh Dent, schoolmaster, and to John F. Danby, my first year tutor as an undergraduate at Bangor, I owe an interest in Wordsworth that has lasted almost sixty years. In unsimpling *The Simple Wordsworth* so unpretentiously, John Danby stimulated much of the Wordsworth renaissance of the sixties and seventies. Like most students of Wordsworth, I find myself perpetually 'discovering' some facet of Wordsworth which in reality Geoffrey Hartman expressed definitively long ago. The work of Paul Sheats and Stephen Parrish in recovering Wordsworth's experimental art, of Mary Jacobus and Alan Bewell and David Simpson in placing that art in significant contexts, and of Jonathan Wordsworth in recovering not only Wordsworth's texts but those of his age, have had immeasurable effects. Parts of this book got started with the aid of advice from Mary Wedd, and from P. W. Davies at the National Library of Wales. Without the lights cast by Prys Morgan, A. L. Owen, Nora Chadwick, T. D. Kendrick and Gwyn Williams the Welsh *terra* would be as wholly *incognita* to me as it is to most English and American readers. Stephen Gill's biography, re-read in 2001, has been infinitely suggestive.

I owe, as do many others, an enormous debt to Richard and Sylvia Wordsworth, whose Wordsworth Summer Conference (continued by the Wordsworth Conference Foundation which I co-founded for that purpose, with a team of Trustees) has for almost over forty years provided each Summer with its warmest and brightest moments. Participants in this event who have fed my thoughts on Wordsworth include John Beer, Tony Brinkley, David Bromwich, Mark Bruhn, Annette Cafarelli, Heather Glen, Kenneth Johnston, Thomas McFarland, Lucy Newlyn, the late W. J. B. Owen, Joel Pace, Adam Potkay, Daniel Robinson, Nicholas Roe, David Simpson, Gordon Thomas, E. P. Thompson, Nicola Trott, Robert Woof, Jonathan Wordsworth and Duncan Wu. For needful encouragement to continue with this work at various junctures in the 1990s, Frederick Burwick, David Erdman, Norman Fruman, Kate Fullbrook, Marilyn Gaull, Molly Lefebure, Chris Moss, Michael O'Neill, Yvonne Pearson and Seamus Perry are especially culpable. Over many years (indeed over more than two decades) I received much expert help from the late Pete Laver, Jeff Cowton, Stephen Hebron, and other staff at Dove Cottage Library.

Quotations from Dove Cottage manuscripts are by permission of the Trustees. Quotations from Geoffrey Hill's *Collected Poems* are by permission of the poet, Penguin Books and Houghton Mifflin. Chapter 6 is reprinted (revised) with permission of the editors of *Romanticism* (where it appeared as 'Tintern Abbey and the System of Nature') and chapter 5 is based more loosely on 'Lyrical Ballads (1798): Wordsworth as Ironist', first published in *Critical Quarterly.* Numerous other chapters were first aired as lectures at the Wordsworth Summer Conference or Winter School. A version of the epilogue was composed for Mary Wedd's 90th birthday issue of *The Charles Lamb Bulletin*.

I live now in the village where Wordsworth's grandfather, aunt, brother and nephew lived, withn daily sight of Blencathra and of Penrith Beacon, and near the homes of Sir Lancelot Threlkeld (who sheltered the Shepherd Lord), Thomas Wilkinson the Quaker poet, and Thomas Clarkson the anti-slavery campaigner.

For that, and for the deepest joys of my life, I thank Fiona, who first introduced me to the Lake District (and its tinkling crags and muttering rocks) almost exactly forty-six years ago.

Tirril, December 2014

Abbreviations

1816	*Thanksgiving Ode, January 18, 1816. With other short pieces, chiefly referring to recent public events.* London: Longman, Hurst, 1816
Bewell	Alan Bewell, *Wordsworth and the Enlightenment: Nature, Man and Society in the Experimental Poetry.* New Haven and London: Yale University Press, 1989.
Bialostosky	Don H. Bialostosky, *Making Tales: The Poetics of Wordsworth's Narrative Experiments.* Chicago & London: University of Chicago Press, 1984
BL	*Biographia Literaria*, ed. James Engell and Walter Jackson Bate. 2 vols. London and Princeton: Routledge & Kegan Paul and Princeton University Press, 1983.
Borders	Jonathan Wordsworth, *William Wordsworth: The Borders of Vision.* Oxford: Clarendon Press, 1982
Borderers	*The Borderers,* ed. Robert Osborn. Cornell, 1982.
BWS	*Bicentenary Wordsworth Studies*, ed Jonathan Wordsworth. Ithaca, NY & London: Cornell University Press, 1970.
CLB	*Charles Lamb Bulletin*
Cintra	*Concerning the Convention of Cintra: a Critical Edition*, ed. W J B Owen and Richard Gravil. Penrith: Humanities-Ebooks, 2008.
CN	*The Notebooks of Samuel Taylor Coleridge, Volume 1, 1794–1804*, ed. Kathleen Coburn. London: Routledge Kegan Paul, 1957.
Cornell	The Cornell Wordsworth. General Editor: Stephen M. Parrish. Ithaca, NY: Cornell University Press.
CWRT	*The Poems of William Wordsworh: Collected Reading Texts from the Cornell Wordsworth*, ed. Jared R Curtis. 3 vols. Penrith: Humanities-Ebooks, 2009.

Danby	John F. Danby, *The Simple Wordsworth: Studies in the Poems, 1797–1807*. London: Routledge & Kegan Paul, 1960.
EPF	*Early Poems and Fragments, 1785–97*, ed. Carol Landon and Jared Curtis. Cornell, 1997.
EW	*An Evening Walk*, ed. James Averill. Cornell, 1984.
Excursion	*The Excursion, 1814*. Oxford & New York: Woodstock Books, 1991.
EY	*The Letters of William and Dorothy Wordsworth: The Early Years*, ed. Ernest de Selincourt, 2nd edn, rev. Chester L Shaver. Oxford: Clarendon Press, 1967.
FN	*The Fenwick Notes of William Wordsworth*, ed. Jared Curtis, 2nd edition, revised and corrected, Penrith: Humanities-Ebooks, 2007.
Gill	Stephen Gill, *William Wordsworth: A Life*. Oxford: Clarendon Press, 1989.
Griggs	*Collected Letters of Samuel Taylor* Coleridge, ed. Earl Leslie Griggs. 6 vols. Oxford: Clarendon Press, 1956–71.
HG	*Home at Grasmere*, ed. Beth Darlington, Cornell, 1977.
Jacobus	*Mary Jacobus, Tradition and Experiment in Wordsworth Lyrical Ballads, 1798*. Oxford: Clarendon Press, 1976.
LBOP	*Lyrical Ballads and Other Poems*, ed. James Butler and Karen Green. Cornell, 1992.
LY	*The Letters of William and Dorothy Wordsworth: The Later Years*, ed. Ernest de Selincourt, 2nd edn, 4 vols, rev. Alan G Hill. Oxford: Clarendon Press, 1978–88.
McFarland	Thomas McFarland, *William Wordsworth: Intensity and Achievement*. Oxford: Clarendon Press, 1992.
Moorman	Mary Moorman, *William Wordsworth: A Biography*. 2 vols. Oxford: Clarendon Press, 1957.
MY	*The Letters of William and Dorothy Wordsworth: The Middle Years,* ed. Ernest de Selincourt, 2nd edn, 2 vols, rev. Mary Moorman and Alan G Hill. Oxford: Clarendon Press, 1969–70.

OHWW	*The Oxford Handbook of William Wordsworth.* ed. Richard Gravil and Daniel Robinson, Oxford University Press, 2015.
Parrish	Stephen Maxfield Parrish, *The Art of the Lyrical Ballads.* Cambridge MA: Harvard University Press, 1973.
P2V	*Poems, in Two Volumes, 1807.* Poole and Washington DC: Woodstock, 1997.
PELY	*Poems Chiefly of Early and Late Years.* London: Edward Moxon, 1842.
Potts	Abbie Findlay Potts. *Wordsworth's Prelude: A Study of its Literary Form.* Ithaca NY: Cornell UP, 1953.
Prelude	*The Prelude: The Four Texts (1798, 1799, 1805, 1850),* ed. Jonathan Wordsworth. Harmondsworth: Penguin, 1995.
PW	*The Poetical Works of William Wordsworth*, ed Ernest de Selincourt and Helen Darbishire. 5 vols. Oxford: Oxford University Press, 1940–49.
PrW	*The Prose Works of William Wordsworth*, ed. W. J. B. Owen and Jane Worthington Smyser. 3 vols. Oxford: Clarendon Press, 1974. Vols 2 & 3.
RCP	*The Ruined Cottage and the Pedlar*, ed. James Butler. Cornell, 1979.
Sensibility	Richard Gravil, *Wordsworth and Helen Maria Williams; or, the Perils of Sensibility.* Penrith: Humanities-Ebooks, 2010.
Simpson	David Simpson, *Wordsworth's Historical Imagination: The Poetry of Displacement.* New York & London: Methuen, 1987.
SPK	*Shorter Poems, 1807–1820*, ed. Carl H. Ketcham. Cornell, 1989
SPP	*The Salisbury Plain Poems*, ed. Stephen Gill. Cornell, 1975.
TWC	*The Wordsworth Circle*
WD	*The White Doe of Rylstone*, ed. Kristine Dugas. Cornell, 1988.

Woof	Robert Woof, *William Wordsworth: The Critical Heritage*. London & New York: Routledge, 2001.
WPW	*Wordsworth's Political Writings*, ed. W. J. B. Owen and Jane Worthington Smyser. Penrith: Humanities-Ebooks, 2009.
Wu	Duncan Wu, *Wordsworth's Reading, 1770–1779*. Cambridge: Cambridge University Press, 1993.

Introduction

SCREAMING SEAMEWS and a blasted tree; storm clouds and a cruel wind from the east; the flanks of Snowdon, adorned with a truant henge; bodies of apprentice bards and druids strewn from recent massacre; the distant army of Edward the Bardicide making its way through a mountain pass; and Gray's bard. His hand stretched, as if to say 'no pasaran', the Bard foretells the triumph of the Tudors and the revival of British poetry by Talisesin's distant heirs, before plunging to his death into the unseen river Conway. Thus, on the cover of this book, Thomas Jones of Pencerrig realizes the scenario imagined in Thomas Gray's *The Bard* of 1757, the defining pre-Romantic image of the Romantic poet, his purpose and his lineage.

Poets, according to Wordsworth in *The Prelude*, are 'even as prophets, each with each / Connected in a mighty scheme of truth', within which scheme each poet has 'for his peculiar dower, a sense / By which he is enabled to perceive / Something unseen before'. This sense of an unbroken bardic inheritance introduces the ostensibly modest plea:

> forgive me friend,
> If I, *the meanest of this band*, had hope
> That unto me had also been vouchsafed
> An influx— (*1805*, 12.301–5)[1]

Readers of Thomas Gray will recognize my added emphasis. Wordsworth aptly echoes the humility of the British bard, Aneirin, as he sings in Gray's powerful translation of the momentous defeat of 300 Britons at Catterick:

> But none from Cattraeth's vale return,
> Save Aeron brave, and Conan strong,

---

1 Quotations from *The Prelude* (identified as *1805* or *1850*), are, unless otherwise indicated, from *The Prelude: The Four Texts (1798, 1799, 1805, 1850)*, ed. Jonathan Wordsworth (Harmondsworth: Penguin, 1985).

(Bursting through the bloody throng)
And I, the meanest of them all,
That live to weep and sing their fall—[1]

Aneirin, as David Jones put it in his great verse novel *In Parenthesis*, was the poet of 'that time of obscurity when north Britain was still largely in Celtic possession'.[2] The deeds and the poetry of 'the men of the north', of Cumbria and Strathclyde, forgotten in Saxon England, lived in Welsh memory and enjoyed a Romantic resurrection in Wordsworth's youth.

A minor aim of this book is to illumine Wordsworth's career-long fascination with that eighteenth-century re-invention of the Northern Bards and the Ancient British Druids; the major one is to demonstrate the integrity of Wordsworth's sense of poetic vocation, and the kind of 'natural piety' whereby traces of his earliest minstrelsy endure throughout the career. My starting point in Part 1, which is a kind of overture, is the sublimation in Wordsworth's oeuvre of the antiquarian impulse that raged during his youth. (Readers impatient with the antiquarian may wish to skip these chapters: for which reason I thumbnail them in the next few pages). Ossian may well have been a 'Phantom', as Wordsworth said in his best joke, 'begotten by the snug embrace of an impudent Highlander upon a cloud of tradition' (*Prose Works*, 3: 77, 'Essay Supplementary') but Taliesin—whether an individual or, as some modern scholars believe, a generic figure—and Aneirin, whose work he knew, are another matter. Wordsworth's scepticism about the recovery of any authentic ancient British history appears in the title of the ecclesiastical sonnet *Uncertainty*. Like Milton, he never subscribed to the truth-claims of the wilder antiquarians. Milton remarked in his *History of Britain* that of British affairs 'from the first peopling of the iland to the coming of Julius Caesar, nothing certain, either by Tradition, History, or Ancient Fame hath hitherto been left us' but he nonetheless devoted Book 1 of his history to reviewing such non-history.[3] Wordsworth pronounced decisively in the *Ecclesiastical Sonnets* that no such researches have led to 'an unquestionable source'. But finding life in our embers (as in *Intimations*)

1   Thomas Gray, cited from Edward Jones, *Musical and Poetical Relicks of the Welsh Bards: Preserved by Tradition, and Authentic Manuscripts* (1794) 2nd edn (London: 1794), 17.
2   David Jones, *In Parenthesis* (Faber & Faber, 1963), 191.
3   *Complete Prose Works of John Milton*, Volume 5, *History of Britain*, ed. French Fogle (New Haven & London: Yale UP 1971), 2.

was always important to Wordsworth. Wanting to believe, he struggled like the eighteenth-century antiquarians against what Camden called 'the iniquitie of time'.[1]

So the 'Sacred Bards and wise Druides', as Drayton called them, appear in Wordsworth's work at regular intervals from 1787 to 1842. In *The Vale of Esthwaite*, in *Salisbury Plain*, in *The Prelude* and *The Excursion*, druidic reveries provide a major climax. The variety of druidism selected by Wordsworth's imagination sometimes resists the prevailing liberal or even Jacobin reconstructions of druidism in the late eighteenth century, reverting to 'a more than Roman' sense of druids as men of power. Fostered alike by beauty and by fear, he sometimes adopts Lucan's picture of druids as barbarous priests who worship 'dreadful power' and 'lustrate every tree with human gore',[2] while at other times he portrays druid rites as worshipping nature herself, or an androgynous duality of sky-god and earth-goddess. Both visions coexist in *Salisbury Plain*. Even in *The Prelude*, the genial druidism so prominent in the work of eighteenth-century poets, cohabits with the anatomizing, divining, and generally unsoftened image presented by the Roman military historians.[3] Wordsworth seems as unwilling to resolve this ambivalence as he is to anatomize the hiding places of his power in the personal 'spots of time'.

It is much the same with the bards, in so far as bards and druids can be separated in Wordsworth's day. The poet figures himself in his reveries

---

1   Camden, *Britannia*, 4; cited by John E. Curran Jr in 'The History Never Written: Bards, Druids, and the Problem of Antiquarianism in Poly Olbion', *Renaissance Quarterly* 51 (1998) 498–525, 502. Curran cites Camden on the problem of reliance on lost oral traditions: the Druids 'were supposed to have known all that was past' and the Bards 'used to resound in song all valorous and noble acts' yet the proper conclusion to be drawn from such sources as Caesar and Gildas is 'that no authentic trace of ancient British life exists, thanks to "the iniquitie of time"'.

2   Marcus Annaeus Lucan. *Pharsalia*, tr. Nicholas Rowe (London 1779), 1.597–8.

3   A. L. Owen summarized the matter in a much-quoted (and misunderstood) passage: 'Curiously enough, since he was interested in Druid stones, in the Druids who knew the secrets of Nature, the Druids who had known the Patriarchs, the Druids who lived in Drayton's "darksome groves" and the Druids who waved Toland's white wands in his vision on Salisbury Plain of the long-bearded teachers, his only point of contact with the Druids as they had been described in the original [that is, Latin] sources is with the sacrificers of men.' *The Famous Druids: a Survey of three centuries of English Literature on the Druids* (Oxford: Clarendon Press, 1962), 166. This passage is usually quoted as if it means that Wordsworth's druids are always Roman: Owen's point, I think, is that the poet seemed unaware of Roman sources for other aspects of druidism.

as Minstrel or apprentice Bard, a professional associate of the druids, and as a descendant, therefore of Taliesin and Aneirin, bards who belonged as much to Cumbria as to Cambria, if not more. Wordsworth's bards duly lament the fallen, but they also prefer swords to harps. In referring to Taliesin, Wordsworth pays little attention to Taliesin's Pedlar-like early life as a herdsman, educating himself—one Celtic scholar says—'by close observation of all visible phenomena in earth and sky'[1] Nor does he respond to the legendary Llywarch Hên or Myrddin the Caledonian as poets of Nature. A dawn description ascribed to Taliesin in Wordsworth's day inspired the post-Romantic J. G. Evans to this encomium: 'sun and smoke alike awake that homing instinct which sees beyond the horizon, obliterating the present in the future. Truly, the magnificats of the mountain induce that mystical lucidity of mind and soul which transfigures life and its destiny' (J. G. Evans, xxxix.) No such tribute to bardic sweetness appears in Wordsworth. Perhaps, given his claim to have been vouchsafed 'something unseen before', a new vision of the features of the common world invested with transcendent significance by the imaginative and loving mind, Wordsworth cannot afford to recognize in his bardic forebears what he wishes to present as his own 'peculiar dower'. So, one might argue, his Bards are blood-stirring, and his Druids remain blood-letting, despite a century of poetic reclamation, because he can permit them to retain only what he does not share with them.

The problem with this mildly Bloomian argument is that he does share—spasmodically—this warlike vein. In 1802 and 1815 Wordsworth studies whole-heartedly in the sinew-stiffening school of Bardic utterance, just as in 1793 and 1805, on Salisbury Plain, he shares their 'daring sympathies with power'. His work absorbs and fuses both the hard and the soft primitivisms of his forebears. The soft primitivism, not always recognized as such, produces such characteristic poems as 'It is the first mild day of March', the Lucy poems, *Nutting* and even *The Poem upon the Wye*. The hard primitivism produces sonnets to the 'Men of Kent' and of 'Killikranky', and odes to the sublime sacrifice of Waterloo.

It is hard to read accounts of druidic lore, as collated and elaborated by some scholars (and forgers) of the eighteenth century without feeling that one is getting, essentially, a spiritual profile of William Wordsworth. Stukeley's druids are much closer to Christian orthodoxy

1   J. G. Evans, ed. *Facsimile and Text of The Book of Taliesin* (Llanbedrog, 1910), xxxv–vi.

than Wordsworth often comes, but his are exceptional; the doctrine-free spirituality of *On revisiting the Wye* (to give it Wordworth's alternative title), sits comfortably with mainstream accounts. This great overture to Wordsworth's philosophic song might even be termed the apotheosis of druidism—the liberal humanist guise in which Iolo Morganwg's religion of nature passed into the Victorian psyche cleansed of all such association with the forged, the suspect, or the antiquarian. The Gauls had some savage customs, Pomponius Mela wrote in 50 AD, but there were among them 'teachers of wisdom called druids'. These professed to know 'the greatness and shape of the earth and the universe, and the motion of the heavens and of the stars'; they taught in their caves or 'secluded groves' that 'souls are everlasting, and that among the shades there is another life'.[1] If Mela's druids sound Wordsworthian, it is because Wordsworth's intercourse with the 'motion' of the earth and of the clouds, and 'that uncertain heaven / Received into the bosom of the steady lake', and his intimations of pagan immortality in what he variously called 'the narrow house', 'the sunless land' or the 'fields of sleep', had a long ancestry.

Having seen himself in *Prelude* Book 12 as 'the meanest of the band' (as quoted above), Wordsworth is already, in ascending Snowdon in Book 14, 'the foremost of the band', confident that he has seen something unseen before and fit to be transmitted. Part of that something is *The Prelude*'s theme of 'genuine liberty', the marriage of Imagination and Love. Part of it is announced in the 'Prospectus' to the Recluse. In a passage which explains obliquely the conspicuous absence from his poetry of the detritus of classical mythology Wordsworth announces a human-centred mythopoeia which promises to restore to men and women in whom love and imagination are co-operant, a saving access to three realms: realms of innocence, realms of the blessed, and realms of the heroic dead, or, in the familiar triad, 'Paradise and groves / Elysian, Fortunate Fields'. These three terms, well-known to all Wordsworthians but cordially ignored by most, open windows upon doctrinally diverse worlds. They might be glossed with reference to Milton in his 'holiest mood', to Virgil, or to the legends of the Celts whose 'fortunate isles' lay to the West of Ireland. All three, in the new mythus, will be no longer 'A history only of departed things, / Or a mere fiction of what never was,' but rather 'A simple produce of the common day.' It is an enigmatic dec-

---

1   *De Chorographia*, Book 3, cited in Nora Chadwick, *The British Heroic Age: The Welsh and the Men of the North* (University of Wales Press, 1976), 29.

laration but a helpful one. Frequently, in Wordsworth's most familiar and most impressive poems, the Elysian sublime counterpoints the Paradisal: the theme of Elysium, as the abode of the blessed after death, is disconcertingly pervasive.

Part 1 of this Book, 'The World of Shades', investigates what might be termed Welsh Wordsworth. There has been much work on Wordsworth and Wales, but as far as I can see, none that recognises that the Welsh poetry he knew of may have been largely the creation of the kingdoms either side of the Solway Firth in the heroic age when the land of Wordsworth, Scott and Burns was known as Rheged. I look at the traces in Wordsworth's work of a long fascination with druidical and bardic lore as received in Wordsworth's day (I deal less with their authenticity, which is negligible, than with their contemporary 'historicity'). Anyone reading Wordsworth chronologically will note that his early work is invariably touched, in one way or another, by druidical hauntings, glimpses of Elysium or bardic elegy. Chapter 1 sketches how Wordsworth and his precursors and contemporaries saw druidism. Chapter 2 considers the ancient kingdom of Rheged, and why one might claim that Wordsworth felt some affinity with its part-historical, part-legendary bards—Taliesin, Aneirin, Llywarch Hên, and Myrddin. Chapter 3 reads a selection of works, some of which are obviously, some less obviously, impregnated with such concerns.

Part 2, 'The Bond of Nature' (the phrase comes from *Salisbury Plain*) attends to the this-worldly Wordsworth of 1793–98. Revising the ahistorical readings of some new historicists I read Wordsworth's defence of the people, in *An Evening Walk*, *Salisbury Plain*, *The Ruined Cottage* and *Lyrical Ballads*, in the light of a Jacobinical sense of Nature as synonymous with Liberty. As a poet of nature and the poet of human suffering, Wordsworth in the 1790s discovers these two themes simultaneously, in part because natural religion and natural rights are ineluctably combined in the liberal culture which created, at the same time, Commonwealthman politics, and the 'history' of Druidism.

Part 3, 'The Living and the Dead', considers that Elysian Wordsworth who peopled Cumbria with shadowy survivors, elegized Lucy and her cousins, and translated minstrelsy into a modern key. Lucy, herself iconic of Wordsworth's memorial poetry, haunts a spot on the margin between Paradise and Elysium. Her poems leave us free to see their heroine as born of *terra genetrix*, and reborn into the living world in the very act of separation; or to see her as an Elysian presence—related perhaps to the Solitary Reaper or to the woman on Penrith Beacon. Her ultimate archetype is Kore, as the Solitary Reaper's is Demeter, whose worship, according to some of the ancients, centred in Britain. Another such figure is the Discharged Soldier; another the Leech-Gatherer. In *The Prelude* the Soldier emerges from a distant region of the poet's soul, having been significantly transformed from the Gothic spectre of the juvenile *Vale of Esthwaite*. He no longer bears a harp, or a key to the womb of Helvellyn, yet he stills bears messages from the realms of the dead, concerning pestilence and war, and has about him the peace of the dead. Such figures rise in Wordsworth's mythopoeic art to answer needs and they have the longevity of archetype. His minstrel figures, however, seem anticipatory rather than memorial. Harrowing the realms of minstrelsy and romance, Wordsworth in poems from *Hart-Leap Well* to *The White Doe of Rylstone*, spends the first decade of the new century reconfiguring the tribal past to reflect a more pacific, milder future.

At this point in the book, a triptych of chapters on *The Prelude* might have seemed desirable. After all, if bards are in the business of seeing 'something unseen before', yet fit 'fit to be transmitted', *The Prelude* must be the fullest exposition of what that 'something' is. To adopt an analogy once used (I am told) by a speaker at the Wordsworth Conference, its fourteen books are structured like a sonnet.[1] It devotes an opening quatrain of books to the building up of a human spirit at Cockermouth, Penrith, Hawkshead and Cambridge—mythologised as the formation of a chosen spirit, as it it were a modern or apocryphal *Mabinogion*. Its second 'quatrain' tests that spirit by exposing it to contrary models of human existence, in London, France and Cumbria: human nature 'melted and reduced to one identity'; human nature 'seeming born again' and 'faifhful to itself under worst trials', and shepherds as 'an index of delight'. This eight-book *Bildungroman* attributes sanity to nature's empirical education through the senses, and shows why in Wordsworth's prose writings he shares Eduardo Pestalozzi's contemporary conviction that despotism lies in wait for those who succumb to the vitiation and dissolution wrought by detaching words from things.[2]

---

1   The notion of a thirteen-book *Prelude* is an editorial back-projection: Wordsworth clearly decided upon the fourteen book structure in 1805 (see *Prelude*, 636 n) for which reasons I refer to its versions by the still familiar, if approximate, *1805* and *1850*.

2   For the cultural meaning of nature's education of man see my '"Knowledge not Purchased with the Loss of Power": Pestalozzi and the "spots of time"', *European Romantic Review*, 8:3 (1997), 231–61.

To pursue this sonnet analogy, the first 'tercet' of the fourteen-book structure, its crisis narrative, concerns the end of civilization, and a final tercet offers a formula for restoring the waste land. Our hero, in Books 9–11, travels through what he terms 'a country in Romance', a young Dion apprenticed to Beaupuy's Plato, intent not merely on singing high deeds in the name of liberty but performing them. The great experiment in human engineering, however, ends in something between Quixotic failure or Frankensteinian monstrosity, and Books 12–14 of *The Prelude* therefore presents a poet in rehab, as it were, still in search of 'something fit to be transmitted'.[1] In the final book of *The Prelude*—which announces how Wordsworth's bardic mission will be to discourage the nations from their 'trek from progress'—the bard-elect receives the gift of Genuine Liberty, the wedding of Imagination and Intellectual Love, atop Mount Snowdon (Snowdon is not merely the Parnassus but the Ararat and Sinai of the ancient Britons). 'Intellectual Love', I argue briefly in chapter 12, is all that separates the poet-hero from his otherwise imaginative shadow, Oswald, whose loveless liberty is expounded in *The Borderers*. There is truth in this configuration of *The Prelude* as a quest narrative, but to fit all that into this already lengthy book, would burst its seams.

Part 4, 'Wordsworth and Kindliness', is an account of Wordsworth after the Peace of Amiens, and seeks to demonstrate the continuity and integrity of Wordsworth's bardic vocation in his defence of the British people, and his various attempts to vocalize an Englishness transcending the political factions of his day. An alternative title for this book was *Wordsworth's Two Consciousnesses*. The textual recognition of 'two consciousnesses' occurs, of course, in book 2 of *The Prelude*, where it refers to the consciousness of the man writing and reflecting, and of the child experiencing. The phrase applies with equal force, however, to Wordsworth's philosophising in that work, and to his portrait of the French Revolution: the power of Books 9, 10 and 11 of *The Prelude* arises from their being written by a post-Jacobin in dialogue with his Jacobin self. What power *The Excursion* has—I argue in chapter 10— derives, similarly, from continuing arguments between paganism, stoicism and Christian belief, a dread of change and the desire for change,

---

1   On Wordsworth and France see '"Some other Being": Wordsworth in *The Prelude*', *Yearbook of English Studies*, 19 (1989), 127–43. I have developed this argument, and traced Wordsworth's indebtedness to Helen Maria Williams somewhat further, in *Wordsworth and Helen Maria Williams; or, the Perils of Sensibility* (2010).

his Alfoxden and Grasmere selves. That it philosophises through dialogue, a four-way dialogue between persons of variant beliefs, about the struggles of human beings in quite different stations and predicaments, itself symbolises a concern above all with 'the kind'.

The anti-hero of Chapter 11 is Napoleon. Wordsworth's celebrations of National Independence and Liberty are, of course, overtly bardic utterance—these poems do precisely what bardic poems are supposed to do. My chapter agrees with those who see the sonnets of 1802, the *Convention of Cintra* and the Iberian sonnets as all of a piece; but its brief recuperation of the notorious *Thanksgiving Ode* of 1816 may scandalize some readers. Wordsworth's sombre 'celebration' of Waterloo was, however, a watershed in his own work, marking a positive if still qualified engagement with an establishment he still suspected.

The highlights of his publishing activity after *The Excursion*, *The White Doe of Rylstone*, and *1816* were in a sense posthumous. Though published in 1819–20, *Peter Bell* looks back to 1798, *The Waggoner* to 1806 and *Vaudracour and Julia* to 1805.[1] Chapter 12 attends to *Guilt and Sorrow* and *The Borderers* as even more revelatory works, conceived in the Jacobin Age and addressed to a Chartist one. The 1842 texts of these works are addressed to the nation (not that the nation appears to have noticed) in a particular historical crisis, 'When unforeseen distress spread far and wide / Among a people mournfully cast down.' In this crisis Wordsworth offers his final collection as likely to augment 'Kindly emotion tending to console / And reconcile'. It is a signal instance of natural piety, since 'Kindly emotion' looks back to *Simon Lee,* which, in 1798, challenged the polite reader to recognize kinship in a superannuated huntsman. One may read the 1842 volume as sustaining the project inaugurated in *On revisiting the Wye*—itself designed to 'console and reconcile' the sundered enthusiasts for revolution. 1842 is the year of the main action of Elizabeth Gaskell's *Mary Barton*, and the most Wordsworthian feature of that novel is that it tells of a good man betrayed into murder by the unfeeling times. Wordsworth's message to his countrymen in 1842 is essentially the work of the poet of 1794–1796 witnessing how people can be ground between economic disaster and political theory. In the 1840s, of course, the political theory was begotten on Malthusianism by the likes of Harriet Martineau.

---

1   The subversiveness of *Peter Bell* and *The Waggoner* has been well recognised and for that reason receive little attention in this study. Alan Bewell's work on *Peter Bell*, especially, seems likely to remain definitive.

The *Postcript* of 1835 and *Poems* of 1842 are one part of a pincer attack on such theory, of which the other was provided by Wordsworth's admirer John Stuart Mill.[1]

I have puzzled over where to place a new chapter on the *Ode: Intimations of Immortality,* which has obvious thematic continuites with Part 3, but decided in the end that as it was the last written, and as Wordsworth's lifetime editions generally treated the *Ode* as a sort of climax, or as a thing *sui generis*, I would follow suit. It is good a place to end as any.

Wordsworth had become, by the time of Tennyson's debut, the pre-eminent national bard, though perhaps no longer a poet of the people, as he had been in 1793–98 or in a rather different sense in 1802–7. A Bard may be a poet of his tribe, of his nation, or of the people, and 'the people' may be as defined by either Paine or Burke or both. At different stages of his career Wordsworth saw himself as Bard to his people in each of these senses. Henry Reed, Wordsworth's American editor, said in his lectures on *English History and Tragic Poetry as Illustrated by Shakespeare*:

> Every people as they rise in virtue and intelligence, crave a history of their own; and, for lack of that which is authentic, they welcome the imaginative legend and the rude chronicle. The genuine dignity of the nation grows as its history gathers, and there is a moral power in the mere memory of an heroic age. The spirit of a people must be fed with its historic associations; its natural food is the story of the good and great men of their blood; deprived of that it languishes and dies.

A generation that separates itself from the past, Reed continues,

> does so to its own grievous degradation. It is better that legendary associations with the past should be created, if historic associations cannot be found; for a nation stands on its highest moral station when, looking back, it can appropriate the poet's words—

> > The thought of *our* past years in *me* doth breed
> > Perpetual benediction.[2]

---

1   See Mill's contemporaneous attack on Martineau for enunciating her narrow notions of political economy 'with as little qualification as if they were universal and absolute truths'. *Monthly Repository* 8 (1834) 319.

2   Henry Reed, *English History and Tragic Poetry as Illustrated by Shakespeare* (London: 1856), 32, 33.

Wordsworth, whose phrases permeate Reed's throughout the lectures, does not appear to offer such an argument in historical terms, unless one notes the shifting pronouns I have italicized here in Reed's quotation from *Intimations*. The same effect haunts a familiar passage of *The Prelude*:

> The days gone by
> Return upon *me* almost from the dawn
> Of life; the hiding places of *man's* power
> Open; I would approach them, but they close.
> I see by glimpses now; when age comes on
> May scarcely see at all; and *I* would give,
> While yet *we* may, as far as words can give,
> Substance and life to what *I* feel, enshrining,
> Such is my hope, *the spirit of the Past*
> For future restoration. (*1850*, 12.277–286, my italics)

That '*I* would give while yet *we* may' is a remarkable and characteristic glide. In Wordsworth's poetry '*I*' and '*we*' are as prone to confusion as in the bardic utterance of the much more overtly Ossianic Walt Whitman. Ostensibly personal references in such phrases as 'the days gone by', 'the spirit of the past', 'our past years' and 'natural piety', have more often than one might suspect a national dimension and a reference to 'the kind'.

In literary criticism, T. S. Eliot might have said, the ostensible argument is usually a sort of bone thrown to the guard dog to amuse him while the burglar is at work. The 'bone', in this case, is Wordsworth's flirtation with Bardism-Druidism. My burglarious intent is to celebrate his unity in multeity and the integrity of his career, while noting the variety of his poetical practice, and his mastery of a wider variety of poetic forms and strategies than has been attempted by any other poet in English. Within *Lyrical Ballads*, Wordsworth rarely uses one narrative strategy more than once, or a metre more than twice, and *Poems, in Two Volumes* employ an unparalleled output of lyrical variety—unparalleled until Hardy at least. For all its diversity, however, his output of elegies, twice-told minstrelsy, loco-descriptive poetry, lyrics, ballads and lyrical ballads, blank verse narratives, celebrations of 'national independence and liberty', sonnets and philosophizing, does seem to me to manifest a self-consciously bardic vocation.

Wordsworth's Bardic Vocation, then, is not a book about 'sacred bards and wise druides'. It is an attempt to say something responsible and holistic about a poet who saw himself as shepherd of the people, and to present him whole, or as whole as can be, with so unprecedentedly diverse a poet. To do that requires giving some attention to a surprising variety of contexts, some less familiar than others. Wordsworth's contexts include not only Jacobinism, Nature, and the continental struggle with Napoleon, but also antiquarian researches, gender revision, and the rise of Chartism. As Ted Hughes and Seamus Heaney once suggested in televised debate, he was—with the possible exception of Tennyson— England's last *national* poet. He approached antiquarian dreams and fancies about his country's nationhood with commendable scepticism. But in other ways he had a genuine claim to the mantle of Aneirin, who in the year 600 or so, lamented those who marched to Cattraeth.

Part 1

The World of Shades

and since that time
The world of shades is all my own

—The Vale of Esthwaite

Chapter 1: 'Among the Men of Old'

Wordsworth's Primal Scene

IN AUGUST 1793, having been separated from his companion William Calvert, Wordsworth is crossing Salisbury Plain on the way to Wales. He is in a compound state of anxiety about the future of the nation (which is now preparing a fleet for war with France), his lover and daughter, and the fate of the revolution in France, where the first steps have been taken towards the great Terror.

In France, the Committee of Public Safety already exists. The Girondins have been expelled from the Convention; Wordsworth's hero Jean-Baptiste Louvet is in hiding; other leaders are being hunted down, and they will be executed in October, starting with Gorsas on 7 October. Wordsworth may or may not be working out whether he can somehow return to France before the year ends (if there is any truth in the legend that he does, he will arrive in Paris in time to witness the first of these executions).[1] It is a year since the invasion of the Tuileries by radical Parisian 'sections', when on 10 August 1792 some four hundred sansculottes were slain by Louis XIV's Swiss Guard, who were themselves slaughtered in reprisal. It is eleven months, more or less, since the September Massacres. Then, according to Helen Maria Williams, the authorities colluded in the murder of 1,088 political and criminal prisoners, ostensibly to pre-empt any treasonable activities while the army of the revolution was on its way to defeat the Duke of Brunswick.[2]

Alone on Salisbury Plain, Wordsworth may, or may not, like the anonymous traveller in the 1794 text of *Salisbury Plain*, have been warned by some kind of barrow-wight to avert his face from the 'mountain-pile'

---

1   The evidence is reviewed by Kenneth R. Johnston in *The Hidden Wordsworth: Poet, Lover, Rebel, Spy* (New York: W. W. Norton, 1998), 358–400.
2   Helen Maria Williams, *Letters from France…Particularly Respecting the Campaign of 1792*, Vol 3, 2nd edn (London, 1796), 13–14. Cited from *Letters from France,* intr. Janet M. Todd. 2 vols (New York: Delmar, 1975), vol 1, n.pag.

of Stonehenge:

> *For oft at dead of night*, when dreadful fire
> Reveals that powerful circle's reddening stones
> *Mid priests and spectres grim and idols dire,*
> *Far heard the great flame utters human moans,*
> Then all is hushed: again the desert groans,
> A dismal light its farthest bounds illumes,
> *While warrior spectres of gigantic bones,*
> *Forth-issuing from a thousand rifted tombs,*
> Wheel on their fiery steeds amid the infernal glooms.
>
> (SPP, 23–24, stanza 11)

The stanza offers two tonally contrasted scenes. The first reeks of Gaul. The poet, or the Gothic voice, envisions the famous giant wicker in which, according to such prejudiced sources as Caesar and Strabo, druid victims, captives or prisoners, were offered to the gods as burnt offerings. Wordsworth is likely to know the charmingly implausible illustration by Aylett Sammes (shown on the next page) of a giant wicker in human form, its limbs filled with living victims, based on Caesar's equally implausible hint.[1]

Nor were such practices wholly antiquarian. Wicker giant forms, according to Frazer, formed part of traditional mid-summer processions in some regions of France and Belgium, until well into the early years of the nineteenth century.[2] In Brie a wicker giant was burnt annually on midsummer's eve. In Paris and elsewhere the preferred date was the nearest Sunday to the 7th July. In many areas animals—usually cats—substituted for the human sacrifices. In September 1792, however, London newspapers had carried reports of revivals of human sacrifice: the Countess Perignan and her daughters (it was claimed) had been burnt alive to the amusement of onlookers.[3] By the time Wordsworth arrived in North Wales at the end of August—that is, some time before he thought

1   Aylett Sammes, *Britannia Antiqua Illustrata* (1676) 105; Caesar, *De Bello Gallico* 6.16.

2   Sir James George Frazer, *The Golden Bough: a Study in Magic and Religion* (London: Macmillan, 1963), 856, 858.

3   Alan Liu, *Wordsworth: the Sense of History* (Stanford: Stanford University Press, 1989) 151. Sacrifice, Liu writes, 'appears to have been statistically the most important radical of violence', especially in the frequency of its occurrence in speeches of Marat and Robespierre, 152. *Salisbury Plain* is the subject of a complex and exhaustive treatment in Liu, 190–201.

Aylett Sammes, *Britannia Antiqua Illustrata* (1676) p. 105

of 'writing up' his Stonehenge experience—this picture may have fused with a more topical colossus. On 10 August 1793 the official artist of the Convention, Jacques Louis David designed a pageant of National Unity in which a Herculean figure strikes down the Monster of Federalism (or regional autonomy)—which autonomy the now proscribed Girondin deputies were busy promoting. In 1798 James Gillray would trope revolutionary indifference to human suffering in his cartoon of a French Colossus, guillotine in hand, devouring the people until struck down by Britannia's thunderbolts.[1]

1   See *Works of James Gillray* (London 1851; repr. New York and London: Blom,

In the second half of the stanza, Wordsworth alludes to a different class of victim. 'Gigantic bones' invariably imply, in the antiquarian writers Wordsworth knew, ancient Britons. According to Clarke's *Survey of the Lakes*, the remains of King Arthur (supposedly buried in Glastonbury) and of Owain of Cumbria (supposedly buried in Penrith) were reported to be of superhuman stature.[1] And Stonehenge, according to a story that originates with the Northumbrian chronicler Nennius, and is elaborated by Geoffrey of Monmouth in the twelfth century, was built by Merlin to memorialize the massacre of over four hundred British chieftains by the perfidious Saxons.[2] Detailed accounts of this event—entertained by John Thelwall as a topic for a poem, and versified by Chatterton in 'The Battle of Hastings'—appear in such works as Camden's *Britannia*, and William Hutchinson's *History and Antiquities of Cumberland* (1794).

1968) plate 213. Gillray's 'Destruction of the French Colossus' (November 1798) shows the 'Image' of France as a giant man, holding a toy guillotine in one hand and 'The Religion of Nature' in the other. While the image is that of a hollow bronze colossus its function suggests the wicker man.

1   'In …1188 or 1189, King Henry II, finding an account of Arthur's burying place in the songs of the old Welsh Bard Thaliessin [sic]… caused the ground to be opened, that he might see the remains of that celebrated warrior. Externally there appeared two columns similar to these standing at Penrith [where a similar burial has just been described]. After digging, some say seven, others sixteen feet, they came to a prodigious large flat stone. When turning it they found on the under side a leaden cross with this inscription: "Hic Iacet Inclitus Rex Arturius, In Insula Avalonia". …[Giraldus] Cambrensis (who lived at that time) relates, on the authority of the Abbot of Glastonbury, that the shin bone being placed by the leg of a very tall man, reached three fingers above his knee. His skull was likewise found of vast, but proportionable size, and upon it appeared ten wounds [received in Arthur's ten battles against the Saxons]. James Clarke, *A Survey of the Lakes of Cumberland, Westmorland and Lancashire* (London: 1789), 19n. Clarke's survey is a major Wordsworthian source in *An Evening Walk*. For a modern view see J. Carey, 'The Finding of Arthur's Grave: A Story from Clonmacnoise?' in Carey, ed., *Ildánach Ildírech. A Festschrift for Proinsias Mac Cana* (Andover & Aberystwyth, 1999), pp.1–14.

2   The *Historia Brittonum* attributed to Nennius is supposed to have been begun c. 700 in the time of Ida's wars with Urien of Rheged and completed by a variety of hands. It exists in a variety of manuscripts including a Vatican copy of 945—the year Cumbria ceased to exist as a separate kingdom—and another of 1100. It is the earliest evidence for the existence of the North British Bards, Aneirin and Taliesin, in the 6th century. See D. N. Dumville, 'Nennius and the *Historia Brittonum*' in *Studia Celtica* 10/11 (1975–6), 78–95. Geoffrey of Monmouth's *Historia Regum Britanniae*, c. 1136, continues and embellishes Nennius, reinventing Arthur as a national hero, and converting the Caledonian bard Myrddin into the prophet Merlin.

What links the two scenes in the stanza is bloody murder, whether of 400 British chieftains or of the 1,088 Parisian prisoners whose number seems closer to 'a thousand rifted tombs'. Either way, the tone of horror belongs less to the poet than to the dramatized voice of superstition.

When the same matter is elaborated by the Female Vagrant in stanzas 20–22 of *Salisbury Plain*, it is not merely distanced but dignified. The Female Vagrant, we learn from the narrative voice, has encountered an old man, who tells her of a young Swain (a mask for the poet himself) who has seen and heard 'Gigantic beings' striding across the wold (*SP* 20), 'the sacrificial altar fed | With living men' (21), and 'long bearded forms' charming the desert and the moon alike (22). This tripartite vision is almost identical with the version Wordsworth develops in *The Prelude*. In the 1805 text the Salisbury Plain vision recurs, astonishingly, both in his own voice and as an explanation of what Wordsworth means when he says that the poet

> hath stood
> By Nature's side among the men of old
> And so shall stand for ever. (*1805*, 12.296–8)

Now it is explicitly Wordsworth who is crossing the Plain, on his way to Wales in 1793. The Druids, with their Bardic associates, are now recognized as precursors with whom a modern poet must be connected in a mighty scheme of truth.[1] Book 12 situates the experience in a solitary journey, made at a time when Wordsworth thirsted for the destruction of the British fleet, and when he was experiencing 'daring sympathies with power' (*1850*, 10.457)—the power, that is, of the revolutionary Terrorists whose execution of the monarch Wordsworth has already condoned,[2] and who, in October 1793 and early 1794 would be calling

---

1   Bards and druids coexist in Wordsworth's poetry, because it was widely believed at the time he was writing (a) that the British Druids, who were already in decline at the time of the Roman conquest, had nevertheless survived to be contemporary—in their last days—with the Welsh Bards in the post-Roman period; (b) that *The Book of Taliesin* (despite being six or seven centuries too late to have served this purpose) enshrined cabbalistically much of the religious belief of the druids; and (c) that the language of the Bards is that of the Patriarchs preserved by the Druids.

2   'I am sorry that you attach so much importance to the personal sufferings of the late royal martyr', Wordsworth wrote in his *Letter to the Bishop of Llandaff*. Had the bishop reflected, 'so far from stopping to bewail his death, you would rather have regretted that the blind fondness of his people has placed a human being in that monstrous situation [of absolute monarchy]. Any other sorrow for the death of Louis is irrational and

both innocently and heinously for 'Head after head, and never heads enough' (362).

Violent emotions, provoked in part by the treachery of a liberticide British ministry and in part by guilt-laden identifications with those already employing terror to stamp out domestic treason in France, made his imagination acutely apocalyptic:

> There on the pastoral downs without a track
> To guide me, or along the bare white roads
> Lengthening in solitude their dreary line,
> While through those vestiges of ancient times
> I ranged, and by the solitude o'ercome,
> I had a reverie and saw the past,
> Saw multitudes of men, and here and there
> A single Briton in his wolf-skin vest,
> With shield and stone-ax stride across the wold;
> The voice of spears was heard, the rattling spear
> Shaken by arms of mighty bone, in strength
> Long mouldered, of barbaric majesty.

Bearing in mind Geoffrey of Monmouth's 'night of the long knives', that 'single Briton' might have been the *dux bellorum* Ambrosius Aurelianus, or Uther his brother, or even Vortigern making his way to Dinas Emris, his magical citadel in Snowdonia, and the site of Merlin's prophecies of the fall of the Britons and of the (eventual) Tudor restoration. Vortigern's situation, of course, accords best with the poet's own. Like Wordsworth (who visited Dinas Emris with Robert Jones), Vortigern was making his way West after captivity in London, and both were doing so (in rather different senses) as fugitive regicides.[1] Wordsworth's favourite poet, Edmund Spenser, lists all three candidates—Aurelius, Uther and Vortigern—within three lines of *The Faerie Queene* (Book 2, 10.67), treating Stonehenge as the burial place of Aurelius, and a monument to 'the eternal marks of treason'. That this topos was associated with

weak'. *WPW*, 25–6.

1 Hutchinson cites Camden on the detail that Vortigern was held captive by Hengist after the massacre at Stonehenge (which his treasonable deal with the Saxons had enabled) and made his way to Wales on his release in AD 439. *The History and Antiquities of Cumberland* (2 vols. 1794), 1: 234. Vortigern came to power in the first place after having a hand in the assassination of King Constans. See Damian Walford Davies *Presences that Disturb* (Cardiff: University of Wales Press, 2002) for a thorough treatment of this topos.

Stonehenge in Wordsworth's mind is amply shown in lines 428–9 of *Salisbury Plain*: 'Though treachery her sword no longer dyes | In the cold blood of truce'.

In the second phase of the *Prelude* version of the vision on Salisbury Plain, the masterful poet parodies divine fiat, cries 'let there be night', and willingly confronts the sacrificial altar fed with living men, in a ceremony performed 'for both worlds, the living and the dead':

> *I called upon the darkness*, and it took—
> A mighty darkness seemed to come and take—
> All objects from my sight; and lo, again
> The desart visible by dismal flames!
> It is the sacrificial altar, fed
> With living men—how deep the groans!—the voice
> Of those in the gigantic wicker thrills
> Throughout the region far and near, pervades
> The monumental hillocks, and the pomp
> Is for both worlds, the living and the dead.
>
> (1805, 12.315–336)

Under the Druids, or under Robespierre, whose treasonable victims were 'penned in crowds | For sacrifice' (*1850*, 10.406–7), sacrifice remains a bloody business, and 'too near the ancient troughs of blood', as Geoffrey Hill's Ovid opines, 'innocence is no earthly virtue'.[1]

Between 1793 and 1805 Wordsworth treats the theme of human sacrifice in several variants of two major texts. There is, however, a difference in tone between the evocation of sacrifice in *Salisbury Plain* and in *The Prelude*. The anonymous voice of 1793–94 (removed from the 1797 *Adventures on Salisbury Plain*) is clearly horror-struck; Wordsworth in 1804–05 seems rather impressed. Throughout the eighteenth-century rehabilitation of the druids, human sacrifice was perceived as a problem but by no means an insuperable one. William Hutchinson, in his *Excursion to the Lakes in Westmoreland and Cumberland*, in writing about Long Meg and her Daughters (the stone monument near Little Salkeld in Cumbria), argues that druid sacrifice was performed essentially in a spirit of justice, solemnity and propitiation, and that the victims were, in any case, 'criminals guilty of the most atrocious crimes against the commonweal and society' ('commonweal' is of course a key word

---

1   Geoffrey Hill, 'Ovid in the Third Reich', *Collected Poems* 61.

for Wordsworth). As Thomas Love Peacock would also do, Hutchinson compares druidic sacrifice with contemporary Tyburn executions in a way that reflects credit on the druids.[1] In William Mason's *Caractacus, a Dramatic Poem* (1763), the British hero Caradoc promises not to disgrace his Roman prisoners of war by exhibiting them in chains. Solemn sacrifice, he argues, is not cruelty, but love:

> We give you therefore to the immortal Gods.
> To them we lift you in the radiant cloud
> Of sacrifice.[2]

The argument is not far removed from that of the later Wordsworth in his sonnets on capital punishment, and it would be hard to show that Wordsworth was more bothered by druidical sacrifice than either Hutchinson or Mason. After all, despite a common assumption that the Wordsworth of *Salisbury Plain* is aghast at sacrifice,[3] its author has just exonerated revolutionary violence in the *Letter to the Bishop of Llandaff* (June 1793)—his last work before visiting Salisbury Plain. In both works, he seems willing enough to take his place at the side of the sacrificers rather than the sacrificed. Pitt's victims, in the treason trials of 1794, were not guilty. Robespierre's, in 1792–3, are presented in *The Prelude* as the 'snakes' around the Herculean Republic's cradle, destined to necessary sacrifice along with the monarchy they sought to restore.[4] Stonehenge—mythologically—memorializes real, as opposed to constructive treason, and in the testimony of a century of antiquarian writings, it also symbolizes native British jurisprudence, and national

---

1   'What are our executions at this day? The comparison takes away all stigma.' William Hutchinson, *An Excursion to the Lakes in Westmoreland and Cumberland* (London 1776), 112–13. Hutchinson is writing about Long Meg, the subject of one of Wordsworth's most impressive meditations on 'druid' remains. According to Robert Osborn (*Borderers*, 18) Wordsworth consulted the 1794 edn of this work in 1796.
2   'Caractacus, a Dramatic Poem', in *Poems* (1763) 271. Mason was known to Wordsworth, from West's *Guide*, as the discoverer of the famously picturesque lower fall at Rydal. William West, *A Guide to the Lakes in Cumberland, Westmorland and Lancashire* (1778), 80.
3   See, for instance, Stephen Gill, 'The Original Salisbury Plain: Introduction and text', in Jonathan Wordsworth, *Bicentenary Wordsworth Studies,* 142–79, 148–9.
4   Alan Liu argues that 'the poetic of sacrifice is part of the bedrock argument of violence in the *Letter [to the Bishop of Llandaff]*' and that by assimilating Racine's *Athalie* to his argument Wordsworth becomes 'something like a Corday of the left: a devotee of hallowed violence', 575–6 n.

independence and liberty from both Saxon and Roman depredations.[1] If anything, that underground voice of outrage and superstition ('avert thy face' and 'fly') represents Bishop Watson rather than Wordsworth: 'I fly with terror and abhorrence even from the altar of Liberty', said the Bishop, 'when I see it streaming with the blood of the monarch himself' (*WPW*, 28). While the poem of 1793–94 concludes by wishing to see the dungeons of oppression emptied, and superstition banished, it also wishes to see the altars of Stonehenge preserved for eternity.[2]

Wordsworth justified regicide. He condoned necessary terror against domestic treason. It reminded him at times of the sublime pleasure he imagined the ancient prophets experienced when they accomplished the doom of cities. He was, however, aghast when Robespierre turned it against his friends (he does refer to 'lamentable' and 'heinous' acts) and he complained bitterly when Pitt likewise abused 'the guardian crook of law' as 'a tool of murder'. He vacillated, similarly, between fierce and mild versions of what druidical faith entailed, but seems willing to associate himself with either. In the 1829 poem *Humanity*, for instance, he reflects on the supposed use by the Druids of judicial 'rocking stones', like the Bowder Stone in Borrowdale:

> What though the Accused, upon his own appeal
> To righteous Gods when man has ceased to feel,
> Or at a doubting Judge's stern command,
> Before the Stone of Power no longer stand—
> To take his sentence from the balanced block,
> As, at his touch, it rocks *or seems to rock*;[3]
> Though, in the depths of sunless groves, no more
> The Druid-priest the hallowed Oak adore;
> Yet, for the Initiate, rocks and whispering trees

---

1   According to Hutchinson, 'The great merit of King Alfred was, not his creating, but restoring the ancient laws of Britain' (*The History and Antiquities*, 1: 252), laws associated in Camden and Milton with such British Kings as Gorbonian, and in the history of Rheged with Urien's kinsman Rhydderch Hael.

2   In the 1850 *Prelude* another religious relic, the Chartreuse, is 'listed' for preservation. The poet is still keen that the sword of justice should prosper, and its 'purging fires | Up to the loftiest towers of pride ascend', but he concurs reluctantly with nature's plea for these 'courts of mystery': '"Let this one temple last, be this one spot | Of earth devoted to eternity!"' (*1850*, 6.430–451).

3   My emphasis. Wordsworth's cautious scepticism is not found in Mason's *Caractacus*, where the rocking stone 'moves obsequious to the touch of him whose breast is pure'.

Do still perform mysterious offices!

The notion that the accused, himself, might wish to appeal to this ancient lie-detector is a charming one, and the transition from rocking-stone-justice and oak-worship to the 'mysterious offices' of rocks and whispering trees powerfully validates the former as, in some sense, genetically informing his own poetic endowment. In the *Prelude* 'spot of time' the moment of terror, itself redeemed by recognition of its reconciling 'pomp', gives way to a milder and still more obviously valorized sequel:

> At other moments, for through that wide waste
> Three summer days I roamed, when 'twas my chance
> To have before me on the downy plain
> Lines, circles, mounts, a mystery of shapes
> Such as in many quarters yet survive,
> With intricate profusion figuring o'er
> The untilled ground (the work, as some divine,
> Of infant science, imitative forms
> By which the Druids covertly expressed
> Their knowledge of the heavens, and imaged forth
> The constellations), I was gently charmed,
> Albeit with an antiquarian's dream,
> And saw the bearded teachers, with white wands
> Uplifted, pointing to the starry sky,
> Alternately, and plain below, while breath of music
> Of music seemed to guide them ...
>
> (*1805*, 12.337–53)

Dreaming 'antiquarians' from John Leland to William Stukeley associated all druid circles, especially Stonehenge, with astronomical learning, but it seems from this passage that Wordsworth's bearded teachers—whose functions include officiating at ritual sacrifice—are not merely licensed by Renaissance scholars but approved by Nature herself.

As if this primal scene had not occupied sufficient space in his poetry it recurs most surprisingly of all, as if Wordsworth felt constrained to publish some version of it in his lifetime, as the climax of *The Excursion*. Book nine of that work transposes the Salisbury Plain 'spot' to the Vale of Grasmere, and bestows the vision (with appropriate ideological shifts and distancings) on the Pastor. The vision has so far belonged to 'a Swain', a wandering sailor, a female vagrant and the poet. Now, sitting on Loughrigg, a Christian Pastor imagines pre-Roman Britain, where

> Amid impending rocks and gloomy woods—
> Of those terrific Idols some received
> Such dismal service, that the loudest voice
> Of the swoln cataracts (which now are heard
> Soft murmuring) was too weak to overcome,
> Though aided by wild winds, the groans and shrieks
> Of human victims, offered up to appease
> Or to propitiate. And, if living eyes
> Had visionary faculties …

—'visionary' has this sanguinary sense in Wordsworth more often than one might think—

> Aghast we might behold this cristal Mere
> Bedimmed with smoke, in wreathes voluminous,
> Flung from the body of devouring fires,
> To Taranis erected on the heights
> By priestly hands, for sacrifice performed
> Exultingly, in view of open day
> And full assemblage of a barbarous host;
> Or to Andates, female Power! who gave
> (For so they fancied) glorious victory.

In the Pastor's eyes, contemporary worship is wholly changed, not least in the proper subordination of that troubling 'female power', and the new faith 'derived through Him who bled | Upon the cross' appears a 'marvellous advance | Of good from evil; as if one extreme | Were left, the other gained' (*Excursion*, 9.691–724; *PW*, 5: 309–10). The Solitary does not point this out, but this transition from atonement to atonement might impress a sceptical mind (or a follower of Stukeley) with the sense of contiguous rather than disparate theology, especially when one considers the sacrificial appeasement of heaven's wrath that will soon take place at Waterloo. This deconstructive undertow is amplified when the priest goes on to claim that the modern rites are performed in St Oswald's (Grasmere's temple to a robustly martial martyr, an effficient slayer of Celts) both for 'ye who come | To kneel devoutly in yon reverend pile … and ye who sleep in earth'. The pomp of St Oswald's, like that of Stonehenge or the Cumbrian monuments at Castlerigg or Long Meg, is for both worlds, the living and the dead.

This motif of 'the living and the dead' manifests itself more often in Wordsworth's poetry and prose than in anyone else's but Whitman's. It occurs in various forms but is perhaps best articulated in the lines of Book 10 of *The Prelude* where Wordsworth sees the poet as ineluctably enrolled in the 'one great society' of 'the noble Living and the noble Dead' (*1805*, 10.969). The idea that the living and the dead are co-existent—that formal religion is above all concerned with negotiation between the sundered parts of this society, and with due propitiation of the dead majority by the maintenance of proper rites—may not be central to most people's sense of what the Anglican creed implies when it speaks of Christ coming to judge 'the living and the dead'. It is, however, integral to Wordsworth's sense of the Church in England, and it is bound up not only with his treatment of the poetic genius and the mysteries of the Druids but (and rather intriguingly) with the way he situates himself as regards the central political controversy of the 1790s, that between Paine, contending for the rights of the living, and Burke, champion of the dead, whose perceptions he simply unites.

Varieties of Druidism

'The light of God, which at the creation was imparted to man', wrote a knowing author in 1824, 'hath never been extinguished. From the patriarchs it descended to the prophets, and from the prophets to the apostles; but there were many who wandered and lost the light, and their offspring became inheritors of darkness. Thus it fared with our forefathers.' Yet 'there is reason to believe that they [our British forefathers] brought with them some glimmerings of patriarchal faith' before at length they fell into idolatry.

> Their priests, the Druids, are said to have retained the belief of one supreme God, all-wise, all mighty and all-merciful, from whom all things which have life proceed. They held also the immortality of the soul. Whatever else they taught was deceit and vanity.

Pretended magic, worship of Baal, and human sacrifice are laid to their charge. Then, with the great mountain-fringed stone circle at Castlerigg, Keswick, in mind, the author alleges: 'Naked women, stained with the dark blue dye of woad, assisted at these bloody rites.' Sexual depravity was institutionalized: 'A wife was common to all the kinsmen of her husband ... nor did any child know its father.'[1]

Robert Southey's remarks, in this first chapter of his monumental *Book of the Church*, blend an eighteenth-century desire to believe that the heirs of the patriarchs set foot in Britain, with an almost Victorian revulsion from the idea that the Church of England might be a simple evolution from earlier priestcraft. His moral outrage marks a hardening of attitude towards druids compared with most of the Renaissance and Augustan accounts, and certainly by comparison with the poems of William Mason from which the young Wordsworth probably received his formative first impressions of nature's priesthood. The orgiastic depravities which Southey deprecates are authenticated mainly in Gilpin's *Tour,* and before that by the Reverend William Borlase who spoke, in his *Observations of the Antiquities of Cornwall* (1754), of druidical indulgence in Bacchanalian 'luxury and debauch'.[2] Southey was as well educated as anyone in the liberal tradition of druidism, having researched it for *Madoc*, but by this date he has turned game-keeper. The priapic campaigner John Wilkes and the notorious orgiastic excesses of French libertarians have fused for Southey as they did for Coleridge.[3] In Southey's apostastic syllogism, Druids = Welsh Jacobinism; Jacobinism = licence; licence = debauch. Therefore, Druids were debauched.

All Southey's debauchery is derived, ultimately, from a single remark in Pliny the Elder's *Natural History* to the effect that the ceremonial cutting of the medicinal mistletoe would be followed by a banquet.[4] What Borlase's fevered imagination made of this 'banquet' was first implanted in the Lake District by William Gilpin, who visited Castlerigg stone

1   Robert Southey, *The Book of the Church*, 1824, vol. 1: 1, 4, 8.

2   William Borlase, *Observations of the Antiquities of Cornwall* (1754), 85. The idea that Britain worshipped Bacchus was commonplace. Aylett Sammes had also imagined that nocturnal sacrifice to 'Infernal Deities' (Pluto and Proserpina are the erotic duo he has in mind) led to 'horrid lusts and unnatural incests', *Britannia Antiqua* 138.

3   See Kathleen Wilson, *The Sense of the People: Politics, Culture and Imperialism in England, 1715–1785* (Cambridge: Cambridge University Press, 1995), on the libertinism of such as Wilkes; Richard Cobb, *Reactions to the French Revolution*, London 1972, on that of France; and Samuel Taylor Coleridge's despicable libel on almost anyone of Jacobin persuasion as 'th'imbrothell'd Atheist' (*Religious Musings*, line 150).

4   Pliny, *Natural History*, tr. J. Bostock and H. T. Riley, Bohn's Library (London: Henry G. Bohn, 1857), 16. Aylett Sammes had also imagined that nocturnal sacrifice to 'Infernal Deities' (Pluto and Proserpina are the erotic duo he has in mind) led to 'horrid lusts and unnatural incests', *Britannia Antiqua*, 138.

circle in 1772 and found in 'these ancient vestiges of architecture'

> strong proofs of the savage nature of the religion of these heathen priests. Within these magical circles we may conceive any incantations to have been performed ... It is history as well as poetry when Ossian mentions the circles of stones, where our ancestors, in their nocturnal orgies, invoked the spirits which rode upon the winds—the awful forms of their deceased forefathers.[1]

Gilpin's imagination was not exceptional: every age has found in these bronze age funerary monuments, with their protective stones, a reflection of its own fears and desires. Thus, although Wordsworth grew up at a time when the druids had been envisioned and revisioned and rehabilitated by Drayton, Milton, Collins, Temple, Thomson, Mason, Gray and Cowper, he knew more than most of these about the soul of man under revolutionary impulses and so chose—or was chosen by—one particular image: that of the druids as the sacrificers of men. More strangely still, in the many poems in which Wordsworth refers specifically to bards and the bardic function, the focus is less upon their elegiac than upon their martial theme. To some authorities, such as Owen Pughe and Iolo Morganwg, bards were so pacific that the presence of one was enough to suspend hostilities; but to Evan Evans and Sharon Turner they were warriors. Wordsworth's bards in the *Ecclesiastical Sonnets* exhibit his own divided sense of self. Wordsworth claimed that had he not been a poet he would have gone in for soldiering. In extremis, his bards prefer swords to harps. To Wordsworth a bard is one who urges upon his tribe what the hymnwriter called 'The love that asks no question | The love that pays the price'. His interest in druids seems in fact to have developed most dramatically while devising his guerrilla-war drama, *The Borderers*.

On page 49r of DC MS 12, otherwise devoted exclusively to *The Borderers*, Wordsworth wrote out this curious bibliography:[2]

> Druids.—
> C. Comment.Lib 6

---

1   William Gilpin, *Observations, Relative Chiefly to Picturesque Beauty, made in the year 1772, On several Parts of England, particularly the Mountains and Lakes of Cumberland and Westmorland* (3rd edn, 1792), vol 2, 28. Wordsworth was at school with Gilpin's nephew.

2   It is reproduced in Cornell *Borderers*, 420–21. The list has little to do with anything else in the manuscript, and may predate work on the play.

Plin. Nat. Hist: Lib 16 c 44—Lib 29 c3
Dray. Poly-Olbion. Ninth Song—
Mona Antiqua 338
Dion Chrysostom.—
Tac. Annals L 14th.c.29
Luc. Phar. L.3
Ammianus Marcellinus Lib 15th
Procopius. Goth. Lib 4

The first seven items in this bibliography, down to Lucan, are copied precisely from the notes to Mason's *Caractacus*. The last two titles might have been taken from one of the many works available to Wordsworth in the substantial Racedown library—for instance Carte's *History of England* (where all the above except Drayton are cited), Camden, or Selden's notes to Drayton's *Poly-Olbion*. It is likely that the copying down of these *Caractacus* references was either for revision of *Salisbury Plain* or for future use (there is nothing much to do with druidism in *The Borderers*, though human sacrifice in the name of liberty is part of the play's theme).[1] But the terrain of *The Borderers* is precisely that of the bardic culture both Mason and Wordsworth would have associated indissolubly with druidism: Rivers / Oswald and his associates act out their peacekeeping and / or levelling roles as a form of ad hoc people's militia, in the northern badlands between the two Roman walls, where in 5th-, 6th- and 7th-century Cumbria, the land of the Cymri, the authentic bardic literature of 'Wales' enjoyed its florescence.

Wordsworth read not merely these sources but virtually every antiquarian source available to him when preparing himself for *Ecclesiastical Sonnets* over two decades later, and his library at Rydal also contained three of the more important omissions from this early shortlist of classical authorities on druidism—namely Strabo, Clement of Alexandria and Eusebius. But whether he actually read (or re-read) any of these titles at Racedown in 1796, and for what purpose, can only be conjectural. He had *already*, one supposes, written the druid reverie of *Salisbury Plain*. But if he had already determined on recycling this material on some future occasion, one confronts the intriguing possibility that the expanded (1804) reverie of *The Prelude* book 10 was conceived in Racedown in

---

1   A. L. Owen, in *The Famous Druids*, notes a specific borrowing from *Caractacus* in *Descriptive Sketches* 1793. Caractacus makes a belated appearance in Wordsworth's poetry in 1842 in 'The Eagle and the Dove'.

1796, some three years before *any other part* of the autobiographical poem except the Ossianic passage on the death of his father which itself remodels another druidical reverie of 1787.[1]

As a bibliography, Wordsworth's Racedown list is far from complete, and in most respects one would not have thought that a person of Wordsworth's classical education would have needed reminding of its contents. Caesar, Pliny, Tacitus and Lucan are routine enough. Drayton and Rowlands are very well known. The references to Dion, Ammianus Marcellinus and Procopius of Caesaria are more unusual. Together, these two groups represent two distinct branches of ancient druidology, the Roman and the Alexandrian, emphasizing barely compatible facets of druidism corresponding to the sacrificial and astronomical stages of Wordsworth's 'vision'.[2] Caesar, Pliny and Tacitus offer an Imperial justification for suppression of the druids. Rowlands, Dion, Ammianus and Procopius, on the other hand, lament the loss entailed in that suppression.

What they signify, as a compendium of druid lore, is as follows. The sixth book of Caesar's *De Bello Gallico*, is the most substantial classical account of the druids and of their status in Gaul. What Wordsworth would have gleaned from *The Gallic Wars* is that under an elected national leader, the arch-druid, the order constituted the more powerful of Gaul's two dominant classes—the other being warrior chiefs. Caesar's druids are responsible 'for divine worship, the due performance of sacrifices, public and private, and the interpretation of ritual questions' (*De Bello Gallico*, 6.13).[3] As the ruling caste of a sort of Holy Gallic Empire, they also instruct youth, and determine criminal and civil legal questions. 'It is believed that their rule of life was discovered in Britain and transferred thence to Gaul; and today those who would study the subject more accurately journey, as a rule, to Britain to learn it' (6.13). Caesar is also responsible for the image of the druids as guardians of an unwritten hermetic culture, transmitted through some twenty years of instruction, mostly in the form of memorised verse, and for the earliest formulation (clarified in latter accounts, including Lucan's) of the druid belief in the

---

1   Compare *Prelude* 11:35–89 and *EPF* pp 446, 548.

2   The primary accounts include A. L. Owen, *The Famous Druids* (1962), Nora C. Chadwick, *The Druids* (Cardiff: University of Wales Press, 1966), T. D. Kendrick *The Druids: a Study in Keltic Prehistory* (London: Methuen, 1927), and Stuart Piggott, *The Druids* (London: Thames & Hudson, 1968).

3   Citations from *De Bello Gallico*, tr. J. H. Edwards (Loeb Library, 1917) are taken from T. D. Kendrick, *The Druids*, 77–78.

immortality of the soul:

> The cardinal doctrine which they seek to teach is that souls do not die,
> but after death pass from one to another; and this belief, as the fear of
> death is thereby cast aside, they hold to be the greatest incentive to
> valour (6.14).

Perhaps because he is prejudiced—as a military commander—by this
gloomy reflection, Caesar also reports the druids as presiding over human
sacrifice. The Romans encountered the druids of Gaul and Britain mainly
as the ruling caste of the Celtic world and the only effective opposi-
tion to Rome (rather as the Catholic Church was in communist Poland),
and well able to organize resistance, a fact which undoubtedly preju-
diced their accounts (Chadwick 72). Caesar associates them with the use
of that most extraordinary and implausible of sacrificial tools the Giant
Wicker, 'figures of immense size, whose limbs, woven out of twigs, they
fill with living men and set on fire, and the men perish in a sheet of living
flame' (6.16). Strabo and Diodorus Siculus stress the practice of divina-
tion from the death throes of a man stabbed in the throat for this purpose.
Pliny and Tacitus, in the latter part of the first century A.D., round off the
Latin accounts in statements redolent of imperial satisfaction at having
abolished that nasty Northern business of ritual murder and such un-
Roman practices as divination from human entrails.

Item 6 in Wordsworth's bibliography, the fourteenth book of the
Annals of Tacitus, provides the sensational account of the destruction
of the druids of Anglesey (aided by their far more frightful womenfolk)
by Suetonius Paulinus, Governor of Britain, in A.D. 61, who was deter-
mined to destroy Mona as a refuge for fugitives:

> The enemy lined the shore: a dense host of armed men, interspersed
> with women clothed in black, like the Furies, with their hair hanging
> down, and holding torches in their hands. Round these were the Druids,
> uttering dire curses and stretching out their hands towards heaven.
> These strange sights terrified our soldiers. They stood …as if paralysed,
> offering their bodies to the blows. At last, encouraged by the General,
> and exhorting each other not to quail before a rabble of female fanatics,
> they advanced their standards, bore down all resistance, and enveloped
> the enemy in their own flames. Suetonius imposed a garrison upon the
> conquered, and cut down the groves devoted to their cruel superstitions:

for it was part of their religion to spill the blood of captives on their altars, and to enquire of the Gods by means of human entrails.[1]

This massacre was avenged for a time by the successes of Boudicca, until Suetonius secured a major victory over a British army of 80,000 warriors. If Bardism-Druidism was, in its day, almost as influential an ideology as Marxism-Leninism in the twentieth century, this is its archetypal scene. Tacitus's account of it is endlessly retold, among others by William Sotheby, in his *Tour* of 1794. In the Romantic era the Mona Massacre becomes iconographically indistinguishable from subsequent atrocities, such as the sack of Old Bangor in 607 by the Saxon Ethelfrith, and Edward's twelfth-century massacre of the last bards, which last event (via the mention in Carte's *History*) inspired Thomas Gray whose poem 'The Bard' did much to inspire the recovery of this entire 'history' of Bards and Druids. It even reverses itself somewhat farcically in the French invasion of Pembrokeshire in 1797, when the descendants of Tacitus's wild Welsh women of the hills inflicted a humiliating defeat on the new invader.

For whatever reason, Tacitus, Lucan and Pliny agree on the symbolic necessity of the destruction of druidic groves—from Mona to Marseilles—and in the major Latin sources subsequent to the suppression of the druids under Claudius, druids are associated with secret and remote retreats. Pomponius Mela agrees with Lucan in situating druid academies in 'secluded dales'. Lucan, nevertheless, praised the bards as oral historians, and gives the most concise account of how the druid version of immortality involved transmigration of souls within the world of all of us, rather than departure to 'the silent land of Erebus and the pale halls of Pluto'. As we shall see (in chapter 3), Lucan's account of druid groves in his *Civil War* undoubtedly informs Wordsworth's account of one in 'Yew-Trees'.

Pliny's *Natural History* (A.D. 77) is largely responsible for representations of the druids as magicians. In Lib 30, Pliny praises Tiberius for putting down the druids of Gaul and 'all that tribe of wizards and physicians', even though such persecution has merely driven the problem across the ocean into 'the void recesses of Nature'. There, 'At the present day, struck with fascination, Britannia still cultivates this art [of divination] and that with ceremonials so august that she might almost seem to

---

1   Tacitus, *Annals*, tr. George Gilbert Ramsay (John Murray, 1909) Book 14, ch. 29

have been the first to communicate them to the people of Persia'.[1]

The third and fourth items in Wordsworth's bibliography represent nationalistic British reclamations of Druidism. Michael Drayton's *Poly-Olbion* (1622) is a lively antiquarian tour of Britain as mythologized in Camden's *Britannia*, and equipped with notes—provided by John Selden—from most of the classical authorities. Its Ninth Song laments in particular, the passing of Mona Antiqua into the modern Anglesey and Wordsworth may have sympathised with 'Mona's' complaint about her new fangled name: he was himself inclined to rescue some ancient Celtic names that had become overlaid with more prosaic ones—preferring Blencathra, for example, to the familiar Saddleback. Why page 338 of Henry Rowlands's *Mona Antiqua Restaurata* (1723) should be cited is a puzzle: elsewhere, however, Rowlands not only celebrates the druid culture of Mona but is responsible for one of innumerable eighteenth-century attempts to demonstrate the identity of Welsh or British and Hebrew, thus proving that 'the local tongue was still … the venerable language of Noah'.[2]

Pliny's *Natural History* concedes grudgingly a possible link between the druids and Persia, in a way that flatters neither. But the *Orations* or *Discourses* of Dion Chrysostom (c. AD 100) associate them with the Persian magi, the Egyptian priests and Indian Brahmins, as an instance of a priestly caste of greater power than the kings or chieftains they ruled: 'In all these cases the kings were not permitted to do or plan anything without the assistance of these wise men, so that in truth it was they who ruled.'[3] Since these wise men are barely distinguishable from poets one sees the attraction to this particular unacknowledged legislator. Perhaps more significantly, if one thinks of Wordsworth's poetic celebrations of lost maidens in the Lucy poems, especially the Plutonian 'Three Years she Grew', Dion Chrysostom is one of the authorities, alongside Strabo, for the belief that Britain was, if not the original home, then certainly a centre, of the rites of Ceres and Proserpine, or the mysteries of Samothrace. Dion is the major inspiration for Edward Davies's highly

1   Pliny, *Natural History*, tr. J. Bostock and H. T. Riley, Bohn's Library (London: Henry G Bohn, 1857), Lib 30.c.4

2   A. L. Owen, 73. For instance, 'cairn' or 'carnedde' = Hebrew keren nedh. Moreover, Hercules = Erchyll, and Apollo = Ap haul.

3   Dio Chrysostom, *Discourses*, tr. H. Lamar Crosby, Loeb's Classical Library (Heinemann, 1946), Discourse 49, 301.

inventive *Celtic Researches* and *Mythology and Rites of the British Druids*.

More secular antiquarians warmed to Ammianus Marcellinus, who reported in the 4th century AD, a much earlier, first century account by Timagenes, of how in the Celtic regions 'study of the liberal arts flourished, initiated by the Bards, the Euhages, and the Druids':

> Now the Bards sang to the sweet strains of the lyre the valorous deeds of famous men composed in heroic verse, but the Euhages, investigating the sublime, attempted to explain the secret laws of nature. The Druids, being loftier than the rest in intellect, ... were elevated by their investigation of obscure and profound subjects, and scorning all things human, pronounced the soul immortal.[1]

While the Romans credit the druids with some learning in physiology (entrail gazers must be granted a professional acquaintance with the human form) and a belief in immortality, it is in the third century that druids become popularly associated with the teachings of Pythagoras on the subject of metempsychosis. Milton himself gave credence, in *Areopagitica*, to the idea that 'the school of *Pythagoras* and the *Persian* wisdom took beginnings from the old Philosophy of this Iland'.[2] Hippolytus and Clement of Alexandria, major omissions from Wordsworth's bibliography, are the sources of this tradition, which was based no doubt on the coincidence that Celtic mythology is much concerned with tales of heroes being reborn after multiple metamorphoses, as in Taliesin's famous 'boast', which remains a potent motif in Welsh poetry.[3] Hippolytus claims that the druids adopted Pythagoras, while

1 Ammianus Marcellinus, *History*, tr. J. C. Rolfe, Loeb's Classical Library (Heinemann, 1950) Bk 14, chapter 9 'Of the Origins of the Gauls', 4-8 (c.f. Strabo, *The Geography,* Book 4, 4.4).

2 *Complete Prose Works of John Milton*, Vol. 2, ed., Ernest Sirluck (New Haven & Oxford: Yale University Press, 1959) 551.

3 Taliesin boasts at the Court of Maelgwyn: 'I carried the banner before Alexander; I was in Canaan when Absolom was slain; ... I was on the high cross of the merciful Son of God; I was the chief overseer at the building of the tower of Nimrod' (cited from Arnold *Celtic Literature* [London: Dent, 1910], 59–60). Compare Dai Greatcoat's five-page boast in David Jones's magnificent *In Parenthesis*, which begins 'I was with Abel when his brother found him, under the green tree |... | I built a shit-house for Artaxerxes.| I was the spear in Balin's hand, that made waste King Pellam's land'. Dai's boast concludes—lest we forget what such 'boasts' account for—'I was in Michael's trench when bright Lucifer bulged his primal salient out'. *In Parenthesis* (London:

Clement goes so far as to claim that the druids of Gaul were the origin of the Pythagorean philosophy (Chadwick, *The Druids*, 59). If Milton's patriotic spirit led him to entertain these classical hints, with some scepticism, writers in the age of the noble savage were eager to elaborate and liberalise the image of druidism.

The oddest and most suggestive of Wordsworth's references is the last, to Procopius of Caesarea. The Rydal Mount sale catalogue lists *Procopii Caesariensis de Rebus Gothorum Persarum ac Vandalorum* in an edition of 1531. My schoolboy Latin gleans nothing to the point from this volume, but according to Nora Chadwick, Procopius (who was Secretary at the Byzantine Court during the reign of Justinian I) reports that the spirits of the dead are conveyed to Britain by fishermen periodically summoned to this duty, who travel at supernatural speeds when on this service, making the crossing in an hour.[1] The idea that not merely Borrowdale (as in Gray's account) but Britain as a whole might be yclept a Vale of Elysium, or the Fortunate Isles, casts some light, perhaps, on Wordsworth's desire that his poetry should make such legendary spheres of existence, or post existence, 'the simple produce of the common day'. Given that both Charlotte Corday and Jean-Baptiste Louvet saw themselves as bound for Elysium in 1793, the one to converse with Brutus, the other with Sidney, such concern has a more contemporary (and more political) ring than one might imagine.[2]

Natural Supernaturalism?

St John's College, Cambridge, may not have been aware in October 1787 that it had just enrolled, in the precocious author of *The Vale of Esthwaite*,

> a young Initiate who had seen
> Thrice sacred mysteries mid Druid groves
> Or where grey Temples stood on native Hills[3]

Faber, 1978) 79, 84. See, also, R. S. Thomas's poem 'Taliesin 1952'.

1   Nora Chadwick, *The British Heroic Age: The Welsh and the Men of the North* (University of Wales Press, 1976), vii.

2   *European Magazine*, August 1793, 165 and Louvet's *Narrative of the Dangers to which I have been exposed, since the 31st of May, 1793* (London: J. Johnson, 1795), 109.

3   *The Prelude*, ed. E de Selincourt, 2nd edn., rev. Helen Darbishire (Oxford: Clarendon Press, 1959), 76 *app. crit.* Book 3, ms.A draft.

but had it been advised of Wordsworth's adherence to the ancient order of British Druids, or his status as 'a bard elect' (that is, one trained to celebrate in sympathetic verse primeval mysteries), it may not have been greatly surprised. Almost every poet of that date was so apprenticed. As A. L. Owen noted, Wordsworth describes himself here in phrases drawn from William Owen's *Heroic Elegies of Llywarch Hên* (1792), promoting himself rapidly in adjacent drafts from 'vernal green' robes to 'cerulean' ones—a revisionary self-promotion from the lowest to the highest of the Bardic classes.[1] A well-read admissions tutor might have regarded such apprenticeship an adequate guarantee of a proper patriotism. Cowper's *Boadicea*, for instance, looks pityingly on the Roman Empire as no more than a dress rehearsal for the British: 'Regions Caesar never knew | Thy posterity shall sway'. And in Whitehead's strident *Verses to the People of England* (1758), a druidically instructed muse rouses the Bards from torpor:

> But when War's tremendous roar
> Shakes the Isle from Shore to Shore,
> Every Bard of purer fire
> Tyrtaeus-like should grasp the Lyre.

They also represented a certain pride in lineage. Although in some eyes the original druids were migrating Titans, most agreed that they were of the line of the patriarchs. The quarrel was between those who felt that their religion had degenerated and those who felt that it was pure. Edward Davies, in his *Celtic Researches*, insisted that while 'the religion of the patriarchs had been deformed ... by all nations' the druids 'appear to have retained many of its vital and essential principles'.[2] Others Christianized them. Drayton insisted on their monotheism; Selden, his annotator, shows them familiar with the crucifixion; Stukeley gives them a trinity and finds it symbolized in the architecture of Avebury (Owen 124). For Stukeley, the druids were not merely the repository of primitive religion but the fountainhead of Christian faith. 'These famous philosophic priests came hither as a Phoenician colony in the very earliest times, as soon as Tyre

1   A. L. Owen, 164. William Owen Pughe, in his introduction to *The Heroic Elegies of Llywarch Hen, Prince of the Cumbrian Britons* (1792), describes the three orders of Bards as wearing, blue, white and green robes respectively. *Heroic Elegies*, xxxvi–xl.
2   Edward Davies, *Celtic Researches on the Origin, Traditions and Language of he Ancient Britons* (London, 1804), 119.

was founded: during the life of the patriarch Abraham, or very soon there-after' and the only difference between their religion and Christianity was their belief that the Messiah was yet to come.[1] Stonehenge, to Stukeley, was both a place of dread and 'the house of God ... the gate of heaven' (Owen, 126). Possessors of the pure religion of Abraham, the druids who had migrated to Britain in Abraham's lifetime, preserving in Welsh an uncorrupted Hebrew, served collectively as a John the Baptist to English Christianity.

Edward Davies gave little credence to all this Christianizing, but his *Celtic Researches* affirmed of the druids that

> Their studies embraced those elevated objects which had engaged the attention of the world in its primitive state—the nature of the Deity—of the human soul—of the future state.... Their conceptions were great and sublime, their speculations comprehensive in their sphere .... Perhaps there was no order of men amongst the heathens, who preserved the history and the opinions of mankind, in its early state with more simplicity and more integrity.[2]

For poets, too, especially those in search of an alternative to Augustan mythology—borrowed wholesale from the classics and soiled by over-use—the druids had much to offer. John Clelands's *Specimens of an Etymological Vocabulary* (1768) credited the druids with cleansing mythology of its named godkins and goddesslings and Gray compli-mented Mason on a passage in *Caractacus*, concerning mysterious rites atop Snowdon. He liked it all the more 'because it seems like a new mythology peculiar to the Druid superstition, and not borrowed of the Greeks'.[3] As Blake's work shows, a new Pantheon similar to, but dis-tinct from, that of Rome and Greece, and employing unfamiliar names,

1   William Stukeley, *Stonehenge: A Temple Restored to the British Druids* (London, 1740), 2.]
2   *Celtic Researches*, 120. Nora Chadwick shares this enthusiasm: 'The druids are the most advanced of all intellectual classes among the peoples of ancient Europe beyond the Greek and Roman world.... It is in fact this deep concern with spiritual and intel-lectual matters which constitutes the chief lasting claim of the druids on our attention. Education was in their hands and rarely has it been carried on with more sustained and prolonged assiduity. Rarely has it been devoted to matters less utilitarian or more majestic. Their central subjects were nature and the universe; their leading doctrine, the immortality of the soul' (*The Druids*, vii–viii).
3   *Letters*, ed. Tovey, 1: 337, cited Edward D. Snyder, *The Celtic Revival in English Literature 1760–1800* (Gloucester, MA: Peter Smith, 1965), 5

can energize the mind by requiring one to interpret story lines afresh. Alternately, one could see classical myth as a corruption of British faith: Blake's contemporaries were persuaded by hints in such classical figures as Procopius, Dion Chrysostom and Strabo that Britain was the true home of the mysteries of Samothrace. Aylett Sammes cites Onomacritus, otherwise known as Orpheus, to the effect that the Britannic Islands were 'the seat of Queen Ceres', and half confirms Camden's suggestion that they were also supposed by the ancients to be the Fortunate Islands, and the domain of the Elysian Fields.[1] When nocturnal sacrifices were performed, Sammes surmises, they were devoted to Pluto and to Proserpine.

Whatever the Pastor may feel, when he disparages 'Andates' in *The Excursion*, one can feel that for Wordsworth, Taranis the Thunderer (Jove) and Andates offer an alternative way (alternative to Milton's and the Pastor's) of conceiving power and terror 'put forth in personal form'. United, they make up an androgynous deity—one much closer to Wordsworth's way of presenting the sense of God throughout *The Prelude*. Andates or Andraste appears frequently in poetry of the turn of the century. She is invoked as the spirit of Mona, in Sotheby's *Tour* (1794) along with 'viewless harps' and 'aerial murmurs' as heard by Wordsworth on Salisbury Plain:

> Though mute the voice
> Of Druid, nor an oak now rear aloft
> It's head, beneath whose gloom the white-robed priest
> Hymned his fierce gods, and with infernal rites
> Poured forth the sacrifice of human blood
> At dread Andraste's fane; yet sudden heard
> To viewless harps aerial murmurs sound
> Mourning the desolated shrines.[2]

As Wordsworth could have known directly at almost any date from Dion Chrystostom, who is listed in his Racedown 'bibliography', antiquarians tended to associate Andates or Andraste with Hecate, with Minerva, and with Venus, both as goddess of victory and mother of the Gods. She was, most famously, invoked by Boudicca before her battles with the Romans.[3] Wordsworth invokes her most effectively in the opening stan-

1   Aylett Sammes, *Britannia Antiqua Illustrata*, 2; c.f. Camden *Britannia*, iii, iv.
2   William Sotheby, *A Tour Through Parts of Wales, Sonnets, Odes and Other Poems* (London: R. Blamire, 1794), 37.
3   Sammes, on the relatedness of Celtic and Roman deities, glosses Taranis as Jupiter,

zas of *Resolution and Independence* merely by focusing upon the hare, from whose course when released Boudicca divined the favour of the Goddess. And it is surely as bizarre to read the Lucy Poems without *some* consciousness of the abduction of Persephone, as to read Blake's *A Little Girl Lost* in entire ignorance of the mysteries of Samothrace. Indeed the Lucy poems may help one understand how the Persephone myth arose in the first place. Geoffrey Hartman has commented that even the opening lines of something as naturalised as *Michael* can lead us 'unexpectedly to a Greek prototype' in Theocritus and Leonidas, and that 'even a song as bare as "Tintern Abbey" is based on the superstition of spirit of place':

> At the end of the poem ... he speaks as if he were one of the dead who exhort the living in the guise of the genius loci. But the archaic for-mulae are now generated from the natural soil of the meditation. We feel that a superstition of the tribe has been genuinely recovered and purified. There is nothing patently archaic or poetically archaizing in Wordsworth's use of a belief which he grounds so deeply in the human passion for continuity, for binding together the wisdom of the dead and the energy of the living. (*The Unremarkable Wordsworth*, 41, 42)

Wordsworth's sense of the poet as standing by Nature's side among the men of old—rather than by the side of supernature—goes some way to explain why he does not, in his poetry, tend to give supernatural names to what in nature he experiences. The primacy in his religious sense of a giant Mother (a phrase he uses in his poem on Long Meg) almost always designated 'she', and displaced only occasionally by a more masculine and chastising power, is something we all know from our reading of *The Prelude*: a poem whose supernatural machinery, though at its most pagan in the earliest *Two-Part* version, is never wholly Christianized, if it is at all. And when Wordsworth says of the education of the Pedlar in the 1798 version that 'he did not feel *the God*: he felt his works' he appears to be echoing the un-English usage of the definite article in George Richards's

---

and relates him to Thor, Donner, etc., Hesus as Mars, Tutates or Toutatis as Mercury or Hermes, Belisama as Diana, Hu or Hues as Bacchus, Belenus as Apollo, and (citing Dio) Andraste as Venus Victrix. *Britannia Antiqua Illustrata*, 126–36. (Students of *Asterix the Gaul* may recall three of these deities being invoked by Panoramix the Druid: 'par Belenos, Toutatis et Belisama…'). Camden's *Britannia* (1586, 1695) xxv and Edward Davies, *Mythology and Rites of the British Druids* (1809), 617 cite Dio on the identification of Andates, and William Sotheby, in his *Tour*, opined that sacrifice was made to her in the Isle of Mona.

similar equivocation regarding deity in *The Aboriginal Britons* (1791):

> Yet gazing round him he beheld *the God*
> Hold in all nature's works his dread abode:
> He saw him beaming in the silver moon
> Effulgent burning in the blaze of noon,
> On the dark bosom of the storm reclin'd
> Speaking in thunder, riding on the wind,
> And, mid the earthquake's awful riot hurled
> Shaking the deep foundations of the world.

'In part a Fellow-citizen, in part | An outlaw and a Borderer of his age' Wordsworth called himself ('Prospectus' MS, *PW*, 5: 6 app crit.). He remained one in his religion: not least because, as a true poet, he is as troubled as Robert Graves says the true poet always is, by the banishment of the Goddess, or even of 'the God', or the gods. The surfacing of Triton, or Pan, in Wordsworth's poems is rare, and when it happens, can cause the hairs to rise on the back of one's neck—as classical allusions in eighteenth century poetry tend not to. It is confined mostly to occasional sonnets (Triton appears most memorably in 'The World is too much with us', Pan makes a startling appearance among the reeds in *Composed by the side of Grasmere Lake*). But without 'familiars' of the lakes, and 'presences' and natural forms performing 'mysterious offices' Wordsworth would not be Wordsworth: he trumps Drayton's local deities ('Ye genii of these floods, these mountains and these dales') with his own tutelary spirits.[1] Such effects are intimately related to the late eighteenth century's desire to naturalise a sense of the divinity of nature that had become confined to decorative allusion to alien classics, but they are altogether more integral to his own imagination. One feels that whereas eighteenth-century poets borrow from the druids or Greece as a picturesque resource, Wordsworth does exactly what *The Excursion* says the Greeks did: he personifies in order to give appropriate embodiment to felt recognitions. Edward Young's *Conjectures on Original Composition* had counselled poets to imitate Homer, not his works: to 'drink where he drank … at the breast of Nature'.[2] When Emerson, energized by *The Tables Turned*, challenged his book-ridden contemporaries to 'close up these barren leaves' and cultivate their own 'original relation to the uni-

---

1   *Poly-Olbion*, ed. J. William Hebel (Oxford: Blackwell, 1933), Song 30.
2   Edward Young, *Conjectures on Original Composition* (1759; Leeds: Scolar, 1966), 21.

verse', Wordsworth is undoubtedly the model.[1]

God, in Wordsworth's poetry, is often required to co-habit with deities of other, if lesser, orders, and with spirits of undistinguishable modes. The localized 'beings of the hills' who, in the *Two-Part Prelude* of 1799 are made responsible for the early 'spots of time', do give place on occasions to the more deistical 'wisdom and spirit of the universe', but even in the 1850 version Wordsworth's climactic vision upon Mount Snowdon is granted to 'spirits of the night' as well as 'three chance human wanderers'. God may exist as a remote celestial first cause, but nature's local spirits act on him: 'I believe | That there are spirits' (*1799*, 1.68–9). He interacts with 'beings of the hills, | And ye that walk the woods and open heaths' (130–31). He attributes his education to 'Ye powers of earth, ye genii of the springs, | And ye that have your voices in the clouds, | And ye that are familiars of the lakes | And of the standing pools' (186–89). Even when in 1805 these powers and genii become 'presences' he still finds solace in 'the souls of lonely places'. Asked by a local constable to help with his enquiries about a stolen boat on Ullswater his excuse is that 'They guided me'. 'They' in this instance may be his own vital spirits, or local spirits of the lakes, or the former giving rise to the latter; after all, they are all one life (in *1805* the excuse is that he is 'led by *her*'). How else would deities, minor or major, local or universal, come into being? As Anthony Harding has argued, one may wish to doubt Wordsworth's 'I believe that there are spirits', but to dismiss the animism of the *Two-Part Prelude* as merely conventional is to miss its function in presenting the young Wordsworth as a child of the people, and sharing in folk perceptions.[2] One might add that it is the animist experience of the child in Part 1 of the *Two-Part Prelude* that qualifies Wordsworth to write the Pedlar's speech on pagan imagination in *The Excursion*, which in turn kick-started Romantic Hellenism. When Part 2 of the same work ascribes some of the same effects—including voices on the winds—to imagination, the revisionary terminology merely confirms one's sense that for Wordsworth paganism is not merely an archaic stage in human

1   *Nature* [1836], *Norton Anthology of American Literature*, 5th edn, Vol. 1, ed. Nina Baym et al.(New York: Norton, 1998), 1073. As the opening poems in *Lyrical Ballads* (Philadelphia, 1802), *Expostulation and Reply* and *The Tables Turned* came to exemplify Wordsworth's 'mission statement' in America.

2   See 'Imaginative Animism in Wordsworth's 1798–99 *Prelude*', chapter 2 of Anthony John Harding, *The Reception of Myth in English Romanticism* (Columbia MO and London: University of Missouri Press, 1995) 60–87.

history but a necessary stage in personal history.

If Wordsworth's poetry is less overtly mythological than much eighteenth-century writing this may because he generally absorbs, so that we do not see it as druidic, the substance of eighteenth-century druidism, whose practitioners were gentle haunters of the woods, as familiar as Wordsworth himself with muttering rocks and whispering trees and correspondent breezes. In some accounts—including that of Mircea Eliade—we might see the druid-bards as poets of a paradisal myth, distinguished precursors. They shared a function which Wordsworth called healing and connecting, and which, post-Hughes, we might be inclined to call Shamanistic. Their role was to commune with the invisible world, and to reassure the tribe that paradise can be the simple produce of the common day. The gentle druids of Thomson, Mason and Collins look back, A. L. Owen writes, 'to Sir William Temple's druids, whose "lives were simple and innocent, in woods … and hollow trees"'. So in Mason's 'solemn groves' in *Caractacus*:

> Reside the sages skill'd in Nature's lore:
> The changeful universe, its numbers, powers,
> Studious they measure, save when meditation
> Gives place to holy rites. (*Poems*, 175)

Like the true poet described in Wordsworth's MS.W, these druids were 'familiar with the essences of things', and like the boy of *The Prelude* they listened to 'The ghostly language of the ancient earth'. Taliesin, whose legendary boyhood prefigures some of Wordsworth's own, assumes that it is the function of a bard 'to relate the great secrets of the world we inhabit'.[1] In Hutchinson's *Antiquities*, the druid 'taught the adoration of the divine essence, and deduced his arguments, from examples displayed in the book of nature'.[2] For druids, Wordsworth concedes in the late poem *Humanity*, 'rocks and whispering trees' performed 'mysterious offices'.

Patriarchs or Jacobins?

The recovery of the lost culture of Wales in the eighteenth century was largely the work of two gentleman scholars, Lewis Morris and Evan

---

1   Edward Davies, *Mythology and Rites of the British Druids* (1809), 47.
2   William Hutchinson, *History and Antiquities of Cumberland* (2 vols. 1794), 1: 5.

Evans, who built a genuine archive of ancient poetry while deprecating the fabricated 'Ossian'.[1] It was made pertinent to Romantic poets in part by the comparative mythologist Edward Davies, whose works were consulted by both Southey and Wordsworth at various dates, and in part by the Welsh Jacobin, Edward Williams.[2] Edward Williams's bardic name (inherited, he insisted, from five hundred years of unbroken succession from the mediaeval Welsh bards, despite the worst efforts of Edward the Bardicide), was 'Iolo Morganwg'. Aided by the gullibility of Blake's associate William Owen Pughe (an elder of the church of Joanna Southcote), Williams adulterated the work of Morris and Evans. He manufactured more and more editions of supposedly authentic relics, and developed a complete system of druidism. He expounded this system in the history of bardism he contributed to William Owen's *Heroic Elegies of Llywarch Hen* (1792, dedicated to Thomas Pennant), and in his own *Poems Lyric and Pastoral* (1794, dedicated to the Prince of Wales). From a Romantic point of view, Iolo's is the more interesting 'case', and not only because of his connections with Southey, Mrs Barbauld, Horne Tooke and Coleridge.[3] His ongoing debate with Edward Davies did for druidism what Tom Paine and Edmund Burke did for Nature—they made it capable of bewilderingly contrary ideological inflections.

In *Celtic Researches on the Origin, Traditions and Language of the Ancient Britons* (1804)—consulted by Southey for *Madoc* and Wordsworth for *Ecclesiastical Sonnets*—Edward Davies proclaimed the druids as authors of 'great and sublime' conceptions, guardians of 'the

---

1   For the achievements of both Lewis Morris and Evan Evans see Edward D. Snyder, *The Celtic Revival*, 17–33. Thomas Carte, the historian, owed much of his Celtic lore to Lewis Morris. To Evan Evans's *Some Specimens of the Poetry of the Antient Welsh Bards* (1764) we owe Thomas Gray's translations and imitations. Evans's celebration of 'Ifor Hael' inspired, by linguistic misprision, Wordsworth's Ivor Hall in *Simon Lee*.

2   For William Owen (Pughe), Iolo Morganwg and the invention of Wales see Prys Morgan, *The Eighteenth-Century Renaissance* (Llandybie: Christopher Davies, 1981), Gwyn A. Williams, *The Search for Beulah Land: the Welsh and the Atlantic Revolution* (London: Croom Helm, 1980), and Morgan's 'From death to a view: the hunt for the Welsh past in the Romantic period', in Eric Hobsbawm and Terence Ranger, eds, *The Invention of Tradition* (Cambridge, 1984), 43–100. Iolo Morganwg has more recently become the focus of widespread research project as evidenced in the twenty-two essays of Geraint. H. Jenkins, ed., *A Rattleskull Genius: The Many Faces of Iolo Morganwg* (Cardiff: University of Wales Press, 2005).

3   Coleridge had met Williams by 13 May 1796 'probably at Estlin's' and 'may have known his bookshop in Cowbridge'. *CN*, 1, 174 (16) n. and 605 n.

history and opinions of mankind in its early state' (119). In *Mythology and Rites of the British Druids* (1809), dedicated to the Bishop of Llandaff, Davies claimed that 'the ancient superstition of Druidism, or at least some part of it was … preserved in Wales without interruption, and cherished by the Bards, to the very last period of the Welsh Princes' (25). In a lengthy analysis of the 'Hanes Taliesin' (189–224) he sees it relating to 'a succession of ceremonies, by which the ancient Britons commemorated the history of the deluge; and concludes imaginatively 'that these ceremonies had a constant analogy with the mystical rites of Ceres and Isis, which our best mythologists regard as memorials of the same event'.

But in the more radical 1790s Edward Williams had forged (in both senses of the term) a much more dynamic model of druidism. Edward Davies, despite his own fanciful conjectures concerning the helio-arkite mysteries and the rites of Bacchus and Ceridwen, found Iolos's version outrageously inauthentic. He spent some sixty pages of *Mythology and Rites* attempting to separate what could be known and believed in from what was claimed by Iolo and by Pughe. In their 'history of Bardism' Davies amusingly detects some later adhesions to druid doctrine:

> The principles here announced seem to go rather beyond the level-lers of the seventeenth century, and to savour strongly of a Druidism which originated in Gaul, and was thence transported into some corners of Britain not many ages before the year 1792 when the memorial of Bardism made its appearance. (*MR* 57)

Citing Taliesin, Caesar and Sharon Turner's *Vindication* (1803) as to the martial quality of the bards, Davies will have nothing to do with Iolo's egalitarianism or with his pacifism: 'It therefore rests with the advo-cates of this *chair*, to inform us whether [egalitarianism] was introduced into their code by the levellers of the seventeenth century, or fabricated during the late anarchy of France' (59), As for pacifism, 'I do not recol-lect to have seen this doctrine … promulgated by any code, before a cer-tain period of the French revolution' (60).

In *Poems Lyric and Pastoral* Iolo claimed, inter alia, to possess a manuscript synopsis of Druidism 'by *Llewellyn Sion, a Bard*, written about the year 1560' and entirely conformable to the ideas of 'TALIESIN in the sixth century, whose poems exhibit a complete system of DRUIDISM' (*Poems* 2: 194). This manuscript enjoined some thirty maxims, condu-cive to liberty and the pursuit of happiness, and strikingly suggestive

of the Romantic and liberal Jacobin agenda. Along with metempsycho-
sis, Iolo's druids believed in necessitarian progress to the good. They
asserted man's perfect recollection in eternity of all he has been (a sort
of Keatsian 'repetition in a finer tone' of the bliss each person attains);
a materialist belief in the circulation of life force from one living form
to another, enjoying a sort of immortality; and a libertarian code strik-
ingly adapted to—say—the *Political Lectures* of John Thelwall or the
'Proverbs' of William Blake: 'Our infallible rule of Duty', say Iolo's
Druids, is, not to do or desire any thing but what can eternally be done
and obtained in the Celestial states, wherein no evil can exist. The Good
and happiness of one Being, must not arise from the Evil, or misery,
of another'. As Owen Pughe's friend William Blake insisted in *The
Marriage of Heaven & Hell*, 'Hindrance is not an act', and as Thelwall
taught, 'What I have a RIGHT to demand for myself, it is my DUTY to
secure to others'.[1]

In short, where Edward Davies sought among the druids the purest
preservation of the traditional beliefs of mankind, amalgamating venera-
tion for Noah with the mysteries of Samothrace, Edward Williams found
in them a blend of Romantic, Unitarian and Jacobin ethics.

Iolo, to use his bardic name, was a one-man Romanticism. His con-
tacts range from the Welsh equivalent of the Society for Constitutional
Information, the Gwynneddigion or 'Men of North Wales', to Joseph
Priestley and numerous other emigrants, to the Paris Welsh in the form of
David Williams (the forgotten British Jacobin), to Citoyen Brissot, and
to Citoyen Dupré, official sculptor of the French republic, who designed
some of the medals used during the efflorescence of Eisteddfodau in
those heady years between 1789 and 1798.[2] He amply deserves Gwyn
Williams's wonderful (and headlong) eulogy:

> Out of this lovely, open but frustrated society [of South Wales] living in
> the interstices of gentry politics and so similar in intellectual and social
> tone to that Philadelphia which was the spiritual capital of most of
> them, came the maimed and towering genius *Iolo Morganwg*, Edward
> Williams the stonemason Bard of Liberty who invented the Gorsedd of
> Bards and the no less Jacobin and Unitarian Druids of a 'revived' tradi-

1   John Thelwall, *The Rights of Nature against the usurpations of establishments. A
series of letters to the People of Britain, occasioned by the recent effusions of The Right
Honourable Edmund Burke* (3rd edition, 1796) 2: 40.
2   Prys Morgan, 'From death to a View', 60.

tion and offered the Welsh a revivification of that 'tradition' which was in truth the driving ideology of a new and radical nation built on the principles of the American and French revolutions.[1]

Moreover, Iolo's career, which paralleled Blake's in its consistency, rather than the apostatic trajectory of Wordsworth, Coleridge and Southey, was fired by a vision of the status of poets that all four of these English poets shared: 'Welsh poets, Iolo perceived, had not been poets as the English used the word; they were the directive spiritual elite of a society, the people's remembrancers' (Gwyn Williams, 32). That vision of the poet was one Ioloesque notion that Wordsworth embraced with increasing tenacity.

---

1   Gwyn Williams, *The Search for Beulah Land,* 33. Iolo went on promoting Eisteddfodau, with all their bardic associations, throughout the period of high Romanticism. In the year Blake piped his *Songs of Innocence* there were three Eisteddfodau, in Llangollen, Corwen and Bala; in the year of Shelley's *Ode to the West Wind,* Iolo married his druidical Gorsedd of Bards to the Eisteddfod in Carmarthen in an attempt to politicise the latter. In his hands, Gwyn Williams writes, 'Druidism itself took on the lineaments of Rousseau's natural religion, a unitarian creed uncorrupted by priestcraft' (Williams, 15). See also, Prys Morgan, *The Eighteenth-Century Renaissance,* 115.

Chapter 2: 'Unforgotten Lays'

> Majestic Skiddaw round whose trackless steep
> Mid the bright sun-shine darksome tempests sweep,
> To you the patriot fled: his native land
> He spurn'd when proffer'd by a conqueror's hand:
> In you to roam at large; to lay his head
> On the black rock, unclad, unhous'd, unfed
> —George Richards, *The Aboriginal Britons* [1]

DESPITE THE RECURRENCE of his primal scene of druid sacrifice at intervals between 1787 and 1842,[2] one would not say that Wordsworth ever made the subject of Druids and their beliefs, or Bards and their work, the central focus of any of his major work. Speculative expositions of the alleged beliefs and values of the Druids and their Bardic successors have little purchase on him. When one thinks of the output of antiquarian verse between Drayton's *Poly-Olbion* (1622) and Cottle's *The Fall of Cambria, a poem in Twenty Four Books* (1808), Wordsworth's investment in 'The Matter of Britain' can seem belated, insignificant and even, until the scrupulously researched *Ecclesiastical Sonnets*, ill-informed.[3]

While the evidence of Wordsworth's library is late, his friendships and his travels nevertheless suggest a life-long interest in Wales.[4] His early

1 *The Aboriginal Britons, a Poem* (Oxford, 1791), 17.
2 Apart from the visionary moments in *The Vale of Esthwaite, Salisbury Plain, The Prelude*, and *The Excursion*, ancillary motifs appear in *An Evening Walk, Yew-Trees, A Weight of Awe* (on Long Meg and her daughters), *Humanity, The Pass of Kirkstone*.
3 The output included Mason's *Caractacus* and *Elfrida* (1752), Thomson's *Castle of Indolence* (1748), Gray's 'The Bard' (1757) and his transcreations of Aneirin, Robert Holmes's *Alfred* (1778, in which Saxon Alfred inherits druid wisdom), Cowper's *Boadicea* (1782), George Richards's *Songs of the Aboriginal Bards* (1791), James Boaden's *The Camro-Britons* (1798), William Sotheby's *The Cambrian Hero, or Llewellyn the Great* (c. 1800), Thelwall's 'The Fairy of the Lake' (1801), and Southey's enormous investment in *Madoc* (1805).
4 Three venerable articles addressing this topic are: H. Wright, 'Wordsworth and Wales', *Welsh Outlook* 11 (1924) 103–5 and 127–29. T. H. Bowen, 'Wordsworth's

allusions to the druids are based, in the main, on picturesque guides, such as West, Gilpin and Pennant, and on Mason's *Caractacus*. His later ones are enriched by the work of such serious Celtic scholars as Sharon Turner and Edward Davies. His circle of friends included Southey and Thelwall, and more remotely, Sotheby and Cottle—all distinguished Celtophiles and writers on matters Welsh. And in July–September 1790 he went on a lengthy walk, to Switzerland and back, with Robert Jones, a fellow student. They spent all of the Summer of 1791 together in Wales, at Plas-yn-Llan, near Ruthin, planned to meet up in France in 1792, and were together again in North Wales in September 1793. There may have been a cooling in the early years of the nineteenth century, but Wordsworth visited Jones's Oxfordshire Parsonage in 1820 (commemorated in the poem *A Parsonage in Oxfordshire*), and William, Mary and Dora enjoyed Jones's company again in Wales in 1824. Jones visited Grasmere in 1800, and Rydal in 1831.[1] In between these visits, Jones provided Wordsworth with gifts of books on and in Welsh—including William Owen's dictionary of Welsh, at the poet's request—and a Welsh *Paradise Lost*. And in 1829 Wordsworth became an honorary member of the Cymmrodorion.[2]

There is little direct evidence that Jones and Wordsworth ever exchanged a word about Welsh literature, or the matter of Britain. Yet in 1791 they toured North Wales with Thomas Pennant in hand—i.e. accompanied by readings from Drayton and his sources—and visited the antiquarian en route.[3] And introducing *Descriptive Sketches* (1793),

Welsh Friend', *English* 8:43 (1950) 17–21; and D. Myrddin Lloyd, 'Wordsworth and Wales', *National Library of Wales Journal*, 6:4 (1950), 338–52. Neither these nor later work have recognized Wordsworth's awareness that much 'Welsh' literature belongs as much, if not more, to Cumbria.

1   D. Myrddin Lloyd (342–45) adds that there were several dashes into Wales from Somerset in 1797–98 (including the visit to Thelwall's hermitage), and ongoing communication between the Wordsworths and Thomas Hutchinson in Radnorshire and John Monkhouse at Stowe, near Hay-on-Wye, between 1809 and 1841. .

2   For the Cymmrodorion see *LY*, 2: 11; for Pughe's *Abridgment of the Welsh-English Dictionary* (1806), *see LY,* 2: 650: 'I often wish to consult a book of that kind'.

3   In 1793 Jones and Wordsworth encountered a Reverend Thomas who boasted of the concision of Welsh as compared to English. The inebriated Reverend produced only one example; that 'tad' [dad] is Welsh for 'father'. When Wordsworth smiled at this, the cleric brandished a carving knife and cried 'You vile Saxon ... to come here and insult me an ancient Briton on my own territory'. Wordsworth revenges himself on this parochial ancient Briton, who seems unaware that his guest was from the land of the Cymri, in a letter of 14 May 1829 (*LY 2*: 77–79), by when Wordsworth's knowledge of

Wordsworth apologizes for not *yet* having touched in poetry on

> The sea-sunsets, which give such splendour to the vale of Clwyd, Snowdon, the chair of Idris, the quiet village of Bethgelert, Menai and her druids, the Alpine steeps of the Conway, and the still more interesting windings of the wizard stream of the Dee.[1]

In 1825, after the 1824 tour in Wales, Wordsworth was still planning to redeem this pledge, but now in the form of a companion volume to his *Guide to the Lakes*, offering an 'analysis' of the cultural integrity of 'Snowdon, Cader Idris and their several dependencies' (*LY*, 1.172).[2]

The places itemized in these two passages are not merely picturesque viewing stations. Menai was recognized by Tacitus as the last line of defence of the druids when Suetonius confonted them (and her druids make a belated appearance in Wordsworth's verse in the 3rd Ecclesiastical Sonnet). Pennant's guide treats Snowdon as a northern Parnassus (2.323–4)—the very place to seek a revelation of the eternal mind.[3] It was also, in druid lore, the equivalent less of Parnassus than of Ararat, a place where imagined seas might indeed lick one's feet.[4] The Chair of Idris, another mountain-top, has its own legend—that to spend a night on that rocky chair will render one mad, dead, or a poet. Idris, as an astronomer, was, like Wordsworth, conversant with the stars, and how at evening they 'moved along the edges of the hills'. Bethgelert is near the source of the Conway: it was at nearby Dinas Emris, according to Pennant, that Merlin Ambrosius 'foretold the fall of the Britons to the hapless Vortigern in the 5th century'.[5] The phrase 'the wizard Dee' is Milton's but her peculiar powers and interesting windings are splendidly celebrated by Drayton, in whose topographical poem *Poly-Olbion* the speaking voice of nature assumes variously the accents of Royal Snowdon, the Severn, the 'ominous' Dee, and the 'lascivious' Wye. The lewder sort of Wye tourist was

his Celtic inheritance was much enhanced.

1   Matthew Arnold has a similar, if more learned, passage in *Celtic Literature*, evoking 'Diganwy, where Mael-gwyn shut up Elphin', 'God-daeth, the place of feasting, where the bards were entertained', and 'Llanrwst ... and Taliesin's grave' *On the Study of Celtic Literature and Other Essays* (London: J. M. Dent, 1910), 14.

2   Lloyd notes this ambition, 346–47, but deplores Wordsworth's lack of understanding of the culture of Wales, as compared to Cumbria.

3   Thomas Pennant, *Tours in Wales*, 3 vols (London 1810), 2: 323–4.

4   Edward Davies, *Mythology and Rites*, 323.

5   Pennant, 2: 351, citing *Poly-Olbion*.

already wont, if Drayton is to be believed, 'her passages to view, | As wantonly she straines in her lascivious course'. In a passage cited in full by Pennant, who has much to say about hydromancy, Drayton presents the 'sterner Dee', whose 'holinesse begun, | By his contracted front and sterner waves, to show | That he had things to speak, might profit them to know'.[1]

Each element of Wordsworth's as yet uncelebrated landscape, then, is pregnant with imprecations, divination, prophecy, revelation, illumination, or omen. And if *The Excursion* is to be believed, the Wales he visited with Robert Jones, in successive walking holidays, was still a bardic land. As a wandering youth, he writes,

> I listened with delight
> To pastoral melody or warlike air,
> Drawn from the strings of ancient British harp
> By some accomplished master.
>
> (*Excursion*, 7: 9–12)[2]

So did Thomas Gray, whose *Bard,* inspired by the art of Blind John Parry, in turn inspired John Martin, Thomas Jones and De Loutherberg. No doubt Wordsworth's memory is coloured by Beattie and by Gray, as well as by Pennant and Iolo Morganwg, but as a matter of historical fact he could have heard such 'time-hallowed minstrelsy' even though the performers were most likely to be itinerant London Welsh, sponsored by the Cymmrodorion or by Iolo Morganwg and his North Walians. Heard or unheard, the minstrelsy is valorized in key Wordsworthian terms, for 'Strains of power | Were they, to seize and occupy the sense' (22–23).

Three of Wordsworth's most formative experiences—a meeting with a little girl at Goodrich Castle in 1793, for whom he was still looking in 1841, the return to the Wye in 1798, and the ascent of Snowdon in either 1791 or 1793—belong to Wales. Otherwise, Wordsworth pays scant attention to Wales as such. *Simon Lee* alludes to bardic Cardigan, and *Anecdote for fathers* to John Thelwall's hermitage at Llyswen, and the 1824 tour with Jones produced the sonnet *To the Torrent at the Devil's Bridge*, with its emotion-fed links to 'the throbbing rocks of Viamala'.[3]

1   Drayton, *Poly-Olbion*, ed. J. William Hebel (Oxford: Blackwell, 1933), 10.200f.
2   Whether Wordsworth heard such bards, or relied upon Pennant's testimony that one could, is a moot point. See Pennant, 2: 242.
3   See Geoffrey Hartman's masterly essay, 'Blessing the Torrent: Wordsworth's later Style', in *The Unremarkable Wordsworth*.

That is all. One reason for this sparse output may be the poetic over-crowding. A year after Wordsworth promised to poeticize Wales at some future date William Sotheby published his by no means uncompeti-tive *A Tour Through Parts of Wales*. Sotheby not only climbs Snowdon (glimpsing the real landscape beneath a sea of mist), but celebrates 'the genius of wild Llangollen' in a style already less *Vale of Esthwaite* than *The Poem upon the Wye*:

> Genius of wild Llangollen! once again
> I return to thy rude haunts, …

Here, 'Mid the grey cliffs that o'er yon heights impend…',

> At distance from the murmur of mankind,
> I sooth to peace the cares of life awhile,
> And woo, lone Nature's long-forgotten smile.

As Wordsworth develops his sense of Cumbrian archaeology, revising *An Evening Walk* in 1794, Sotheby has already done the same for 'the wizard Dee'. Beside the Dee, where Arthur 'once listened to the wizard's lore' fancy still 'wanders unconfined, | And visionary day-dreams sooth the mind'. As in Wordsworth's Cumbria, where such relics inform the lives of poets and shepherds alike, Sotheby finds signs of long-mould-ered 'British forts' where 'The rich grass spiring o'er the sheep-fed heath, | Points out the levelled turrets sunk beneath' and 'Year after year the ver-dant circles spring, | And shepherd boys retrace the fairy ring.'[1]

All in all, Wordsworth might well have felt that Drayton, his beloved Dyer, Gray, and Sotheby had already done Wales quite enough justice, as compared with Cumbria. Wordsworth, who rarely did anything twice, even as regards rhyme schemes, followed directly in others' footsteps still more rarely. The antiquarian field was heavily over-subscribed, and after *The Bard* very little of it is worth saving from the next flood. Wordsworth, in any case, knew very well that much of what was claimed as classical Welsh literature in his day belonged, in reality, less to Wales (geographically speaking) than to the warlike Romano-British kingdom of Rheged, where Taliesin, Aneirin and Myrddin celebrated, inter alia, the exploits of Arthur and Urien, as they withstood, in the hills and val-leys of Cumbria and West Yorkshire and the forests of Caledonia north

---

1   William Sotheby, *A Tour Through Parts of Wales,* 112–13. For Arthur and Merlin Sotheby refers the reader to *Faerie Queen*, book 1, canto 1.

of the Wall, the advance of the Northumbrian Saxons. One reason for Gray's priority is the symbolic resonance of his theme. Thomas Carte, in his *A General History of England*, on which Gray based his poem, comments on Edward's victory over Llewellyn in A.D. 1282 in these terms: 'Thus was Wales at last subdued; after having contended bravely for her liberty, with a power much superior to her own, for above 800 years'.[1] *The Bard* is not merely a lament for bards. It is also, as Arthur Johnston says, a poem about 'the cycle of history represented by the restoration of the descendant of Arthur, Henry Tudor, to the throne of Britain', as prophesied by the last bard to be extinguished by the Plantagenets. It dramatizes—in Romantic terms—'The man of power and the man of genius ... face to face'.[2] The prophecy mythologized by Gray belongs as much to Cumbria as to Cambria. But intimidated, perhaps, by Gray's priority, Wordsworth's treatment of this particular historical topos is characteristically oblique and understated: it takes the form of a Lancastrian minstrel's brief and indirect allusion to Bosworth Field in *Song at the Feast of Brougham Castle*, at which I will glance in chapter 9.

The Kingdom of Rheged, a Wordsworthian Ethnoscape

> In Carleile dwelt king Arthur,
> A Prince of passing might;
> And there maintained his table round,
> Beset with many a knight.[3]

When Wordsworth returned to Cumbria in 1799, after a winter in Germany, he devoted much time to the naming of places, as if knowing the place for the first time, and concerned in tribal fashion to endow each 'point of land, every bay of water' with its 'legendary story'.[4] It was, perhaps, since the task was designed to be shared with Coleridge, a quasi-pantisocratic gesture, and it certainly mimics the landscape practice of

1   Thomas Carte, *A General History of England* (4 vols, London: 1747), 2: 195. For Gray's use of this passage see Arthur Johnston, *Thomas Gray and the Bard*. An Inaugural Lecture [at Aberystwyth]. Cardiff: University of Wales Press, 1966.

2   Arthur Johnston, 18. Gray's use of the prophecy of the return of a *British* dynasty to post-Plantagenet *England* parallels Drayton's frequent use of that same motif—though Drayton associates the prophecy with Merlin.

3   Thomas Percy, *Reliques of Ancient English Poetry* (4th edn., 3 vols, 1794), 3: 340ff.

4   George Copway, *The Traditional History and Characteristics of the Ojibwa Nation* (London: Charles Gilpin, 1850), 8.

Native Americans, in whose cultural practices Wordsworth had come to interest himself. More broadly, however, one might see Wordsworth's mature sense of his region in the terms defined by Anthony D. Smith. He perceives not landscapes, or even mindscapes (as we have long thought), but ethnoscapes: 'landscapes endowed with poetic ethnic meaning through the historicization of nature and the territorialization of ethnic memories'.[1]

He had grown up in Arthurian territory, or territory claimed by local antiquarians and by folklore as Arthurian. In Arthur's time, Saxon advances had broken the Celtic world into three fragments (the others being Wales and Cornwall). These fragments still spoke a common language which spread as far as Brittany (the 'Armorica' to which the Celts of Cornwall emigrated and from which the legends embroidered by Geoffrey of Monmouth returned) and parts of Spain. 'British' at that date was still a lingua franca for the Western fringe of Europe.[2] His own imaginative country, which extends from Galloway to Camelford, with retrospects of old Sarum and Glamorgan, is historically as well as imaginatively an entity. His earliest spot of time is couched in knight and squire terms partly because it involves Penrith Beacon, established by the Normans to summon local knights and their retainers against marauding Scots, and partly because it is set not far from the 'round table', which was established in A.D. 516 by the British leader 300 yards from Lowther bridge, at least according to Clarke's *Survey of the Lakes* and local belief.[3] From hereabouts, the supposed British *Dux Bellorum* won a series of victories on the Scottish side of what is now the border, until his fatal battle with Mordred in 542.[4]

1   Anthony D. Smith, *Myths and Memories of the Nation* (Oxford: Oxford University Press, 1999), 16.

2   See Nora Chadwick, *The British Heroic Age,* passim, and Sir Ifor Williams, *The Beginnings of Welsh Poetry*, ed. Rachel Bromwich, 2nd edition (Cardiff: University of Wales Press, 1980).

3   James Clarke, *A Survey of the Lakes,* 8. A transcript of the 1787 text is online at http://www.geog.port.ac.uk/webmap/thelakes/html/clarke/cl13tit.htm.

4   From Wordsworth's time until very recently scholarship was concerned with recovering a historical Arthur from the legendary one. Now this 'historical Arthur' is seen by some as an equally suspect back projection from the legendary one. For scholarly surveys of the historicity of Arthur, Aneirin, the sources in Gildas, Galfridi, Nennius, see *inter alia,* R. Bromwich, A. O. H. Jarman, and B. F. Roberts, eds, *The Arthur of the Welsh. The Arthurian Legend in Medieval Welsh Literature* (Cardiff: University of Wales Press, 1991), D. N. Dumville, *Histories and Pseudo-Histories of the Insular*

Wordsworth lived nearer the beginning than the end of the search for the historical Arthur, which continued unabated well into the twentieth century, and he knew much of the antiquarian lore reviewed in the last chapter.[1] The debates that raged between defenders and detractors of Welsh literature in Wordsworth's time also exercised Matthew Arnold's generation. It was Arnold's response to what he called the 'natural magic' of Wordsworth (in *The Cuckoo* and *Nutting*), Keats (in *To a Nightingale*) and Shakespeare's 'On such a night', and the passion of revolt in Byron, that led him to champion *The Study of Celtic Literature* as a way of grasping why, though both are supposedly Germanic, English poetry differs

Middle Ages (Aldershot, 1990) and T. D. Griffen, *Names from the dawn of British legend: Taliesin, Aneirin, Myrddin/Merlin, Arthur* (Felinfach: Llanerch, 1994), in which work only Aneirin survives as a historical figure. Thomas Green concludes in his exacting review of sources that 'there is no reason to believe that the concept of Arthur as a 5th-/6th-century warrior is anything other than a secondary development of the legendary/mythical Arthur', 'The Historicity and Historicisation of Arthur', online, http://www.users.globalnet. co.uk/~tomgreen/Arthuriana. For the legendary exploits of the legendary Arthur see John Lewis, *The History of Great Britain,* book 6, and, inter alia, John Leland, whose credo-like title reads: *The Assertion of Arthur. A Learned and True Assertion of the original Life, Actes and death of the most Noble, Valiant and Renowned Prince Arthur, King of great Brittaine. Who succeeding his father Uther Pendragon, and right nobly governing this land six and twentie years, then dyed of a mortall wounde receyued in battell, together with victory over his enemies. And was buried at Glastonbury, An 543* (London, 1582). Buried, that is, for the time being?

1   Wordsworth knew, from schooldays, West's *Guide,* Gilpin's *Observations,* and Hutchinson's *Excursion.* West and Gilpin recycled large quantities of Camden and Stukely. He refers to Mason's *Caractacus* in *Descriptive Sketches.* He travelled in Wales with Thomas Pennant's *Tour* in hand, and visited him in 1791. He quotes from James Clarke's *Survey* in *An Evening Walk* and used it extensively for *The Borderers,* when he also relied on Joseph Nicolson and Richard Burn, *The History and Antiquities of the Counties of Westmorland and Cumberland* (1777). Clarke's *Survey* shows an interest in precisely the kind of local tradition that interested Wordsworth in 1794 and again in 1800. It would be astonishing if he knew neither Hutchinson's *History and Antiquities* nor Thomas Carte's *History of England,* which owed its Celtic scholarship to Lewis Morris. Carte's *History* and John Lewis's *The History of Great Britain, from the first Inhabitants thereof 'till the death of Cadwallader, Last King of the Britains; and of the Kings of Scotland to Eugene V* (1729) were standard historical fare. By 1805 he evidently knew Pughe's *Llywarch,* which contained much of Iolo Morganwg's speculations, and may have consulted either Sharon Turner's *History of the Anglo-Saxons* (1799) or his *Vindication* (1803) on which he certainly relied sixteen years later for *Ecclesiastical Sonnets.* Virtually everything I refer to in chapter 1 is quoted or referred to in these volumes, along with Camden, Gildas, Geoffrey of Monmouth, Leland, Giraldus Cambrensis, Rowlands and Stukeley.

from German. Like Wordsworth, Arnold perceived that the Celtic inhab-
itants of such regions as Rheged were less displaced by than absorbed
by the Saxons. Enslaved at first, but in the course of time emancipated,
having lost political and linguistic existence, but not their genetic endow-
ment or their tales, they leavened the Saxon genome.[1]

Where, what and when was Rheged? Antiquarian histories use the
terms Rheged and Cumbria almost interchangeably, though the term
Cumbria (for the land of the Cymri, or Kimbri) or Cumberland enters the
records only towards the end of the ninth century, when it lost its inde-
pendence. Lear-like, Arthur divided the territory he brought under con-
trol into a loose federation of three kingdoms, one of which was Rheged,
or Cumbria. Cumbria is, according to Sir Ifor Williams, 'the equivalent
of "the old North" of Welsh tradition, and it originally encompassed a
large area of north-west England (Cumberland, Westmorland and North
Lancashire), and Strathclyde'.[2] Wordsworth's earliest authority for local
history states that in the early years after the Roman withdrawal, 'the
most considerable kingdom among the Britons was that of the *Strath
Clwyd* Britons, called generally the kingdom of Cumbria', which then
included all the western Lowlands of Scotland and most of Lancashire.[3]

The work Wordsworth relied on most when writing the *Ecclesiastical
Sonnets*, Sharon Turner's *History of the Anglo-Saxons*, states:

> In some part of the district between the Humber and the Clyde was a
> state called Reged, which Urien the patron of Taliesin governed. In the
> parts nearest the Clyde were three other sovereigns, Rhydderc the gen-
> erous, Gwallog the son of Lleenog, and Morgant. Llywarch Hen also

---

1   My 1910 Everyman copy of Arnold's *The Study of Celtic Literature* (1867) includes
appendices from 'D. W. Nash's forgotten book on *Taliesin*' which testified to the exten-
sive manuscript base of the *Myvyrian Archaiology* (16,000 ms pages of verse and
15,300 of prose) but dwelt on the gap of six hundred years between the period when the
earliest poetry was said to have been composed and the earliest surviving manuscripts.
Nash reviewed the testimony of William Owen, Iolo Morganwg, Edward Davies and
Sharon Turner, along with further scholarly quarrels of the 1850s, touched off in part by
Lady Charlotte Guest's 3 volume *Mabinogion* (1838–49), and his scepticism provoked
Arnold's reply. The Everyman edition itself belongs to a fresh Celtic Renaissance,
whose landmarks include the publication of Oxford facsimiles of *The Red Book of
Hergest* and *The Black Book of Carmarthen*, the work of Standish O'Grady and Lady
Gregory, Sir John Rhys's *Studies in the Arthurian Legend* (1891) and the earliest work
of Jessie L. Weston, whose *From Ritual to Romance* followed in 1920.
2   Sir Ifor Williams, *The Beginnings of Welsh Poetry*, 71.
3   Nicolson and Burns, *History and Antiquities,* 2: 3.

enjoyed a little principality in Argoed. Aneirin the Bard, was chief of a district called Gododin. And Mynnyddawg ruled in a part near the friths at Eiddyn [Edinburgh].[1]

The exact relation between these figures is unclear, since there is no record of who ruled what, and precisely how Urien stood towards his associates. Taliesin calls Urien 'ruler of monarchs',[2] so the Arthurian title *dux bellorum* might be appropriate. But whatever their relations, these are names to conjure with. It was Mynnyddawg's mead that fired up the 300 British warriors who gave their lives at Cattraeth in battle with the Saxons, c. 600, and thus inspired the great poem of the age, Aneirin's *Y Gododdin*. Nennius treats Urien Rheged and his sons, especially Owain ap Urien, as the greatest warriors to contest the region with the Northumbrian Ida and his sons, and acknowledges the 'renown' of the British bards Taliesin and Aneirin in the same period (Ifor Williams, 43). Urien, called Lord of Cattraeth (by Aneirin), and Yrechwydd's Lord (by Taliesin), is supposed to have had his capital in Carlisle, within reach of the territories north and south of the Solway Firth, partly because (as Percy and the historians of Wordsworth's day believed) Carlisle had also been Arthur's military headquarters, whence he fought his twelve great battles with the Saxons. The warfare of Urien and his five sons with Ida constitutes the main historical matter of classical 'Welsh' literature.

Sharon Turner's *A Vindication of the Genuineness of the Ancient British Poems of Aneirin, Taliesin, Llywarch Hen, and Merdhin* was made necessary because the spuriousness of Ossian ensured a sceptical reception for the labours of Evan Evans and Lewis Morris in recuperating Welsh poetry. The *Vindication* makes two telling points about the content of this poetry: 'If Welshmen of the twelfth century had forged these poems, it would have been an inevitable consequence that Wales and Welshmen would have been the objects extolled. But it is singular that Wales is scarcely mentioned in them' and 'if these poems had been forged in the twelfth century [that is, after Geoffrey of Monmouth] they would have betrayed themselves by their panegyrics on Arthur'.[3] Turner

---

1   Sharon Turner, *History of the Anglo-Saxons*, 4th edn, 3 vols (London: Longman et al, 1823), 1: 285.
2   Cited from Joseph P. Clancy, *The Earliest Welsh Poetry* (Macmillan 1970), 27.
3   Sharon Turner, *Vindication of the Ancient British Poems of Aneirin, Taliesin, Llywarch Hen, and Merdhin, with Specimens of the Poems* (London: Edward Williams, 1803), 157, 160.

took the much greater prominence of Urien of Rheged in the poems of the four Bards as proof that they really were of the sixth century, uncontaminated by later legend:

> Llywarch the Aged, who lived through the whole period of slaughter, and had been one of the guests and counsellors of Arthur, never displays him in transcendant majesty .... [H]is elegy ... scarcely mentions the commander whose merit, in the frenzy of later fables, clouds every other. ... In the same manner Arthur appears in the Afallenau of Merdhin; he is mentioned as a character well known, but not idolized ... not a single epithet is added from which we can discern him to have been that whirlwind of war, which swept away in its course all the skill and armies of Europe. That he was a courageous warrior is unquestionable; but that he was the miraculous Mars of the British history ... is completely disproved by the temperate encomiums of his contemporary bards. (*History of the Anglo-Saxons*, 275–6)

Unlike Arthur, however, the historical Urien inspired eulogies from both Taliesin and Aneirin, and elegies attributed to Llywarch Hen. His assassination by Morgant in 570 is referred to in the mediaeval Welsh triads as 'one of the three villainous deeds of the isle of Britain'.[1] After Urien, Rheged's most distinguished leader was Rhydderch Hael, who in 573 'established himself in Dumbarton as ruler of the territory from the Derwent to the Firth of Clyde', becoming by the close of the century 'monarch of the north'.[2] His domain was by now quite separate from a diminishing Wales, squeezed between Irish imperialism on the West coast, and the Saxons.

As Wordsworth stood on Helvellyn or Blencathra looking towards Burns and Scott territory across what was once known as 'the sea of Rheged', now the Solway Firth, he contemplated a federal land, whose Bards, Taliesin, Aneirin, and Myrddin served such local princes as Rhydderch and Morgant, and their commander-in-chief Urien. Their terrain was the joint inheritance of Wordsworth and his poetic neighbours, Robert Burns (one of Pitt's excisemen), and the local warlord Sir Walter Scott. This factor becomes particularly significant in 1803 when

---

1   William Owen [Pughe], *The Heroic Elegies of Llywarch Hen, Prince of the Cumbrian Britons* (London: 1792), x.

2   William F. Skene, *The Four Ancient Books of Wales, containing the Cymric Poems attributed to the Bards of the Sixth Century*, 2 vols (Edinburgh: Edmonston and Douglas, 1868), 57, 67.

Wordsworth visits the Scottish half of Rheged, during alarms of invasion and returns emulating Sir Walter by joining the Ambleside volunteers. Scott wrote (that year) in his *Minstrelsy* that:

> In 570 [the year of Urien's death], if we may trust the Welsh Bards, … in their account of the wars betwixt the Saxons and Danes of Deira and the Cumraig [sic], imagination can hardly form any idea of conflicts more desperate than were maintained on the borders, between the ancient British and their Teutonic invaders. Thus the Gododin [sic] describes the waste and devastation of mutual havoc, in colours so glowing as strongly to recall the words of Tacitus, 'et ubi solitudinem faciunt, pacem apellant'.[1]

And that 'solitude ... called peace' was Cumbria's golden age. After another seven centuries of desolation Urien's overlordship looked even more distinguished. The later history of Wordsworthshire is, in its way, as eventful as that of, say, Mexico. Bede narrates how Ethelfrid and Edwin of Northumbria successively, in the first quarter of the 7th century, 'subdued and destroyed more of the British nation than any of the other English princes'.[2] For the rest of the century the North was mastered successively by King Oswald, the warrior patron saint of Grasmere, the brutal Northumbrian King Egfrid, and by the scholarly Irish-educated Aldfrid. Aldfrid's victory over Egfrid, in 685, in alliance with the Scots, brought about a brief period of British resurgence in Rheged, which lasted into the lifetime of the venerable Bede who wrote in 721. Despite the final reduction of Northumbria in 894, by the great patriot king Alfred, some form of Cumbrian autonomy seems to have survived until 945, when Edmund King of England 'having wasted all Galloway, and entirely subdued the Britons in Cumberland, gave that principality to Malcolm King of Scotland, on condition of guarding the Northumbrian territories' (Nicolson and Burns, 2: 3). Edmund's victory, associated with confused accounts of Edmund putting out the eyes either of King Dunmail, or of his sons, is told by Nicolson and Burns, in West's

---

1   Sir Walter Scott, *Minstrelsy of the Scottish Border* (1803), 9. Algernon Sidney's version of the Tacitus quotation had been restored to public circulation by Joseph Johnson's reprinting in 1795 of the *Discourses on Government*, published on 14 July 1795: 'It is ill that men should kill one another in seditions, tumults and wars; but it is worst, ... to give the name of peace to desolation'.

2   Bede, *The History of the Primitive Church of England, from its origin to the year 731*. tr. Rev. William Hurst (London: 1814), 95, 161.

Guide, Clarke's *History* and in Hutchinson's *Antiquities*, and from one or other of these sources it finds its way into Wordsworth's first long poem, *The Vale of Esthwaite*.

In 1069, William Rufus re-annexed Cumberland to England. King Stephen restored it to the Scots. Henry II, who is credited with discovery of the remains of King Arthur, in 1188 or 1189, demanded it back. Under Norman rule the famous beacons, including Penrith Beacon, were established to summon knights and their retainers. Nonetheless, Cumbria experienced Scottish invasions or depredations throughout the reigns of Edward II, Edward III, Richard II, and so on, indeed right up until the time of Queen Anne and the rising of 1745, a fact reflected in the sturdy and defensible domestic architecture of the region and in the action of Wordsworth's tragedy *The Borderers*. A century or more of local history is evoked in Wordsworth's *Yew-Trees* by the single word Umfraville. One Umfraville is mentioned in Henry's *Magna Charta Hiberniae* in 1216. Sir Gilbert Umfraville, a Northumbrian, became Earl of Angus in 1243. A later Umfraville, from Cockermouth, fought with Edward II at Bannockburn, in 1314 and another with Edward III at Halidon Hill, in 1333 when the English wrested Berwick from the Scots. Wordsworth, as a parishioner of St Oswald's, Grasmere, had reason to feel the history of the place. He did not write that history until 1821, however, and when he did so, he chose to celebrate the contribution of Druid, Celtic, Saxon and Roman cultures to the rise of the church.

Rheged's Bards

To claim for Cumbria all of the poetry *attributed* to Taliesin, Aneirin, Llywarch Hen, and the bard Myrddin (as opposed to the Magician Merlin) would be misleading. Most of this corpus of poetry does belong in reality to Wales and to bards of the ninth to twelfth centuries, especially to bards celebrating the resistance of a new generation of heroes to the Plantagenets. But its topoi, frequently, are Cumbrian. One explanation of the impact of 'The Men of the North' on the literature of Wales is that as the North disintegrated, refugee warriors from Rheged—among them Llywarch Hen, Prince of the Cumbrian Britons—assisted in the liberation of large tracts of Wales from Irish colonists in the seventh century and the Saxons in the ninth century.[1]

1   'Maelor, The Vale of Clwyd, and other parts of Gwynedd, according to Brut y

The legendary Llywarch Hên, or Llywarch the Old, is supposed to have been at the court of Arthur in his youth, i.e. early in the sixth century, and to have lived to the second half of the seventh, losing twenty four sons in battles for Rheged and Powys.[1] He is described in *The Gododdin* as the epitome of 'the North's true valour'[2] and he ended his days in Wales, not far from Robert Jones's 'vale of Clwyd', passing into bardic legend as—most thought in Wordsworth's days—the author of his own heroic elegies. These were published by William Owen Pughe in 1792, and known to Wordsworth in that form as *The Heroic Elegies of Llywarch Hen, Prince of the Cumbrian Britons*. 'His' work is now attributed to the ninth and tenth centuries, and to Wales,[3] but Wordsworth would have supposed Llywarch himself to be the author of this astonishingly haiku-like triad, typical of poems in *Red Book of Hergest* attributed to him:

> Bright are the ash-tops; tall and white will they be
> When they grow in the upper part of the dingle;
> The languid heart, longing is her complaint.
>
> (Skene, 576)

Numerous haunting elegies for Urien of Rheged, such as this, are attributed in Turner's *Vindication* to Llywarch Hên, who here represents himself having severed Urien's head from his body to save it from desecration:

> I bear by my side a head;
> The head of Urien!
> The courteous leader of his army;
> But on his white bosom the raven is feeding

Tywysogion of 890, were liberated from the Saxons by exiled men of the North, whose kingdom of Strathclyde had been ravaged repeatedly in c. 875.' Skene, 182.

1   William Owen, in *The Heroic Elegies,* claims that Llywarch 'was born about the commencement of the sixth, and lived to the middle of the seventh century; being about a hundred and fifty years old at the time of his death', and that he was alive at the time of Arthur's death in 542, and of Cadwallon in 646 (vi). C.f. Sharon Turner, *Vindication,* 14–15.

2   Aneirin, cited from Clancy, *The Earliest Welsh Poetry,* 48.

3   Patrick K. Ford concludes that Llywarch Hên 'was the creation of a functionary in the court of some Welsh prince of the late ninth or tenth century; ... to legitimize the rule of the dynasty then in power and to glorify it through celebration of the deeds of its heroic ancestors'. *The Poetry of Llywarch Hen* (Berkeley: University of California Press, 1974), 4.

> I bear a head from the mountain:
> The lips foaming with blood.
> Woe to Reged from this day.
>
> My arm has not shrunk
> But my breast is greatly troubled.
> My heart! is it not broken?
> The head I bear supported me.
>
> (Turner, *History*, 290)

Aneirin, with whom Wordsworth identified when referring to himself as 'the meanest' of the bardic band, also retreated to Wales, becoming it is thought, a monk. This sole survivor of the disaster at Cattraeth treats in the spasmodic and fragmented utterance of *The Gododdin* of how 'some 300 warriors, the bodyguard of Mynyddawg Lord of Dineiddyn [Dunedin, or Edinburgh], travelled to Cattraeth [Catterick or Richmond] to recover it from the English or die in the attempt' (Ifor Williams, 69). What they did when they got there, Sir Ifor Williams beautifully continues, 'we do not exactly know, further than this; they were loyal and brave, and true; their mothers wept for them, their kinsmen sorrowed for them, and their countrymen have remembered them for over thirteen hundred years.'

The third of the famous bards, Myrddin, became a forest recluse after a major inter-tribal battle, the battle of Arfderydd (573) in which his lord, a semi-pagan, was slain in battle with the Christian Rhydderch Hael. Myrddin becomes 'Welsh' only by accident. Since his isolation in the Forest of Celyddon (the Caledonian forest), and his resentment of the Christian victor, led to madness and to wild prophecies, he elides in Geoffrey of Monmouth's 'cooked histories', as David Jones calls them, with the Welsh 'Merlin', or Myrddin Ambrosius—the one who magically built Stonehenge and assisted at Uther Pendragon's siring of Arthur.[1] Myrddin Sylvestris, or Myrddin the Caledonian, may come to mind when we examine Wordsworth's celebration of Waterloo, in 1816, in which he reminds whatever deity he was worshipping by that date,

---

1   As Thomas Parry points out: 'though we know today that Myrddin did live at some time (more than probably in the sixth century) and was a poet, no poetry now exists under his name except the prophecies attributed to him centuries after his time'. *A History of Welsh Literature*, tr. H. Idris Bell (Oxford: Clarendon Press, 1955), 27. See also, Meic Stephens, *The New Companion to the Literature of Wales* (Cardiff: University of Wales Press), 1998, 522.

'Yea carnage is thy daughter'.

Myrddin's poem *The Avellanau* (Sweet Apple Tree) though sweetly named, is bloody and prophetic enough:

> On the Saxons there will be a slaughter with ashen spears
> And their heads will be used as balls to play with. (Skene, 371)

The writing of these bards is concerned with heroic feats of arms, with the defence of *British* culture against *English* barbarians, with declining power, with recollections of Celtic tranquillity, and remnants of Celtic tribal story and belief within a Romanized social order. In its Cumbrian and its Welsh phases British poetry fills the age between the retreat of Rome and the complete triumph of the Norman Conquest. The most authentic period of Welsh literature dates from an era rather like Wordsworth's own—certainly his own as he increasingly came to see it in the Napoleonic era—in which the Celtic fastnesses in the West of Britain, especially that almost legendary commonwealth of Rheged, represented the only manly and civilized order North of the Alps. It is a point worth remembering when Wordsworth, always self-consciously a Man of the North, speaks of 'the flood of *British* freedom' while exhorting *England* to abandon its 'emasculating food'.

Theirs is a genuine border poetry, of the kind hinted at in Oswald's flattering address to Marmaduke in *The Borderers*:

> we have seen you
> Stand like an isthmus 'twixt two stormy seas
> That oft have checked their fury at your bidding.

Indeed, given Urien's role in managing the recalcitrant Welsh, the fickle Scots and the savage Northumbrians, the description might well have been sung in his praise, by an earlier British bard. Taliesin, who *did* celebrate Urien, was somewhat more partisan:

> England's men know him
> When they encounter:
> Death is their portion
> And pain in plenty,
> Their houses blazing,
> Their garments taken,
> And heavy losses,
> And grievous hardship,
> No mercy granted

> By Rheged's Urien,
> Rheged's defender,
> Famed lord, land's anchor [1]

One of Urien's major battles with Ida took place at 'the mound of Gwenystrad, literally the pleasant valley' (*Vindication*, 289). Here, according to Taliesin, the 'master of word-craft', as Aneirin called him in *The Gododdin*:

> Like a wave raging against the shore—
> I saw the tumult of the perishing hosts;
> The blood springing forward and moistening the ground…
>
> Like the bird of rage was his sword on their bucklers:
> It was wielded with deadly fate.[2]

No wonder Wordsworth chose the term 'impetuous' for the song of Taliesin. And while this epithet (in *Ecclesiastical Sonnets*) is clearly a distancing one, one remembers Wordsworth's claim that when *The Prelude* is written, the epic of the mind is chosen only after contemplating earlier heroic themes, including the kind of matter treated by the first Cumbrian bards:

> tales of warlike feats
> Where spear encountered spear, and sword with sword
> Fought, as if conscious of the blazonry
> That the shield bore, so glorious was the strife.

Not until the 1821 series of *Ecclesiastical Sonnets* do Rheged's bards leave a direct imprint on Wordsworth's poetry. Nevertheless, he is not being too economical with the truth when he claims to have relinquished the traditionally heroic with reluctance. His earliest efforts at poetry were in the heroic vein, and his first major poem, *An Evening Walk*, was more

---

1   'In Praise of Urien', in Clancy, 26..

2   Taliesin, *The Battle of Gwenystrad*, cited from Sharon Turner, *History*, 289. Thomas Stephens identifies Gwenystrad as Winsterdale in Westmorland. He places Urien's battle of Argoed Llwyvain, celebrated by Taliesin, at Leavington, next to the forest of Durham, and the battle of Arderydd, 'at which battle Rhydderch Hael ensured the triumph of Christianity over the pagan Gwenddolau, and his bard Merddin, who took refuge in the woods of Celyddon' at Airdrie, nr Glasgow. Stephens, *The Gododin of Aneirin Gwawdrydd, an English Translation*, ed. Thomas Powel (Printed for the Honourable Society of Cymmrodorion. London, 1888) 67, 72, 73, 78.

bardic in revision than in its first conception.

An Evening Walk

The version of *An Evening Walk* published in 1793 was largely the work of 1789, at Cambridge. It is a turgid piece, full of Thomsonian 'vistos' and descriptions of Gilpinesque 'stations', barely touched by radical sentiment. The version in *Poetical Works* is the product of numerous revisions. Its most interesting text is the work of 1794, a revision undertaken at Windy Brow, in Keswick, by the newly politicized author of *A Letter to the Bishop of Llandaff.*

As Wordsworth sat in Keswick revising and jacobinizing his loco-descriptive poem, the Romantically prescient Iolo was issuing through their shared publisher, Joseph Johnson, his *Poems Lyric and Pastoral.* These include a poem in praise of laudanum, one *To the Cuckoo*, with whose voice 'returns the vernal morn', and another *On the Destruction of a favourite thicket. A pastoral. In the Welsh manner.* This is based upon a similarly Nuttingesque model by Taliesin, referred to by Edward Davies, in which the Bard warns against prematurely raiding sacred groves for the emblems of maturity. Iolo's *Poems* also include a celebration of *Escape from London*, an *Address to the Inhabitants of Wales, Exhorting them to emigrate with William Penn, to Pennsylvania* (the volume also popularizes the discovery of America in 1170 by Prince Madoc),[1] an elaborate *Vernal Ode* celebrating the escape from 'tainted cities' and invoking Caractacus much as Wordsworth's *Vernal Ode* will invoke St George, and most charmingly, *A Song Written in 1785, for the Use of a little select Society of Journey-Men Masons, that met weekly to spend*

---

1   Iolo's Madoc is an enterprising Pantisocrat modelled on Thomas Cooper the land agent: 'America was discovered, about the year 1170, by Madoc.... We have manuscript accounts of this discovery that were written before the birth of Columbus. Dr David Powel, in Queen Elizabeth's time, says, in his History of Wales ...that Madoc, in hopes of discovering the lands beyond the Atlantic (of which there were ancient manuscript accounts ... in Wales), and of finding there a retreat from the horrors of intestine wars which then deluged all Wales with blood, resolved on a voyage of discovery.' Having discovered 'a fine fertile country, destitute of inhabitants' he left a hundred men, came back to Wales, and set out again 'with a fleet of ten ships, full of such persons of both sexes as preferred peace to discord'. Edward Williams, *Poems Lyric and Pastoral*, 2: 64 n. Iolo is responsible for the unpublished and more radical version of Southey's *Madoc*, in which the pantisocratic flight from religious and political tyranny is enacted by twelfth century Bardic Unitarians.

a chearful hour at the moderate and restricted expense of fourpence.
Having opened so much poetic territory for Wordsworth, Coleridge and
Southey, Iolo also offered the pithiest possible manifesto for poetry in the
new age (or, as he claimed, in the Bardic ages) in the form of an ancient
Welsh triad asserting that:

> *The three primary and indispensible requisites of* POETIC GENIUS *are,
> an* EYE THAT CAN SEE NATURE, *a* HEART THAT CAN FEEL NATURE, *and a*
> RESOLUTION THAT DARES FOLLOW NATURE.

Equally germanely, bearing in mind Wordsworth's poetics in 1799–1800,
Iolo 'found' among his ancient *Bardic Triades* the following remark-
ably up-to-date maxim of the *Ancient British Philosophers*, which he
Englished as follows: 'Three things restored will prolong a man's life;
| The country where in childhood he was brought up, | The food that in
childhood nourished him, | And the train of thought that in childhood
amused him (2: 36).

Whether or not Wordsworth knew Iolo Morganwg's work at this date
(Duncan Wu suggests that he did so by 1797–98)[1] the list of subscribers
Iolo claimed for his volumes includes numerous names much celebrated
in Wordsworth studies: Mrs Barbauld, Lady Beaumont, the Reverend W.
L. Bowles, Citoyen Brissot, Dr. Charles Burney, James Boswell, John
and Edward Calvert, Thomas Cooper (of Pantisocratic connections), the
Bishop of Llandaff,[2] Hannah More (whose bourgeois didacticism inspired
Wordsworth's riposte in *Goody Blake and Harry Gill*), Thomas Pownall,
advocate of American liberty, the Reverend Dr. Price, whose name is
synonymous with ancient British liberties, Samuel Rogers, Granville
Sharpe (the anti-slavery campaigner), and Washington, the one contem-
porary liberator who for Wordsworth remained untarnished. In short, this
imaginative exercise in liberal druidism addressed itself to a consider-
able cross-section of the Anglo-American cultural establishment.

Imbibing no doubt 'the spirit of the season' (Iolo's work was not the
only sign of exceptional druid resurgence in 1794)[3] Wordsworth pro-

1   Wu, 161. Coleridge had met Iolo by May 1796 (Griggs, 1: 214) and Iolo presented
him with a copy. Iolo Morganwg's dealings with Coleridge, Godwin, Southey and
others are extensively examined in Damian Walford Davies's *Presences that Disturb*
(University of Wales Press, 2002).
2   Richard Watson, a Cumbrian, inspired, by a process of reaction, Wordsworth's most
Paineite production. His name also graces Jones's *Relics* and Davies's later *Researches*.
3   The same year, 1794, saw the publication of Jacob des Moulins' *Antiqua Restaurata:*

ceeded to embellish *An Evening Walk* in several interesting directions: he made it more personal, in the sense of giving it a stronger sense of poetic mission, in the guise of a reclusive poet not unlike Myrddin Wyllt in his Caledonian forest, or Milton after the restoration; he made it more social, in the sense that he develops passages related to both *The Female Vagrant* and *The Ruined Cottage*; he radicalized it, giving vent to critiques of war and property and devising cutting techniques to add emotional force to his critique; and he elaborated a nature philosophy that may, as some claim, be little more than an adaptation of Akenside, but is certainly compatible with that of the French Encyclopaedists.[1] These facets of the poem I shall touch upon in chapter 4. For the moment I attend only to those revisions which elaborated on matters of local history and legend—not excluding the Skiddaw 'faeries' who reappear in *The Waggoner*—and give greater symbolic resonance to our friends the famous Druids, revisions which, as it happens, almost double the poem's length.

In 1793 Wordsworth had devoted just one line to druid stones (171), in which 'the druid stones their lighted fane unfold', together with a note recommending the druid monument at Broughton (visited by the Hawkshead schoolboy on one of the unspecified excursions in Book 2 of *The Prelude*, but as yet unmentioned in the picturesque 'tours'). Now, however, in lines 324–7:

> Refulgent on the mountain top appear
> The naked druid stones, and, curling near
> From piles of burning fern, still smoke aspires,
> Where once the savage viewed mysterious fires.[2]

It is a little early, but he seems to be writing the first draft of the pastor's reverie in Book 9 of *The Excursion*. As the sun sets, in 1794, Wordsworth

---

A Concise Historical account of the Ancient Druids, William Sotheby's *Tour Through Parts of Wales*, and the second edition of Edward Jones's very important *Musical and Poetical Relicks of the Welsh Bards* (1784) with its bardic transcreations by Thomas Gray. These followed hard on William Owen's edition of *The Heroic Elegies,* dedicated to Pennant.

1 H. W. Piper, *The Active Universe* (London: Athlone Press, 1962), 70.

2 'Refulgent': Wordsworth may have remembered this word from Cumberland's 'Ode to the Sun' quoted in West's *Guide*, where it is used twice, along with the equally potent word, 'diurnal'. Wordsworth's setting sun makes a brief appearance from behind clouds, while Cumberland's fought its way through storm clouds on Skiddaw.

addresses its guiding spirit or active principle:

> Spirit, who guid'st that orb and view'st from high
> Thrones, towers, and fanes in blended ruin lie
> Roll to Peruvian vales thy gorgeous way;
> See thine own temples mouldering in decay;
> Roll on till, hurled from thy bright throne sublime
> Thyself confess the mighty arm of Time.
>
> (*EW*, 142, ll. 333–338)

The idea that even major systems of superstition 'set' like the sun itself leads however into a further and contrary expansion. He uses the idea also at the close of the first *Salisbury Plain*, fair copied at Windy Brow while *An Evening Walk* was being revised. *Salisbury Plain* appeals to the 'Heroes of Truth'—Paine? Godwin? Priestley? Price?—to pursue their march until 'not a trace | Be left on earth of Superstition's reign, | save that eternal pile which frowns on Sarum's plain'. 'Superstition', at this date, certainly includes that professionally represented by such as the Bishop of Llandaff whose 'foul Error' (*Salisbury Pain*, 545) regarding the French Revolution Wordsworth had recently denounced in his Paineite *Letter* to that cleric. The evidence of both poems, then, is that Wordsworth regarded Druidism as superstition—but as the one superstition he would save from the flood.

The 1793 *Evening Walk* (lines 177–90) contained an obscure and perfunctory ten-line account of the apparition of a troop of visionary horsemen. His note refers the reader to Clarke's *Survey of the Lakes* for 'a description of an appearance of this kind … accompanied with vouchers of its veracity that may amuse the reader'. James Averill comments , misleadingly, that 'whatever Clarke thinks, for Wordsworth the "visionary horsemen" are only quaint and amusing local superstitions' (*EW*, p. 54) , but 'amuse', according to the *OED*, means '*to cause to muse or to puzzle*', which reading works for most usages encountered in the 1790s (Wordsworth sends Coleridge two Lucy Poems with the suggestion that they will 'amuse' him [*EY*, 236]). Clarke's *Survey* conjectures that these apparitions may have been designed to warn of 'approaching tumults' since they were first seen in 1744, that is, shortly before a rebellion 'intended to subvert the liberty, the law, and the religion of England'.[1] In the context of 1794, war having been declared between

---

1   James Clarke, *Survey,* 56. Clarke's intriguing 'vouchers' are detailed, extensive and

Britain and France, the shepherds have plenty of reason to be apprehensive of 'tumults', perhaps on an even greater scale than 'the 45'.

In 1794 the brief passage beginning 'a desperate form appears' is expanded to 65 lines (ll.345–409) now comparable in structure and importance to the Salisbury Plain vision of *The Prelude* and its ensuing meditation. It now consists of the original horseman vision, relating to 1745; an apt application of this to shepherds anxious about civil strife in 1794; a scene of flocks playing on ancient burial mounds; then a new vision—resulting from some further study of Clarke—of some possibly Arthurian form: 'There rent the fen before him and—behold | A horseman skeleton of giant mould … | An unknown being of forgotten years…'. Clarke devotes considerable space to Penrith as the alleged burial place of Torquin, a brutal giant with a taste for virgins, who was felled by Lancelot du Lac at Arthur's command, and is led thereby into associating this giant burial to that of Arthur.[1] To George Richards, all ancient Britons, it seems, were 'By untam'd nature cast in giant-mould' (*Aboriginal Britons*, 11). Wordsworth's sense that rending the fen, or the fell, might lead to unexpected revelations is undeveloped here, perhaps because it has already been used dramatically in the barrow scene of *Salisbury Plain*. But it recurs in the *Guide to the Lakes* in a rather enthralling conjecture that the poor country cousins of the major metropolitan stone circles of lakeland—Long Meg, Castlerigg, Broughton, etc—probably lie *all around one* at no very depth beneath the soil (*PrW* 2: 191).

Finally, at the close of the poem, Wordsworth develops a moonlight scene into a contrast between a shepherd's quiet perception of the moonlight on his sheepfold and the poet's vision of 'shapes sublime'. In this lengthy and entirely new passage he asks:

> What Bards, in strains more faint at every close,
> Pour griefs which once the troubled winds scarce bore
> To meet the languid battle's dying roar,
> When freedom here beheld the Bird of Rome

---

corroboratively witnessed. He concludes: 'This country … abounds in the aniles fabellae of fairies, ghosts, and apparitions; but [unlike this] these are never even fabled to have been seen by more than one or two persons at a time…. Speed tells of something indeed similar to this as preceding a dreadful intestine war. Can something of this nature have given rise to Ossian's grand and awful mythology?' (56)..

1   For Clarke's account of these burials see note on page 35 above.

> O'er her last barrier shake his deepest gloom,
> And sighes from every fountain shade and cave
> Wept the last remnant of the great and brave?
>
> (*EW*, 154, ll. 717–736)

The dimpling surface of the lake is sensitive to every entering rill, and streams 'unheard till now, now hardly heard', as the poet witnesses 'at the stillest watch of night' 'slow-gliding forms of light' and catches 'echoes whispered from each hill and shade'. The long-dead, to whom the land owes its present peace, pursue their watch and rove 'haunts once their pleasure, mountain, lake or grove'. 'But the dead maintain their ground—', as Geoffrey Hill lugubriously says, 'That there's no getting round—'.[1]

In 1794, it seems, the Cumbrian living owe their tranquillity to Rheged's virtuous dead. The visionary horsemen, the giant bones, the druids and bards manifested in water, snow and light, the last memories of the great and the brave, all hint at a Cumbrian landscape peopled as much by the noble and pre-Imperial dead as by their living remnants. In this war-haunted territory, Wordsworth's poetic imagination is not merely 'amused by' local legend or superstition; it takes fire from them. *An Evening Walk* in its *1794* expansion is a fascinating illustration of just how inseparable Wordsworth's radicalism, his visionary imagination, his primitivism and his humanism, really are—as they were for Iolo Morganwg and many admirers of the primitive. Had Wordsworth sent the lengthened work to Joseph Johnson, to take its place in his list alongside Morganwg's *Poems Lyrics and Pastoral*, they would have belonged self-evidently to much the same dissident culture.

In a late interlinear revision of *The Vale of Esthwaite* Wordsworth had written a line comparing 'the white hair'd mist' to 'druids pale' (*EPF*, 200: MS 5, 4r). In *An Evening Walk*, simile is transcended. In casting his druids as 'Dim as the mellowed foam of falling streams' and 'Cresting yon mountain head like vernal snows' his imagination fuses the landscape and its history, making the most evanescent (and ubiquitous) element of Cumbria—its water—into a sort of Ossianic presence of Rheged in its Romano-British prime. Buried lightly under the surface, and living mercurially on that surface, sharing its present life, are—and it is a stunning avowal—'the last remnant of the great and brave'. In prac-

---

1   Geoffrey Hill, *The distant fury of battle*, from *For the Unfallen* (London: Andre Deutsch, 1959) in *Collected Poems* (Harmondsworth: Penguin, 1985) 26.

tice, Wordsworth's immediate inspiration may be Macpherson's ghost of Connal ('his face is like the beam of the setting moon; his robes are of the clouds of the hill') or Hugh Blair's *Critical Dissertation*: 'The ghosts of departed bards continue to sing. The ghosts of departed heroes frequent the fields of their former fame'.[1] In 1835 at the Cave of Staffa, Ossian is certainly in Wordsworth's mind when he writes 'If eyes be still sworn vassals of belief | Yon light shapes forth a Bard, that shade a Chief'. But there were also more local and authentic precedents. In the words of the Llywarch Hên elegies concerning the hearth of Rheged:

> This hearth, green sward conceals it,
> When Owain and Elphin lived
> Its cauldron seethed with prizes...
>
> This hearth, reeds conceal it,
> More common, once, were gleaming
> Tapers and true companions.[2]

Or in still more eloquent lines from *The Book of Taliesin*:

> If there is a cry on the hill,
> Is it not Urien that terrifies?
> If there is cry in the valley,
> Is it not Urien that pierces?
> If there is a cry in the mountain,
> Is it not Urien that conquers?[3]

Last Bard of Rheged?

Was Wordsworth in any sense self-consciously the last Bard of Rheged, as Yeats was the last Romantic? If he was, he doesn't say. In order to tri-angulate a sort of subterranean identification, one has to collate his brief references to Rheged's celebrated prince and his bards, and covert allu-

1   *The Poems of Ossian* (Edinburgh, 1792), 33, 399.
2   From the *Llywarch Hen Saga*, Clancy, 68. Owain and Elphin were sons of Urien.
3   Skene, 'The Book of Taliesin', *The Four Ancient Books of Wales*, 1: 349. Wordsworth is likely to have read a version of these lines in Sharon Turner's *History of the Anglo-Saxons*, 290: 'If there be a sigh on the mountains; | Is it not Urien who conquers? | If there be a sigh on the slope of the hills; Is it not Urien who wounds? | If there be a sigh of dismay; | Is it not from the assault of Urien? | There is no refuge from him; | Nor will there be from famine, | To those who seek plunder near him!'.

sions to Llywarch Hên, another Prince of Cumbria, and link them back to the climactic episode in *The Vale of Esthwaite*—the murder of the Princes of Cumbria by the Saxon Edmund at Dunmail Raise. But he had a strong sense of lineage. If any three figures in British literature strictly merit the term 'Bard' they are Taliesin, Aneirin and Myrddin, of the Men of the North. All are associated with the golden age of Romano-British resistance to Saxon hegemony, and with the name and fame of Urien, 'Rheged's defender | Famed Lord, land's anchor'. Wordsworth applied the term 'bard' selectively enough: Virgil and Theocritus, Ossian (with real misgivings), Taliesin and Aneirin, Chaucer, Spenser, Shakespeare, Milton, Thomson, Burns. Gray's poem claimed Spenser, Shakespeare and Milton, as authentic heirs to his prophetic Bard, in a line re-established by the Tudors. But none of these was qualified to lodge, as Wordsworth was, a claim to the Bardic Chair of Rheged. Gray, Thomson, Collins, Beattie might play at the role, and dabble in antiquarianism. Iolo Morganwg simply anointed himself heir to an unbroken line of bardic apostles. True bards do not specialize in pleasing fictions.

Percy's preface to *Reliques* described the minstrels of England as heirs to and associates of the Celtic Bards, and his original dedication claimed that 'By such bards …was the infancy of genius nurtured and advanced, by such were the minds of unlettered warriors softened and enlarged, by such was the memory of illustrious actions preserved and propagated.'[1] Percy's focus is mostly Saxon, but the matter of his third volume is Arthurian and the collection as a whole endeavours self-consciously to raise the status of the Saxon minstrel to that of the Norse scald or the Celtic bard. He asserts that minstrels from the time of Alfred, the earliest Saxons and Danes, through the Normans, down to Elizabeth 1, were successors to the Bards of the Celts, as they existed throughout both Celtic and Gothic Europe: 'they were protected and caressed because their songs tended to do honour to the ruling passion of the times [chivalry], and to encourage and foment a martial spirit.'[2]

As Abbie Findlay Potts argued long ago, the template for *The Prelude* is James Beattie's design for his poem *The Minstrel, or The Progress of Genius*, which poem set out 'to trace the progress of a poetical genius,

---

1   Thomas Percy, *Reliques of Ancient English Poetry*, first edition (1765), 1, vii. This dedication to the Countess of Northumberland was in the edition used at Hawkshead.
2   *Reliques*, 4th edn, 1794, xxi (this is the edition Wordsworth bought in Hamburg in 1798).

born in a rude age, from the first dawning of fancy and reason, till that period at which he may be supposed capable of appearing in the world as a Minstrel, that is, as an itinerant poet and musician'.[1] As Kathryn Sutherland has shown, Beattie's ambition was itself born of a fascination with the portrait of the minstrel heritage in Percy's *Reliques*—a work to which Wordsworth and Scott proudly acknowledged their obligations. Not only is the hero of *The Prelude* following such a programme as Beattie's, but his alter ego, the Pedlar, also nature's child, was in his 1799 form less given to tireless moral discourses than to bursting into 'The songs of Burns or many a ditty wild | Which he had fitted to the moorland harp | His own sweet verse'.[2]

One thinks of Percy both when reading the numerous poems in which Wordsworth does something conspicuously revisionary to the matter of minstrelsy—as in *The White Doe, Hart-Leap Well* and *Song at the Feast of Brougham Castle*—and when faced with the volume of poems surrounding the notorious *Thanksgiving Ode*. Indeed Wordsworth's sense of his poetic function may owe much to reading, perhaps at Hawkshead, Percy's eloquent lament, which seems to underlie his own sense of the dignity of poetry in 1798 and 1815: 'much greater honours seem to have been heaped upon the northern SCALDS, in whom the characters of historian, genealogist, poet and musician were all united, than appear to have been paid to the MINSTRELS and HARPERS of the Anglo-Saxons, whose talents were chiefly to entertain and divert; while the Scalds professed to inform and instruct, and were at once the moralists and theologues of their Pagan countrymen' (Percy, xxv).

The late eighteenth century was a period of frequent calls for the replacement of neo-classical poetry by something of the earth, earthy: a new bardic poetry capable of summoning the blood and stiffening the sinews. The simplicity and directness of *Lyrical Ballads*, as received by Hazlitt, for example, fulfils—as did the barbaric yawp of Whitman half a century later—something of that demand, though not quite in the expected manner. Wordsworth's response to a demand for the bardic was to not add to the accumulation of pseudo-antiquarian verse but to rec-

---

1 Abbie Findlay Potts, *Wordsworth's Prelude: A Study of its Literary Form*, 68.
2 Kathryn Sutherland, 'The Native Poet: the influence of Percy's Minstrel from Beattie to Wordsworth', *Review of English Studies,* n.s. 33: 132 (1982) 414–33, 418, 432. Sutherland demonstrates persuasively the genetic continuity between Percy's conception of the bard | minstrel, and Wordsworth's pedlar / wanderer.

reate poetry on the model of the bards themselves. He exercises rather than imitates the bardic function, and he functions increasingly (to adapt Gwyn Williams's expression for Iolo Morganwg's concept of bardism) as 'spiritual counsellor' and 'the people's remembrancer'. To be a bard in the nineteenth century must mean more than versifying Geoffrey of Monmouth's cooked histories. It ought to mean forging the conscience of one's race.

Wordsworth's bardic vocation is authenticated by a mythic poetic education amounting to election, a modern Mabinogion—or tale of the hero's boyhood—mythologized like Taliesin's. Taliesin, in George Borrow's version of the legend, was found among the rushes in a coracle, like another national voice, and 'on a salmon weir in the domain of Elphin'.[1] Wordsworth's orphaning followed more usual courses, but his vocation expresses itself in an unparalleled nature poetry, declaring the life of mountains and rivers, rocks and stones and trees. It involves the creation of elysian elegies, codifying the tribe's experience of loss and endurance, and lamenting the aged and the fallen. In these respects it perpetuates the most affecting elements of Taliesin, Myrddin, and the poetry attributed to Llywarch Hên. It also means celebrating an entirely new and democratized brand of folk hero. Once in a while, it is true, the bardic genome manifests itself more overtly and the poet has to seize the patriotic lyre, singing of national independence and liberty. Eventually, it means researching and recording the spiritual history of the race, chanting the genealogy of the tribe, uniting the living and the dead, and binding the present and the past in natural piety. Viewed in that light, nine tenths of Wordsworth's oeuvre sublimates the bardic.

---

1   George Borrow, *Celtic Bards, Chiefs and Kings* (London: John Murray, 1928) 39.

Chapter 3: 'Indignant Hills'

WE KNOW FROM De Quincey's *Recollections* that Wordsworth's morning walks at Hawkshead with his schoolfriend Fleming were spent eclaiming Goldsmith and Gray, and the young poet who asserted in *The Vale of Esthwaite* manuscript that 'Friendship and Fleming are the same' also expresses a wish to lie in peace in such a churchyard 'as heard the pensive sigh of Gray'.[1] The fact that his mature poetry is devoted to the realization of 'Paradise, Groves Elysian, Fortunate Fields'[2] (terrain at least two-thirds other-worldly) may stem from knowing at an early date that his native region enclosed what Thomas Gray—equally torn between the classical and the ethnic—called the 'Vale of Elysium'.[3] For a grammar school boy growing up in Elysium it may seem natural to write of Elysium as conceived in the tradition of Catullus, Ovid and Virgil, quite as much as that of Macpherson, which is precisely what his juvenile production does. One would not have needed an especially prophetic soul, in 1789, to foretell that Wordsworth would specialize in endurance, loss and death. One *would* have needed considerable foresight to prophesy that his mature oeuvre—until *Dion* and *Laodamia*—would be free of overtly classical reference, even when (or perhaps especially when) his muse recalls him to the themes of loss, separation, and grief, which are the concern of the classical verse of his schooldays. Translating that classical sense of his region into indigenous ethnoscape took him until the 1820s.

'Black Helvellyn's inmost Womb'

Amid Wordsworth's juvenilia lie the remains of *The Vale of Esthwaite*,

---

1   Thomas De Quincey, *Recollections of the Lakes and the Lake Poets*, ed. David Wright (Harmondsworth: Penguin), 166.
2   'Prospectus' to *The Recluse*.
3   William West, *A Guide to the Lakes*, 203. West includes Gray's Journal, 1769, as edited by Mason in the *Memoirs*, as an Appendix.

an ambitious wreck which like any ruin, fragment, or clouded hill-top, teases the imagination. Inscribed on his manuscript title page—which heads not the poem itself but a series of extracts from it—are two lines from Beattie's *The Minstrel* (lxii), 'Adieu ye lays that *fancy's* flow'rs adorn | The soft amusement of the vacant mind', to which Wordsworth responds, in part demurral, 'What though my griefs must never flow |For scenes of *visionary* woe | I trust the Bard can never part | With Pity, Autumn of the heart'.[1] *The Minstrel*, as Abbie Potts pointed out, contained a contributory sketch of the climactic Snowdon vision.[2] It might

---

1   DC.MS.2. Although MS2 is made up of a series of extracts from the poem, the fact that these lines follow thematically from the apparent epigraph for the poem suggests that they might, in fact, have been its opening lines. The first line of 'the poem' in MS3— '[?] avaunt! With tenfold pleasure | I ga[ze] the landskip's varied treasure' [*EPF* 422] is barely satisfactory, not least because *VE* gives much less account of 'landskip' than of 'visionary woe' and 'Pity, Autumn of the heart'. The version of the poem which appears in *Poetical Works*, Volume 1, and with a few emendations in Hayden's two volumes, was very largely a work of editorial conjecture. The Cornell editors (in *Early Poems and Fragments*, ed. Carol Landon and Jared Curtis) have had to produce an even sparer text by removing many lines placed there, on the best of intentions, by de Selincourt. The Cornell *Vale of Esthwaite* offers a reading text based on MS3 only, though omitting some of its sketchier passages, whereas de Selincourt interpolated a selection of passages from MS2 and MS5 which appear in the Cornell edition under such headings as 'Additional Pieces', 'Affinitive Pieces', and 'Extracts'. De Selincourt sometimes substituted clearer versions from MS2 or MS5 for illegible or torn passages in MS3. As hinted above, it is not clear that Wordsworth's first major poem opened as both the published texts do. Where the poem ends is also guesswork. Although de Selincourt's lines 379–415 may not belong where he puts them, it is not clear that Wordsworth's poem went from 'The world of shades is all my own' to 'No spot but claims the tender tear' as in the Cornell reading text. Both de Selincourt and the Cornell editors include the lines to Dorothy beginning 'Sister for whom' (possibly continuous but in different ink and in a larger hand) and those to Fleming beginning 'What from the social chain' and ending 'Friendship and Fleming are the same' (which are in different ink and discontinuous). But whereas Landon and Curtis prefer *VE* to end with the sentiment 'Friendship and Fleming are the same', de Selincourt follows the manuscript a little further. Generally, although MSS 2, 3 and 5 contain numerous draft passages linked thematically and imagistically with the chunks of the poem as we have it, no arrangement of these fragments seems likely to produce anything like a complete and satisfying whole. Whether the Cornell text should leave out all that it does is doubtful, but the fragments taken by de Selincourt from MSS 2 and 5 to pad out *The Vale* are certainly best left as the Cornell editors leave them—as 'additional' or 'affinitive' pieces. A computer might generate numerous fascinating collocations of what we have, but none of them would be a poem by Wordsworth.

2   Abbie Findlay Potts, *Wordsworth's Prelude*, 71–72. For the version in *Descriptive*

also be regarded as providing the inspiration for the entire *Esthwaite* enterprise, in the lines (Book 1 stanza 32):

> When the long-sounding curfew from afar
> Loaded with loud lament the lonely gale,
> Young Edwin, lighted by the evening star
> Lingering and listening, wander'd down the vale.
> There would he dream of graves and corses pale;
> And ghosts that to the charnel-dungeon throng,
> And drag a length of clanking chain, and wail,
> Till silenced by the owl's terrific song,
> Or blast that shrieks by fits the shuddering isles along.

If great poets steal, Wordsworth mastered that part of the art very early. In so far as *The Vale of Esthwaite* gives signs of having any more of a plot than Edwin's mobile reverie, its more immediate model is Helen Maria Williams, from whom Wordsworth borrowed assiduously.[1] Her tautologically entitled *Part of an Irregular Fragment*, inspired by contemplation of a long-closed door in the Tower of London, presents models for three of Wordsworth's most dramatic motifs. In Part 3 of Williams's poem, the impressionable speaker is approached by spirits whose spectral forms are reflected in the stanza lineation:

> Ye visions that before me roll,
> That freeze my blood, that shake my soul !
> Are ye the phantoms of a dream ?
> Pale Spectres! are ye what ye seem ?
> They glide more near—
> Their forms unfold !
> Fix'd are their eyes, on me they bend
> Their gleaming look is cold![2]

The closest thing to an incident in the first section of Wordsworth's poem takes the same form, except that instead of dream phantoms his imagination is working on woodland shades. Seeking at noon 'the gloomy glades

---

Sketches, see Jonathan Wordsworth in 'The Climbing of Snowdon', *BWS*, 452.

1   My *Wordsworth and Helen Maria Williams; or, the Perils of Sensibility* documents how her *Letters from France* provided some of the central metaphors for his treatment of the French Revolution, and argues that the legacy of her poetry in his may account for much of the critical opprobrium directed at his *Poems, in Two Volumes*.

2   Helen Maria Williams, *Poems in Two Volumes* (2nd edn, 1791), 2: 6.

| Religious woods and midnight shades', as he will do in *Yew-Trees*, he mistakes foaming cataracts for druid robes. 'Why roll on me your glaring eyes', he addresses one such cataract. 'Why fix on me for sacrifice?'

> And hark the ringing harp I hear
> And lo! her druid sons appear.
> Why roll on me your glaring eyes?
> Why fix on me for sacrifice?
> But Lo the stream's loud genius, seen
> The black arch'd boughs and rocks between
> That brood o'er one eternal night,
> Shoot[s] from the cliff in robe of white.
>
> (*EPF* 424, ll. 31–38)

Having been re-energized in *Salisbury Plain*, this metamorphosis will be recycled more imaginatively in the 1794 revision of *An Evening Walk*.

Williams's hero, after numerous speeches by numerous spectres regarding numerous violent or suspicious deaths, is invited to penetrate further into the glooms beneath the Tower of London:

> But whence arose that solemn call?
>   Yon bloody phantom waves his hand
> And beckons me to deeper gloom—
>   Rest, troubled form! I come—
> Some unknown power my step impels
> To horror's secret cells—

whereupon the spectre reveals to him a selection of the regal dead, and perhaps, Death himself, before the youth retreats, just in time, eyed by 'two sullen shades half seen'.

Wordsworth's reworking of this passage takes the form of the primary spot of time in *The Vale of Esthwaite*. He has entered a turreted mansion surrounded by storm-tossed trees that seem like 'Gigantic Moors in battle joined' (*EPF*, line 146; *PW*, 1: 219), wherein—but only in Ernest de Selincourt's interpolations from MS.5—he meets a spectral woman with a blue taper in 'a haunted castle's panelled room' (241). She leads him to a dungeon, shakes her head mysteriously thrice and shows him 'an iron coffer marked with blood' (261):

> The taper turn'd from blue to red
> Flash'd out and with a shriek she fled.
> With arms in horror spread around

> I mov'd—a form unseen I found
> Twist round my hand an icy chain
> And drag me to the spot again. (*PW*, 1: 262–67)

All this build up leads precisely nowhere. But at de Selincourt's line 307 (*EPF* 198) Wordsworth finds himself back in a vault, where, as the Cornell editors point out, effects from Walpole's *Castle of Otranto* and Macpherson's *Ossian* jostle for room, until, scared by a 'hollow-howling blast | I started back' (*PW* 326) from a ghostly form:

> —when at my hand
> A tall thin Spectre seem'd to stand
> [Li]ke two wan wither'd leaves his eyes
> [B]lack were his bones seen through his skin
> As the pale moonbeam wan and thin
> Which through a chink of rock we view
> On a lone sable blasted yew
> And on his feeble arm he bore
> What seem'd the poet's harp of yore
> He wav'd his hand and would have spoke,
> But from his trembling shadow broke
> Faint murmuring sad and hollow moans
> As if the wind sigh'd through his bones.
> He wav'd again, we entered slow
> A narrow passage dark and low,
> The mountain seem'd to nod on high
> Shriek'd loud then groan'd a hollow sigh

(Here de Selincourt's 'I heard the mountain heave a sigh | Nodding its rocky helm on high', though borrowed without real authority from MS.5, catches the improved reference to Helm Crag)

> And on we journeyed man[y] a mile
> While all was black as night the while,
> Save his tall form before my sight
> Seen by the wan pale dismal ligh[t]
> Around his bones so [*trochee*] shed
> Like a white shroud that wraps [the dead].
> Now as we wandered through the gloom
> In Black Helvellyn's inmost womb
> The spectre made a solemn stand,
> Slow round his head thrice wav'd his [hand]
> And cleaved mine ears then swept his [lyre]

> That shriek'd terrific shrill an[d] [dire]
>
> *(EPF*, ll.218–245)

'Thrice wav'd' is not a premonition of *Kubla Khan,* but an echo of the female spectre's triple head-shaking in MS.5, cited above. Derived from Virgil. It matches Cyrene's three oblations in Book 4 of *The Georgics,* in the tale of Orpheus and Eurydice which the orphaned Wordsworth translated movingly at Hawkshead. It belongs, too, with 'Thrice with my arms I strove her neck to clasp' (*Aeneid* 2.1055, in Wordsworth's later translation of Aeneas's attempt to embrace the ghost of Creusa), and with 'Then thrice around [Anchises'] neck his arms [Aeneas] drew | And thrice the flitting shadow slipped away' in (Dryden's) *Aeneid* Book 6. And it anticipates Wordsworth's remarkable (and again Virgilian) *Laodamia* (1814), in which the passionate heroine forfeits Elysian bliss by making three forbidden attempts to embrace her husband's apparition. Each triple gesture pertains to interviews with the dead or passages through the portals of Erebus. In the *Vale,* a clumsy associationist logic gestures towards the poet's loss of his father and his mother; in *Laodamia*—'which cost me more trouble than almost anything of equal length I have ever written' (*Fenwick Notes,* 67) —the empathy with Laodamia's inconsolability is charged, transparently, with grief for Catherine Wordsworth.

The 'fiend' now shudders (it is unclear whether the bardic Spectre has now *become* a fiend or rather been replaced, in the poem's dreamwork, *by* a fiend); the vault echoes with the song; 'my breaking soul could bear no more', and 'with a thunderous sound | That shook the groaning mountain round | A massy door wide open flew'. The poet remains troubled 'each night' by what happens next, and 'ridden' by shapeless terrors (terrors that will later become naturalized as the uncanny 'forms that do not live like living men' in the Ullswater spot of time). In the poem's nightmare-logic, the personal becomes the historical: Wordsworth's orphaning at his father's house takes the form of the end of the house of Dunmail. The fatherly, harp-bearing, spectre-fiend accords him a vision of the assassination by Saxon Edmund of the last 'royal brothers' of the line of Urien, following their defeat on Dunmail raise.

> I saw the ghosts and heard the yell
> Of every Briton [blank] who fell

> When Edmund deaf to horror's cries
> Trod out the royal Brothers' eyes.[1]

And so:

> While Terror shapeless rides my soul
> Full oft together are we hurled
> Far, Far amid the shadowy world—
> [And since that hour, the world unknown
> The world of shades is all my own.]

(EPF lines 262–71)

This conclusion owes much, all editors have noted, to the opening of Collins's *Ode to Fear*—'Thou, to whom the World unknown | With all its shadowy Shapes is shown'—but it improves upon the borrowing, and it stands, it seems to me, as an appropriate manifesto for the 'Poet of Elysium' that Wordsworth's apprentice output (here and elsewhere) shows him to be. The claim that 'The world of shades is all my own' manifests greater self-recognition than any other self-imaging line in Wordsworth's poetry until, perhaps, *Tintern*'s 'a worshipper of Nature' or *The Prelude*'s 'I became a patriot'. Indeed, as the appropriate talisman of his poetry it outlasts either of these.

In De Selincourt's *Vale of Esthwaite*, an obscure bridge passage depicting a Cumbrian version of the River Styx, overlooked on each sable rock by 'Forms' of wild terrific mien, leads into the poem's final piece of ore, the first version of what will become the Christmas spot of time, in which Wordsworth pays 'the mighty debt of grief' for his dead father. There is in fact no obvious continuity except in the implication that there has been throughout, that Wordsworth's underworld journey is modelled less on anything in Williams or English Gothic than on Virgil's inspirational accounts of Aeneas's search for the shade of his father in Book VI of the *Aeneid*, and Orpheus's descent in the *Georgics* in quest to redeem Eurydice, the two scenes that most inform Wordsworth's dedication to the world of shades, his sense of Elysium, and his dedication to both the living and the dead.

In this version, the episode is undeveloped. All that we are told is that sheltered by a naked rock,

---

1   Because de Selincourt misreads the adjective as 'cruel' there is a persistent notion that these lines refer to Gloucester's blinding in *King Lear*. Sans blinding, the scene recurs in *The Waggoner* (1806–1819) lines 201–20.

> Long, long my swimming eyes did roam
> For little horse to bear me home
> To bear me—what avails my tear?
> To sorrow o'er a father's bier.

When he does develop it, in *The Prelude*, he will—rather surprisingly perhaps—Ossianize the scene. William Gilpin, who visited Castlerigg stone circle in 1772 found in its 'ancient vestiges of architecture'

> strong proofs of the savage nature of the religion of these heathen priests. Within these magical circles we may conceive any incantations to have been performed ... when our ancestors, in their nocturnal orgies, invoked the spirits which rode upon the winds—the awful forms of their deceased forefathers. (*Observations*, 28)

The same equation of mists and the souls of the departed is found, with no particular personal application, in the closing passage of *An Evening Walk*, and it recurs in the *Guide*. If one remembers that Wordsworth attended Hawkshead Grammar School with Gilpin's nephew, Charles Farish, it becomes less surprising that this Ossianic image fathered one of the most powerful moments in Wordsworth's poetry, the spot of time in *The Prelude* (*1805,* 11: 344–84) in which, as the boy reimagines the spot where he waited anxiously for the horses to bear him home for the Christmas holiday—culpably wishing away precious moments in his father's last few days—wind and mist advance along 'each of these two roads | … in such indisputable shapes', to manifest the accusing spirit of a dead father, as they manifest the presence of innumerable fallen heroes in the poems of Ossian.

Nor, by way of *ur-Prelude*, does that exhaust the poem's riches. Before the *Vale of Esthwaite* closes it has moved from the scene of orphaning to that uncanny moment in *The Two-Part Prelude* where the boy represents himself at the point of death. He imagines that he will remember how the setting sun 'A lingering lustre softly throws | On the dear hills when first he rose'. Though transferred to Coniston in *The Prelude*, here is one instance, at least, of a sentiment later applied to youth having a textual presence there. Even the pursuit of imaginary terrors at the start of the poem—the fear of the youthful poet that he is destined for sacrifice—presents the motif of the fated poet in startlingly literal terms. Later he will use the same motif, but no longer innocently—rather with the implication that the man of imagination (Robespierre, say, or his Jacobin apologists), may stand beside the sacrificer, not the sacrificed. However Gothically, Wordsworth is already seeing the poet, as Hölderlin does, as one whose task is to stand atop the mountain, grasp the very lightning-flash, and pass, wrapped in song, the divine gift to the people ('and thereof come in the end', in the Chattertonian variant of this motif of the fated poet, 'despondency and madness'). Nor are 'the people' as they later appear in *Lyrical Ballads* and *The Ruined Cottage*, absent from the *Vale*. As Duncan Wu, who has mined the early Wordsworth more productively than anyone, has pointed out, the so-called 'affinitive pieces' on Madness, Suicide, Despair and Horror, with their interest in extreme mental states contain the seeds of the radical humanist poetry of the next decade.[1]

Given the models provided by such poets as Beattie, Collins, Gray and Helen Maria Williams, for reasonably structured pieces of anguished sensibility, the textual remnants of *The Vale of Esthwaite* may seem, even for a 17-year-old, remarkably incoherent. Yet the poetry has a mesmeric power, not found in its generally distanced models, that goes far beyond such exercises in convention. Despite the greater assurance of Williams's writing in her *Poems in Two Volumes*, and her not uninteresting treatment of royal secrets (in *Part of an Irregular Fragment*), Wordsworth's *Vale* is still the more haunting performance. Joseph Cottle in *The Fall of Cambria*, twenty years later, has his Caradoc exclaim over the fallen Bards:

> In the hour of stormy woe,
> Iron war hath laid you low!—
> While I am left, forlorn, alone,
> To heave the sigh, and pour the groan.

Juvenile Wordsworth comes much closer to a Virgilian anguish, and avoids any line quite as bad as the last.

In 1787 Wordsworth signalled his poetic terrain in a visionary encounter with an Anchises figure who haunts his major works and who led him into a local Hades a little above Thirlmere. Fifty-five years later, in a fit of insight, Benjamin Robert Haydon depicted the 72-year-old poet 'in the act', Wordsworth said, 'of climbing Helvellyn': the painting shows a poet with his arms folded, his head cast down, still gazing into Helvellyn's womb. Helvellyn, by the way, was mined in the seventeenth century: guided exploration of her womb may qualify as the first authentic spot of time.

---

1   Duncan Wu, *Wordsworth: an Inner Life* (Oxford: Blackwell, 2002), 3.

'Glaramara's inmost Caves'

Despite the evidence of *The Vale of Esthwaite* and *An Evening Walk* the pedestrian panorama is not Wordsworth's stock in trade. Both poems demonstrate that the characteristic topoi, both of *Lyrical Ballads* and of the spots of time, are present in Wordsworth poetry from the outset, but it is clear that for a psyche as turbulent as Wordsworth's and a conscience as engaged, the loco-descriptive mode of Thomson, Cowper and Akenside will not do.[1] The elements of introspection and human pathos which mix so uneasily with the panoramic in these poems require either to be fused or sundered. They will be fused, eventually, by the kind of mythopoeia developed in *The Ruined Cottage, The Discharged Soldier, Michael,* and *The Leech-Gatherer*. One fruit of their tactical severance is the production in 1799 of two poems which half belong to *The Prelude*, namely *Nutting* and *There was a Boy*. Another is the long struggle in 1803–14 with a poem which half belongs with them, *Yew-Trees*. As in the *Prelude* 'spots of time', these affinitive pieces involve significant interaction with place. *Nutting* and *Yew-Trees*, especially, depict a naturally sacred spot, where the boundaries between inner space and outer space, or between personal time and tribal time, are relaxed.

Given that the primary signification of *Nutting* is, when all is said and done, nutting, it might be reasonable, one would have thought, to consider 'hazels' in this context. It would be absurd to discuss *The Thorn* without recognizing that in folklore the hawthorn is associated with witchcraft, with chastity and with female sexuality; or *Yew-Trees* without cognizance that the yew is in one frame of reference the provider of longbows and in another the death tree of Hecate. Yet in all the discussion of the variant MSS of *Nutting*—often vitiated by a semiotically myopic assumption that there is something feminine about a grove of erect hazels hung with clusters of nuts—there has been, as far as I can find, no attention whatever to the fact that what the sexually undifferentiated Wordsworth and Dorothy have *both* been prone to ravage is a grove of hazels, emblematic of authority, wisdom, judgement and art. Traditionally, the hazel was

---

1   'Away, away, it is the air | That stirs among the withered leaves; |… | Away, and take the eagle's eyes, | The tyger's smell, | Ears that can hear the agonies |And murmurings of hell;… | Then tell me if the thing be clear, | The difference betwixt a tear | Of water and of blood'. *LBC*, 285. Whether written as dramatic empathy or autobiographical utterance, these lines illustrate the extreme chords out of which Wordsworth's passionate harmonies are made.

arbiter or judge in the battle of the trees. Its nuts symbolize knowledge or art, as concentrated wisdom (and are for this reason associated with rites of initiation). Its rods have been used throughout the British Isles, from time immemorial, for purposes of divination—both of water and, until the seventeenth century, of guilt—and by the druids as heraldic wands. The tree of poets, priests and kings, it is subject to ritual harvesting only by true successors. For the pretender, pillage of the tree itself—and nuts are manifestly not the issue—is punishable by death. The association of hazels, in bardic times, with what Graves refers to as the 'nine hazels of poetic art', and Yeats calls 'the tree of Life or of Knowledge' is one reason why, in the heroic age, ravage of a hazel copse could carried the death penalty. *Nutting*, that is to say, offers one pertinent answer to the *Vale of Esthwaite*'s rhetorical question, 'Why fix on me for sacrifice?'[1] Some of this lore would be available to a Cumbrian schoolboy, certainly enough to make him aware of a spirit in the place and to give rise to the most *Prelude*-like moment in the poem: 'unless I now | Confound my present spirit with the past, | … I felt a sense of pain'.

Applied to rape, the prime burden of the criticism, though not of the poem, this twinge of conscience is not good enough. The legitimate question, as in *The Prelude*, is whether Wordsworth's responsiveness to nature's spirit can really be energized as early as this—whether indeed the sympathetic spirit can possibly coexist with the 'glad animal' phase of a boy's existence—and whether, if so, it is innate. The doctrine of growth in *The Prelude* suggests as a whole that in the development of the spirit certain kinds of sympathetic feeling, though innate, have their own season—that the predatory atavisms of boyhood are a necessary repetition of the savage childhood of the race. That such savagery is quite as much a part of the sister's endowment as her brother—in the manuscript version of the poem Wordsworth's boyhood memory is provoked by Dorothy ravaging a hazel copse—is of course where the poem engages with the contemporary argument between Hannah More, Mary Hays and Mary Wollstonecraft concerning sexual identity.[2] The explicit argument of the poem, with or without its cancelled opening, is that what is possible for the brother is also possible for the sister and is wrong for both. In the concluding lines (which in the short version are as surprising as

1   Robert Graves, *The White Goddess* (London: Faber, 1961), 73, 75, 181, 182.
2   The excised portion of *Nutting*, in which Dorothy's ravage provokes the poem, is available in *PW* 2: 504–6, and there is a full transcription of MS.15 in *LBOP*, 302–05.

the address to Dorothy in the fifth movement of *The Poem upon the Wye*)
the brother invites his sibling to share the moral he has learned: 'Then,
dearest Maiden, move along these shades | In gentleness of heart; with
gentle hand | Touch—for there is a spirit in the woods.' Gregory Jones
concludes in his fine essay on what he calls the uncensored *Nutting*, that
this final plea 'is primarily a demonstration ... that female sexuality need
not be determined by anything less than the imagination'.[1] In fact, surely,
it is *primarily* a demonstration that, like their brothers, and like not-yet-
Ancient Mariners, sisters may need reminding that everything that lives
is holy. Even sisters who have always feared to brush the wings of butter-
flies may not yet feel the one life within us and *all* things, which sublimer
awareness is their birthright too. As in *Yew-Trees*, a habit of listening to
'the ghostly language of the ancient earth', or simply 'the language of
things', results in his speaking for a threatened copse.

In later years, when Sir George Beaumont disposed of some property
at Loughrigg, Wordsworth applied part of the proceeds to a little remem-
bered gift to Grasmere. He planted around St. Oswald's church eight yew
trees, with the hope that they might one day rival those of Borrowdale
(this now seems unlikely; in 2001 they were looking as if something
in their diet did not agree with them). In the *Fenwick Notes* (203–4)
Wordsworth devotes more space to recording in punctilious detail how
this was done than he does to almost anything else in his career.

> There is a Yew-Tree, pride of Lorton Vale,
> Which to this day stands single, in the midst
> Of its own darkness, as it stood of yore:
> Not loth to furnish weapons for the bands
> Of Umfraville or Percy ere they marched

---

1   Gregory Jones, '"Rude Intercourse": Uncensoring Wordsworth's "Nutting"',
Studies in Romanticism 35 (1996) 213–43, 239. Of all Wordsworth's poems, *Nutting*
is the one that will take longest to free itself from the retreating shadows of Freud and
Lacan, although it is perhaps, like Rossetti's *Goblin Market*—with all those luscious
globes and juices—a text that should make one wary of supposing that symbolism,
before Freud, worked hermeneutically in as monotone a fashion as it does a century
after. Sometimes, Freud is supposed to have said, 'a cigar is just a cigar', and even
when that is not the case, a phallic symbol, Freud insisted, does not symbolise the
phallus—it symbolises what the phallus also symbolises. Jones's essay is refreshingly
free from interpretive mechanism, but it doesn't entertain for a moment the notion
that *Nutting* may be about nutting. Wordsworth described himself innocently to Miss
Fenwick, as 'an impassioned nutter' (*FN*, 62). What *did* she suppose him to mean by
that—and what *would* she have made of Dorothy being another?

To Scotland's heaths; or those that crossed the sea
And drew their sounding bows at Azincourt,
Perhaps at earlier Crecy, or Poictiers.
Of vast circumference and gloom profound
This solitary Tree! a living thing
Produced too slowly ever to decay;
Of form and aspect too magnificent
To be destroyed. But worthier still of note
Are those fraternal Four of Borrowdale,
Joined in one solemn and capacious grove;
Huge trunks! and *each particular trunk a growth*
Of intertwisted fibres serpentine
Up-coiling, and inveterately convolved;
Nor uninformed with Phantasy, and *looks*
That threaten the profane;—a pillared shade,
Upon whose grassless floor of red-brown hue,
By sheddings from the pining umbrage tinged
Perennially—beneath whose sable roof
Of boughs, as if for festal purpose, decked
With unrejoicing berries—*ghostly Shapes*
May meet at noontide; Fear and trembling Hope,
Silence and foresight; Death the Skeleton
And Time the Shadow;—there to celebrate,
As in a natural temple scattered o'er
With altars undisturbed of mossy stone,
United worship; or in mute repose
To lie, and listen to the mountain flood
Murmuring from Glaramara's inmost caves.

Yew-Trees occupied Wordsworth from 1803 to 1814. It was, he said, one of his best poems 'for the imaginative power displayed', meaning, presumably, that it is one of those in which the invisible world—in this case an Elysian one—usurps most boldly upon the quotidian.[1]

1   According to Crabb Robinson's *Diary* for 11 September 1816 Wordsworth considered that 'by the imagination the mere fact is exhibited as connected with that infinity without which there is no poetry', from which Robinson concludes that 'imagination is the faculty by which the poet conceives and produces—that is, images—individual forms in which are embodied universal ideas or abstractions' (1. 278–9.) For major readings of 'Yew-Trees' see Cleanth Brooks and Robert Penn Warren, *Understanding Poetry* (New York: Holt, Rinehart and Winston, 1960), 274–8; Michael Riffaterre, 'Interpretation and Descriptive Poetry: A Reading of Wordsworth's "Yew-Trees"', *New Literary History* 4 (1973) 229–65, Geoffrey Hartman, 'The Use and Abuse of Structural

Motifs of the bardic strain and of the druidic conjoin in an evoca-
tion of the invisible world, the world of Virgilian and more specifically
in this case Lucanian, shades. The covertly intertextual method is con-
tiguous with that of *Nutting*. *Nutting*, in Gregory Jones's justly cele-
brated reading, tacitly evokes the bowers of *The Faerie Queene*, *As You
Like It* and *Orlando Furioso*.[1] It does so, I would add, while endors-
ing Andrew Marvell's love of trees (in Marvell's presciently Romantic
and Keatsianly sensuous poem *The Garden*, 'Apollo hunted Daphne so
| Only that She might Laurel grow'). *Yew-Trees*, similarly, celebrates a
vegetable life 'vaster than empires and more slow' by naturalizing not
only this arboreal motif from *To his Coy Mistress,* but more vital ones
from *Paradise Lost*, *The Aeneid* and *Pharsalia*.

The poem borrows the 'Pillar'd shade' of Milton's fig-tree, apply-
ing it to sublimer trees, and as Brooks and Warren pointed out long ago,
fuses Milton's adjacent 'pines' and 'umbrage' into a punningly 'pining
umbrage'.[2] Its 'ghostly shapes' recall those who surround the dreaming
elm at the gate of Virgil's underworld—'Revengeful Cares and Sullen
Sorrows ... Toils and Death, and Death's half-brother Sleep'.[3] Behind
these, deeper within darkness (to borrow a phrase from Hughes's *Pike*),
lie the archetypal speaking tree in *The Dream of the Rood*, itself 'not
loth' to share in Christ's mankind-changing Passion, and more recently
the voicing of nature in Drayton. Like Drayton's Dee—but with none of
his quaintness—Wordsworth's yews borrow the poem's consciousness
to voice their 'phantasy'. They, too, have 'things to speak, might profit
[us] to know'. Yet, as in *Nutting*, the poem's allusive texture is sublimi-
nal, a world away from overt raids on the poetry of sensibility in the *Vale*,
the *Walk* and *Descriptive Sketches*.

Wordsworth's gift to Grasmere, it seems, as he surrounded St
Oswald's with eight twinned Yews, was what Seamus Heaney might
call a door into the dark: temporally the imaginative landscape of the
poem is one in which a Christian world—even one as primordial as the

---

Analysis: Riffaterre's Interpretation of Wordsworth's "Yew-Trees"', *New Literary
History* 7 (1975) 165–89, and Tim Fulford, in *Landscape Liberty and Authority:
Poetry, Criticism and Politics from Thomson to Wordsworth* (Cambridge: CUP, 1996),
197–206.

1   Jones, 227, 229, 231, 233, 234.
2   Brooks and Warren, 276. While noting the borrowing, they do not observe that it
exemplifies imaginative fusion—or a double pun on both 'pining' and 'umbrage'.
3   *Aeneid*, Book 6, in Dryden's translation.

Anglo-Saxon—yields to something much more primordial. The transhistorical reference moves backwards from mediaeval battles recollected in tranquillity—Umfraville would have set out from Cockermouth, joining Northumbrian Percy, to fight at Bannockburn in 1314—to the destruction of sacred groves in Mona and Marseilles.[1] The Fenwick note apprises us that a Yew similar to the ones in the poem had always seemed to Wordsworth 'as old as the Christian era', and that 'Hutton, the old Guide, of Keswick ... used gravely to tell strangers that there could be no doubt of its having been in existence before the flood' (61–2). Such trees, if ever young, were so at the time of Rome's suppression of Gaul and invasions of Britain. Through such associations, the 'fraternal four' of Borrowdale become survivors of, or recoverers from, Suetonius's or Caesar's systematic destruction of druid groves, contemporaries of those at Marsillia, described by Lucan in the 3rd book of *The Civil War*:

> A grove there was, untouched by men's hands from ancient times, whose interlacing boughs enclosed a space of darkness and cold shade, and banished the sunlight far above ... gods were worshipped there with savage rites.... Legend also told that ... serpents twined and glided round the stems.... This grove was sentenced by Caesar to fall before the stroke of the axe.[2]

Closer to Wordsworth's appropriately Latinate trees (an unusual case of Latinism *as* concreteness) is Nicholas Rowe's verse translation of 1719:

> The baleful yew, though dead, has oft been seen
> To rise from earth, and spring with dusty green;
> With sparkling flames the trees unburning shine,
> *And round their boles prodigious serpents twine.*
> The pious worshippers approach not near,
> But shun their gods, and kneel with distant fear:
> The priest himself, *when, or the day or night,*
> *Rolling have reached their full meridian height,*
> Refrains the gloomy paths with weary feet,
> Dreading the Daemon of the grove to meet;

1   *Yew-Trees* is Poem 5 of 'Poems of the Imagination'. Poem 25, *Song at the Feast of Brougham Castle*, concerns the restoration of Lord Clifford, whose ancestor, the first Lord Clifford, accompanied Umfraville at Bannockburn. I owe this point about the Clifford-Umfraville connection to Professor Masanori Yoshida.
2   Marcus Annaeus Lucanus, *The Civil War*, tr. J. D. Duff, Loeb, 1928, p 143.

> Who, terrible to fight, at that fix'd hour,
> Still treads the round about his dreary bower.[1]

Wordsworth's curious noontime haunting, like his incorporation of 'prodigious serpents' into the nature of the trees themselves, betray a consciousness of Lucan. The moral of Lucan's lengthy treatment is that only someone prepared to violate the gods would take an axe to such a grove, as Caesar does, and that he does so only because (like his avatar Napoleon, who is still laying the axe to the fabric of time) Caesar has already violated the values of the Republic.

In Lucan, the onlookers, aghast at Caesar's sacrilege, comfort themselves by spelling out the thought implied in Wordsworth's cancelled ending:

> They hope such power can never prosper long,
> Nor think the patient gods will bear the wrong.

In the manuscript version of *Yew-Trees* Wordsworth substitutes Mona for Marseilles and (by implication) Sertorius for Caesar:

> Pass not the [Place] unvisited—ye will say
> That Mona's Druid Oaks composed a fane
> Less awful than this grove: as earth so long
> On its unwearied bosom has sustained
> The undecaying Pile: as Frost and drought,
> The Fires of heaven have spared it, and the Storms,
> So for its hallowed uses may it stand
> For ever spared by man.   (*PW*, 2: 210)

Like other cancelled Wordsworthian conclusions, and the close of *Nutting*, which follows this poem in Poems of the Imagination, this one may prod the reader too overtly—it lacks the kind of enigma that permits the conclusions of *Simon Lee* or *Resolution and Independence* to stand (*why* 'mourning'? 'think' *what* of the leech-gatherer? and *what* precisely is learned from the boy of *Anecdote for fathers*?). The Fenwick note, lurking in the penumbra of the poem, nudges the reader more gently.

The 'altars undisturbed of mossy stone' are nature's art work, as in the 1814 sonnet, *Mark the Concentred Hazels*, where another mossy stone seems to frame 'the very image … of a tomb | In which some ancient

---

1   Marcus Annaeus Lucan, *Pharsalia,* tr. Nicholas Rowe, Johnson's poets Vol. 27. 2 vols (London 1779), p 130: 619–30 (the entire passage is 3.591–663).

chieftain finds repose'. Sympathizing with 'Time's forlorn humanities' they hint that this is a temple erected by nature, or in David Jones's sense, is a place 'set up' by and for nature, appropriate to natural religion. The named celebrants lead the reader on a curious route of conjecture. The antithetical abstractions Fear and Hope fade partially into the more compatible Silence and Foresight only to take form again in the almost interchangeable Death and Time—which pair tend to merge in traditional representations. These 'ghostly shapes' seem to retain possession of the scene less as ghosts than as representatives of the human heart by which we live. Like the youthful and conflicted Wordsworth, who also sought out at noon 'the gloomy glades | Religious woods and midnight shades', or the infant Wordsworth whose thoughts were 'composed' by the shallows of the fairest of all rivers, or the boy of *Nutting* charmed by 'fairy water-breaks' for ever murmuring, these conflicted abstractions of a war-torn culture seem to have the power of being active and passive at once. Like the synchronic alternatives in *Nutting* ('a little while I stood ... or beneath the trees I sat'), perhaps they 'celebrate united worship', or perhaps they listen to a 'mountain flood' murmuring from Glaramara's inmost caves. Kubla, seated in his sunny dome, midway between the fountain and the caves, heard 'ancestral voices prophesying war'. In Wordsworth's long meditated answering poem, much is reversed. It is both more and less exotic—Abyssinian-Ethiopian gives place to Romano-British, but the invisible world is more Celtic than Platonic—and what Stopford Brooke aptly called 'the ghostly masters of mankind'[1] are assuaged by the murmur of that mountain flood.[2]

A Visionary Republic

Wordsworth's references in *An Evening Walk* to 'the last remnant of the great and brave'—which poses the question whether Umfraville and Percy in *Yew-Trees* are already too belated to share these qualities—are further glossed in Wordsworth's most successful and many-versioned prose work. The *Guide to the Lakes* began its published existence in 1810 as the text accompanying Joseph Wilkinson's *Select Views in Cumberland, Westmorland and Lancashire*. While finishing the intro-

---

1   Stopford Brooke, *Theology in the English Poets* (London, 1896), 259.
2   I have expanded this reading in *The Oxford Handbook of William Wordsworth* (2015), in a joint essay with Daniel Robinson on *Daffodils* and *Yew-Trees*.

duction for this project, in November 1809, he conceived a future inde-
pendent *Guide*, which he published as *A Topographical Description of
the Country of the Lakes*, as the final part of the *River Duddon* volume
in 1820. It appeared independently, as *A Description of the Scenery of
the Lakes*, in 1822, and finally as *A Guide through the District of the
Lakes in the North of England*, 1835. By this time he had considered
writing a companion work on the historical geography of Snowdonia, to
redeem his twenty-year-old promise to Robert Jones that he would one
day celebrate his friend's legendary landscape. Its composition, there-
fore, bridges the interval between his great defence of the Iberian people
in *Concerning the Convention of Cintra* (1809), and his research for
Ecclesiastical Sonnets. Its publishing history extends to the time of the
1835 'Postscript'—his most considered assault on the naively heartless
political economy of his offcomer neighbour, Harriet Martineau. The
Guide is becoming recognized as a work of central importance to the
development of human ecology, and a particular inspiration to a further
instalment of that genre, Thoreau's *Walden*. Its brilliance as a description
of lakeland as a living system, shaped by nature and by human occu-
pation, cannot be overstated, and the diamond precision of some of its
notation of the ways lakes are shaped, and how both flora and fauna have
responded to human activity is what appealed to Thoreau's trained eye—
the eye of a land surveyor.

At the beginning of section 2 of *The Guide*, 'Aspect Of the Country,
as Affected by its Inhabitants', Wordsworth cites West's *Antiquities of
Furness* (1774) on 'the empire of beasts' and comments:

> Such was the state and appearance of this region when the aboriginal
> colonists of the Celtic tribes were first driven or drawn towards it, and
> became joint tenants with the wolf, the boar, the wild bull, the red deer,
> and the leigh, a gigantic species of deer which has been long extinct.

The inner parts of the region, he claims, were too secluded to 'participate
much of the benefit of Roman manners' and

> When the Romans retired from great Britain, it is well known that these
> mountain-fastnesses furnished a protection to some unsubdued Britons,
> long after the more accessible and more fertile districts had been seized
> by the Saxon or Danish invader. (*PrW*, 2: 194, 195)

Nature, in time, replaced this British culture—the end of which is memorialized in *Ecclesiastical Sonnets* in 1821—by a similarly robust Saxon one: indeed, according to Wordsworth, 'a perfect Republic of Shepherds ... a pure Commonwealth ... whose constitution has been imposed and regulated by the mountains which protected it' (2: 206). Although Wordsworth does not say so, this human ecology follows something of the process that patriotic historians, such as Samuel Williams and Thomas Jefferson, had observed in America. Europeans, having dispossessed what Natty Bumppo would always recognize as the true owners of the land, inherited, under the promptings of nature, the same democratic tendencies, and the same natural republicanism, as had been apparent in the dignified and eloquent conduct of the native peoples. Lakeland's Saxons and Vikings, similarly, inherited—under nature's tuition—the dauntlessness of those they had displaced and/or absorbed. This ancient repository of Britishness possesses, therefore, its own version of the laminated virtues sought by the Pantisocrats.

In a note on Lakeland's Roman and Celtic monuments, Wordsworth speculates on the notion that though only a few druid circles remain, such circles might have been numerous and that many might lie 'under no deep covering of soil', rural chapels to the cathedrals of Long Meg[1] and Karl Lofts at Shap.[2] The architectural metaphor which he later used to describe the relation of his shorter poems to *The Recluse* is thus used first to describe the buried spiritual history of his poetic territory. Continuity in that spiritual history is also implied: commenting on the ruined chapel

---

1 For the definitive piece on 'Long Meg and her Daughters' see Tim Fulford, *The Late Poetry of the Lake Poets* (Cambridge University Press, 2013) 258–74.

2 *PrW*, 2: 195. I imagine that Wordworth was aware of Lady Lowther's sketch of the great avenue at Shap, as well as William Stukeley's account of its vanishing grandeur in *Itinerarium Curiosum*. When Stukeley visited Long Meg in 1725, he saw not only the extant stone circles of Long Meg, Little Meg and Glassonby, but a fourth to the South West of which no trace remains. Similarly, his survey of Shap, Mayburgh Henge, Arthur's round table and its adjacent circus, is the most valuable record of exactly how things stood in the locality a century before Wordsworth, and exactly what was happening to ancient monuments in this era: stones buried by people fearful of their powers; stones blown up or sawn into millstones; stones incorporated at a frightening rate into farms, houses, walls, and roads—and of course the township of Shap itself which obliterated most of the astonishing ceremonial avenue of some 400 stones. This avenue, 1.3 miles long, 70 feet wide, with a stone on each side every 35 feet, must have rivalled Avebury and almost eclipsed Stonehenge itself. *Itinerarium Curiosum; or, An account of the antiquities, and remarkable curiosities in nature or art, observed in travels through Great Britain* (1725).

of Boredale Hause he says 'scarcely did the Druids, *when they fled to
these fastnesses*, perform their rites in any situation more exposed ....
the rustic psalmody must have had the accompaniment of many a wildly-
whistling blast' (248). Again there is that note of 'the last remnant of
the great and the brave' driven to 'these fastnesses', with its clear par-
allel implication that in the feeble polity of contemporary Britain—the
writing is more or less contemporaneous with the *Cintra*—this is where
steadfastness and genuine liberty are still to be found. Finally, beneath
the roman camp of Castle Crag in Borrowdale, Wordsworth delivers the
coup de grace to imperial pretensions:

> And behold the eagle upon the wing, retaining her empire when
> that ambitious people who adopted her image for their standard have
> for ages been but a name... (*Unpublished Tour; PrW*, 2: 345).

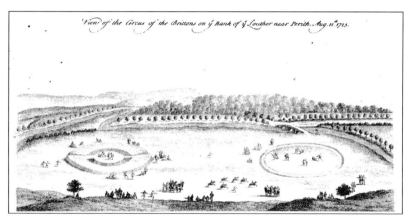

Stukeley's 1725 sketch of Arthur's Round Table at Eamont Bridge, under two
miles from the Wordsworth property in Sockbridge. About 90% of the circle on
the left remains; the other was obliterated by a gatehouse to Lowther Park.

A Short History of Wordsworthshire

Introducing *The Ecclesiastical Sonnets of William Wordsworth* (1922),
Abbie Findlay Potts quotes aptly from the *Cintra* Wordsworth's belief
that 'there is a spiritual community binding together the living and the
dead: the good, the brave, and the wise of all ages. We would not be
rejected from this community, and therefore do we hope'.[1] *Ecclesiastical*

---

1   Abbie Findlay Potts, ed., *The Ecclesiastical Sonnets of William Wordsworth* (New
Haven & London: Yale University Press and Oxford University Press, 1922), 10, citing
The Convention of Cintra (*WPW*, 229; *Cintra*, 218)).

Sonnets is the most concentrated effort Wordsworth made to see the national present in significant relation to its past, to trace its 'natural piety'. Sonnets 1–14, especially, work the same imaginative territory as Melvyn Bragg's novel, *Credo*, and like *Credo*, they work with a variety of historical sources, of which the greatest is Bede's *Ecclesiastical History*.[1] While Wordsworth's overall purpose in this work is to memorialize the Church *in* England (his own preposition)—and, by occasion, to justify his belated adhesion to the present form of that church by treating it as the organic product of nature and the people—one can feel that his imagination is most at home in the first, pagan, dozen. Borrowing Pope's 'once a heretic, always a heretic', Walter Bagehot aptly remarked 'sound men are sound from the first ... and Wordsworth began wrong'.[2]

In a curious way, the opening pages of the *Ecclesiastical Sonnets* replay the opening pages of any chronologically arranged Wordsworth— returning to the early hauntings of the druidic, the bardic, and glorious strife. Now, however, the result is a thorough essay in pre-history, equipoised between research and desire. The result is often prosaic, but a dense, allusive, elliptical prosaism, compressing great swathes of history into quatrains as demanding as anything Wordsworth wrote, and (like the Eiger or *The Waste Land*) approachable only with much apparatus.[3] Alluding to his prior sonnet sequences—both among the best received of his work, and at times equally gnomic—Wordsworth markets these sketches as integral to the work of the poet who has already 'accompanied with faithful pace | Cerulean Duddon from its cloud-fed spring' and 'essayed the nobler Stream to trace | Of Liberty'.

Like another Romantic for whom the power of prophecy meant seeing 'Past things, revealed like future' Wordsworth questions the historians:

> Did holy Paul, a while in Britain dwell,
> And call the Fountain forth by miracle,
> And with dread signs the nascent Stream invest?
> Or He, whose bonds dropped off, whose prison doors
> Flew open, by an Angel's voice unbarred? (*Conjectures*)

1 In Bragg's novel (London: Hodder & Stoughton, 1996), Bede himself is an orphan of the stock of Urien, cannily handed over to the Saxon monks in order that he might survive the ethnic cleansing of Cumbria after the joint victory of Edwin over the British and the Roman Church over the Celtic Church.

2 Cited from W. J. Harvey and Richard Gravil, eds, *Wordsworth: The Prelude*, in the original Casebook series (Houndmills: Macmillan, 1972), 55.

3 The apparatus required is provided in Potts, *The Ecclesiastical Sonnets*.

'And did those feet...?'? No, it isn't quite Blake, and Wordsworth's answer to his own question is a rather uninspiring 'probably not'. A note comments bluntly, 'Stillingfleet adduces many arguments in support of this opinion, but they are unconvincing'. Nonetheless, 'The latter part of this Sonnet refers' (lukewarmly and in verse that adds nothing to the prose) 'to a favourite notion of Roman Catholic writers, that Joseph of Arimathea and his companions brought Christianity into Britain, and built a rude church at Glastonbury...'. Druids, however, are much more than 'a notion', and as Wordsworth looks back in sonnet 3 they are themselves peering forward in some trepidation:

> Screams round the Arch-druid's brow the seamew—white
> As Menai's foam; and toward the mystic ring
> Where Augurs stand, the Future questioning,
> Slowly the cormorant aims her heavy flight,
> Portending ruin to each baleful rite,
> That, in the lapse of ages, hath crept o'er
> Diluvian truths, and patriarchal lore.[1]
> Haughty the Bard: can these meek doctrines blight
> His transports? wither his heroic strains?

It is a canny performance. Picking his way delicately between Edward Davies's enthusiasm for the arkite mysteries and the prophetic powers of the druids, and more critical accounts such as Sharon Turner's, Wordsworth puts together this not unregretful account how a heroic mythology based upon atoning sacrifice makes way for a slave morality based on atoning sacrifice, but only at the prompting of 'the Julian spear', and at the cost of 'chains' which cannot but remind of later missionaries:

> But all shall be fulfilled;—the Julian spear
> A way first opened; and, with Roman chains,
> The tidings come of Jesus crucified;
> They come—they spread—the weak, the suffering, hear;
> Receive the faith, and in the hope abide.

This equivocal treatment of heroic strains replaced by meek doctrine is underlined by adopting for the druids a distinctly Catholic term, in

---

1   Wordsworth's note informs the reader (following Edward Davies, whose own ultimate authority is Taliesin), that while the Seamew 'was, among the Druids, an emblem of those traditions connected with the deluge that made an important part of their mysteries', the Cormorant 'was a bird of bad omen'.

sonnet 4, 'Druidical Excommunication'. In the working out of the theme, Wordsworth sympathizes with both the hapless excommunicant, cut off from 'fire and food', and the druids' desire to serve appropriately 'the Ancient of days'.[1] Blake's picture of that personage comes not unhelpfully to mind:

> Yet shall it claim our reverence, that to God,
> Ancient of days! that to the eternal Sire,
> These jealous Ministers of law aspire,
> As to the one sole fount whence wisdom flowed,
> Justice, and order.

That their intimations of deity are dated back to when 'the stars were shaped' relates the druids to Wordsworth's own sense of duty in the *Ode to Duty*, despite the equivocal qualification:

> And still, 'mid yon thick woods, the primal truth
> Glimmers through many a superstitious form
> That fills the Soul with unavailing ruth.

Wordsworth's even-handedness between his authorities, and between confession of ignorance and a strong desire to penetrate the darkness—to reach the hiding places of our power although we know them to be closed—comes out powerfully in Sonnet 5, *Uncertainty*. In this sonnet's invocation of the sublime, its range of reference, its conjunction of association-laden place-names, we read the marks of a more than fleeting desire that shadows may prove substantial. In *The Prelude* of 1805, where Wordsworth himself employs that mode of prophecy which sees the past revealed as future, he had called on darkness and stood by Nature's side among the men of old. In 1821–22 it is still dark. Out of the unknown comes the known, lacking the power of the unknown's sense of 'something evermore to be revealed'.

> Darkness surrounds us; seeking, we are lost
> On Snowdon's wilds, amid Brigantian coves,
> Or where the solitary shepherd roves

---

1   Potts cites helpfully balanced testimony: according to Davies (*Celtic Researches*, 172), 'Amongst their disciples, these druids could at all time ensure peace by holding up the rod of excommunication', whereas in Turner (*History of the Anglo-Saxons*, 1.83–4 [1.72 in later editions]) druids 'interdicted' miscreants, and such interdiction was the severest punishment, as the interdicted person was shunned as 'impious and wicked'.

> Along the plain of Sarum, by the ghost
> Of Time and shadows of Tradition, crost;
> And where the boatman of the Western Isles
> Slackens his course—to mark those holy piles
> Which yet survive on bleak Iona's coast.
> Nor these, nor monuments of eldest name,
> Nor Taliesin's unforgotten lays,
> Nor characters of Greek or Roman fame,
> To an unquestionable Source have led;
> Enough—if eyes, that sought the fountain-head
> In vain, upon the growing Rill may gaze.
>
> (*Uncertainty*)

The glide between the personal *I* and the tribal *we* is always disconcerting. Here something of the same kind takes place invisibly. For once, that worn 'mapping' trope seems appropriate. This *tour de force* maps onto the topography of the sacred sites of the tribe a personal poetical history. It tallies Wordsworth's journeys with Jones in Snowdonia, and alone on Salisbury Plain, and with Coleridge and Dorothy in search of Burns and Ossian. The Brigantian coves, incidentally, might well include the Leven Estuary,[1] where verses from Gray's *Elegy* were engraved on the headstone of Wordsworth's schoolmaster. These 'holy piles' are more ambiguous than they look. Druids held Iona long before the Christians and the 'holy piles' might belong to either. 'We will grieve not, rather find...', the final couplet seems to say, as in *Intimations*, making the Christian 'Rill' a consolation for loss of the druidical fountain-head.

After two sonnets on Roman persecutions under Diocletian, and the recovery of Romano-British Christianity 'in many a re-constructed fane',[2] the 8th sonnet returns to a theme broached in *The Guide*, and in the political sonnets: Rome, like Napoleon, emasculated to rule. The theme is handled vigorously by William Hutchinson, citing the very best authorities:

> In Stewart's discourse prefixed to second edition of Sullivan's Lectures, it is said 'The Britains were debauched into a resemblance with a most

---

1   'The Brigantes, according to Roman writers, possessed a very large tract of country on the western coast of Britain; but ... it is enough for us to observe, they inhabited the district now called Cumberland', William Hutchinson, *History and Antiquities*, 3.

2   This notion is based, according to Potts, on Eusebius, *Ecclesiastical History* (1585)—a work listed in the Rydal Mount Sale Catalogue.

corrupted people. They renounced the fatigues of war for the blandish-
ments of peace. They forsook their huts for palaces; affected a costliness
of living, and gave way to a seducing voluptuousness.' (*Antiquities*, 2)

Samuel Daniel, on whose prose the sonnets frequently rely, quotes from
Cornelius Tacitus on the measures adopted by Agricola for the subjuga-
tion of Britain. Agricola determined to bring about 'by degrees, a general
collapsion into those softenings of vices, fair houses, baths, and delicate
banquets' all of which 'by the ignorant, was termed humanity, when it
was a part of servitude'.[1] Thus, the sonnet adopts the watchman tone:

> Watch, and be firm! for, soul-subduing *vice*,
> Heart-killing luxury, on your steps await.
> *Fair houses, baths, and banquets delicate,*
> And temples flashing, bright as polar ice,
> Their radiance through the woods— may yet suffice
> To sap your hardy virtue, …

Rome's arts, 'though fondly viewed | As humanizing graces' are 'instru-
ments of deadliest servitude!' The departure of Rome—with much of
the Romanized British technological and military elite—leaves a land
afflicted by ancient feuds, new heresies and strange allies. Sonnet 1.9
refers to two heresies (neither of which Wordsworth admits to here)
namely that of 'Pelagius, a Briton [who denied] the assistance of divine
grace' (Potts) and 'the gangrene' of Arianism, as Fuller called it in his
Church History. At the same time, 'The Pictish cloud darkens the ener-
vate land | By Rome abandoned', and 'strange Allies', the Saxons, will
soon 'become more dreaded enemies'.

Nonetheless, what may have been Rheged's finest hour inspires the
finest sonnet in the series, a collage of British history:

> Rise!—they have risen: of brave Aneurin ask
> How they have scourged old foes, perfidious friends:
> The Spirit of Caractacus descends
> Upon the Patriots, animates their task;—
> Amazement runs before the towering casque
> Of Arthur, bearing through the stormy field
> The virgin sculptured on his Christian shield:—
> Stretched in the sunny light of victory bask
> *The Host that followed Urien as he strode*

---

1   Samuel Daniel, *History of England*, 5th edition (London, 1685), 3.

> *O'er heaps of slain*;—from Cambrian wood and moss
> Druids descend, auxiliars of the Cross;
> Bards, nursed on blue Plinlimmon's still abode,
> Rush on the fight, to harps preferring swords,
> And everlasting deeds to burning words!

Each dash in this stirring evocation of what the political sonnets called 'altar, sword and pen' connotes a different episode, and indeed location. 'Patriots' is an interesting term. It elides Milton's and Mason's celebration of Caradoc, the most successful of those who resisted Roman occupation in the first place, with the Iberian heroes of the *Cintra*. Caradoc's battles with the Romans in the South elide with Arthur's post-Roman border wars as remembered by Rheged's Aneirin, though the shield of the Virgin comes, in the first place, from Geoffrey of Monmouth.[1] Sharon Turner's *History of the Anglo-Saxons* cites Taliesin on Urien of Rheged's victories: Wordsworth is probably thinking of 'the tumult of the perishing hosts; | The blood ... moistening the ground' in Taliesin's *The Battle of Gwenystrad*.[2] Wordsworth now sides overtly with those (including William Stukeley) who elided Druidism and Christianity, so that Christianity becomes a sort of organically evolving native faith. The sonnet's final scene, in North Wales, is generalized enough to collate resistance to Suetonius or Ethelfrid, but the warlike bards suggest Wordsworth's agreement with Sharon Turner that 'these Bards were warriors; their songs commemorate warriors; and their feelings and sentiments are wholly martial' (*Vindication* 207).

Bede's account of the Scottish victory gained by 'Germanus' and a valiant few by shouting 'Hallelujah' (Sonnet XI) provides a momentary stay against wider defeats, but the mound-dwelling Saxons—in another motif influenced by Samuel Daniel—'Content, if foss, and barrow, and the girth | Of long-drawn rampart, witness what they were', drive the superior culture to the hills.[3] This cultural night is nowhere more feelingly described than in sonnet 12, *The Monastery of Old Bangor* (Bangor in Flintshire), which draws from Wordsworth his closest approximation—outside the *Thanksgiving Ode*—to the staccato half lines he associated with Taliesin's unforgotten lays:

---

1   Geoffrey, *Historia Regum Britanniae,* Book 9, chapter 4.
2   *Ecclesiastical Sonnets*, 218 n.
3   Daniel, 9, depicts the extirpation by the Saxons of all trace of Roman architecture.

The oppression of the tumult—wrath and scorn—
The tribulation—and the gleaming blades—
Such is the impetuous spirit that pervades
The song of Taliesin; —Ours shall mourn
The unarmed Host who by their prayers would turn
The sword from Bangor's walls, and guard the store
Of Aboriginal and Roman lore,
And Christian monuments, that now must burn
To senseless ashes.

Lines 1–2 adapt the version of Taliesin found in Sharon Turner's *History of the Anglo-Saxons* (1:32): 'I saw the oppression of the tumult; the wrath and tribulation; | The blades gleaming on the bright helmets; | The battle against the Lord of Fame in the dales of Hafren; | Against Brocmail of Powys, who loved my muse'.[1] Wordsworth's own note cites Turner as follows:

> 'Ethelforth reached the convent of Bangor, he perceived the Monks, twelve hundred in number, offering prayers for the success of their countrymen: "if they are praying against us," he exclaimed, "they are fighting against us;" and he ordered them to be first attacked: they were destroyed; and, appalled by their fate, the courage of Brocmail wavered, and he fled from the field in dismay. Thus abandoned by their leader, his army soon gave way, and Ethelforth obtained a decisive conquest. Ancient Bangor itself soon fell into his hands, and was demolished; the noble monastery was levelled to the ground; its library, ... the collection of ages, the repository of the most precious monuments of the ancient Britons, was consumed; half ruined walls, gates, and rubbish were all that remained of the magnificent edifice.'[2]

Taliesin's supposed presence at the battle which preceded this desolation accounts for the imitation of the opening, and the complementary lines in which Wordsworth adds his own and Sharon Turner's lament. As for Bede, who justified the depredations of Rome-inspired Northumbrians against the Celtic church, and congratulated Ethelfrid on having 'made a very great slaughter of that heretical nation',[3] Wordsworth comments

---

1   *Ecclesiastical Sonnets*, 220. Potts adds that 'Davies in the Appendix to *MR*, 502, prints a similar version of this song'. See also, Skene, *Four Ancient Books*, 1.274–5.
2   Turner, *History*, 1.321 In the later edition, 1.319–20, Ethelforth is corrected to Ethelfrid.
3   Bede, *Ecclesiastical History*, tr. A. M. Sellar, Bohn's Library (1912), 87–8.

drily: 'The account Bede gives of this remarkable event, suggests a most striking warning against National and Religious prejudices'. Since the slaughter at Chester and the razing of Bangor were justified in English eyes—and Augustine's—by the 'gangrene' of Arian and Pelagian heresies, Wordsworth, one might say, is writing an elegy for himself.

At this point in Wordsworth's history, Celtic Britain is over. The battle at Chester marks the final severance of Wales from the Men of the North. Since the series celebrates the march of Christianity it passes to the conversion of Northumbria, adopting Bede as the guide and central consciousness, in a story of which Augustine, Paulinus and Edwin, zealously promoting a Rome-centred faith, are—temporarily—the heroes. But this last sonnet on indigenous faith is not quite over and there are a few lines for a lament:

> Mark! how all things swerve
> From their known course, or vanish like a dream;
> Another language spreads from coast to coast;
> Only perchance some melancholy Stream
> And some indignant Hills old names preserve,
> When laws, and creeds, and people all are lost!

'Indignant hills'? Wordsworth grew up nurtured by the Derwennydd, Saxonized as the Derwent, which was in Rhydderch's time the Southern border of a diminished Rheged. As William and Dorothy made their way to Windy Brow, in Keswick, in 1794, at the outset of Wordsworth's career as last Bard of Rheged and first Bard of Wordsworthshire they would have passed *Arthur's Seat* and *Helm Crag*—their daily neighbours once they moved to Grasmere—then walked up *Dunmail Raise* and past *Helvellyn*, with a view facing them, once they crossed the raise, of the fell which Wordsworth called by its ancient name *Blencathra*.[1] The local poem *Song at the feast of Brougham Castle*, one of the poems most devoted to grasping the local ethnoscape, celebrates the young Lord Clifford's sequesterment under Blencathra, and the same tale echoes in *The Waggoner* (629–39).

Nor is the Wordsworths' Celticism only local. Dorothy's last letter of 1799 looked back upon the scenery of Pillesdon Pen, the highest point

---

1   Among mountains, Blencathra and Helvellyn are certainly Cumbric, Skiddaw probably so. Among rivers, the Derwent certainly, and probably the Eden, Cocker and Esk. Among major towns, the Celtic/Cumbric origin of Penrith (Pen Rhydd) is easier to detect than that of of Carlisle (Caer Luen).

in Dorset, and the earthwork of Lambert's Castle, as among the factors making Racedown 'the place dearest to my recollections upon the whole surface of the island' (*EY*, 281). At Alfoxden they had been in daily sight of Glastonbury Tor—'before our eyes during more than half of our walk to Stowey; and in the park wherever we go … it makes a part of our prospect' (*EY*, 191). As they knew well enough from Clarke, if not from Leland himself, *Hic Iacet Inclitus Rex Arturius, In Insula Avalonia*. And from Windy Brow they looked towards the head of Borrowdale past Saint Herbert's Island towards (Goidelic?) *Glaramara*'s inmost caves.

The *Ecclesiastical Sonnets* are not an easy read, but they explain much. And 'there is at times', says Geoffrey Hill in *For the Unfallen*—and Geoffrey Hill's poems often give one words for what the troublous Wordsworth brings to mind—there is at times

> some need to demonstrate
> Jehovah's touchy methods, that create
> The connoisseur of blood, the smitten man.[1]

One might wonder: did Wordsworth plant yews in the churchyard at St Oswald's merely to compensate for the tree-felling which caused him much outrage some years before? Or was it also an attempt to reinforce a Christian temple with a natural one; to remind the national church of its auxiliars and associate a martial saint with his erstwhile foes? Is it a literal-minded piece of landscaping, or one 'not uninformed by Phantasy'? If the latter, Wordsworth's gift to Grasmere expresses a characteristic desire that the religious insights of a people, especially a mongrel people such as the British, should be bound each to each in natural piety.

Just as Wordsworth subscribes to that very British pattern whereby those with any sense of history tend to identify successively with the British Arthur, the Saxon Alfred, and Hereward the Wake as national heroes resisting Saxons, Danes and Normans respectively, so in his account of the church in England he associates British, Roman and English memorials in a way that rebukes 'national and religious prejudice'.

---

1   Geoffrey Hill, *Of Commerce and Society, 4,* in *For the Unfallen*, 51 (*Collected Poems*, 49).

Part 2

The Bond of Nature

'Tis a bad world, and hard is the world's law;
Each prowls to strip his brother of his fleece;
Much need have ye that time more closely draw
The bond of nature, all unkindness cease,
And that among so few there still be peace:
Else can ye hope but with such numerous foes
Your pains shall ever with your years increase

—Adventures on Salisbury Plain

Chapter 4: 'And of the Poor'

> many rich
> Sank down, as in a dream, among the poor,
> And of the poor did many cease to be,
> And their place knew them not.
>
> —*Excursion*, 1.574–7[1]

WHETHER OR NOT 'love of nature' led to 'love of man' in Wordsworth's affections, as *The Prelude* claims, it is true that he first found a style that convincingly renders an acute observation of natural appearances while taking his first steps towards an adequate poetry of human suffering. Both accomplishments progress notably in the 1794 revisions of *An Evening Walk*.[2] At line 191 of the 1794 text Wordsworth develops an analogy between human and watery sensitivity, in his first tentative use of the symbolism of waters for the mind's activities:

> Blest are those spirits tremblingly awake
> To Nature's impulse like this living lake,
> Whose mirrour makes the landscape's charms its own
> *With touches soft as those to memory known*;
> While *exquisite of sense*, the mighty mass
> All vibrates to the lightest gales that pass. [ll. 191–6]

Five years later, in *The Boy of Winander*, Wordsworth makes the mirroring of uncertain heavens in the bosom of the 'steady lake' analogous to the boy's reception of both lake and heavens into memory. Nor is this observation without some basis in thought, a theory of the living landscape. Revising a routine celebration of the lower fall at Rydal, Wordsworth first paraphrases Horace (on animal sacrifice) then comments of the spirits of lakeland that:

> The mystic Shapes that by thy margin rove

---

1 *CWRT*, 2: 324., as in *RC* MS. D 141–44.
2 *An Evening Walk*, ed. James Averill (Ithaca, NY: Cornell University Press, 1984).

A more benignant sacrifice approve; …
Harmonious thoughts, a soul by Truth refined,
Entire affection for all human kind;
A heart that vibrates evermore, awake
To feeling for all forms that Life can take,
That wider still its sympathy extends,
And sees not any line where being ends;
Sees sense, through Nature's rudest forms betrayed,
Tremble obscure in fountain, rock, and shade;
And while a secret power those forms endears
Their social accents never vainly hears [*1794*, 117–32]

He is writing in a way that in the view of some scholars reflects recent exposure to the ideas of the Encyclopaedists with their gospel of an active universe, or Volney's 'puissance mysterieux qui anime l'univers' or 'âme universelle des êtres'.[1] Whether being awake to 'feeling for all forms that life can take' is, or is not, quite the same as 'in all things | I saw one Life' (*Prelude 1805*, 2.429–30), and whether Wordsworth could possibly have arrived at such a feeling without the assistance of Coleridge, is one of those questions that Wordsworthians and Coleridgeans love to fall out over. It is clear, however, that Wordsworth in 1794 is already beginning to formulate the view of nature and its enjoyments that informs the lyrics of 1798, while also developing his own distinctive theory of imagination. In eight lines of *An Evening Walk*, intensified in the revision, he combines the underlying thought of 'It is the first mild day of March' with an anticipation of *The Prelude*'s 'higher minds':

How different with those favoured souls, who, taught
By active Fancy or by patient Thought,
See common forms prolong the endless chain
Of joy and grief, of pleasure and of pain.
With them the sense no trivial object knows;
Oft at its meanest touch their spirit glows
And, proud beyond all limits to aspire,

---

1   H. W. Piper, *The Active Universe* (London: Athlone Press, 1962), 70. Others have found similar sentiments in the Commonwealthman writings of Akenside and Thomson. This dispute may be more apparent than real. The poetry of these rather conventional poets does at times express, loosely intertwined with a sense of the life of things derived from Virgil and even Newton, adhesion to the Commonwealthman or True Whig strain of republicanism that inspired both American liberty and the French Revolution. Nature, whichever way you look at it, is republican at this date.

> Mounts through the fields of thought on wings of fire.
>
> (203–210)

Newly aware of the 'social accents' of such forms, Wordsworth is feel-
ing towards the most portable thesis of *Lyrical Ballads*, 'If this be of my
creed the plan, | Have I not reason to lament | What man has made of
man?'

The most successful passage of *An Evening Walk* (1793) was a sus-
tained celebration of the connubial bliss of swans. Swans play a curi-
ously important role in Wordsworth's poetry. His juvenile poems include
a bemused comparison, in 'Beauty and Moonlight':

> Then might her bosom soft and white
> Rise upon my swimming sight
> As these two Swans together heave
> Upon the gently swelling wave

(Heave and wave, by the by, is an exact local rhyme, half way between
'standard' pronunciation of either). The same thought later thrust itself
into a lascivious description of the female vagrant in *Salisbury Plain*:
'like swans, twin swans, that ... | 'Mid Derwent's water lilies swell and
sink | In union, rose her sister breasts of snow'. In *An Evening Walk*
(1793) the swans are described first in and for themselves, as the mother
calls her cygnets near 'and with affection sweet | Alternately relieves
their weary feet; | Alternately they mount her back, and rest | Close by her
mantling wings embraces prest' (215–18). Standing in for Nature, who
never did betray the heart that loved her, the swans are complimented on
their parental solicitude: 'Ye ne'er like hapless human wanderers, throw
| Your young on winter's winding sheet of snow'.[1] *1794* intensifies the
erotic charge of the description ('swells', 'burning', 'tender', 'furtive',
'wanton', 'embraces'). The swans still 'crush with broad black feet their
flowery walk' (*1793*: 232) but the poet exhorts them:

> Involve your serpent necks in changeful rings,
> Rolled wantonly between your slippery wings (*1794*: 460-61).

When the poet turns from this voyeurism to the vagrant and her dying
children, the revision intensifies the transition between nature and death
into a shock transition between sex and death, of the kind beloved by
experimental film-makers in the 1960s.

---

1   This clumsy aspersion on the mother is disposed of later by having her envy the
swans 'and call thee blessed' (*1849*; 251).

The *Walk* of 1793 already contained a harrowing account of a war-widow, whose husband lies 'asleep on Bunker's hill' while for her 'Chok'd is the pathway, and the pitcher broke' (*1793*: 254, 256; *1794*: 481, 483). Toiling, arthritically in one version, through winter snows, denied even 'hut or straw-built shed' by unsocial man in all versions, she is helpless as her children freeze to death, 'Thy breast their death-bed, coffin'd in thine arms' (*1793*: 300; *1849*: 278). Numerous variant drafts fail to find an adequate response, relying on attempts to capture the physical attitudes of death, and leaving the woman without the kind of voice her sisters achieve in *Lyrical Ballads*. She is characterized most by her attempt to amuse the children with 'the glow-worm's harmless ray | Tossed light from hand to hand'. This silent vagrant, whose husband is 'Asleep on Bunker's charnel hill afar' is immediately related to the voluble Female Vagrant of *Salisbury Plain*, who lost both husband and children in the American War, if not on Bunker's hill, and who becomes her poem's dominant voice. The silent mother is also a prototype of Margaret in *The Ruined Cottage* in which work new techniques will be found to intensify both the inwardness and the maturity of contemplation of such harrowing subject matter, the victim will be empowered to correct her narrator, and a powerful symbolic use will be found for both halves of the promising line 'Chok'd is the pathway, and the pitcher broke'.

Numerous other contributions of *An Evening Walk* to *The Excursion* might be mentioned as proof of the integrity of Wordsworth's development, and Mark Bruhn's forthcoming work provides startling evidence that the poem already contains, in 1794, much of the philosophical argument hitherto assumed to be Coleridge's contribution to *The Prelude*. One further passage of 1794 revision is worth mentioning, however, because it focuses the blend of nature and thinking, the role of nature as (in John Danby's phrase) 'a partner in the thinking', that differentiates Wordsworth's poetry before and after this personal watershed at Windy Brow. In treating the idea of reclusiveness it is seminal for both *The Poem upon the Wye* and *Home at Grasmere*, though it has all the difficulty of Wordsworth's syntax at its most challenging. A classroom test as to who or what is the referent of 'thy' and 'thou' in the following lines might elicit numerous answers, including the owl, the moon, a generalized 'meek lover of the shade', or 'Quiet', all merging into 'Virtue', unless the reader notices that inconspicuously in the last clause of the prior sentence 'the glow-worm fades'. It is s/he who 'in Quiet's breast' sits 'With thine own proper light sufficed' and who inspires this socially accented prayer:

> May each rude foot thy hermit cell revere;
> Thy bower may wings of whirlwinds never crush,
> Nor on thy path the devious torrent rush;...
> Oh! may'st thou, safe from every onset rude.
> Irradiate long thy friendless solitude.
> So Virtue, fallen on times to gloom consigned,
> Makes round her path the light she cannot find,
> And by her own internal lamp fulfils,
> And asks no other star what Virtue wills,
> Acknowledging, though round her Danger lurk,
> And Fear, no night in which she cannot work;
> In dangerous night so Milton worked alone,
> Cheered by a secret lustre all his own....[1]

It is a rare instance of an observation where the signification grows organically out of the object: for most of the lines of this passage the subject really *is* a glow-worm, before the applicability to Milton (and to Wordsworth, who is sheltering at Windy Brow while Pitt's government rains terror upon Thelwall, Hardy, and Horne Tooke) occurs to the poet. The glow-worm was already glowing in 1793; sympathy for her leads to the human-hearted imagination of the meditation of 1794.

Calls to issue forth from this retirement and join the Heroes of Truth in the battle for 'Science, Freedom and [if one is Coleridge] the Truth in Christ' are muted in this poem, even in its revised version, partly because this theme has already been expressed roundly enough in the stark conclusion of the fair copy of *Salisbury Plain*, a poem which frequently encroaches upon the descriptions of an *An Evening Walk*.[2] Nonetheless, every kind of rural worker makes an appearance—from quarrymen to

---

1   This passage is central to Nicola Zoe Trott's superb essay on 'Wordsworth, Milton, and the Inward Light', in Lisa Low and Anthony Harding, eds., *Milton, the Metaphysicals, and Romanticism* (Cambridge: Cambridge UP, 1994), 114–35, one of the 'must read' Wordsworth articles of the 1990s.

2   In one cross-textual raid, the *Salisbury Plain* bustard, 'forcing against the wind its thick unwieldy flight', influences the *Evening Walk* swans, who in revision, 'Force half upon the wave their cumbrous flight'. The giant forms emerging from Salisbury Plain's rifted tombs certainly energise the archaeological perceptions of *An Evening Walk*, giving rise (textually) to the giants under the soil and druid forms in Cumbrian mists and snows.

iron workers—as in the first edition, and the *Prelude* theme of nature's wish, recently discovered in Blois, 'to recompense the lowly child of toil' comes out starkly in the new closing lines. The 1793 text had already lamented the fate of a stream constrained to power a mill beside a ruined abbey, where 'the distant forge's swinging thump profound' echoes from Thomson. Now he adds the anti-clerical thought that the labouring poor deserve a more refreshing sleep than 'yon dark abbey's tenants ever drew | From the soft streamlet idly murmuring near'. Why so much difference? '1793', throughout this brief discussion, has really meant 1789/91—the date of original composition of *An Evening Walk* at Cambridge before Wordsworth became 'a patriot' in his rural seminars on the banks of the Loire with Michel Beaupuy. The difference between the published text and the version of 1794 is France.

Salisbury Plain, 1793–1798

Despite its similar date, therefore, *Salisbury Plain* represents later thinking, and of course a far more urgent inspiration. Having read and admired *Guilt and Sorrow* long before *Salisbury Plain* and *Adventures on Salisbury Plain* became widely available, my reading of their relative power constitutes a minority report. Perverse I may be, but I have no doubt that in most respects the late text arrives at a truer realization of the poem's essential vision, and achieves the optimum balance between the Hardyesque description of an alienated traveller on Salisbury Plain, his encounter with an indigent woman whose heart-rending tale recalls him to active social sympathies, and his decision to take upon himself responsibility for an involuntary crime against humanity. Moreover, it is only in revision that the brilliantly conceived landscape is trusted to make its own points about alienation, uninterrupted by clumsy accidentals of plot. The result is a sustained depiction of a wounded mind at large on Salisbury Plain, comparable in its power to Philip Larkin's surreal simile for damaged consciousness in the title poem of *The Less Deceived*, 'Your mind lay open like a drawer of knives'.

Composed soon after Wordsworth's solitary walk across Salisbury Plain, when he was brooding on war preparations in Portsmouth and the prolonged separation from Annette and his child, the original *Salisbury Plain* of 1793–94 mounts a vivid, thoroughly Paineite assault on 'the system', which assault is continued with greater specificity and new

Godwinian adhesions in *Adventures on Salisbury Plain* 1795–99. Neither *Salisbury Plain* as written by the thoroughly *engagé* author of *A Letter to the Bishop of Llandaff*, nor *Adventures* as revised at Racedown by his more Godwinian self, is a better poem than the version published in 1842. This, when all is said and done, still mounts a vivid Godwinist attack on 'the system' and does so without allowing the poet's self-pleasuring rhetoric to detract from the twin tragedies of his defrauded sailor or the female vagrant. But the early texts are undoubtedly more charged with relevant and contemporary rancour.

In *Salisbury Plain* the sailor who strides across an accusing landscape has no tale to speak of. He is there only to contribute a parallel sensibility through which to depict the landscape of the plain itself, before providing a listener for the heroine. Her tale, the details of which were 'faithfully taken from the report made to me of her own case by a friend', was published in 1798 as *The Female Vagrant*.[1] The sailor, that is to say, stands in for the briefer role of the poet in such poems as *The Last of the Flock* and *The Mad Mother*. When anything needs saying, by way of pointing a theme, the poet says it *in propria persona* (as Coleridge thought poets should), as in the opening and closing stanzas. Thus the sailor enters as an illustration of the thesis, reminiscent of Burke's *Vindication of Natural Society*, that while savage life was hard, at least everyone shared the hardships alike, whereas those dispossessed in the lottery of civilized life are beset by worse torments in the form of 'pleasures flown' or meditations on inequity. The poetry establishes Salisbury Plain as a waste through which the sailor wanders, resigning all hope of any sign of the social world, until he stumbles on its symbol in the 'antique castle' of Stonehenge, a place of 'priests and spectres grim and idols dire' (*SP*, stanza 11). Taking refuge in a lonely Spital, now 'the dead house of the plain', he and the vagrant first frighten then reassure each other. She tells—rather pointlessly, since in this version the sailor is not yet a murderer—of rumours that a new murdered corpse had been discovered hereabouts, and then encapsulates the Swain's triadic vision of 'Gigantic beings'(20) of 'the sacrificial altar fed | With living men' (21), and of 'long bearded forms' charming the desert and the moon alike (22).

The Female Vagrant's story occupies stanzas 26–44 of the early text, and it indicts the loss of her father's fishing rights, Britain's war against American liberty, the rounding up of 'want and pain' by press gangs as

---

1   See *PW*, 1: 330, or *SPP*, 6.

sacrificial offerings on altars of royal pride (34–36), the Vagrant's long Atlantic torment (40–43) and her return to a homeland in which 'homeless near a thousand homes I stood, | And near a thousand tables pined and wanted food'. Now, she says, 'across this waste my steps I bend: | O tell me whither, for no earthly friend | Have I, no house in prospect but the tomb'. As the two wanderers are directed (by the narrator) to partake of an allegorical picnic (consisting of Spenserian bread and milk in a lowly cot) the narrator sets about an eight-stanza digest of Price and Priestley, indicting want, empire (from the Andes to India), war and state terror (stanza 58 appears to envisage political executions), before calling upon the 'Herculean mace of Reason'—one remembers France as an infant Hercules in *Prelude* 10—to make an end of dungeons, palaces and superstition. It is all splendidly idealistic, especially in the idea (shared by Priestley and Price in 1789) that the example of France would put an end to greed, war and empire, but it is also perfunctory and inconsequential. It is perfunctory in the sense that the sailor has very little to do but feel lonely and sympathetic. It is inconsequential in that compared with the manner in which Wordsworth derives a constitutional programme from the girl with the heifer in Book 9 of *The Prelude*, and mounts an attack on poor relief through the shepherd's tale in *The Last of the Flock*, it is hard to see how the Vagrant's tale necessarily produces all this bombast.

Her own story is (as it remains in the unvarnished and unsoftened version published in *Lyrical Ballads*) powerful enough. Its only blemishes as a dramatic conception are in hijacking the woman to be the vehicle of Wordsworth's own druid reverie, making her guilty of some awful poetic diction (her first stanza speaks of her father's 'finny flood' and her own 'fleecy store'), and having her speak the impressive but improbably tutored eloquence of stanza 35:

> Oh dreadful price of being! to resign
> All that is dear in being; better far
> In Want's most lonely cave till death to pine
> Unseen, unheard, unwatched by any star.
> Better before proud Fortune's sumptuous car
> Obvious our dying bodies to obtrude,
> Than dog-like wading at the heels of War
> Protract a cursed existence with the brood
> That lap, their very nourishment, their brother's blood.

Most of the lines that make the 1798 version so peculiarly impressive are already there, and in language the poet of the 1800 preface would not need to apologize for. It took a little tweaking to get from 'Viewing our glimmering cot through tears that never ceased' to the inwardness of 'through tears that fell in showers, | Glimmered our dear-loved home', but her part of the poem is basically that published in *Lyrical Ballads*.

At Racedown, in 1796, while reading in the republican library of the Pinney's 'True Whig' residence, Wordsworth decided to add to her tale a number of additional perceptions indicting old corruption.[1] Now, in *Adventures on Salisbury Plain*, her father's expulsion is the result of 'a mansion proud' acquiring cottages and pastures and buying out peasant rights (34–35, Gill 133); her own starvation leads her to hospital, where she experiences, uncomplainingly, the neglectful and callous treatment of the poor; she finds among gypsies her 'first relief'; tired of vagabonding, she learns 'to live upon the mercy of the fields'; and her story ends with what Geoffrey Hill has identified as one of Wordsworth's profoundest rhythmical insights:

> She ceased, and weeping turned away,
> As if because her tale was at an end
> She wept; —because she had no more to say
> Of that perpetual weight which on her spirit lay (*ASP*, 62).

At the heart of *Salisbury Plain* and of *Adventures*, as of the eventual *Guilt and Sorrow*, remains the compelling story he published in *Lyrical Ballads* as the most sustained exhibition of sorrow by a tragically defeated woman. She speaks on behalf of the tortured figures of *The Vale of Esthwaite*, the vagrant in *An Evening Walk*, and Martha Ray in *The Thorn*, and she forms with Margaret of *The Ruined Cottage*, and the less developed but solo figures of *The Mad Mother* and *Forsaken Indian Woman* a more compelling quartet of female *voices* than was created before, then or since by any English poet, male or female—outside Felicia Hemans's *Records of Women*. For which effrontery, Wordsworth has been accused of colonizing female space.

In keeping with the increasing specificity of this harrowing narrative, and in order to create one significant relationship at the heart of

---

1   John Williams sees Wordsworth turning to the Commonwealthman ideology of Milton, Sidney, Gordon, Franklin and Jefferson, and 'tacitly abandoning Painite and French models for revolution', 'Salisbury Plain: Politics in Wordsworth's Poetry', *Literature and History* 9:2 (1983) 164–93, 177, 178. See my *Sensibility*, chapter 1, for further discussion of what it meant at the time to identify with the Commonwealth.

the poem, Wordsworth also develops the sailor from a rather shadowy if sympathetic character into a complex portrait of what Browning would call 'the tender murderer'. His drama, enclosing the vagrant's, is a parallel tale of being abused by the state, trained to kill, defrauded of his pay, and set adrift without the means to support himself or his family. Having murdered a traveller, he becomes an outcast. Yet he speaks the moral of this version of the poem, as of *Guilt and Sorrow*, and of much Wordsworth's poetry in the intervening forty-four years:

> ''Tis a bad world, and hard is the world's law;
> Each prowls to strip his brother of his fleece;
> Much need have ye that time more closely draw
> The bond of nature, all unkindness cease;
> And that among so few there still be peace:
> Else can ye hope but with such numerous foes
> Your pains shall ever with your years increase.' (*ASP*, 72)[1]

At the time Wordsworth wrote *Salisbury Plain* he was beginning to persuade himself that the bonds of nature were of more account than the abstract rights of man. Sensitivity to what *The Poem upon the Wye* will call 'the still sad music of humanity' grows as *The Ruined Cottage* displaces *Adventures on Salisbury Plain*. Wordsworth founds a poetry of personal encounter upon the central event of *Guilt and Sorrow*. The mutual solicitude of the Vagrant and the Sailor anticipates his own meetings with a Discharged Soldier and a Leech-Gatherer. 'Meeting' becomes his forte. Moreover, like the Discharged Soldier of 1798/1805, and The Leech-Gatherer of 1800/1802, the Sailor of 1795/1842 seems morally distinguished by his alienation. He seems to stand outside society in quite as monitory fashion as they, and to have strange power of speech. In Gary Harrison's admirable formulation, Wordsworth's 'treatment of the poor as a class ... capable of philosophical utterance and deep feeling really did break through a dominant wall of prejudice'; his refusal to 'police the borders of the once privileged space of the poem' challenged class as well as genre categories.[2]

In sum, while the narrator is generally silenced in *Adventures*, the poem's tragic intensity is greatly deepened and its social indictment

---

1   *Guilt and Sorrow*, stanza 57, changes only the first two lines: 'The world is bad, and hard is the world's law | Even for him who wears the warmest fleece'.
2   Gary Harrison, *Wordsworth's Vagrant Muse: Poetry, Poverty and Power* (Detroit: Wayne State University Press, 1994), 178.

is broadened. Paine (in the vagrant's cautionary tale of what comes of making war upon liberty) and Godwin (in the parable of man reduced to an implement of war and punished for so being) are meshed in a highly class-conscious Wordsworthian tale of encounter. The archaisms are reduced. Wordsworthian diction inhabits comfortably the Spenserian stanza, which retains its power of suggesting that what the characters represent is archetypal (or in Coleridge's roundabout way of putting it, suggest 'the depth and height of the ideal world').[1] And while Wordsworth found the technique to marginalize himself and his opinions, he also put those erotically charged swans in their proper place, in the vagrant's own description of her lakeside garden.

Joseph Cottle may have been right: the poem Cottle would have published in 1796, but for Coleridge's dilatoriness with the manuscript, was, in parts, one on which 'Mr Wordsworth might most advantageously [have rested] his fame as a poet'.[2] But *Adventures on Salisbury Plain*, like many of Wordsworth's revisionary endeavours, is a matter of loss as well as gain. It gains a powerful telling of the sailor's story, to balance that of the vagrant, and enrich the drama of their encounter and their mutual aid (it's the poor that help the poor, Mrs Gaskell would be demonstrating at around the time the poem finally saw the light of day). But it suffers from a proliferating plot tending towards Whitehall farce, with bewildering exits and entrances. In 1796 the sailor meets an ancient soldier, equally adrift on Salisbury Plain (in this version *everyone* wanders aimlessly about the plain as if waiting for Godot) and pops him onto a cushion in a postboy's cart where, like Betty Foy but ludicrously in this context, 'all his body trembled with delight'. It is extremely hard to see why anyone would regard *Adventures on Salisbury Plain* as this poem's definitive text. Nonetheless, when Wordsworth returned to the poem in the 1830s, prior to publication in 1842, it needed little weeding to reveal its strengths, which strengths I will return to in chapter 12.[3]

1   *Biographia Literaria*, 1: 80.
2   Joseph Cottle, *Early Recollections; Chiefly Relating to the Late Samuel Taylor Coleridge* (2 vols; London 1837), 1: 314 n., cited *SPP*, 9. For the failure to publish *Adventures on Salisbury Plain* in 1796, see Gill, *William Wordsworth: A Life*, 100.
3   For a recent assessmernt of the three texts see Quentin Bailey, 'The Salisbury Plain Poems (1793–1842)', *Oxford Handbook of William Wordsworth* (2015) 135–51.

The Ruined Cottage, 1797–1804

Uncertain how to deal responsibly with harrowing matter, Wordsworth took from 1797 to 1804 to decide on the correct balance between narrator, auditor and heroine in *The Ruined Cottage*, that is, between a family sacrificed to wartime economics, a narrator qualified by his professional acquaintance with rural decay, and an auditor newly sensitized to the still sad music of humanity. He began, in 1797, with equitable treatment of Margaret and her husband Robert. Then he developed the histories of both Margaret and the Pedlar-narrator, so that the poem becomes balanced between its heroine (now far more central than the undeveloped husband) and the narrator. Then he carved out two separate but overlapping poems, allowing Margaret's story to emerge again as the central, but not exclusive, focus of *The Ruined Cottage*, while *The Pedlar* allowed the narrator's story (and his philosophy) to expand and coalesce more and more with the poet's own. Finally, he recombined them in a sustained act of revision in 1802–4 as a three part poem (MS.E) which is more or less the text that appeared (without the overt three-part structure) as Book 1 of *The Excursion*. One by-product of all this work is the extraordinary sophistication of narrative voice in *Lyrical Ballads*.

Some, including Jonathan Wordsworth, see the separated version of Margaret's tale in MS.D (1799), a spare performance in which the Pedlar's character is implied rather than developed, as the 'best' version of the poem; others, including Peter Manning, see the poem's *Excursion* format as a more subtle but equally compelling creation in which Margaret's defeat, the Wanderer's exemplary but slightly unnerving stoicism, and the Poet's efforts to reconcile his responses to both, are superbly combined as an exploration of the question, how, in a world like this, does one live?[1] More Shelleyanly, if it is the poet's function to feel

---

1   Jonathan Wordsworth, *The Music of Humanity* (New York: Harper, 1969) argues that both Margaret and the Pedlar benefit from their 1799 divorce, since the Pedlar's biography—especially as it proliferates in 1798 in the excitement of 'the One Life'—has little bearing on Margaret's story (xii). Peter J. Manning's 'Wordsworth, Margaret and the Pedlar', *Studies in Romanticism* 15 (Spring 1976) 195–220, reprinted in *Reading Romantics: Text and Context* (New York: Oxford University Press, 1990) 9–34, is a classic treatment of the evolution of Book 1 of *The Excursion*, informed by a microscopic eye for the imagistic connections between the various MSS and their forebears and an impressive sense of the relation of Margaret's abandonment to the poet's own orphaning. The psychology has never been explored more tellingly.

'the else unfelt oppressions of the earth', how is one to be adequately responsive to suffering yet still feel able to write? In a world of 'want and pain', the female vagrant's phrase, is there a middle way between being paralysed by feeling, or living by ceasing to feel? Critics may feel that Wordsworth ought to have faced more sophisticated questions than these, but they do seem to be at the heart of his vocation (no other poet ever spoke of metre, as he does in the 1815 *Essay Supplementary*, as it if it were a kind of shock absorber, necessarily employed to soften the effect of all-too-painful subject matter). But then, no poet, certainly no Romantic poet, was ever inclined to suffer so much *with* his characters. Much of Wordsworth greatest poetry asks the question of *Resolution and Independence*, 'how is it that you live, and what is it you do?' or sounds the note expressed at the end of *Michael*:

> There is a comfort in the strength of love;
> 'Twill make a thing endurable which else
> Would overset the brain, or break the heart.

The Ruined Cottage sounds the note most bleakly in a way that, as Shelley recognized, and as Wordsworth's tetchy opening lines indicate, touched on the question of the indifference of both the natural universe and of the social world to human suffering.

The circumstances of the tale told by the Pedlar are similar to those of *The Female Vagrant*: Margaret's husband takes the King's shilling, in consequence of the fact that his family faces economic ruin if he does not. Robert's self-worth has been destroyed by the ruination of his livelihood, and like the shepherd of *The Last of the Flock*, as that livelihood is taken from him, his love for his children becomes deformed. Two years of famine, combined with war taxes in 1794, drove many agricultural people to enlist. Robert's departure fixes Margaret to the spot, in which the decay of her home, her parenting, her pride, and of everything except her tormenting hope for his return, is depicted in remorselessly accumulating detail. The economic circumstances are set out quite clearly at the start of every version of the poem, so that we are required to read Robert's story as simply one instance of a generalized suffering and Margaret's martyrdom as a direct consequence of an unequal economic system, war, and heavenly indifference. As the point is made in Book 1 of *The Excursion*:

> Not twenty years ago, but you I think

> Can scarcely bear it now in mind, there came
> Two blighting seasons, when the fields were left
> With half a harvest. It pleased Heaven to add
> A worse affliction in the plague of war:
> This happy Land was stricken to the heart!
> A Wanderer then among the cottages,
> I, with my freight of winter raiment, saw
> The hardships of that season: many rich
> Sank down, as in a dream, among the poor;
> And of the poor did many cease to be,
> And their place knew them not.[1]

It became fashionable in the 1980s to criticize this poem for marginalizing of history, to which metaphor one might reply that that margins are tactically equivalent to frames and frames work best, in the main, when they do not obscure the picture.[2] One poignant phrase in this frame echoes in Shelley's *Mont Blanc*, from whose glaciers 'the race | Of man flies far in dread; his work and dwelling | Vanish, like smoke before the tempest's stream, | And their place is not known.' Nature can be quite as inexorable, Shelley is arguing, as what Wordsworth in MS.E and *The Excursion* calls, on the Pedlar's behalf, 'the unthinking masters of the earth'.[3]

In John Rieder's summary of the poem as it stood in 1797, the impact of bad harvests and the plague of war on Robert 'is completed by the excruciating close-up of Robert's unemployment, disease, and nervous imbalance, climaxing in his selling himself to the army' while Margaret's

---

1   *Excursion,* 1: 566–77 (*CWRT*, 2: 324); c.f. MS.B.185–96 (*CWRT*, 1: 275).

2   Jerome McGann sees the poem enacting 'the subtle transformation of Wordsworth's 1793–4 world—including the social and political discontents which dominated his life at that time, into the changed world of 1797–8'. The revision of *Salisbury Plain* into the more, not less, politicized *Adventures on Salisbury Plain* in 1796–97 suggests that this is a falsification of Wordsworth's political history. To sustain it, McGann has to misread *The Poem upon the Wye* also. McGann deplores the fact that Margaret's story produces 'an overflow of sympathy and love for the sufferer rather than as in 1793–94, a sense of outrage, and an overflow of angry judgment on those whom Wordsworth at the time held accountable' (*The Romantic Ideology: a Critical Investigation* [Chicago: University of Chicago Press, 1983], 82–85). James Chandler, astonishingly, finds in the poem 'no sense whatever of human complicity in the causes of her suffering and death' (*Wordsworth's Second Nature: a Study of the Poetry and Politics* [Chicago and London: University of Chicago Press, 1984], 135).

3   Both poets reverse the Old Testament source, in which it is the crowned and their captains (those locusts and grasshoppers) whose 'place is not known' (Nahum 3: 16).

tale 'hammers home the themes of victimization and the ruination of the virtuous poor'. The 'whole poem renders quite poignantly the cottage weaver's vulnerability to economic disorders and the way the military's opportunistic purchase of manpower destroys the very basis of a healthy community'. At the same time 'Their economic catastrophe poisons their love for each other … by transforming its very persistence into a "reckless" abandonment of home and children'.[1] I borrow so much from Rieder because as a summary of the political and economic plot of Wordsworth's 1797 poem this would be hard to better: but, contrary to critical mythology, it is equally true of the poem as developed in 1798–1804 and published in 1814.

One sad side-effect of the Cornell editions is that criticism tends to focus more and more on manuscripts, rather than published poems. Thus Rieder attributes to MS.A, as if it were unique, the narrator's bitter conflation of economic and political disaster as what 'pleased Heaven' (Rieder 153). Yet this phrase, and what it conflates, appears in every text of the poem, in all lifetime revisions. So indeed does the Pedlar's last vision of Margaret:

> Seest thou that path?
> (The greensward now has broken its grey line;)
> There, to and fro she paced, through many a day
> Of the warm summer: from a belt of flax
> That girt her waist, spinning the long-drawn thread
> With backward steps. (MS.B, 493–8)

These lines, copied by Coleridge into a letter of 10 June 1797, remain untouched in any revision except that 'grass' finally replaces 'greensward'. They show, as a generating image of the poem, a representation informed by the anger of 1793–94 as it was expressed in *An Evening Walk* (in the enigmatic 'the path is broken') and *Salisbury Plain* (in the figure of a man whose life's business was to stand in a field with a gun to scare crows) and as it would be expressed in the stark vision of a girl used as a mobile tethering post, her life governed by the desires of a grazing heifer, in *The Prelude* of 1805. The germinal passage continues (here quoted in the 1845 text):

1   John Rieder, *Wordsworth's Counterrevolutionary Turn: Community, Virtue and Vision in the 1790s* (Newark and London: University of Delaware Press and Associated University Presses, 1997), 151–52.

> Yet ever as there passed
> A man whose garments showed the Soldier's red,
> Or crippled Mendicant in Sailor's garb,
> The little Child who sate to turn the wheel
> Ceas'd from his task; and she with faltering voice
> Made many a fond enquiry; and when they,
> Whose presence gave no comfort, were gone by,
> Her heart was still more sad.
>
> (*Excursion* 1.922–29)

Framed thus, *in all versions of the poem*, Margaret's tragedy is, in its instigation, a social one, brought about by an unjust state of society. She is a victim of 'the unthinking masters of the earth'. Such lines do not bulk large in the poem. But one notes that while just five lines of *The Brothers* (212b–213a, and 296–9) deal with the destruction of the thousand year patrimony of the Ewbanks, precipitating the tragedy that poem so tactfully narrates, *all* of Wordsworth's commentary on that poem in his letter to Charles James Fox dwells on their significance (*EY* 314–15). Perhaps the poet felt that in poetry as understated as his own usually is, describing the 'sacred' property of the poor as 'buffeted with bond | Interest and mortgages' is a sufficient reading instruction for the historically aware. A rash assumption, as criticism in the 1980s showed.

The immediate victim of the state of affairs that 'it pleased heaven' to inflict is Robert, and the moral effects of his economic impotence are duly shown in part one of the poem:

> at his door he stood
> And whistled many a snatch of merry tunes
> That had no mirth in them

and

> One while he would speak lightly of his babes
> And with a cruel tongue: at other times
> He played with them wild freaks of merriment
> And 'twas a piteous thing to see the looks
> Of the poor innocent children.
>
> (MS.B, 213–43; MS.D, 161–85)

Again, the lines remain unchanged as the climax of the first instalment of the Wanderer's tale at line 591 of Book 1 of *The Excursion*. In all versions, the rest of the tale of Margaret is told in a series of vignettes as the Pedlar / Wanderer is drawn back to the cottage, hapless witness of Margaret's decay. Changes in the telling are very minor; only the space given to directly characterizing the Minstrel / Pedlar / Wanderer varies. Wordsworth's problem is that from the outset he wished to treat not only sorrow but also sympathy. The poem is concerned both with the sufferings and the moral paralysis of Margaret, and with dramatizing the contrast between the Pedlar's response to his story and the poet's. The Pedlar knows one cannot give up life because of one case of human waste, and that this is just one of innumerable such tales. MS.E enlarges on this in a way Book 1 of *The Excursion* retains: he was a specialist in

> the progress and decay
> Of many minds, of minds and bodies too,
> The history of many families,
> And how they prospered; how they were o'erthrown
> By passion or mischance, or such misrule
> Among the unthinking Masters of the earth
> As makes the nations groan.   (MS.E. 333–39)

Like the victim-murderer-sailor of *Adventures*, and the female vagrant, abused and self-abused, Margaret is the victim both of those 'unthinking masters' and of her own 'passion'.

While Wordsworth does not forget that *The Ruined Cottage* is historically engendered, it is true that it does not read as a 'protest poem'. It does not use Margaret as the girl with the heifer will be used in *The Prelude*, or as the human scarecrow is used in *Salisbury Plain*—even though Margaret, in a passage cited earlier, uses herself as a sort of bobbin. In no version of the poem does Wordsworth foist upon Margaret, as he does on the hapless female vagrant, the kind of language and opinions one might expect of a Cambridge student recently returned from France. *The Ruined Cottage* shows rather than tells. Almost all of our impression of Margaret, which is close and intense, comes through the Pedlar's description of her cottage in its various stages of decline. Even when the burden of the poem is economic process, or psychological responses, that burden is communicated through objective correlatives. Wordsworth discovers that the image is capable of standing in for the kind of abstraction that critics assessing late eighteenth-century poems still think themselves entitled to find. Where any other poet at this date would have resorted to personified Labour, Want, Penury, Grief, sad-eyed Despair, delusive Hope and so forth, to tell us what is being suffered or felt, Wordsworth presents the most subtle nuances of feeling through concrete (not necessarily natural) imagery. The method, much of the time, is astonishingly unobtrusive. Where, however, Eliot's theory of the objective correlative implies (over-optimistically) some automatic process of meaning-precipitation within the reader, Wordsworth's narrator assumes that the tale will be 'scarcely palpable to him who does not think'.

From the outset, the meaning of the pedlar's tutorial has, in part, to do with reading the natural world as telling the still sad story of humanity, or as he puts it, 'reading the forms of things'. The pedlar reconstructs for us the story of the simultaneous decay of the woman and her cottage, as we sit amid the ruins, focusing alternately on the past and the present in that spot. The desolation surrounding the double narrative is the conclusion towards which the whole poem tends, and it is introduced very poignantly before we have any story as such. The method is announced in the wonderful opening words of the Pedlar as the poet returns from drinking at Margaret's well, an act which now becomes a kind of intimate trespass. The Pedlar says 'I see around me here | Things which you cannot see' and with that he begins to charge the surroundings with feeling. Re-describing the half-choked well spring at which the poet has just drunk he says

> When I stooped to drink
> A spider's web hung to the water's edge,
> And on the wet and slimy foot-stone lay
> The useless fragment of a wooden bowl

This 'broken pitcher', now liberated from *An Evening Walk* and developed to its full resonance, as a memorial to Margaret's life and her generosity to travellers, travels through the nineteenth century where it will be joined eventually by Silas Marner's broken pot, the sole thing other than his gold with which his mind—in Charles Lamb's imaginative phrase for imaginative process—has been able to 'make friends'.

The triumphs of this narrative, its other lessons in reading the forms of things, are so often treated that I will simply enumerate them. They include Margaret's speechless sorrow on the Pedlar's first visit when he learns of Robert's enlistment (MS.B, 304–10); the Pedlar's reduction to fearful auditor of Margaret's own narrative (311–337); her long absences from her decaying cottage, leaving the Pedlar time, on his next visit, to note the weeds, the crying infant, and the reddle stains upon the door-posts, and giving ourselves time to construe his constructions (360–94); and Margaret's own self-accusing and self-deluding perceptions (398–414). She is never the silent object of his narrative; indeed at times she takes charge of it. For instance, her own reading complements, deepens and in part upbraids the Pedlar's reading of the 'young apple tree' (458–65). The blend of intentionality in the Pedlar's account, and writer-liness in the poet's handling of that account, makes for the most involving of reading experiences. If we at times 'shape' things in a way other than the Pedlar expects us to, that is only to exercise the freedom that Wordsworth's vital style makes possible.

No hope is permitted: the two figures are sitting on a bench once occupied by the heroine, and she—we are told at the start—is dead. Her 'torturing hope' is part of the poem's subject. The problem propounded is how to cope with the ineluctability and subjective infinity of human suffering. It is not obvious that the poem actually answers this question, though it offers a model of quasi-Christian stoicism in the figure of the pedlar-narrator. One is no more obliged to accept his view of providence than that of the editorial voice in the gloss to *The Ancient Mariner*. Wordsworth made numerous attempts to find a way past the last lines of MS.B, all of them, as Stephen Gill suggests, provisional. None of them make it any easier for the reader to feel that Margaret's story is done with than it was for Margaret to feel that she must have done with Robert and, in the cliché, 'move on'.

>   — Yet still
> She loved this wretched spot, nor would for worlds
> Have parted hence; and still that length of road
> And this rude bench on torturing hope endeared,
> Fast rooted at her heart, and here, my friend,
> In sickness she remained, and here she died,
> Last human tenant of these ruined walls.

MS. B ends here. In MS. D and in *The Excursion* the Wanderer finds consolation of sorts in 'the high spear-grass on that wall, | By mist and silent rain-drops silver'd o'er', and feels that sorrow, despair and 'the grief | The passing shews of being leave behind' are but 'an idle dream that could not live where meditation was'. This may not suffice. The Poet's non-corroboration of his Pedlar is perhaps eloquent enough. Elizabeth Palmer Peabody, the Boston blue-stocking, and very clearly a reader 'neither too petulant to submit to a genuine poet nor too feeble to grapple with him', articulated the poem's artful invitation as well as anyone—'Would the state be *good* which would allow me to read the story of Margaret with an unfaltering voice? Did you not *mean* that Simon Lee's gratitude should leave the reader "mourning"?'[1] The 'heartfelt chillness' experienced by the Poet at mid-point in all versions (MS.B, 271; MS.D, 213; Book 1, 619) is part of the answer.

In one reading text which has disappeared from view in recent years, Wordsworth did come close to resolving the problem—namely Ernest de Selincourt's. This is perhaps the best way to read the 1798 poem, because it is the only one in which the key term 'meditation' is adequately glossed at the appropriate moment in the reading experience. It includes Wordsworth's three brief attempts to write an adequate ending, followed by the brilliant 'Addendum to MS.B' of which the close of MS.D is merely a fragment. In the three brief sketches we see the poet struggling to express a sense of being 'disciplined' by the journey on which the Pedlar has taken him, into a vision of things as 'consecrated' by the Pedlar's words, so that (alluding to *The Ancient Mariner*) 'to myself | I seemed a wiser and a better man' (*PW*, 5: 400). In the Addendum itself, the Pedlar speaks of the efficacy of 'quiet sympathies with things that hold | An inarticulate language', of the discipline of man by such sympathies so that he 'seeks for good and finds the good he seeks', and—pointedly—of nature's encouragement of the mind's 'excursive power', of drinking in 'the soul of things' in a kind of natural eucharist, and of drawing 'new energies' from such communion. In this expanded context, the Poet's glimpse of 'the secret spirit of humanity' surviving amid nature's 'calm oblivious tendencies'—as if Margaret was indeed one 'who could not die'—does something to explain how Wordsworth can close her story with the line we '*chearfully* pursued our evening way'. Margaret's tale is a tragedy, but in specifying what 'excursive power' it was her tragic flaw to lack, feeding on a single passion of delusive hope instead of achieving the Pedlar's meditative 'discipline', the conditions of a provisional catharsis are brought about.

---

1   DC MA A/Peabody/2, 27 March 1829. For annotated transcriptions of this correspondence, which is not in the only edition of Peabody's letters, see Margaret Neussendorfer, 'Elizabeth Palmer Peabody to William Wordsworth: Eight Letters', *Studies in the American Renaissance* (1984) 181–211. And for a brief discussion, Richard Gravil, *Romantic Dialogues* (2000), 62–7 and 2015 (118–26).

That delusive shadow, 'The Recluse', is no doubt the villain of the piece. Wordsworth was required by his scheme for a four book 'Recluse' (*The Prelude*, *Home at Grasmere* as a fragmentary 'Recluse Part 1', *The Excursion*, and the imagined 'Recluse Part 2') to minimize over-lap and repetition. He therefore removed from MS.B some of its most visionary passages, in which the Wanderer's capacity for insight into the heart of things is most triumphantly asserted, for more pressing duty in *The Prelude*. These excisions leave him a rather uneasy blend of lapsed Calvinist and natural religionist, whose bursts of hatred for nature (in the form of weeds, nettles and adders) are somewhat bewildering. Moreover, before it ever became part of a fair copy manuscript of *The Ruined Cottage* or *The Pedlar*, much of the *Addendum* was sidelined for Book 4 of *The Excursion*, 'Despondency Corrected'. Were the perfec-tion of *The Ruined Cottage* the only issue, had the categorical impera-tive of writing *The Recluse* not been imposed upon him, he might have brought about the final reconciliation of the two tales, Margaret's and the Pedlar's, that all his manuscript labours were tending towards. But *The Excursion* required one tragic exemplum of defeated humanity if books 2–9 were to have a raison d'être. So the Pedlar | Wanderer remains a fifty-fifty sort of character, a Calvinist by fits and a prophet of Nature by starts, whose contradictions will eventually ensure the failure—at least in terms of achieving closure—of *The Excursion* itself.

In conception, the fifty-fifty Pedlar was still more bewildering. In MS.B he is a native of Cumbria, prone to burst into old ballads and snatches of Burns in tune with the manuscript epigraph, 'Give me a [sic] spark of Nature's fire, | 'Tis the best learning I desire'. He is recognizably related to the merry Mathew, as well as to actual Packmen of Hawkshead, and remotely—and in his upbringing—to Beattie's Minstrel. In all versions, even after the excision of material needed for *The Prelude*, the Pedlar remains as much the subject of the poem as Margaret is: both are, from the outset, characters in Wordsworth's poem, however much their shares in it vary. Since the Pedlar—not Margaret—is charged with answering Coleridge's challenge, to help a generation recover from the blasting of their hopes for human perfectibility, he needs to have 'seen something unperceived before', but it is not at all clear that Wordsworth ever made up his mind what that something might be. Since 'the eye altering alters all', the precise configuration of that eye which is to see most clearly in the only portion of *The Recluse* ever to be completed is of some moment, if it can be done. But the Pedlar's insights are eclectic enough to have been drawn from the Baron d'Holbach, Dugald Stewart, Immanuel Kant and *The Christian Year*. For critics from Jeffrey to Coleridge, in any case, he remained an unacceptable intermediary, both as an autodidact and *on class grounds*. He is just too combatively configured to please these conservatve arbiters of taste—a hereditary minstrel, with appropriate traces of druidical wisdom, a chosen son of nature, an autodidact, and a man of the people.

In MS.B, as in the final text, some of the most powerful elements in what we are told of the Pedlar are at odds with the poem he tells. It is hard to see how a figure whose education has taught him to give 'To every natural form, rock, fruit and flower ... a moral life' (MS.B, 80) can resent the life of 'weeds and the rank spear-grass', or complain that 'nettles rot and adders sun themselves | Where we have sat together while she nursed her infant at her bosom' (MS.B 157–65).[1] Nor, having thus disburdened himself of rage against the way things are, and lesser forms of the one life, is it easy to see how he can find (or once found) in the speargrass 'by mist and silent raindrops silver'd o'er' an adequate consolation at the close. The tale is not remediable; nor, perhaps—since however much we know we can never know the mind of the poet—was it ever meant to be. We see through the Pedlar's naturalistic eye, not with it; and his way of making things endurable need not be ours. Closure was not—in 1797/99—part of Wordsworth's poetic.

Had *Adventures on Salisbury Plain* and *The Ruined Cottage*, more or less in its MS.B version, appeared as a joint volume in March 1798, the entire curve of Wordsworth's career might have been changed. Instead, Wordsworth remained a virtually invisible poet, whose reception was clouded by years of controversy over the diction and humble subject matter of *Lyrical Ballads*, and worsened almost a decade later by the hostile reception of the 'namby-pamby' *Poems, in Two Volumes*.

Imagination baulks at the thought of a two-volume set of poems containing *Adventures on Salisbury Plain*, *The Ruined Cottage*, *Lyrical*

---

1 Desperate lines may require desperate readings, but John Rieder's remark that 'eroticism and violence ... pervade Armytage's lament. The nettles, worms, and adders reverse his unstated, but clear sexual desire into images of hostile penetration and disgust' and the bare stripped hut and wall represent Margaret's sexual appeal 'as a provocation' (Rieder 170) does seem unduly desperate.

Ballads and *Peter Bell*, but such a body of work would surely have commanded recognition for Wordsworth as the most various poet of the day—capable of tossing off simultaneous masterpieces in widely different modes. Such a comprehensive 'Defence of the People of England' might also have yoked him more firmly to the radicals, pre-empting both Shelley's *To Wordsworth* and Browning's *The lost Leader*. Instead, Wordsworth dithered for years over whether his great tragic poem, *The Ruined Cottage*, told Margaret's story, or her narrator's, or was a step towards *The Prelude*. How should one hear, and how compose, 'the still sad music of humanity'?

Chapter 5: *Lyrical Ballads* and 'The Pathos of Humanity'

> You say that mine is the pathos of humanity ... the very excellence at which I aimed.
>
> —Wordsworth to John Taylor, 9 April 1801

> People in our rank in life are perpetually falling into one sad mistake, namely, that of supposing that human nature and the persons they associate with are one and the same thing. Whom do we generally associate with? Gentlemen, persons of fortune, professional men, ladies, persons who can afford to buy ... books of half a guinea price, hot-pressed, and printed on superfine paper. These persons are, it is true, a part of human nature, but we err lamentably if we suppose them to be fair representatives of the vast mass of human existence.
>
> —Wordsworth to John Wilson, 7 June 1802[1]

THE PEDLAR shows Wordsworth acutely aware in 1798 of the amount of suffering caused by 'the unthinking Masters of the earth', envisaging his narrator as a man of the people, a devotee of Burns, and one educated in what one can only call 'the system of nature'. *Lyrical Ballads*, too, has a radical cohesion that has in recent years been denied.[2] Midway through his *annus mirabilis*, the poet of *Lyrical Ballads* is motivated about equally by two things, both of which stem from his residence in France and his reflections at Racedown: an established belief that the social order must reflect the fact that 'we have all of us one human heart'; and an awareness that for anyone not living under the *ancien régime*, a

1 *LEY*, 315, 355.

2 James K. Chandler, seemingly more intimate with such matters than Jeffrey, Hazlitt and Shelley, concludes that they were all wrong to assume that Wordsworth in 1798–1807 was 'in any important sense either pro-French Revolution or pro-English Reform', '"Wordsworth" after Waterloo', in Kenneth R. Johnston, and Gene W. Ruoff, eds. *The Age of William Wordsworth: Critical Essays on the Romantic Tradition* (New Brunswick and London: Rutgers University Press, 1987), 84–111, 101.

revolution in the French sense may be the worst of all ways to realize fraternity. Such a dual conviction may result in paralysis. In Wordsworth's case it generated a mastered irony.[1]

Despite the (derivative) clerical satire in Book 7 of *The Prelude*, no one would argue that Wordsworth was, could, or ought to have been, a great satirist, even if he had found a way to reconcile satirical modes with his desire to heal, and 'to console the afflicted, to add sunshine to daylight by making the happy happier' (*MY*, 2: 146). In any case, he makes clear in the letter to John Taylor cited above, that he shares Coleridge's disapprobation of 'what you with great propriety call jacobinical pathos' that is, the mode of 'those writers who seem to estimate their power of exciting sorrow for suffering humanity by the quantity of hatred and revenge which they are able to pour into the hearts of their Readers' (*EY*, 326). But an ironic temper will out, even if it chooses modes less conspicuous, and more effective, than satire and invective. Wordsworth's habitual irony conceals itself coolly and ingeniously in the themes and strategies of the poems themselves, but manifests itself in the sardonic vein of the 1798 'Advertisement' to *Lyrical Ballads*, and in the 1800 'Preface'.

The man who wrote *Lyrical Ballads* had been back in England for six years after his experience of revolutionary France. Part of this time had been spent in London, participating in iconoclastic political speculations, and working or planning to work on the periphery of Jacobin journalism. Part of it was spent in long walks through a land which, if one judges from the poems treated in the last chapter, was inhabited exclusively by victims of scarcity and war, most of whom seem to have been deserted mothers. Part of it was spent in a kind of emotional and intellectual convalescence in the West Country with Dorothy (somewhat Bohemian, despite her Royalist sympathies), a still radical Coleridge, and the yet more radical company of Tom Poole and (occasionally) John Thelwall.

---

1   This chapter revises an essay '*Lyrical Ballads* (1798): Wordsworth as Ironist' (*Critical Quarterly*, 1982) which learned much from John Danby's analysis of Wordsworth as 'a superb ironist' in *The Simple Wordsworth* (1959), and Stephen Parrish's classic *The Art of the Lyrical Ballads* (Harvard,1973) but it predated Don Bialostosky's *Making Tales* (1984) and David Simpson's *Wordsworth's Historical Imagination* (1987). As these later discussions have considerably furthered our understanding of the complexities of Wordsworth's simpler poems, I have somewhat reduced my attention to irony, in this revision, while emphasising the radicalism of the ballads, and the historical impregnation of Wordsworth's diction.

For some of his time he was able to concentrate his thoughts on men who were neither political vermin nor narcissistic clerics of the kind treated in *The Prelude*, but men such as one might meet on any public way, 'men as they are men within themselves'. One of his conclusions reflects upon what can be learned from such men and upon the ideology of publishing:

> —Yes, in those wanderings deeply did I feel
> How we mislead each other; above all,
> How books mislead us, seeking their reward
> From judgements of the wealthy Few, who see
> By artificial lights; how they debase
> The Many for the pleasure of those Few.
>
> (*1850*, 13: 206ff)

The evidence of the poems and of the 1800 Preface being corroborative, one can take this to be an accurate depiction of his Alfoxden state of mind. One poem of the period which Wordsworth did not include in any edition of *Lyrical Ballads*, though it appeared in Stuart's *Morning Post*, began with a vituperative assessment of 'the wealthy Few':

> 'Tis not for the unfeeling, the falsely refined,
> The squeamish in taste, and the narrow of mind,
> And the small critic wielding his delicate pen,
> That I sing of old Adam, the pride of old men.[1]

The vehemence (unfeeling, false, squeamish, narrow and small) reveals a man deeply conscious of the ideology of publishing, and troubled by the realization that he was writing about people whose circumstances resulted from the acts of those *for* whom he was writing.[2] His characters are the dispossessed and the settled poor of the still late-feudal society of Dorset and Somerset, whose tenant he then was. The landlords and the 'poetry owners' were the same people, and Wordsworth's radical temper found the fact acutely painful—in *Simon Lee* the relation is more painful still in that the poet is *in loco landlordis*, as it were, to the stricken retainer.

As Charles Lamb insisted, the themes of *Lyrical Ballads* were not

1   *The Farmer of Tilsbury Vale* may have been written as early as March 1797, and is one of several poems which derive from Tom Poole's fertile anecdotes.
2   One may attribute this to disappointed ambition (that of appearing before the public as a tragedian) but he sometimes writes rather in the manner of Emily Dickinson about an aversion to publishing (*EY*, 211, 267).

chosen to experiment with poetical adaptation of 'the language of con-
versation in the lower and middle classes of society': they sprang 'from
living and daily circumstances'.[1] Throughout the nineties, Wordsworth's
imagination had been almost wholly preoccupied by images of distress,
and he was deeply sceptical about the will or the power of society to radi-
cally amend the human condition unless a fundamental shift in imagina-
tive sympathy could first be engineered. The English reading (for 'reading'
read 'ruling') classes, one remembers from the Preface, were at this time
sunk into a state 'of almost savage torpor'. The experiment Wordsworth
was engaged in has more to do with clinical psychology than with sty-
listic decorum, and that experiment is extended in 1800 and 1802, when
the two versions of the Preface extend and deepen his critique of the
audience to which both volumes are addressed, and when he adds more
poems in the same vein. Although the 1798 poems might be regarded as
the more experimental, Wordsworth opened the 1800 volume with an
apparent hunting ballad that involves the vertiginous displacement of a
feudal order of reality by another, conducive to a 'milder day', and closes
it with an implicit comparison of a Grasmere shepherd to the patriarch
Abraham and in a style to match. Other additions in 1800 include *The
Brothers*, a quasi-dramatic dialogue between a homely priest and a shep-
herd-lad turned sailor, couched in the terms of the *utmost* delicacy of
feeling, as if to challenge Jeffrey's celebrated remark that the feelings of
a plebeian cannot possibly be the same as those of a gentleman; and a
tribute to the strength of imagination—that distinguishing mark of man-
kind as progressive being, to borrow Coleridge's definition—in a dis-
placed female called 'Poor Susan'. Indeed *Poor Susan* and *The Brothers*
exhibit Wordsworth's great theme, the creativity of *all* human imagina-
tion. If one wants to know what he meant in the Prospectus by defining
his theme as 'how exquisitely'

> The external world is fitted to the mind;
> And the creation (by no lower name
> Can it be called) which they with blended might
> Accomplish. (*Home at Grasmere*, 1002–14)

one need look no further than Leonard's maritime world, as he hangs
over the ship's side

---

1   Lamb to Wordsworth, 30 January 1801. *The Letters of Charles and Mary Lamb*, ed.
Edwin W. Marrs, 3 vols (Ithaca: Cornell University Press, 1975), 1: 266.

And, while the broad green wave and sparkling foam
Dash'd round him images and hues, *that wrought*
In union with the employment of his heart,
He, thus by feverish passion overcome,
Even with the organs of his bodily eye,
Below him in the bosom of the deep,
Saw mountains, saw the forms of sheep that graz'd
On verdant hills … (*The Brothers*, 53–62; my emphases)

One does not need to be a poet, that is to say, to 'half create' one's own world. When, two years later still, Wordsworth wrote *Beggars, The Sailor's Mother* and *Alice Fell* in a burst of creativity in four days of March 1802, the result is an even subtler testing of class sensitivities in poems of such apparent simplicity and real abstruseness (to borrow Hazlitt's remark) that they had to wait until the 1980s for readers able to negotiate them.[1]

While the 1800 Preface, compared with the excluded *Farmer of Tilsbury Vale*, is a relatively mannerly composition, its latent aggression is worth noting. The poet wishes to trace in incidents of common life 'the *primary* laws of our nature', choosing common life because there 'the essential passions of the heart find a better soil in which they can attain their maturity'. The human mind is '*capable* of excitement without the application of gross and violent stimulants'. His aim is to '*produce* or enlarge this capability'. His work is a modest attempt to counteract the public's '*degrading* thirst after outrageous stimulation'. And he wishes to keep the reader 'in the company of flesh and blood'. He therefore expects his poems to be read with 'more than common dislike' by an audience which prefers its literature to be 'frantic … sickly and stupid … idle and extravagant'. Imploded in this crude fashion, the message of the Preface is plain enough. The 'almost savage torpor' of the reading public calls for surgery, and Wordsworth's surgical instrument will be irony. In irony, Kierkegaard writes, 'the phenomenon is not the essence but the opposite of the essence'.[2] This definition is superior to most in two respects: it relates irony to the quality of truth, which demands the identity of phenomenon and essence, and it grasps that irony is not (or not merely) a figure of speech. Irony, after all, may inhabit stance, gesture,

---

1   See the readings of these three poems in Bialostosky's *Making Tales*. 'Alice Fell' is also superbly read in Simpson's *Wordsworth's Historical Imagination*.
2   *The Concept of Irony*, tr. Lee M.Capel (London: Collins, 1966), p. 264.

look, or a habitual cast of mind. What the ironist does is exploit the non-coincidence between phenomenon and essence (that is, if he happens to be using words, between what is said and what is meant) for purposes of his own. The transparent ironist, of course, presupposes an instancy of understanding: the ironic figure of speech is a self-cancelling strata-gem. But the ironist's purpose may be evasion, or concealment, or the self-satisfaction of remaining misunderstood (for instance by those by whom it might be demeaning to be understood). Or he may, contrariwise, be intent on bestowing the gift of self-consciousness. Positively, irony discloses to the self its hitherto unconscious movements: its function, to Kierkegaard, is to help the personal life 'acquire health and truth'. In literature (outside satire), irony's purpose is not generally the commu-nication of a content but to make the mind aware of its own processes. Not in itself a figure of speech, it employs numerous literary figures and strategies of which the aim is to decoy the reader into a confrontation with himself, or (as Wordsworth puts it in the Preface) with his own 'pre-established codes of decision' or 'habits of association'.

One such strategy is to appear in the world incognito—doing some-thing other than one appears to be doing. For almost every poem in *Lyrical Ballads*, numerous models have been identified, and the term 'parody' is occasionally aired in connection with one poem or another.[1] Indeed a vein of parody runs through nearly all of Wordsworth's poems in the 1798 volume and the volume as a whole gives evidence of a sus-tained parodic strategy. By parody, of course, I mean something more sober than burlesque, although Wordsworth does in fact indulge in some conspicuously comic burlesque of literary balladry and of ballad-tracts and Gothic furniture, and his determination to critique such modes may have led to the controversial exclusion of *Christabel* in 1800.[2] In a sub-

---

1   One of the achievements of Wordsworth scholarship in the 1960s and 1970s was an awareness of how conventional Wordsworth actually was in his choice of form, style and subject matter. Robert Mayo, W. J. B. Owen, Mary Jacobus and others took pains to demonstrate the 'contemporaneity' of the volume, and its marked lack of original-ity, for instance, in choosing the ballad form, or writing about vagrants. See Robert Mayo, 'The Contemporaneity of the *Lyrical Ballads*', *PMLA*, 1965; W. J. B. Owen's Introduction, *Lyrical Ballads 1798* (Oxford: OUP 1969); Mary Jacobus, *Tradition and Experiment in Wordsworth's Lyrical Ballads (1798)* (Oxford: Clarendon Press, 1976).

2   Much mythologizing has taken place of this event. One can read *Christabel* as a poem so interrogative of narrative cliché that it suits the purpose of the volume extremely well. Yet the projected ending described by Coleridge to Dr Gillman (in *The Life of Samuel Taylor Coleridge*, 1838, 301–2) clearly implies a poem not only far

tler sense, however, parody can mean the imitation of a literary mode in order to refine and extend its possibilities, as Wordsworth does with the lyric poem and the loco-descriptive mode—and as Coleridge, it may seem to us today, does in *Christabel*. This is not to claim that work in such modes displays a parodic surface-texture: it is enough to be working within and against a semblance of convention, so as to activate the reader's 'pre-established codes of decision' and to play upon his 'habits of association'. In each of Wordsworth's poems in *Lyrical Ballads* the surface manner courts comparison, to begin with at least, with what his gentle reader—having laid out some portion of a guinea—feels entitled to expect.

Wordsworth's first lines in *Lyrical Ballads* announce the method. Although entitled 'LINES | LEFT UPON A SEAT IN | A YEW-TREE | *WHICH STANDS NEAR THE LAKE OF ESTHWAITE,* | ON A DESOLATE PART OF THE SHORE, | YET COMMANDING A BEAUTIFUL PROSPECT'—the title requires six lines and three levels of typography—the poem really concerns prospects unrealized within a desolate self, and it begins by admonishing the reader somewhat abruptly:

> —Nay, Traveller! rest. This lonely Yew-tree stands
> Far from all human dwelling: what if here
> No sparkling rivulet spread the verdant herb;
> What if these barren boughs the bee not loves;
> Yet, if the wind breathes soft, the curling waves
> That break against the shore, shall lull thy mind
> By one soft impulse saved from vacancy.

The poet who, in 1793, could still write of 'finny flood' and 'fleecy store', now ironizes the 'sparkling rivulet', the 'verdant herb', and those ludicrously alliterative bees and boughs as soft amusements of the vacant mind.[1] This parodic diction deflates a whole tradition of nature-writ-

too long for the collection but threatening to revert to all the clichés of romance. Both Wordsworth and Coleridge seem to have believed in 1801 that a 5-Canto poem was on the point of being realized, and that it would be published in a lavish illustrated edition by Longmans (*EY*, 321 n, 324): 'Christabel is to be printed at the Bulmerian press, with vignettes' writes Wordsworth, 'I long to have the book in my hand it will be such a beauty'. There is no reason to doubt that both Wordsworth and Coleridge *agreed* that the poem, because Coleridge was swimming 'in a current of my own', as he put it, would disrupt the ideology of *Lyrical Ballads*, or to impugn Wordsworth's sincerity in encouraging its separate publication.

1   Paul Sheats uses the term 'parody' in his extended reading of this poem in *The*

ing, a dying aesthetic, to make space for a characteristic Wordsworthian paradox, that of being *lulled into wakefulness* by an as yet unexplained 'impulse'—a complex word that will not be glossed until *The Tables Turned*, five poems from the end of the volume. Meanwhile a curiously difficult discipline is expected of the reader, a self-suspicious and lowly self-reverence of the kind not attained by the proud and loveless hermit, averse from 'the labours of benevolence', whose only memorial this yew-tree is. As this figure is not unrelated to other Wordsworthian selves—his Solitary, for instance—the volume opens with a hidden self-exposure, concealing from any innocent reader in Wordsworth's lifetime the shadow-side of the author, just as its closing poem, *On revisiting the Wye*, leaves clues for the modern reader in search of Wordsworth's political biography.

In *We are Seven*, that litmus test for appreciation of Wordsworth's procedure, the familiar figure of a didactic poet is attempting to argue a pretty child into a conviction of mortality. This may seem a preposterous occupation, and a morbid one, but as Mary Jacobus suggested long ago, it was felt by eighteenth-century readers to be a proper function of poetry: such readers would have been familiar with the *Divine and Moral Songs* of Isaac Watts, and with his sentiment in a poem suggestively entitled 'Against Lying', that it is 'a lovely thing for Youth | To walk betimes in Wisdom's way'. By wisdom, here, we are to understand 'Solemn thoughts of God and Death' (the title of *Divine Song* X). But Watts also taught acceptance of social hierarchy—'Whene'er I take my walks abroad, | How many poor I see! | What shall I render to my God | For all his gifts to me?'—and reverse ageism: 'Let children that would fear the Lord | Hear what their teachers say | With reverence meet their parents' word | And with delight obey'.[1] To Wordsworth, as we know from *The Prelude*, wisdom comes from overt acts of transgression and curfew-infringement, and 'solemn thoughts', while all very well, have their own season. To force them upon the state of childhood is perverse:

Making of Wordsworth's Poetry (Cambridge MA: Harvard UP, 1973), 154–60. It is possible that these lines of the poem were written at school (Wordsworth says that the poem was 'composed in part at Hawkshead') and only kept by the mature poet because they illustrate poetic cliché.

1   Isaac Watts, D. D., *Divine and Moral Songs attempted in easy language for the use of children* (Birmingham, n.d.), Divine Songs XV, X, IV, XXIII. As for the poor they should resolve to be 'modest, neat and clean | And submit when they reprove me', *Moral Song* VII.

Book 5 finely satirizes those who regard the child as merely 'a dwarf man ... | The noontide shadow of the man complete' (5: 297). But readers of 1798 had to approach *We are Seven* with only their native wits, and the hint of a neighbouring poem, to guide them. In *Anecdote for Fathers* Wordsworth detects and chides the errors of adult presumption in himself, or in a compound adult persona (compounded of Wordsworth, Watts and the reader), for demanding of a child answers he himself does not have, to questions of no conceivable interest to childhood—questions of memory, and finely calculated loss and gain.

Both poems are, in the end, precisely what they appear to be: didactic pieces, in which the moral dimension, if not quite 'a moral', is clearly pointed ('A simple child ... what should it know of death?', and 'How the art of lying may be taught'). The irony works at two levels. First, there is the Blakean tactic of reversing the thrust of the didacticism. As Heather Glen has suggested, it is the reader, not the sweep, to whom Blake addresses his troubling moral, 'if all do their duty | They need not fear harm',[1] but Wordsworth's ballads, too, are reverse-thrust cautionary tales, ones which 'every child may joy to hear'. Secondly, there is the ironic self-awareness the poems deploy and commend. The technique may be heavy (Wordsworth did not think his readers likely to be very alert, and nearly two centuries of reception showed him to be right), but it is heaviest when self-directed: 'And five times did I say to him, | Why? Edward, tell me why?' The arithmetic makes us observe that other and more literal exhibition of tenacity in the poem: 'I said and *took* him by the arm ... | I said and *held* him by the arm ... | While *still* I held him by the arm'. How far the material of such poems is, in fact, drawn from Wordsworth's awareness of his own failings is, of course, impossible to say. We do not know how he behaved towards little Basil Montagu, or to the little girl whose resilience makes her the heroine of *We are Seven*. We do know that the mental acts of appropriation and reification in such poems as *The Thorn* and *Old Man Travelling* are such as the poet's mind is prone to. Wordsworth, that is, indicts himself in such use of the first person pronoun, even though we may come to see each of these poems

---

1   Heather Glen, *Vision and Disenchantment: Blake's Songs and Wordsworth's Lyrical Ballads* (Cambridge: CUP, 1983), 101. For a recent transaction with 'We are Seven' in the light of contemporary interrogaton of rural populations see Glen's '"We are Seven" in the 1790s', *Grasmere 2012: Selected Papers from the Wordsworth Summer Conference* (Penrith: Humanities-Ebooks, 2012) 8–33.

as creating a narrator-persona. When he writes 'we err' to John Wilson, he does mean 'we'.

The *Anecdote* ends with a moral learned: questions remain, but self-irony has been acquired by the speaker.[1] *We are Seven* ends with the persona as unenlightened as he began, and subject to a continuing dramatic irony. He persists in answering wrongly the explanatory question with which, thanks to Coleridge, the poem opens: 'A little child ... what *should* it know of death?' The *Anecdote*, based upon Rousseau's sense of lying as a pedagogic outcome, teaches us to read *We are Seven*, which it precedes, and to detect what Blake called 'aged ignorance' in the closing tones of the narrator:

> 'Twas throwing words away; for still
> The little maid would have her will,
> And said, 'Nay, we are seven!'

There is much more at stake in these poems than a little ameliorative fun. The poems address those exigencies of time, and anxieties rooted in the threat of non-being, which are the subjects of Wordsworth's most personal utterances, and they introduce us—as effectively as the most sonorous and transcendental of the spots of time—to the possibilities of modes of relationship which have little to do with the prison-house of Urizenic structures of perception. We may choose to feel that the child in *We are Seven* illustrates 'the perplexity and obscurity which in child-hood surrounds our notions of death' (Preface, 1800)) or we may prefer to regard her as 'the heroine' of the poem (*FN* 39): Wordsworth's divergent 'reading instructions', like his two versions of the origination of *The Thorn*, seem designed to prevent premature closure. But it is hard not to feel that the poet of the Lucy poems, the following winter, is exploring the little girl's imaginative territory, and very hard not to feel that the adult's attempt to wrest her joy from her is felt by Wordsworth not merely as gross impertinence but as gross abuse.

Even if the speaker understood that his religion teaches eternal life (he seems deaf to the contradiction in 'But they are *dead*, those two are *dead* | Their *spirits* are in *heaven*') his incomprehension of the girl's life, and his failure to hear what she is telling him (she is too young to know even the names of the siblings who, to him, are still 'alive' but who to her are without real existence) disqualifies him from spiritual teaching.

---

1   Don Bialostosky questions this in a subtle reading, *Making Tales*, 108–112.

But adults do, as Don Bialostosky implies, say the darndest things.[1] If two 'go' to Conway, and two 'go' or '*are gone*' to sea, how do these states or actions differ from the *going* or the *being* of John who was forced 'to go' or Jane who was 'released' and 'went away'? What 'perplexity' the heroine evinces as she parses the verb 'to go' stems not from her lived experience but from her mother's language, or the inscriptions she sees all round her in the graveyard. Already her employment of two languages (her own and that of her mother) shows that she stands on the brink of euphemism—the adult sin of substituting words for things. Meanwhile 'Their graves are green, *they may be seen*' is not merely the most triumphant line in the poem, one that is echoed precisely in the poetry of Bryant and Whitman, but it proceeds—arguably—from the same metaphysics, the same animism, that finds consolation in the life of 'rocks and stones and trees' or even the same desire that expresses itself in *To a Sexton* (1800) and the *Essays upon Epitaphs*, that we should remain 'neighbours in mortality'. Whatever this six-year-old argued on their first meeting, she was impressive enough for Wordsworth, when revisiting the Wye in 1841, to try to find out what became of her. Poised between animism and pantheism, intinctively aware of Spinoza's position that substance can suffer no diminution, she may even have been the third great influence on his intellectual life.

Several of the lyrics in the collection might have been composed—if Wordsworth had heard of Blake at this date one would be sure they were so composed—as elaborations of Blake's proverb, 'Damn braces! Bless relaxes!' The poem usually called *To my sister* is in every respect except its ploddingly matter-of-fact title ('Lines written at a small distance from my House, and sent by my little Boy to the Person to whom they are addressed') the friskiest of these, and celebrates idleness.[2] Its playful tone is calculated to scandalize the moralist and the semanticist alike:

> No joyless forms shall regulate
> Our living Calendar:
> We from to-day, my friend, will date

---

1   Bialostosky classifies 'Anecdote for Fathers' as a kids-say-the-darndest-things poem in 'Genres from life in Wordsworth's art: *Lyrical Ballads* 1798', in Tillotama Rajan and Julia M. Wright eds, *Romanticism, History and the Possibilities of Genre* (Cambridge University Press, 1998) 115.
2   But is the title plodding? Try saying it respecting Wordsworth's trade-mark sparsity of capitals, and it assumes a wonderful throw-away melody. It swings.

> The opening of the year.
>
> Love, now an universal birth,
> From heart to heart is stealing,
>
> ...
>
> One moment now may give us more
> Than fifty years of reason;
> Our minds shall drink at every pore
> The spirits of the season.
>
> Some silent laws our hearts may make,
> Which they shall long obey ...

'We from to-day, my friend, will date | The opening of the year'? Nobody in 1798, surely, could have encountered this poem without remembering that while in some countries the Gregorian Calendar replaced the less accurate Julian Calendar in 1582, it took 350 years for the rest of the world to fall into line. The French adopted it only in 1760, and then during the Revolution decided to throw out the new calendar and start afresh, dating everything from the Fall of the Bastille, as a sort of universal Spring. The next stanza's 'universal birth' is precisely the kind of imagery that half of Europe had been using just a few years before to describe the French Revolution, and in 1805, Wordsworth would write of 'human nature seeming born again'. That revolution had, perhaps been the product of rather more than 'fifty years of reason': and one is being invited, perhaps to wonder whether this 'moment' is being offered as a parallel or as an antitithetical fresh start, if not for humanity then for a brother and sister in Alfoxden.

The poem invites an idle reading, appearing to offer an idle poetry of flat, unproblematical statement, and its rhythms convey the joy of the Alfoxden Spring, as the lyrics of 1800 / 1802 convey the joy of Grasmere. But it also offers, deadpan, a succession of metaphysical (almost Metaphysical) paradoxes and plays upon figurative possibility. One kind of movement is in that carefree balancing of one moment with fifty years (a very fine excess); another in the intricately figurative manoeuvre which takes us from 'minds' to 'drink' to 'pore', to 'spirits', to 'season'. The effect, surely, depends upon a hermeneutic curve something like this: 'drink' is first loosely metaphorical, when referred back to 'mind'; it then becomes more precisely figurative, in a context of Romantic organicism and Enlightenment science, because of the reference forward to 'pore', an effect instantaneously cancelled by reflection on the oddity of such a conjunction between 'mind' and 'pore' (minds pore, but do they have pores?); so that 'spirits' returns one to the jocular reading of 'drink', until the final 'season' leaves one poised between two ways of construing 'spirits'. One's mind is suspended between simply enjoying the word-play and pondering the possibilities of a reverent animism, when the poem passes us on to a further testing problem—and Wordsworth's Kantianism—that of the casual, unconscious, adoption of laws which bind as deeply as the most categorical imperatives.

Such Jacobin excess, disguised as play, continues in *Expostulation and Reply*. Now bookish morality is allowed to rebuke the poet, but only in terms which the poet has ironically freighted:

> 'Where are your books? that light bequeath'd
> To beings else forlorn and blind!
> Up! Up! and drink the spirit breath'd
> From dead men to their kind'.

Five years earlier Wordsworth had rebuked Burke's piety to the dead as 'a refinement in cruelty superior to that which in the East yokes the living to the dead' and compared Burke's veneration for ancient acts of parliament—all that 'dead parchment'—with a call to 'cherish a corse at the bosom when reason might call aloud that it should be entombed'.[1] It is the living and not the dead, Paine retorted to Burke, who are to be accommodated, and this poem is clearly of Paine's party. Wordsworth is still two years away from adding to the 2nd edition of *Lyrical Ballads* a Latin epigraph aimed at the turncoat lawyer James Mackintosh, suggesting that these Paineite poems 'will not be to your taste, Papiniam'.[2]

The fact that one *cannot* use the phrase 'the living and the dead' in 1798, or address what can or cannot be 'bequeath'd', without invoking Burke and Paine, underwrites one's feeling that the pervasive odour of charnel suggested by the opening lines of *Expostulation* is represented as less than 'wholesome'. Not that the message of *The Tables Turned* seems especially Paineite, unless one recalls Paine's attraction to Pantheism. What the poem offers is revolutionary in a tempered sense. It com-

---

1   *WPW*, 52. Twelve years later, however, he would commend 'the wholesome influence of that communion between living and dead which the conjunction ... of the place of burial and the place of worship tends so effectually to promote', *PrW*, 2: 66.
2   For the significance of this epigraph see *LBOP*, 377.

mends the 'breath' of health and 'the light of things'—the cultivation, in Emerson's phrase, of an original relation to the universe—repaying stale metaphor (that light bequeathed) with paradoxical interest.[1]

Ironically, these four credal lyrics—or are they anti-credal, in casting moral discourse to the winds?—have behind them (in *The Pedlar*) and ahead of them (in manuscripts of *The Prelude*) a weight of Wordsworthian doctrine. His 'wise passiveness' is wise because it involves a discipline of receptivity. A 'heart that watches and receives' suggests a rare attunement to the living universe. An 'impulse from a vernal wood' is no everyday experience. The laws the heart makes for itself are indeed the only ones it is likely to 'long obey'. To 'come forth into the light of things' is a strenuous prescription (it is, after all, the primary theme of Martin Heidegger's metaphysics), and—in the *Lyrical Ballads* context—means seeing as the narrators of *We are seven* and *The Thorn* fail to see. It may, for instance, involve seeing that alternative universe, rooted in the history of European thought from Virgil to the Encyclopaedists and Erasmus Darwin, which is quietly invoked in *Lines written in early Spring*:

> To her fair works did nature link
> The human soul that through me ran…

If nature is indeed the author of our being, if every flower, as in Diderot, enjoys the air it breathes, and if man is free to obey the impulses of his being, why are we in chains? The poems lead inexorably to the exposition of a radical version of Spinozim (aided by Dugald Stewart) in *The Poem upon the Wye*, to which the ahistoricism of the 1980s was culpably deaf.

The dialogue between *To my sister*, *Lines written in early Spring*, *Expostulation and Reply*, and *The Tables Turned* points to a little-noticed feature of *Lyrical Ballads*, the extent of interanimation or hermeneutic reinforcement one finds throughout the work. The homespun animism of *We are seven* leads straight into the tutored animism—both scientific and Jacobin—of *Early spring*. When this latter poem ends with the Burnsian question 'Have I not reason to lament | What man has made of man?' the question has been amply informed by *The Female Vagrant*, *Goody Blake and Harry Gill*, and *Simon Lee*, and leads provocatively into that early masterpiece, *The Thorn*. Similarly, such mutually illumi-

---

1   *Expostulation* and *The Tables Turned* were among the most quoted of Wordsworth's poems during Boston's attempt in the 1840s to recover the moment of Tom Paine.

nating pairs as *The Female Vagrant* and *Goody Blake*, *The Mad Mother* and *The Idiot Boy*, *Old Man Travelling* and *The Complaint of a forsaken Indian Woman*, offer complementary perspectives on particular human conditions—from abuse of property, to mental abnormality, to terminal decay—thus reinforcing the 'more salutary impression' that Wordsworth expects us to receive from his poems. That Wordsworth lends the Indian Woman one of his own favourite words to express her sense of her son's feelings—'a most strange *something* did I see'—is a democratic and anti-racist touch no contemporary reader could be expected to see.

As poems of human suffering, *The last of the Flock* and *The Mad Mother* are belated contributions to a popular genre. Wordsworth knew that his readers enjoyed exercising sympathy, at a comfortable distance, on distressing topics suitably adapted to verse. The representative poem on such themes—the kind of poem to which Wordsworth supposes his readers to be accustomed—is written from the observer's point of view, and in somewhat abstract poetic diction: the interest may be sensationalist or sentimental, appealing at best to pity, at worst to prurience. Decorum, in either case, precludes direct identification with the victim. That genuine poetry had been written about the distressed one would not deny. Both Cowper and Percy furnish examples, and Wordsworth authenticates his style and method in *The Mad Mother* in part by aligning his poem significantly with the magnificent *Lady Bothwell's Lament*: 'Balow, my babe, ly still and sleipe! | It grieves me sair to see thee weipe ...'. But Southey's distanced exploitation of his material in a poem like *Poor Mary* is more characteristic of what the ballad had come to: 'Who is she, the poor maniac...? | She never complains, but her silence implies | The composure of settled distress'. The most salutary feature of *The Mad Mother*, apart from the superiority of its diction to Southey's jigging polysyllables, and its rootedness in medical science,[1] is that in this poem Wordsworth offers nothing at all in the way of outrageous stimulation— nothing corresponding to the 'Bates Motel' opportunism of Southey's *The Idiot*. There is nothing frantic or freakish about his 'poor maniac' and Wordsworth protects both her privacy and her independence. The Fenwick note states merely that the 'poor creature' was reported to him by 'a lady of Bristol' (57). Elsewhere, however, he intimates that the character as envisaged in the poem is no more his 'property' than his

---

1   Erasmus Darwin's *Zoonomia* touches on the medicinal effect of breast-feeding. See *LBOP*, 353.

reader's: 'though she came from far, English was her native tongue—
which shows her to be either of these islands or a North American. On
the latter supposition...' (*LY*, 3: 293). Supposition? Whose poem (one
wants to ask) *is* this?

   Whoever she is, she grounds the *credo* of *The Poem upon the Wye*,
that 'the language of the sense' anchors our moral being:

> Suck, little babe, oh suck again!
> It cools my blood; it cools my brain;
> Thy lips I feel them, baby! they
> Draw from my heart the pain away.

Technically, *The Mad Mother* is one of the first true dramatic mono-
logues, for its third and penultimate stanzas, particularly, leave little
doubt about the speaker's state, or the threat her condition represents
to herself and to her child. This mother hallucinates, and does so alarm-
ingly in the course of the poem; she experiences psychotic delusions of
invulnerability; she will burden her infant with the role of erotic substitu-
tion for the absent father; she is—as the poem proceeds—unable to dis-
tinguish between her baby's need to be burped and demonic possession.
But the poem is less a dramatization than an act of love: Browning's
poems cannot be read without lending some sympathy to their speakers,
but *The Mad Mother* and *The Idiot Boy* cannot be read unless readerly
empathy is unconditional. Inwardness of this order is indeed 'another
and more salutary impression than we are accustomed to receive' from
such subjects. A similar imaginative realism accounts for the peculiar
strength of *The Female Vagrant* and *The last of the Flock*.

   To be addressed so directly, so eloquently, and so illuminatingly,
by social outcasts, was not within the experience of the average reader
in 1798, unless very familiar with the best of Southey's eclogues. Not
until John Barton, in Elizabeth Gaskell's *Mary Barton* (1847), asked
his neighbours what he should tell the parliament folk, while presenting
the Chartist petition, did the 'gentle reader' have so much *viva voce* tes-
timony as to what the poor think when they are not 'being improved'.[1]
Wordsworth's poems engage—and this is why the experimental diction
does matter—to let the reader glimpse the world through the eyes of the
powerless. The effect can be disturbing in several ways, as seeing the

---

1   The phrase is Richard Holt Hutton's in a fine review of *Silas Marner*. Not for noth-
ing does one see Wordsworth in a continuum with Gaskell and George Eliot.

world upside down often is. When, for instance, we have come to terms with the dignity and self-possession of the speaker in *The last of the Flock* and seen his present plight in the perspective of his life, we may feel with the tender Dr Burney that 'if the author be a wealthy man' he should not have suffered the poor peasant to part with his lamb.[1] But *The last of the Flock* is less a plea for private charity than a caustic reflection on an ill-conceived system of relief. Where Blake makes his similar message both explicit and rather abstract ('Pity would be no more, | If we did not make somebody poor'), Wordsworth questions the moral basis of a society in which the price of charity is total destitution. More exactly, however, he offers a piece of apparently unedited testimony, such as one might find in the records of social research.[2] One cannot overestimate the importance, in an age of ideology, of a poet using his art to make others listen and watch—listen to a victim of the Speenhamland system giving testimony vis-à-vis the moral impact of ill-advised measures; watch Simon Lee trying to till the land he was encouraged to 'enclose'; listen to the female vagrant's experience of the property cannibalism that Wordsworth will later summarize in his *Guide* ('Then rose a mansion proud our woods among, | And cottage after cottage owned its sway').

In *Goody Blake and Harry Gill*, property is, manifestly, theft. Once again, a Blakean proverb appears in the form of a parable: his 'prisons are built with stones of law' appears in Wordsworth's tale of how human needs are criminalized by rights of property. This poem has been recognized as openly parodic. Mary Jacobus sees it in relation to contemporary ballad-tracts, and to Hannah More's *Cheap Repository for Publications on Religious and Moral Subjects*, which utilized verse as a means of conveying moral truths to the lower orders.[3] Such poetry chastises intemperance, improvidence and impatience, along with dishonest 'weights and measures'—in More's *The Market-Woman; a True Story*—in the name of solid bourgeois virtues. We may feel therefore that in Wordsworth's equally 'true story'—true because corroborated by

1   *The Monthly Review* XXIX, June 1799.
2   See Regina Hewitt, *The Possibilities of Society: Wordsworth, Coleridge, and the Sociological Viewpoint of English Romanticism* (Albany: State University of New York Press, 1997) for a persuasive assessment of Wordsworth's poetry vis-a-vis the infant science of sociology.
3   Jacobus, 237–9.

the science of that luminary of the Lunar Society, Dr Erasmus Darwin—characters are chosen to activate habitual moral associations. Harry Gill is a respectable farmer, well within his rights. Goody Blake is a conspicuously undeserving, because improvident, old woman:

> Oh joy for her! when e'er in winter
> The winds at night had made a rout,
> And scatter'd many a lusty splinter,
> And many a rotten bough about.
> Yet never had she, well or sick,
> As every man who knew her says,
> A pile before-hand, wood or stick,
> Enough to warm her for three days.

It is striking that this poem is the only one in the collection that condones an onslaught on a property owner—and that the onslaught is brought about by nature, poetry, imagination and science. Harry suffers his chilling torments at the hands of nature and of *two* subversive imaginations, the poet's and his own. Imagination, after all is a second nature, and like Nature (in *The Prelude*, 1850 9.523–4) it desires to recompense the lowly child of toil. Perhaps because *Goody Blake* is a revenge poem (and hence closer than Wordsworth might wish to 'jacobinical pathos') it is the only one of the explicitly 'social' poems that makes use of considerable quantities of humour. In fact the genre of the poem is very hard to place. It has pantomimic qualities (all those coats), elements of the curse poem (Goody Blake with her withered arm upraised in the moonlight), straight economic data on the poverty trap (the price of labour is unpoetically weighed against that of candlelight to work by), gleeful rhymes in a jaunty metre, pointed persuasions to empathy ('Sad case it was, as you may think, | For very cold to go to bed, | And then for cold not sleep a wink'), and one quite unexpected shaft of imagination: Harry Gill's teeth which 'chatter, chatter' throughout the poem finally do so in a brilliant simile, 'like a loose casement in the wind'. One could hardly quarrel with it, or take it ill. Could one? Yet at the close of the poem the property-owning reader is cautioned to 'think', in fear and trembling, 'of Goody Blake and Harry Gill' and one hears in the background Blake's 'so if all *do their duty*, they need not fear harm'. For all the comedy, Dr Burney smelt anarchy: what will become of property, he asked, 'if all the poor are to help themselves, and supply their wants from the possessions of their neighbours'?[1]

All of these poems ask the reader, in the phrase amplified by Conrad in 1897, 'to see, to think and feel'.[2] But Wordsworth's claims for the powers of poetry went further than this. As he wrote to Wilson in 1802, in a letter which made the most revolutionary claims for the function of poetry in any manifesto, not excluding Shelley's *Defence*, 'a great poet ought to rectify men's feelings, to give them new compositions of feeling, to render their feelings more sane'. Moreover, 'It is not enough for me as a poet, to delineate merely such feelings as all men *do* sympathize with but, it is also highly desirable to add to these others, such as all men *may* sympathise with, and such as there is reason to believe they would be better and more moral beings if they did sympathize with' (*EY, 355, 358*). In *Simon Lee*, *The Idiot Boy*, and *The Thorn* his ironic art is applied most strenuously to this maieutic end.[3]

Simon Lee, the Old Huntsman, with an Incident in which he was Concerned, to give it its full and artfully misleading title, deals in a variety of bafflements. In 1800 Wordsworth will offer the reader a hunting ballad, as the opening poem of Volume 2. This later poem, however, turns out to be less of a concession to readerly taste than at first appears. Unexpectedly, it contrasts the atavism of the hunter with the views of a tender shepherd who appears to promise the evolution of a milder humanity. *Simon Lee*, like the later *Hart-Leap Well*, also begins in straightforward ballad style:

> In the sweet shire of Cardigan,
> Not far from pleasant Ivor Hall,
> An old man dwells, a little man,

but it drops at once into the incongruity of 'I've heard he once was tall'. The first stanza ends whimsically, 'He says he is three score and ten, | But others say he's eighty', and what follows for some two-thirds of the poem is a sustained disruption of ballad decorum and the author-reader compact. In the third stanza Wordsworth promisingly modifies the 'pleasant hall' of Romance into the deserted, faintly Gothic, 'hall

---

1   Woof, 76.

2   Letter to Lady Beaumont, 21 May 1807. Compare Conrad's 'My task is …to make you hear, to make you feel—it is, before all, to make you see', Preface to *The Nigger of the Narcissus*.

3   'Maieusis', in Kierkegaard, is a metaphor connoting the role of the ironist as midwife to a new consciousness.

of Ivor'; but this potentially chilling inversion is casually dissipated in another comic rhyme: 'He is the sole sur*vi*vor'. Authentic ballads could, of course, cope with uncomfortable facts, as in 'And though he has but one eye left', but they were not prone to squander such effects in the subsequent jauntiness of 'His cheek is like a cherry'. Wordsworth returns with dogged sympathy to a carefully de-fictionalized hurt two stanzas later—'His hunting feats have him bereft | Of his right eye, as you may see'—and insists on the unpoetical truth that

> His little body's half awry,
> His ancles they are swol'n and thick;
> His legs are thin and dry.

Balladic refrain is abused in the interest of these same ankles some stanzas later: 'For still, the more he works, the more | His poor old ancles swell'.[1] No ballad would address the reader at such a moment in this oddly Swiftian style:

> My gentle reader, I perceive
> How patiently you've waited,
> And I'm afraid that you expect
> Some tale will be related.

Whatever the patient reader may desire, the reader-patient is cautioned, 'should you think | Perhaps a tale you'll make it'. (The needling line ending, 'think', is borrowed from the experimental Pedlar who cautioned the poet that his tale of Margaret would be 'scarcely palpable to one who does not think'). Only when all prospect of a tale is abandoned does the poet offer the anticipated story-telling start, 'One summer's day…'.

The constant shifts of tone induce a sense of insecurity. Generic confidence gives way to bewilderment as to what kind of poem this is intended to be. For half its length it alternates between the romantic past conjured by four lines of each stanza and the raw naturalism suggested in the other four. The dither seems to imply a Wordsworthian reassessment of his recent interest in the antiquarian, for as several scholars have noticed, 'Cardigan', to which this Somerset tale is displaced, was the stamping ground of Iolo Morganwg, where he adulterated the scholar-

---

1 Nor, of course, were gentle readers to be long burdened with the eye-socket, which departed in 1820. The particularly tender quality of his 'little' body was also replaced by the more distant 'dwindled' as early as 1800.

ship of Evan Evans and where both Iolo and Evan Evans celebrated the patronage of Ifor Hael—Ivor the Generous—patron of the great mediaeval poet Dafydd ap Gwilym. Evans, or Ieuan Fardd, the correspondent of Thomas Percy, wrote his own poem *On Seeing the Ruins of Ivor Hael's Palace near Tredegar in Monmouthshire* in which Dafydd ap Gwilym is left alone to lament the loss of the generous patron.[1] Just what are the duties of the radical poet? Can antiquarianism be an adequate answer to what man has made of man? For a Welsh poet who has lost his nation, perhaps. But Wordsworth's naturalistic account of Simon and Ruth displaces the literariness and the antiquarianism to which the opening stanzas half-allude.[2]

While the poem's bathetic structure—the refusal of story in a ballad mode—is, of course, its central irony, there are further ironies in the way the poem actually concludes, or does not conclude. Inviting the reader to conjure a 'tale' out of this 'incident' may imply that there is one way to do this, and that our business is simply to piece together the 'clues'. Or it may not. The poem insists that we think, but we may think in various channels and nothing much will happen until we do. If a poem implies some achieved insight, it really is our choice whether there is or is not to be 'a poem'.

Just what are we supposed to 'mourn'? We may, to attempt one answer, focus on the indeterminate symbolism of the action performed by the narrator. When he follows Paine's advice to 'lay then the axe to the root, and teach governments humanity'[3] a fountain of gratitude springs from a desert of dessication. Simon's gratitude is painfully incongruous both with the slight service the narrator has performed for him, and with the scale of deprivation in which 'all the county' has left him. On the other hand, one might equally mourn the insouciance with which our awkwardly charitable narrator has swept aside this 'overtasked' old man—making as light of the man as of the task. All this before we reach the final lines of the poem: 'I've heard of hearts unkind, | Kind deeds with

1   See Peter Bement, 'Simon Lee and Ivor Hall: a Possible Source', *TWC* 13:1 (1982) 35–6.

2   Wales does of course have a shadowy presence. The borders are the scene of *The Poem upon the Wye* and the home not merely of the little girl in *We are Seven* but also of John Thelwall whose address (misspelt) is planted in *Anecdote for Fathers* for no obvious reason unless as a covert signal to well-informed readers of whose company the author of these poems might be found in.

3   *The Rights of Man*, 80, as cited in this connection by Simpson, 155.

coldness still returning. | Alas! the gratitude of men | Has oftner left me mourning'. We have already been asked to take what is left of the poem 'kindly' and these repetitions undoubtedly push us towards a spirit of 'kindliness' with, and not merely towards, this liveried retainer. Swollen ankles or not, we should consider such men 'with reference to the points in which they resemble us' and not merely 'those in which they manifestly differ from us', as Wordsworth said to Fox.[1] Compared with this internal echo, the faint allusion to Burns's 'Man's inhumanity to man | makes countless thousands *mourn*' might seem a little digressive, except that it prepares us for a subsequent echo of the same Burns passage in *Early Spring* when the poet mourns 'what man has made of man'.[2] It would be hard to summarize the basic theme of *Simon Lee* more adequately than in Burns's 'A man's a man for a' that', though there is also an aesthetic thesis: perhaps the simple facts, those swollen ankles and that swelling heart, may be, in their conjunction more 'marvellous' than either hunting feats or the inventions of Gothic fancy. In such unobviously adroit poems, as in Blake's *Songs*, irony is mastered, and put to humane service.

The device of bathetic structure is also employed in *The Idiot Boy*, with its direct burlesque of the ballad form. Here the stirring ballad rhythms are used to present an ambling plot, in which the poet's rustic representative participates incongruously—manipulating the strings, chiding his characters and his muse, confiding in his audience, and tantalizing them too. A lengthy poem, it leaves open throughout its length the narratological question: who speaks? Like other lyrical ballads this one leaves one in doubt, for a while, whether we are hearing the poet *in propria persona*. That is eventually resolved in the negative, but as in Toni Morrison's *Jazz* the question whether the narrator is also an actor, or a neighbour, never resolves. The 'point of view' in the poem seems only a little ahead of the characters: the neighbour-narrator sees the pony coming before Betty does, and he knows her mind like his own, but tells us nothing that she does not see. Moreover his (her?) manner of addressing characters and readers alike is embarrassingly familiar. His language and manners are much like Betty's and Susan's and he turns to and fro as if negotiating between pantomime characters and the stalls. His mockery

---

1   *EY*, 315. Fox passed this test rather well, taking 'particular pleasure' in *Goody Blake, The Mad Mother, The Idiot Boy* and *We are Seven* (*EY*, 337).
2   See *LBOP*, 346, 349 for critical references to Burns's 'Man Was Made to Mourn'.

(if it is mockery) is generously bestowed upon all and sundry, as foolish Betty sends her idiot boy to a churlish doctor to help a hypochondriacal neighbour:

> There's scarce a soul that's out of bed;
> Good Betty! put him down again;
> His lips with joy they burr at you,
> But, Betty! what has he to do
> With stirrup, saddle, or with rein?

The chiding is applied here, for instance to motherly 'fiddle-faddle', foolishly misplaced pride, and thoughtless generosity. It is applied later to our pre-established codes of how a narrative poem should proceed.

Betty's pride and silliness, and the gentle reader's desires, are chastised alike. What has happened to Johnny? The question leads into a display of parodic power, unleashed in the accents of border balladry:

> Perhaps, with head and heels on fire,
> And like the very soul of evil,
> He's galloping away, away,
> And so he'll gallop on for aye,
> The bane of all that dread the devil.

John Wilson clearly doubted whether a comic poem on the theme of mental deficiency could be in good taste, and many readers share some unease. But the embarrassment the poem can generate arises from a calculated decision to close the distance between reader and character, using that bumbling but artful narrator as intermediary—a narrator who holds the reader by one hand and Johnny by the other insisting that we meet. There is also a strange equivalence between the reader's irrational feelings and those of the mother. The mother's fond pride is comically chastised, and her flights of morbid fancy while she waits for her boy's return are also treated comically—her thoughts of suicide not excepted. But when she finds her son, the narrator prods her forward to embrace him:

> And Betty sees the pony too:
> Why stand you thus good Betty Foy?
> It is no goblin, 'tis no ghost,
> 'Tis he whom you so long have lost,
> He whom you love, your idiot boy.
>
> She looks again—her arms are up—

> She screams—she cannot move for joy;
> She darts as with a torrent's force,
> She almost has o'erturned the horse,
> And fast she holds her idiot boy.

It is comic writing of true brilliance, but also of warmth: a comedy of feeling in which the comic power becomes, after Shakespeare's manner, celebratory. *The Idiot Boy* requires participation in the feelings it presents. A subject is chosen by the poet in the full knowledge that his reader will expect certain kinds of distanced (and illicit) gratification: instead, another and more salutary experience is presented. A poet, Wordsworth also told Wilson, should represent feelings to his readers 'which there is reason to believe they would be better and more moral beings if they did sympathize with': until one does so, this poem may be read with more than common dislike, but to give to the reading public 'new compositions of feeling, to render their feelings *more sane*' cannot be the work of an hour. Only the reader willing to share in the joy of an idiot boy and his feckless mother will be capable of appreciating this poem: it is a carefully selected needle's eye.

'Satire', as Swift discovered, 'is a sort of Glass, wherein Beholders do generally discover every body's Face but their Own', which is why any true ironist, whose concern is to disclose to the reader the refluxes of his own nature, ultimately finds that satire is of little assistance. What the true ironist, suspicious of Swift's corrosive irony, will wish to employ is a mode unrecognizable as satirical, in which the expected accoutrements of satire (wit, point, epigram, invective) have been removed, and only the efficaceous elements of Swift's method—his employment of masks, his reversals of perspective, his techniques of betrayal—are present. In *Lyrical Ballads*, Wordsworth's techniques include some learned from Swift, and some, surely, unfathered. One finds disturbances of tone, the refusal of story, the rupture of decorum; the deployment of paradox and tautology as a method of sending one back into the text in search of something one has missed; the frustration of coyly teased expectations; the subjection of the reader to moral disturbances; the satire of feeling in the service of feeling; the tantalizing dither between sociology and romance; the stepping into the poem and out of his story; the button-holing and the self-mockery; and a range of parodic modes, from the most oblique to exuberant burlesque. Almost all of these features have been recognized in Wordsworth criticism. My point in cataloguing them in this manner is this: they evidence not only irony, but irony of a peculiar richness, including indeed most of the features held to be characteristic of Romantic Irony. Yet there is nothing in Wordsworth's work of the Romantic ironist's 'infinite absolute negativity' (in Hegel's phrase)—nothing of that pathological retreat from commitment of all kinds, to which in Kiekegaard's analysis the Romantic ironist was prey. Wordsworth's irony is deployed in the service of a precise sense of moral and existential health, and indeed a precise sense of historical situation. It is 'mastered' irony.

In *The Thorn* and *Old Man Travelling*, the ironist's scrutiny is applied to nothing less than the operations of Imagination. *The Thorn* begins with three images, laboriously described by a narrator who (according to the poet's note of 1800) is to be imagined as a retired sea-captain of loquacious disposition and tenacious imagination: a thorn tree, a pond, and a heap of moss. One cannot walk five minutes on any elevated tract of English moorland without encountering three such items 'not three yards from the path', but to this sublimely ordinary collation fifty-five lines of exact description are devoted. Mary Jacobus identified a number of analogues for this particular image-cluster, analogues which suggest that Wordsworth chose these particular images because he could rely upon his reader associating them with a particular theme, that of infanticide.[1] He allows his narrator to dwell on them with a lugubrious suggestiveness throughout the opening stanzas. The thorn is described—quite gratuitously—as 'Not higher than a two year's child'; as looking as though it had never been young; as being hung with mosses which are not merely 'melancholy' but also capable of harbouring a 'plain and manifest intent | To drag it to the ground'. Near the thorn is a muddy pond, measured by our meticulous guide, who finds it to be (one is slyly given to understand) long enough to accommodate a body of such dimensions as might equally have been hanged on such a thorn, and buried beneath the nearby heap of moss, which though

> So fresh in all its beauteous dyes,
> Is like an infant's grave in size,
> As like as like can be ...

Something like an infant's grave 'in size' is presumably *equally* like—in that respect—a buried treasure chest, a favourite pet or a carpetbag. Only

---

1   Jacobus, 241–4.

that triple 'like' lends a suggestion of substance to mere dimensions.

There is in *The Prelude* an equally well-known image cluster. It occurs in Book 13 in the passage on the 'spots of time', where Wordsworth recalls a solitary vigil, a little before his father's death, during which 'the single sheep and the one blasted tree | And the bleak music of that old stone wall' were his 'companions'. In retrospect, these simple objects become valued indices of feeling and memorials of a state of being: they acquire, also, a power—or become the hiding-place of power. Nonetheless, they remain unmistakably themselves. One of the (as usual) slightly dissonant explanations Wordsworth gave of the origins of *The Thorn* is that having seen a thorn in impressive atmospheric conditions he asked himself what his imagination could contrive to make it as permanently impressive as it was at that moment. The 'captain' is his means and his representative. He is as like the poet as he is unlike, with only a slightly more 'adhesive' imagination—reluctant to let things go until they are well-coated (or in the critical cant, 'over-determined') by the projection onto them of human fears and dreads.

There is sometimes a tendency to take the Captain at his own estimate: as, in some sense, a reliable witness, or a faithful observer. Paul Sheats, for instance, complains that 'His refusal to move from fact to surmise becomes petty before her unceasing pain'.[1] Yet his role in the poem, if we attend to what he says, is rather to blur the distinctions between fact and surmise. His motive is not to bear witness to a story, but to persuade his listener (the listener within the poem who interjects at stanzas VIII, X, and XX his urgent questions as to 'wherefore', 'what' and 'why') to understand his data *as though* it told a story. 'Now would you see this aged thorn, | This pond and beauteous hill of moss ...' (VI); 'But if you'd gladly view the spot | The spot to which she goes; | The heap ... the pond ... the thorn ...' (IX); 'But to the thorn, and to the pond | Which is a little step beyond, | I wish that you would go' (X). Wordsworth's elderly navigator, like Coleridge's, has strange power of speech, and a strange narrative teleology. That these images are significant, and that what they signify is terrible, and that the woman herself is terrible ('I never heard of such as dare | Approach the spot when she is there') are conclusions towards which the auditor, in whom anxious questions have been implanted that will and must find resolution in a story, is insidiously compelled.

---

1   Sheats, 200.

Coleridge and Byron both took *The Thorn* to be about a deserted mother who murdered her child, and thought it tediously told. Indeed the history of the poem's interpretation says something *both* about Wordsworthian understatement *and* about the strength of our pre-established codes of decision. For the point is carefully, if quietly, made that 'If a child was born or no | There's no one knows, as I have said' (XV). It is by the weight of the narrator's obsessional dreads, and the collective testimony (however conflicting) of the superstitious villagers, that we are led to miss the ironic counterpoint between what is said in stanza XV and the horrors of stanza XX:

> I cannot tell; but some will say
> She hanged her baby on the tree,
> Some say she drowned it in the pond,
> *Which is a little step beyond,*
> But all and each agree,
> The little babe was buried there,
> Beneath that hill of moss so fair.

That the only 'fact' in this stanza is in the line here italicized, is a point almost every reader misses on first acquaintance with the poem, though the poem's repetitions are deliberately foregrounded so that we will wrestle with their meanings. The demurral of stanza XV was itself followed by a characteristic 'But', introducing an irrelevant yet somehow sinister piece of information (the kind of information which becomes 'evidence' as the imagination completes the circle of sublime horrors it is busy inscribing on this scene):

> But some remember well,
> That Martha Ray about this time
> Would up the mountain often climb.

Modulation from the conjectured to the irrefutable is skilfully done: we are played upon in such a way that the fact of the woman's misery becomes sufficient proof of her guilt.

Certainly the poem shows, as Wordsworth said, 'the general laws by which superstition acts upon the mind'. But it is also about how the mind adds up. As in Henry James's tale of a governess engaged in a struggle with demons for the souls of her charges, where we can never be sure whether the governess is telling the truth, whether the children are demonically possessed or not, whether or not there are any ghosts,

Wordsworth leaves us to work out for ourselves the status of the 'facts' in the poem. His object, as John Danby so provocatively suggested, is that we should become aware not only of what we are judging, but of what we are judging with.[1] It is a poem, above all, about story-telling. It is about the manner in which a community (that within the poem, and that being introduced to the community in the act of reading) can be induced to connect a series of dots into a recognizable outline and then believe in the outline they have made. The consequence in this case is that a number of kindly folk conceive a collective fear of a forsaken woman and ostracize her for twenty years. The same 'general laws' burn witches, try people for constructive treason, and institute pogroms.

While hermeneutically the poem is an ironic enquiry into the workings of the human mind (the narrator's, the poet's, and the reader's), existentially it is a stark presentation of isolated pain. For all the villagers who occupy themselves with what this woman may have done, there is none, it seems, who concerns himself with what she is. Wordsworth's anger with society, and his compassion for (and identification with) its outcasts, may be several layers deep in this poem, but they are still its motive force: they occasion the ironic strategies which turn anger into art. The poem asks, in effect, which of us, when confronted with human events of this kind, is able to look steadily at the subject when the subject 'looks at you again'. The evasion of humanity is exactly the issue: the Captain is an ironically scrutinized portrait of the *spectator ab extra*, which Coleridge—who was irony-blind as far as Wordsworth's poems went—perversely, and in a classic case of projection (there are no more credible *people* in Coleridge's poems than in Shelley's) supposed Wordsworth to be.[2]

That is why *Old Man Travelling: Animal Tranquillity and Decay, a Sketch* must have those final lines which explain with painful literalism (about as far from matter-of-factness as could be) *why* the old man was travelling, and which Wordsworth later dropped (or re-dropped, since the earliest manuscript fragment originally ended with 'what the old man hardly feels').

1   *The Simple Wordsworth*, 38.
2   All in all, 'The Thorn' may be the most significant and sophisticated experiment in the 1798 volume. I have enlarged on this reading in 'Old Salts, Elderly Navigators, or What You Will: Writing the Romantic Reader', *The CEA Critic* 74:2–3 (2012). And Nathaniel Hawthorne, I feel sure, founded his famous 'formula of alternative possibilies' on this tale about, well, a hawthorn.

> The little hedge-row birds,
> That peck along the road, regard him not.
> He travels on, and in his face, his step,
> His gait, is one expression; every limb,
> His look and bending figure, all bespeak
> A man who does not move with pain, but moves
> With thought—He is insensibly subdued
> To settled quiet: he is one by whom
> All effort seems forgotten, one to whom
> Long patience has such mild composure given,
> That patience now doth seem a thing, of which
> He hath no need. He is by nature led
> To peace so perfect, that the young behold
> With envy, what the old man hardly feels.
> —I asked him whither he was bound, and what
> The object of his journey; he replied
> 'Sir! I am going many miles to take
> A last leave of my son, a mariner,
> Who from a sea-fight has been brought to Falmouth,
> And there is dying in an hospital.'

Mary Jacobus, speaking for many readers, found it incongruous that the old man 'should emerge from his animal tranquillity to tell a human story' (Jacobus, 180). It is made still more incongruous in 1800 when the title *Old Man Travelling* gives way to the subtitle alone, so that the man's 'travelling' is still more unexpected. The incongruity is with all that is implied by 'a sketch'. The shorter poem, in which the old man is seen but not heard, is certainly beautiful (one only has to pause at the fourteenth line to experience an extraordinary aesthetic accomplishment), but the Wordsworth who wrote *Lyrical Ballads* was concerned crucially with 'men as they are men within themselves', rather than men as they apt to appear to practitioners of the picturesque.

That this old man should be 'insensibly subdued | To settled quiet', that by him all effort should 'seem forgotten', and that patience should 'seem a thing, of which | He hath no need' does indeed 'sketch' a state devoutly to be wished. One can sympathize with a wandering poet, all-too-familiar with things as they are, wishing that is how things were. The speaker's speculation about the old man's insensibility reaches its complacent and tonally hypnotic extreme in the closing line of the poem in its truncated state:

> He is by nature led
> To peace so perfect, that the young behold
> With envy, what the old man hardly feels.

The irony of this is that it is true. He does 'hardly feel' such peace, for
everything after the dash elaborates the inspired fiction of line six. The
old man's vision-disrupting speech also involves a stylistic rupture, one
that Wordsworth as editor, after 1802, found he could not live with. But
these lines are of the essence of the *Lyrical Ballads* poetry. Such shifts of
tone, throughout the work of 1798, are used to signal shifts from illusion
to illumination, and to tease the reader out of passivity so that he will, in
Wordsworth's term 'grapple' with the poem.

It is the mark of a great ironist that his structures are disposable: that
he is willing to mar his finest rhetoric with an appearance of bathos if
such prodigal decreation (a Schlegelian notion) serves a deeper per-
ception. 'The romantic ironist', Irving Babbitt says (in a comment on
Don Juan, 3.107–111), 'shatters the illusion wantonly. It is as though he
would inflict upon the reader the disillusion from which he has himself
suffered.'[1] It is a perceptive comment on the kind of Romantic Irony rep-
resented by Tieck, and of course by Sterne: the Romantic irony which
emphasizes the artificiality of artifice, and suspends Coleridge's willing
suspension of disbelief.[2] Romantic Irony in this sense has two manifes-
tations. First, it perpetually breaks down the sense of order and value
which the work of art is in danger of erecting ('danger' because the
ironist is peculiarly anxious to retain his sense of the ineluctable flux of
perception) by insisting that it, and any particular ethical or metaphysical
orientation on which it may seem to be predicated, are after all illusory
and fabricated. Second, it effects an opposition between the writer and
his work, with the writer constantly intruding to the apparent detriment
of his artefact. It was this factor in the work of Sterne that the Germans
particularly admired and emulated, and the tradition they thereby passed

---

1   Irving Babbitt, *Rousseau and Romanticism* (Boston and NY: Houghton Mifflin,
1919, 265.
2   There are more 'paradigms' of Romantic Irony than are identified in Anne Mellor's
English Romantic Irony (1980), or even in David Simpson's *Irony and Authority in
English Poetry* (1979). My brief and elementary adumbration of these paradigms in
'Romantic Irony and Existential Engagement: Continental Theory and the English
Poets', *Acta Universitatis Lodziensis* 66 (1980) 3–26 was slightly revised from a short
section of my unpublished PhD dissertation, University of East Anglia (1971).

on becomes in due course Brecht's alienation. Romantic Irony is directed not only at everyday illusions, but at the operations of the illusion-making faculty at its most self-aware.

What appears to be bathos in *Old Man Travelling*, I would argue, is quite as tactical as the disruptions in *Simon Lee* and *The Idiot Boy*. The objective, as in *The Thorn*, is to scrutinize the duplicities of imagination. This is, to use Charles Lamb's phrase, a poem about the mind perceiving itself in the act of passing a fiction upon itself. It is a poem, too, in which a sentimental and exploitative imagination (perceiving solely through its own needs) is undercut by a humane—rather than merely aesthetic—intelligence. The deepest irony is that which probes the ironist's own illusions. Here, Wordsworth finds himself using the old man as an object of imaginative reverie, which may be more interesting than using such figures as objects of condescension but is no less culpable, given the aesthetic on which the *Lyrical Ballads* are built. One can find the 'sketch' moving as a fine evocation of a certain kind of imagined peace (the figure has the serenity, almost, of the visionary Danish boy) but in order to become a lyrical ballad, the poem clearly had to be changed. In Gothic writing the portrait walks from its frame. Here the sketched object speaks. Wordsworth is recalled to a world in which centres of selfhood other than his own, live and move and have their being. The poem ends in the shock of recollection of a fractured world, that 'world where in the end we find our happiness or not at all'. The shock is conveyed not least in the socio-political gulf expressed in the single word 'Sir!'—a word speaking across the class gulf to the reader in numerous of these ballads as a reminder of the gentry's ability to discount human suffering (I am revising this in late 2014, four and a half years into the biggest sacrifice of working lives in the interests of the gentry perpetrated in England in my lifetime). It is also conveyed in the abrupt rupture of the reflective style. The old man's speech is simple, but strong enough to discipline the egotistical sublime.

The preface Wordsworth felt unable to write, he says in the one he did write, would have included an account of revolutions in society, which would have involved in turn an examination of 'in what manner language and the human mind react on each other'. Such an explanation might have robbed a poem like *The Thorn* of its power to tease us into thought upon precisely such questions. As it is, we are at liberty to regard it as a piece of feeble pathetic fallacy, or as an ironic masterpiece; and to see *Old Man Travelling* as a fine fragment vulgarized or as completing the critique of the Picturesque begun in *Lines left upon a seat in Yew-Tree* and preparing for its apotheosis in the final piece of blank verse in the volume.

It is not often that one can show a poem or a body of poems responsible for reforming the world. Wordsworth's confessed admiration for Joseph Fawcett's anti-war poetry, of which *Salisbury Plain* and *The Ruined Cottage, Brougham Castle* and *The White Doe* are developments, and for Ebenezer Elliott 'the Corn-Law rhymer', reveals something of a predilection in himself for what is termed 'relevance'. His ballads may have done less than Shelley's rhetorical performances to inspire working class radicalism, but they did rather more to underwrite liberal Chartism's sense of the dignity of the common man. He inspired—alongside Pestalozzi (whose wife translated 'We are Seven')—English and American educational and social reformers. His poems are poems of inclusion in which the barriers created by disability, derangement, idiocy, enfeeblement, destitution, mendicancy, criminality, fecklessness, age, infancy or youth, dissolve. Through the medium of Dorothea Lynde Dix, Joel Pace has shown, Wordsworth's perceptions of mental derangement, enfeeblement and idiocy (in 'The Idiot Boy' and 'The Mad Mother') contributed to the reform of mental care in every part of America.[1] Despite the emphases of literary criticism, Wordsworth's most characteristic, mission-exemplifying, poetry is not in *The Prelude*; it is, as *The Prelude* itself makes explicit, the work most immediately inspired by his change from studying man as he is in Godwininian theory to 'men [of both sexes] as they are men within themselves'. His explorations of the pathos of humanity, in 1798 and 1800, amplified as they were in 1807, not only open up a vision of human possibility, but precipitated—in the imaginations of Gaskell, George Eliot, Hawthorne, Dickens and Hardy—a fundamental democratization of man's perception of man.

Are these poems of the escape from history? I think not. It remained, when the volume was compiled in 1798, to append *The Poem upon the Wye*, which poem expands the Paineite sentiments of *It is the first mild day of March* into a fuller exposition of the doctrine of Nature on which Wordsworth's defence of the people has been based.

---

1   See Joel Pace, 'Wordsworth and America, reception and reform', in Stephen Gill, ed., *The Cambridge Companion to Wordsworth* (Cambridge University Press, 2003) 230–43 and "Wordsworth in America: Publication, Reception, Literary Influence, and Social Reform, 1802–1850" (doctoral dissertation, Oxford, 1999).

Chapter 6: 'Nature' in 'The Poem upon the Wye'

Writing to Catherine Clarkson in January 1815, by when his sympathy with Jacobins (or druids) was a distant memory, Wordsworth repudiated with some heat the notion that he could be termed 'a worshipper of Nature'. The cause of such errors, he insists, is reading 'in coldheartedness' what was merely 'a passionate expression uttered incautiously in the Poem upon the Wye.'[1] Denying, quite implausibly, that there is anything 'Spinosistic' even in his 'simile of the Boy and the Shell' Wordsworth's letter promptly runs into difficulties: 'Where does she [Patty Smith] gather that the Author of the Excursion looks upon nature and God as the same? He does not indeed consider the Supreme Being [*sic!*] as bearing the same relation to the universe as a watchmaker bears to a watch ... there is nothing so injurious as the perpetually talking about *making* by God.' To his own child, Wordsworth says, he has taught the less injurious explanation that God is 'not like his flesh which he could touch; but more like his thoughts'. The child, seeing how 'the wind was tossing the fir trees, and the sky and light were dancing about in their dark branches', exclaims '"There's a bit of him I see it there!"'. And with this perception of God as infinitely fine matter, the *spiritus* or *pneuma* of the ancients, the fond father finds no fault.

It is perfectly reasonable for Wordsworth to deny that the opinions of the speaker in his poem on *The Wye* are his own. When Stephen Gill remarks that 'it is surprising that he should represent 1793 as the time when Nature was all in all and 1798 as the moment when he felt most at one with the cause of humanity' (Gill 153–4) no one can doubt what he

---

1 To Catherine Clarkson, January 1815, *MY*, 2: 188. This epistolary short title for Lines writen a few miles above Tintern Abbey' is a good one, but the one printed in the 1800 *Lyrical Ballads* was perhaps better still: 'On revisiting the Wye' has the great merit of specifying what the poem is about. In 1817 he referred to his 'Lines on the Wye' (*MY*, 2: 385) and in 1823 to his 'poem on the river Wye' (*LY*, 1: 237). The common element is perhap simply 'The Wye'. Had he stuck to his guns we might have been spared some of the sillier readings of the poem. Following Wordworth's example I refer to the poem as *The Wye, On revisiting the Wye, Lines on the Wye*, and *The Poem upon the Wye*.

means, yet there is no reason why the feelings of the anonymous speaker of this poem, with an equally anonymous sister, should correspond to Wordsworth's own, at any date, let alone on any particular date—for instance 13 July 1793. Few readers in 1798 (perhaps at any time before 1983) could have attached any biographical meaning to the line describing the speaker five years before as 'more like a man flying from something that he dreads', though within the codes of lyric utterance it implies clearly enough that nature enthusiasts may be driven by strange fits of passion. No untaught reader of *any* date can be expected to suppose that by 13 July 1793 Wordsworth has acquired, through justification of the terror and regicide, a *dread*ful burden of historical guilts that he needs to escape from.[1] And while he undoubtedly had, it would make no difference to the poem *as poem* if such guilts were acquired as late, say, as 1795, or not at all. But with that caveat, this chapter will suppose, like every other reading of recent date, that the speaker of *The Poem upon the Wye* is William Wordsworth and that his experience is relevant.

Wordsworth's poem *On revisiting the Wye*, in its concluding address to a nameless sister, presents the nameless poet as one who

> so long
> A worshipper of Nature, hither came,
> Unwearied in that service: rather say
> With warmer love, oh! With far deeper zeal
> Of holier love.

Passionate, certainly. But incautious? As the conclusion of some sixty lines of deliberation, rooted in the poem's most 'Spinosistic' experience in lines 94–103, one might rather find the utterance deeply considered, timely, and in the contemporary sense, necessary. Does the heat of Wordsworth's 1815 denial affirm the alignments implied in the timely utterance of 1798?

My purpose is to examine the historicity of Wordsworth's conclusion, in a manner which involves some argument with the influential but anachronistic approaches of Jerome McGann, Marjorie Levinson and John Barrell to the same poem and to many of its lines. What some have

---

1   'It is the knowledge of his complicity in an act of terror that now prompts Wordsworth to describe himself, in a rather shadowy phrase, as 'more like a man | Flying from something that he dreads, than one | Who sought the thing he loved.' David Bromwich, *A Choice of Inheritance: Self and Community from Edmund Burke to Robert Frost* (Cambridge MA: Harvard UP, 1989), 72.

read as a recantation of the politics underlying the Jacobin poems of human suffering is rather, when read in its own moment, a retrospective articulation of the theory underlying that politics and those poems. I shall not stress the point here, but an admirer of Iolo's bardic triads would have found the poem's philosophy both cogent and familiar, an apotheosis of liberal druidism, that fashionable blend of Unitarianism and nature feeling. The poem grounds the future work of one whose poetic agenda (as Thomas McFarland points out) will pointedly and repeatedly, in poetry and in prose, replace the expected, hieratic and traditional triad of 'God, Man, and Nature' with a newly and provocatively centred triad, 'Man, Nature and Society' (McFarland, 121).

The construction of an Idealist Wordsworth, Cartesian / Hegelian in his thinking, concerned more with imagination than with nature or history, was as David Bromwich has suggested, largely a work of the sixties and seventies.[1] The further and even more fictive construction, upon that doubtful base, of something called a 'Romantic Ideology' in which the Romantic Poet is *in flight from* the ruins of history, occupied much of the eighties.[2] To describe Wordsworth's personal negotiation with the competing ideologies of British empiricism, Enlightenment materialism, native benevolence and nascent Idealism would involve difficult discriminations between Stoic, Newtonian, Leibnizian, Priestleyan and Darwinian strands in Wordsworth's intellectual texture, but to dub the outcome either Cartesian-Hegelian as new historicists tended to do, or as 'Hartley transcendentalized by Coleridge', in de Selincourt's famously flip reduction,[3] will not do.

1   David Bromwich, 'The French Revolution and "Tintern Abbey"', *Raritan* 10:3 (1991) 1–23, 7.
2   Unlike Kenneth R. Johnston's germinal essay on 'The Politics of Tintern Abbey' (*TWC*, 14:1 (1983), 6–14), other revisionist readings of the poem have situated it within intellectual domains ideologically far removed from that occupied by William Wordsworth at the moment in question. Jerome McGann, in *Romantic Ideology* (1983) saw *The Poem upon the Wye* as enacting the Romantic flight from history into an autonomous Kantian-Hegelian realm of imagination. Marjorie Levinson saw the theme of the poem as the 'escape from cultural values', arguing that 'its primary action is the suppression of the social': *Wordsworth's Great Period Poems* (Cambridge: Cambridge University Press, 1986), 16, 37, 91 and passim. Both studies preceded David Simpson's needful warning in 1987 that there is 'no such thing [in Wordsworth's writing] as a private or individual imagination capable of complete and entire self-determination' (*Wordsworth's Historical Imagination*, 1).
3   *The Prelude*, ed. E de Selincourt, lxix.

The Glad Preamble (lines 1–23ᵃ)

The impressive canonical lines of *The Poem upon the Wye*'s glad pre-
amble are so familiar, so mesmerizing, that they do indeed serve to con-
ceal their underlying ideology, though whether that ideology is the one
detected by Jerome McGann is another matter. Crowded with barely per-
ceptible metaphor, they build a bridge between landscape and psyche,
while the landscape itself becomes the perfect image of a tranquil mind.
That 'mind', or 'neutral intellect' as Keats would call it, appears to pos-
sess what the observer lacks and is in quest of, and finds no trace of in
the human world; namely, Liberty. In all this landscape, the observer
finds nothing fixed in its own nature, or in isolation, or warped perma-
nently into economic orbits. The implied metaphors (hardly metaphors,
little lines of sportive thought run wild?) define his quest as an escape
not from history but from cultural definition. Amid these cliffs 'which
on a *wild* secluded scene impress | Thoughts of more deep seclusion' he
finds also:

> These plots of cottage-ground, these orchard-tufts,
> Which, at this season, with their unripe fruits,
> Among the woods and copses *lose themselves*,
> Nor with their green and simple hue disturb
> The *wild* green landscape. Once again I see
> These hedgerows, *hardly hedgerows, little lines*
> *Of sportive wood run wild*; these pastoral farms
> *Green to the very door*; and wreathes of smoke
> Sent up, in silence from among the trees ... (my italics)

Marjorie Levinson's biopsy, in *Wordsworth's Great Period Poems*, takes
one half line of this passage as its first tissue sample. Since Wordsworth's
'hardly hedgerows, little lines of sportive wood run wild', with its liber-
tarian concreteness, would do little to support the Cartesian epistemology
Levinson's argument needs her to find, they become, much more ame-
nably, 'hardly hedgerows, little lines'. The poet's liberation of enclosing
hedgerows into native woodland is thus converted into abstraction, and
his polarity reversed.

   The poem, Levinson complains, presents not images of nature but
'beauteous forms'. Most readers would associate Wordsworth's 'forms'
with the way in which he uses the term elsewhere, meaning something
alive and sentient, natural beings, each of which, as Diderot said in the

Rêve d'Alembert, 'has the happiness or unhappiness which is proper to it',[1] or forms as in Robinet's 'formes de l'être'.[2] Levinson, however, gives the term a gloss wholly at odds with Wordsworth's lyrical of poetry of 1798. In this mischievous, perhaps tongue-in-cheek reading, even the lines 'Our meddling intellect | Mis-shapes the beauteous forms of things; | We murder to dissect' (where 'murder' and 'dissection' *require* the supposition that forms are alive and sentient) are pressed into the service of 'cautionary idealism' (43). Wordsworth claims that 'These beauteous forms, | Through a long absence, have not been to me, | As is a landscape to a blind man's eye',[3] and that he has drawn from them 'in hours of weariness *sensations* sweet', but Levinson's reconfigured Wordsworth has no dealings with 'sensations'. She stops this quotation at 'a blind man's eye' on which bereft organ she hangs a disquisition on the poem's 'Cartesian epistemology' (46).[4]

Fifty-six years after Wordsworth, Henry David Thoreau, in his American Grasmere, described his own hermitage in phrases which suggest a much closer reading of Wordsworth's opening lines. It is not merely the repeated emphasis upon seclusion and the wild that prefigures *Walden*. Wordsworth's orchard tufts which can 'lose themselves', his hedgerows which can revert to 'lines of sportive wood run wild', his farms 'green to the very door', put one in mind of Thoreau's home where

1   Cited from H. W. Piper, *The Active Universe* (London: Athlone Press, 1962), 24.

2   *Considérations philosophiques de la gradation naturelle des formes de l'être*, 1768.

3   This 'blind man's eye' is something of a reading block, especially if one thinks of Milton, which takes one nowhere. It is more helpful to remember that, as Mark Booth points out in 'Written and Writing Bards in Eighteenth-century Lyric' (*Modern Language Quarterly*. 53: 4 [1992] 393–408), many Celtic harpers were blind, like the still-famous Irishman Turlough O'Carolan (d. 1783) and the Welshman John Parry, whose visit to Cambridge inspired Gray to finish his stalled draft of *The Bard* (400). Wordsworth may have been alluding quietly to this condition, though it is even likelier that he is thinking of Ossian's (that is, Macpherson's) blindness to nature.

4   Descartes is perhaps brought in because, as Levinson explains in her later essay on 'The New Historicism', whereas the materialism of the eighteenth century was 'revolutionary, demotic', Cartesian idealism 'provided the *ancien régime* with its onto-epistemological model' (in Levinson, ed., *Rethinking Historicism: Critical Readings in Romantic History* [Oxford: Blackwell, 1989], 25). He figures in Levinson's reading, therefore, to block any suspicion that *The Poem upon the Wye* is itself rooted in half a century of rampant materialism. Levinson's later retraction, based on her belated recognition that Wordsworth is a Spinozist, claims that this was not known to Romanticists in 1986. See '"A Motion and a Spirit": Romancing Spinoza', *Studies in Romanticism*, 46:4 (2007) 367–408.

'unfenced Nature' reaches his '*very sills*' ('Sounds'), his field which serves as 'the connecting link between *wild and cultivated fields*', and his beans 'cheerfully returning to their wild and primitive state' ('The Bean-Field').[1] Here indeed, both writers imply, a man might follow where nature leads.

Such conjectural hermitude, in readings of the eighties, became part of Wordsworth's ideological contamination, the sign whereby his dawning apostasy is made flesh. When wreathes of smoke offer 'uncertain notice, *as might seem*, | Of vagrant dwellers in the houseless woods', the phrase 'as might seem' Levinson suggests, hypostasizes these uncertain vagrants out of existence. In the poem, however, the commas make the *notice*, not the *vagrants*, uncertain: the wreathes offer *seemingly uncertain notice* as to whether the woods are full of vagrant dwellers, as they probably were, or whether, more picturesquely, they conceal 'some hermit's cave where by his fire | The hermit sits alone'. 'Uncertain notice', to insist on the obvious, problematizes noticing: it calls attention to how the evidence of human suffering—implicit enough in 'wreathes' and to be returned to in 'the still sad music of humanity'—might be misconstrued by the wishful thinking mind as components in its own complacent landscape. A devotee of the picturesque, such as the persona dramatized and critiqued in 'Old Man Travelling', the previous blank verse utterance in the volume, might well read involuntary vagrants as voluntary hermits.[2]

In fact, neither predicament, with the sufferers open to sky and fields, seems quite so sharp when placed against the prison cells in earlier poems in *Lyrical Ballads*, in which both Wordsworth and Coleridge reflect on political injustice; or indeed the celebrated cell in Chepstow Castle, a

---

1   *Walden and Civil Disobedience: Norton Critical Edition*, ed. Owen Thomas (New York: Norton, 1966).

2   Levinson's reading imagines that Wordsworth in 1798 would have been outraged at seeing 'a national monument overrun with a morally unfixed class', that for him the abbey stood for an ideal, 'a brotherhood of the self-elect, subsidized by the whole society' and that his 'entire experience had led him to conceive of Tintern Abbey (the abbey, not the poem) as the incarnation of a social ideal' (*Period Poems*, 33, 35, 52). Stephen Gill, more pertinently, characterised Wordsworth in 1793 as himself a 'gentleman vagrant' (Gill, 153). For an authoritative, elegant, documented treatment of the condition of the Wye in 1793/98 (disposing of the largely imaginary vagrants, industrial noise, pollution and so forth that materialized in 1980s criticism) see Charles R. Rzepka's 'Pictures of the Mind: Iron and Charcoal, "Ouzy" Tides and "Vagrant Dwellers" at Tintern, 1798', in *Selected Studies in Romantic and American Literature, History, and Culture: Inventions and Interventions* (Farnham: Ashgate, 2010), 199–222.

few miles *below* Tintern, where, as Nicholas Roe points out, the regicide and republican martyr, Henry Marten, lived out his days, making it a shrine with altogether different vibrations.[1] Roe's speculation implies that the reference to vagrant dwellers and hermits conjures other itinerant victims of oppression, a hedge-school of the borders, including of course John Thelwall, a former inmate of the Tower of London, now living on the Welsh border like some Heaneyan 'inner émigré ... | Escaped from the massacre' (Seamus Heaney, *Exposure*). The relevance of Thelwall to *Lyrical Ballads* is, of course, immediate rather than conjectural. Not only does his hermitage at Llyswen Farm make an unexplained appearance in *Anecdote for Fathers*, but were one to gloss *Simon Lee* as a poem about how 'a greedy and unsocial selfishness absorbs our faculties', or *The Female Vagrant* as a poem protesting on behalf of those who 'have either been driven to America for bread, or are pining for want of it at home', or *Goody Blake and Harry Gill* as a poem noting the 'scandalously inadequate price of labour' and the 'unreasonable number of hours through which the labour of the day is protracted', or indeed the opening of *The Poem upon the Wye* itself as expressing the sentiment 'better were savage nakedness, and the dowerless freedom of his woods and caves, than the wretched mockery of such a state of civilization and refinement', one would be borrowing, in each instance, as I have been, from John Thelwall's *The Rights of Nature*.[2]

Once one admits one such martyr, others put in a claim. They might include Algernon Sidney, whose sentence for regicide—unlike Marten's— was not commuted. He died beseeching God's favour for

1   *The Politics of Nature: Wordsworth and Some Contemporaries* (Macmillan, 1992), 130–4. Roe's civil war association has been confirmed by David Chandler's linking of this passage to Thomas Fuller's *History of the Worthies of England* (1662) in which occurs the phrase 'civil war is a vagrant'. Chandler's further suggestion, in 'Vagrancy smoked Out', *Romanticism on the Net* (1998), that Wordsworth associated 'vagrant dwellers' with the civil war of his own 1793 feelings, is powerfully apt. Damian Walford Davies, in '"Some uncertain notice": the Hermit of 'Tintern Abbey'", *Notes and Queries* 241 (1996) 422–4, recalls the sixth century Celtic Hermit-King Tewdrig the Blessed, who was summoned out of retirement to face a Saxon invasion: Wordsworth's prolonged and extensive identification (along with Cottle, Southey and Thelwall) with Celtic resistance, supports this association.

2   *The Rights of Nature against the Usurpations of Establishments*, 3rd edition (London, 1796), 7, 8, 16–17, 46. Wordsworth owed Thelwall an allusion, having been described as 'Alfoxden's musing tenant' in Thelwall's *Lines written at Bridgewater, in Somersetshire, on the 27th of July, 1797* (*Poems, Chiefly Written in Retirement*, 1801).

'that OLD CAUSE in which I was from youth engaged'[1] and lamented, in terms which must have seemed newly minted in the 1790s, that he had lived to see 'the liberty which we hoped to establish oppressed ... the best of our nation made a prey to the worst ... the people enslaved [and] no man safe, but by such evil and infamous means, as flattery and bribery' (*Discourses on Government*, xi). Sidney, whose bust was carried in procession in revolutionary Paris remained for Wordsworth one of the great libertarian martyrs in his sonnets of 1802, and his *Discourses* are fundamental to every strand of libertarian politics in England, France and America in the 18th Century. I mention this because the *Discourses* were republished in 1795—happily enough on 14 July—by Wordsworth's own publisher, Joseph Johnson. Another such martyr who makes a claim to be heard, is one William Hodgson, whose translation of the Girondin 'bible', the Baron d'Holbach's *The System of Nature; or, the Laws of the Moral and Physical World*, also published in London in 1795, announced itself as the work of a man 'now confined in Newgate for sedition, under a sentence of two years imprisonment'.

If there were an Abbey in this poem—and thanks to what Thomas McFarland called the clamour of absence it is now more than ever necessary to insist that in *Lines on the Wye* THERE IS NO ABBEY—it might serve to remind us, except that Wordsworth had not yet written Book 9 of *The Prelude*, that the poet's political tutorials with Michel Beaupuy took place near a ruined convent on the banks of the Loire (*Prelude*, 9.469–532). Wordsworth regrets the ruination of that convent mainly because it offered hospitality to travellers. The passage also associates the notion of a hermitage with ideas of refuge from political injustice. Their talk in this ruin was both Sidneyan (of 'chartered liberties' and the people's right to frame their laws) and d'Holbachian (of 'earth's wish', when rid of royal turpitude and other vices, 'to recompense the patient child of toil'). The two sentiments are connected, and always have been, in republican discourse. Liberty and Justice, to Sidney and Vane, were emanations of Nature. America began the renovation of the political world, as Paine tartly reminded Burke in his slyest dig at the theorist of sublimity, because its landscape 'generates and encourages great ideas'. The 'mighty objects' surrounding man 'act upon his mind by enlarging it, and he partakes of the greatness he beholds'.[2] One might therefore point to

---

1   Algernon Sidney, *Discourses on Government* (London: Joseph Johnson, 1795), xix.
2   Paine, *The Rights of Man* (Harmondsworth: Penguin Books, 1984), 159–60.

numerous texts as annexes to Wordsworth's signally abbeyless poem *On revisiting the Wye*. Not that this poem, when considered *in situ* as concluding a series of Jacobin sketches, needs any such extrinsic references. In a volume whose most audible voices are either vagrant or homeless or close to it—the Female Vagrant, the Mad Mother, Martha Ray, Goody Blake—the echo of that 'houseless poverty', over which (in *King Lear*) monarchy had taken all too little care, gives a sharper note to the still sad music of humanity than the ahistoricism of the 1980s cared to hear.

The 'System' of Nature

William Hodgson in his Newgate cell is relevant not only because, as a political prisoner, he might have envied the inviolate retirement of either a vagrant or a hermit. True, his introduction complains Rousseauistically that 'Man, is in almost every climate, a poor degraded captive ... whom his inhuman gaolers have never permitted to see the light of day' (xxii) and the work he translated does conclude with d'Holbach's recommendation to disappointed patriots: 'If thine unjust country refuse thee happiness ... withdraw thyself from it in silence, and never disturb it'.[1] He does, therefore, effect a bridge between immurement and self-immurement or hermitude. But there are deeper reasons for regarding d'Holbach as not merely *one* of innumerable 'absences' which might, if one chose, be made pertinent to the 'historical moment' of this poem, but as one of several felt 'presences' within it, whose exclusion from 'new historical' discussions of it is peculiarly eloquent.

The terms of Wordsworth's poetry which for many readers convey its peculiar facility for dealings with interactions of the human mind and nature's living forms (and all of nature's forms are for Wordsworth living) are 'motions', 'impress', 'active', 'presence', 'impulse', 'sense'. Wordsworth, in *The Wye* and in the work that follows during the Goslar exile of the following winter, famously describes the interaction of mind and nature in ways which leave one in some doubt as to whether matter is being spiritualized or mind materialized. In transactions with nature, nature's living forms enter 'far into the mind' or 'people' the mind; lakes lie upon the mind 'even with a weight of pleasure'; the mind responds, like lakes, to 'skyey influencings'; and so forth. For such competent read-

---

1 D'Holbach, *The System of Nature; or, the Laws of the Moral and Physical World*, tr. William Hodgson, 4 vols (London: 1795-96), 4: 681.

ers as Hazlitt, Shelley, De Quincey and Pater, this language embodies a literal faith in 'the life of things': Wordsworth's 'forms' are not Platonic entities found in the mind; they enter the mind and take possession of it. It is only because they are substantial that the mind can be 'steadied' by them, and they can blend with what Wordsworth called 'the blood & vital juices' of our very material minds (*PrW*, 1: 113). The question that arises in *The Poem upon the Wye* and *The Two-Part Prelude* is how mind and matter can interact unless they share one substance: and the way in which Wordsworth deals with the matter, while expressed in a fashion unlikely to alarm Coleridge too greatly, is learned from intellectual connections made long before he met Coleridge.

To understand the derivation of Wordsworth's language, and its political significance, one has to turn away from McGann's 'German ideology', that idealizing compound of Coleridge and Hegel, towards those writers in whom Wordsworth himself, at the time in question, and those with whom he associated, were demonstrably interested, and in whom Wordsworth had been interested from the moment he began developing a language to describe the life of Nature in the revisions of *An Evening Walk*.[1] In the twenty-eight years of Wordsworth's life up to the point at which he wrote *On revisiting the Wye*, natural philosophy was a cafeteria.[2] You could go for the straight pantheism of Spinoza and the druidical enthusiast Toland, where God was everything and everything was God, as Wordsworth came close to doing, not least in doodling of that region where 'all beings live with god, themselves are god' (*Prelude*, p 525). Or you could take the Newtonian view that while material elements were inert, their interactions manifest 'active principles' which represent God's agency. Or one could go further, with Leibniz, and suppose that God has lodged a portion of his own will in each particle of matter. One could believe in Volney's 'secret power which animates the universe' (Piper 22), or one could, with Diderot and Robinet, conclude that each form of being has its own sentience and sensibility. On this premise one could conclude with 'Walking' Stewart that human

1   My sense of the poem's 'historical moment' is derived initially from H. W. Piper's *The Active Universe*, enriched by Alan Bewell's *Wordsworth and the Enlightenment*, and confirmed by Nicholas Roe's *The Politics of Nature*. Where Roe emphasises the friends of liberty, I shall emphasise Priestley, the Stewarts, d'Holbach and Volney, the friends of nature *and* of liberty.

2   See H. W. Piper, and Thomas L Hankins, *Science and the Enlightenment* (Cambridge, Cambridge University Press, 1985), 6–15.

beings have a moral obligation to reverence every 'living thing'. Each time Wordsworth uses that phrase, as in his first poem in *Lyrical Ballads* (namely, *Lines left upon a Seat in a Yew-tree*), or proclaims the 'faith that every flower | Enjoys the air it breathes' (*Lines Written in Early Spring*), or says 'I would not strike a flower | As many a man would strike his horse' (Nutting MS, *Prelude*, p. 612; *CWRT* Addendun, 28) you catch the eloquence (De Quincey thought) of this man who became known as 'Walking' Stewart because, having visited India, and imbibed its reverence for created life, he walked back to Europe just in time to form part of the British Jacobin presence in Paris in 1792.[1] His ubiquitousness in the poems of 1798 may betoken other presences from that blissful dawn.

In 1777 'the philosophic Priestley', as Wordsworth called him in his *Letter to the Bishop of Llandaff*, introduced his *Disquisitions Relating to Matter and Spirit* (another Joseph Johnson title) by looking back on the hour of his own thoughtless youth. 'Like the generality of Christians in the present age', Priestley remembers, 'I had always taken it for granted, that man had a soul distinct from his body ... so intirely distinct from matter as to have no property in common with it (ix).' His argument is annotated in Horne Tooke's copy (now in the British Library) by frequent marginalia suggesting that Priestley was plagiarizing from d'Holbach's *Système de la Nature*. The problem Priestley addresses is central also to the work of the Scottish philosopher Dugald Stewart. In a wonderfully wry passage of his *Elements of the Philosophy of the Human Mind* (1792) Stewart looks back on the efforts of philosophers, Christian and Sceptical alike, from Locke to Priestley, to account for 'the communication which is carried on between the sentient, thinking, and active principle within us, and the material objects with which we are surrounded' (64). Stewart seems amused by what he sees as a general principle underlying 'all theories of perception', that since objects are material, and the soul immaterial, there must be 'an intermediate medium between the mind and distant objects' enabling this communication between perception and its objects. These theories, he says:

> all indicate a secret conviction in their authors, of the essential distinction between mind and matter; which, although not rendered, by reflection, sufficiently precise and satisfactory ... had yet such a degree of

---

1   Wordsworth's 'The mind of man is framed even like the breath | And harmony of music' (1805, 1: 352–3) might also owe something to John Stewart's less economical use of this metaphor in *Apocalypse of Nature*, 2 vols (London, J. Ridgway, 1792), 2: 22.

> influence upon their speculations, as to induce them to exhibit their sup-
> posed medium under as mysterious and ambiguous a form as possible,
> in order that it might remain doubtful to which of the two predicaments,
> of body or mind, they meant that it should be referred. (68)

'Predicaments' is delicious. Perception of distant objects involves two
problems. First we must assume 'something emitted from the object to
the organ of sense or some medium to intervene between the object and
organ, by means of which the former may communicate an impulse to
the latter' (the term 'impulse' he attributes particularly to Locke) (79).
Then there is the problem of how the resultant impression is commu-
nicated from 'the organ of sense' to the mind. Are we to imagine yet
another intermediate medium?

> As one body produces a change in the state of another by impulse, so it
> has been supposed, that the external object produces perception, (which
> is a change on the state of the mind,) first by some material impression
> made on the organ of sense; and secondly by some material impres-
> sion communicated from the organ to the mind *along* the nerves and
> brain. (80, my italics)

Something like this, I conclude, is what Wordsworth has in mind when he
talks in *On revisiting the Wye* of that mysterious 'language of the sense'.[1]
    Whether or not Wordsworth's spatial metaphor 'along the heart' owes
anything to Stewart's 'along ... the brain', the general stance of the
Elements, that we simply do not, and cannot know how mind consum-
mates its marriage with nature, is likely to have satisfied Wordsworth.
The depiction of mind/matter communion in *Lines on the Wye* is consist-
ent, or not inconsistent, with almost any of the gradations of material-
ism on offer, including of course, the qualified materialism of a devout
Christian, such as Priestley. As Alan Richardson's contextual research
has shown, Wordsworth's theory and practice as a poet share their his-
torical moment with rapid developments in neuro-science and with an
anti-dualist tendency in the study of human nature.[2] What the verse of
The Poem upon the Wye cannot be made to do, it seems to me, is yield
a *denial* of the materiality of mind, or of the life of *things*, or indeed—

---

1   Proper attention to Stewart is long overdue, and is likely to arrive in forthcoming
work by Mark Bruhn on Wordsworth's philosophical bearings in the mid-1990s.
2   Alan Richardson, *British Romanticism and the Science of the Mind* (Cambridge:
CUP, 2001, 67–73 and *passim*.

whatever editorial footnotes may suggest—any textual *assertion* of a transcendent deity. The *Monthly Review*, consequently, received it with outrage. In Wordsworth's poem, it complained, clearly detecting the perfidious influence of French or Ioloesque theories no longer detectable by modern critics, 'stream, sun, leaf, breeze, torrent, hill, cloud and mountain's brow' are endowed 'with powers of sensation and reflection equal to those enjoyed by ... the most refined and intellectual of his readers'. Not in this way, it proclaimed, will 'misguided mortals' be guided 'back to the precincts of a calm and rational religion' [*Monthly Review*, 66, cited Piper, 5].

Lines on the Wye is the concluding poem in a curiously godless book, one in which (in Wordsworth's contributions) the term 'God' never appears outside quotation marks, where its use represents religious sentiment among the common people. 'God' will not make an appearance in Wordsworth's poetry for some years yet, in any way which requires to be glossed other than as Shelley glosses it in *Queen Mab*, that is, as 'a pervading Spirit co-eternal with the universe'; or as d'Holbach puts it, 'the sum total of the unknown powers which animate the universe' (*System*, 3: 311). Why Wordsworth situated his meditation so close to what Levinson calls a 'national monument', while so pointedly ignoring it, even as a ruin, might indeed be explained by invoking a passage from d'Holbach's peroration:

> Let us then reconduct bewildered mortals to the altars of nature; let us destroy for them those chimaeras which their ignorant and disordered imagination has believed it was bound to elevate to her throne. Let us say to them, that there is nothing, either above or beyond nature. (3: 309, emphasis added)

I do not claim that Wordsworth's views in *The Poem upon the Wye* are the baron's: only that there is nothing in the poem to which d'Holbach could not have assented, or that is radically out of tune with the 'System of Nature' as the Jacobins imbibed it, and as Wordsworth is likely to have imbibed it, whether in his father's library in Cockermouth, or while in France with Beaupuy.[1] Baron d'Holbach, in the Newgate translation, invites his readers to 'consult nature' and 'draw our ideas from nature herself, of those objects that she contains. Let us recur to our senses,

---

1   See Wu, 74-5, and Leslie F. Chard, *Dissenting Republican: Wordsworth's Early Life and Thought in their Political Context* (The Hague: Mouton, 1972) 97–8.

which we have been made erroneously to suspect.' (1: 30). 'Nature' he defines as 'the assemblage of all the beings and motions of which we have knowledge, as well as of many others of which we know nothing, because they are inaccessible to our senses' (36). His Nature, like Leibniz's, is dynamic: 'Everything in the universe is in motion; the essence of nature is to act; and if we consider attentively its parts, we shall see that there is not a particle that enjoys absolute repose'. Even apparently static objects (as static, say, as Wordsworth's living rocks) 'are in fact only in relative or apparent rest; they experience such an imperceptible motion ... that we cannot perceive the changes they undergo' (42).

Matter, then is active. Nor can it have been put in motion (as the long superseded Leibniz and Newton supposed) by anything immaterial. 'How can a being, without extent, be moveable, and put matter in motion?' (1: 156). We have been deceived into supposing a polarity of matter and spirit. The Ancients knew better. By the word spirit they tended to designate 'a matter extremely subtle, and more *pure* than that which acts *grossly* upon our senses': essentially, spirit is a term employed to designate matter which we find imperceptible (and which of course we try to account for in the ways Dugald Stewart finds so evasive). Rather as Blake thought, 'the soul, very far from being distinguished from the body, is only the body itself, considered relatively to some of its functions' (172) and 'in man the nerves unite and lose themselves in the brain; that *intestine* [a term Ted Hughes might have enjoyed] is the true seat of feeling' (178).

What we call 'God' is a projection. D'Holbach's formulation of this must have been the most widespread and influential such formulation in the Age of Wordsworth and of Shelley and indeed of George Eliot:

> It is thus that men, in combining a great number of ideas borrowed from themselves such as those of justice, of wisdom of goodness, of intelligence, &c. have by the aid of imagination, arrived at forming a ideal whole, which they have called the Divinity. (1: 197)

The concept of God is essentially anthropomorphic (3: 299) and d'Holbach's objection to the logical inconsistency of wanting a God who is both immaterial and personal is somewhat Blakean: 'How shall we suppose a being, who hath occasion for nothing ... to have will, passions, desires? How shall we attribute anger to a being who has neither blood nor bile?' (3: 300). Along with God, of course, out goes the notion of an immaterial soul: 'The interior organ which we call our Soul is purely material ... it acquires its ideas, after the impressions which material objects successively make upon our organs, which are themselves material.' Thus d'Holbach resolves the quandary afflicting theorists of perception, without the equivocations Stewart ascribes to them.

None of this would add up to a 'politics of nature' if d'Holbach had not taught, also, a sceptical view of human institutions and the necessity of a social virtue.[1] Necessitarian, in the same sense as Godwin and the early Wordsworth and Shelley, he proclaims that 'although man acts necessarily in every thing that he does, his actions are good, just, and meritorious, every time that they tend to the real utility of his fellow men, and of the society in which he lives.... Society is just, good, worthy of our love, when it procures to all its members their physical wants, security, LIBERTY, the possession of their NATURAL RIGHTS' (2: 410). Consequently, 'of all the objects the most impracticable for a being who lives in society it is that of being willing to render himself exclusively happy' (2: 574).

Much of d'Holbach's writing has the bloodless quality of the French enlightenment, which may be why Wordsworth denigrates his 'meagre tactics' in *The Convention of Cintra* (*WPW*, 219; *Cintra*, 211) but it is also capable of approaching a poetic apprehension. His sense of nature's eternal agitation (*System*, 2: 289) is concrete enough to produce a sense that her dethronement was (to borrow from Hughes's *Crow*) 'a horrible religious error', and that we need to recreate our supreme divinity:

> In distinguishing nature from its mover, men have ... distinguished nature from itself;.... It was the soul of the world, this energy of nature, this active principle which men personified, separated by abstraction, decorated sometimes with imaginary attributes, sometimes with qualities borrowed from their own peculiar essences. (2: 306)

'God', in reality, 'can designate only active nature, or the sum total of the unknown powers which animate the universe, and which oblige beings to act in virtue of their own peculiar energies, and, consequently, according to necessary and immutable laws (2: 311). The key terms—'active', 'active principle', 'powers', 'animate'—constitute a bridge between d'Holbach's vision and the poet's. Wordsworth may not have seen his

---

1 '[T]he savages, in order to flatten the heads of their children, squeeze them between two boards, and by that means prevent them from taking the form which nature destined for them. It is pretty nearly the same thing with all our institutions' (*System*, 1: 265).

boating expedition (in *The Two-Part Prelude*) as a case of 'unknown powers' obliging a young being to 'act in virtue of [its] own energies', but in 1799 he is as likely to have conceived the matter in these terms as in any other.

Whether d'Holbach's nature and Wordsworth's are compatible depends on which passages one selects. Sometimes nature is presented in distinctly impersonal terms. We might like, d'Holbach concedes, to imagine a transcendent deity, in our own image, with 'an aim, ideas, designs', as nature's 'motive power'. Nature, however, 'has no intelligence or end; she acts necessarily, because she exists necessarily'. The whole of which we are a part, 'which we feel, and which acts upon us, is destitute of feeling'. Too chilling a view for Wordsworth? But then, Wordsworth's fisherman in *Point Rash-Judgment* (the most engagé of the 1800 suite of 'Poems on the Naming of Places') draws a sustenance from 'the dead unfeeling lake | Which knows not of his wants'. Despite this lack of feeling, d'Holbach suggests, nature worship is 'the only worship suitable to intelligent beings' (2: 383).

The System of Nature originates, and at times seems to ventriloquize, several Romantic visions. Sometimes a rather Shelleyan 'disciple of nature' engages in tearing down the idols, overturning the temples and altars bathed in tears and smoked with servile incense, so that men may enjoy the right of their own nature (4: 675). Sometimes a Blakean 'apostle of nature' sets about 'extirpating even to the very roots, the poisonous tree, which during so many ages has overshadowed the universe, that the eyes of the inhabitants of this world will be able to perceive that light which is suitable to illumine them' (4: 693). Sometimes, especially in the final volume, a more Wordsworthian voice of Nature invites humanity to cease seeking 'happiness beyond the limits of the universe, in which my hand hath placed thee' (4: 677; it is on earth that we find our happiness, Wordsworth says, 'or not at all') and promises that when her child returns 'She will console thee, she will drive from thy heart those fears which overwhelm thee, those inquietudes that distract thee, those transports which agitate thee, those hatreds which separate thee from man, whom thou shouldst love'. To worship nature is to assist one's fellow men 'to support the sorrows to which destiny has submitted them as well as thee' (678) and allow 'the sensations of humanity [to] interest thee for the condition of man' (679). If one serves nature thus, 'no power on earth will be able to ravish from thee thine inward content' (682). All synopses are prone to intentionality: mine intends to show *The System of Nature* converging with *The Poem upon the Wye*'s 'still sad music of humanity' and 'the chearful faith' of the poem's last two paragraphs.

It was argued against d'Holbach in the 1790s, especially in Royalist quarters, that 'the Universe, transformed into an Eternal being, can never replace for man that father which he believes he will have beyond the perishable world',[1] and for Coleridge this argument became increasingly central. Volney, however, whose traces are indelible in *An Evening Walk* and *Salisbury Plain*, concluded *The Ruins of Empires* by having the people demand 'after so many religions of error and delusion, the religion of evidence and truth'.[2] And d'Holbach, too, reminds his readers where the worship of transcendent deity had led. Nature may be without design, but 'Were it not better' he asks 'to throw ourselves into the arms of a blind nature, destitute of wisdom and of views, than to tremble all our life under the scourge of an omnipotent intelligence who has only combined his sublime plans in such a manner that feeble mortals should [be] the constant victims of his implacable wrath? (3: 383). The Ancient Mariner's associates arguably suffer from an implacable and arbitrary divine wrath: perhaps it is because the Nature worshipped in 'On revisiting the Wye' is without 'designs' that she never *doth* betray the heart that loves her.

Whether or not Wordsworth was a disciple of d'Holbach in 1798, or even—which is likelier—in 1793 or 1794,[3] there is nothing in Wordsworth's poem to prevent the young Shelley, in 1816, finding in *Lines on the Wye* a text wholly in tune with own admiration for *The System of Nature*. Such a perception of the poem's lost ideological bearings would have been available to almost any appropriate reader in its own 'historical moment' and remained so to readers long after Wordsworth had lost it. To announce oneself a 'worshipper of nature' who returns to this scene—on the third anniversary of the republication of Sidney's *Discourses on Government* and of d'Holbach's *System of*

---

1   D. J. Garat, cited, Piper 22.

2   M. Volney, *The Ruins: or, a Survey of the Revolutions of Empires*, 2nd edition (London: Joseph Johnson, 1795), 324.

3   Since Wordsworth rarely found the appropriate form for an intellectual or emotional configuration in much less than five years, it is unsurprising that his expression in 1798 seems so redolent of 1793 (the year from which the poem's energies and convictions derive), or that aspects of his depiction of '93 (its 'aching joys' and 'dizzy raptures') seem more pertinent to '89.

Nature—not only 'unwearied in that service' but with 'far deeper zeal' is to align oneself rather provocatively with all that is implied in the phrase the 'system' of nature, the pursuit of reason, and what the philosophes meant by *the light of things*. For Hazlitt, who knew the spirit of the age more intimately than most of us, being on speaking terms with the universe of things and being wedded to revolution in the social frame, were inseparable ideas. Jonathan Wordsworth, short-circuiting the poem, glosses Wordsworth's 'something far more deeply interfused' as 'God'; to Hazlitt, however, what Wordsworth had grasped and expressed with his 'sense sublime' was none other than 'philosophical necessity'.[1]

'The Language of the Sense'

Of quasi-historicist readings of *The Wye*, John Barrell's 'The Uses of Dorothy' comes closest to recognizing that there might be a radical ground to all this talk of nature.[2] But just as Levinson associates Wordsworth's epistemology with Descartes rather than with the materialists, Barrell associates his theory of language with Hartley rather than with Locke, a fountainhead of thinking about Nature's impulses who was even open to the possibility that matter itself might be capable of thought (see Piper, 18). Warily skirting the evidently pantheist passage about 'something far more deeply interfused, | Whose dwelling is the light of setting suns, | And the round ocean, and the living air, | And the blue sky, and in the mind of man', Barrell does engage with what this 'sense sublime' leads to, namely, the fact that Wordsworth finds

> In nature and the language of the sense,
> The anchor of my purest thoughts, the nurse,
> The guide, the guardian of my heart, and soul
> Of all my moral being.

Recognizing initially that by 'sense' Wordsworth really does mean 'the faculties of physical perception, or sensation as opposed to the higher faculties of intellect, spirit, etc' (*OED*), Barrell then finds that Hartley used 'the *language* of the sense' to mean the language by which we name

---

1   *The Examiner*, 10 December, 1815; *Complete Works of William Hazlitt*, ed. P. P. Howe, 21 vols (London: Dent, 1930–34), 20: 60.
2   John Barrell, 'The Uses of Dorothy: "The Language of the Sense" in "Tintern Abbey"' in *Poetry, Language, and Politics* (London: St Martin's Press, 1988).

objects, and proceeds to limit Wordsworth's implications until they fit that definition: 'the "language of the sense" is first and foremost the language by which we name the things, the material objects, we perceive'. Employing Levinson's technique of truncated quotation (if the lobster won't fit in the box, cut off its claws) he next considers the language of the sense merely as the 'anchor of my *purest* thoughts, the *nurse,* | *The guide, the guardian*'. The troublesome 'and *soul* | Of all my moral being', is quietly dropped, as is the compound beginning of the sentence, so that the anchor guide and guardian are recognized not in '*nature and* the language of the sense' but in 'the language of the sense' alone. Such editing removes the problem of how one recognizes one's 'soul' in 'nature', but at some expense. I have already cited Dugald Stewart's speculation about the materiality of the medium by which objects of perception manifest themselves to perception. This biological medium—that which communicates what we perceive to what we perceive with—is surely a more adequate construction of 'the language of the sense' (in which 'language' is undoubtedly a metaphor) than Barrell's formulation 'the unambiguous way in which the names in the language of the sense refer to their referents' (Barrell, 154).

When Wordsworth recognizes in the 'language of the sense … the anchor of our *purest* thoughts', he summarizes in one of the most subversive syntactical associations in English poetry the promotion of nature, with all its republican associations clustered about it. Wordsworth recognizes in nature and the language of the sense (a) 'the *anchor* of my purest thoughts', (b) 'the *nurse,* | *The guide, the guardian* of my heart', and (c) 'the *soul* | Of all my moral being'. To gloss the apotheosis of the natural being enacted in this series: thought is anchored in the material; nature is both supportively human and instructively superhuman (guide/ guardian is redolent of what Vladimir Propp, in his morphology of folk tales, called the supernatural helper); and 'soul' is located somewhere in the nature/mind/sense continuum Wordsworth is elsewhere committed to. The effect is to redefine God: you cannot, as the putative author of 'The Recluse' ought to have known, have a material soul and an immaterial God.

Tintern Abbey (to give the poem, for once, that tongue-in-cheek title) was famously credited in *The Autobiography of Mark Rutherford* with the recreation of at least one Victorian's supreme divinity, substituting for the old theological entity a sense of divine energy independent of revealed religion.[1] If it had this effect, it seems to me, one must recognize in it the first and perhaps the greatest instance of a mode of writing which is deeply characteristic of Wordsworth, that of writing in such a way as to refuse the polarizing antinomies of his culture. Consider the extraordinary prestidigitation whereby *The Prelude* as a whole and such passages as 'There was a Boy', 'the crossing of the Alps' and the 'Ascent of Snowdon' in particular seem honed so as to accommodate almost any metaphysic, to appeal equally to Lockean empiricists, Coleridgean idealists or Shelleyan materialists. Or, analogously, the astonishing political moment with which he concludes his discussion of the revolutionary terror. When Wordsworth visited the Wye in 1793, in flight from war preparations in Portsmouth, and from patriotic fervour in Anglican pulpits, his political community was polarized between Burke's allegiance to inherited forms of culture, and Paine's mesmeric advocacy of the rights of the living. 'Who is to decide,' Paine asked in his withering refrain, 'the living or the dead?' When Wordsworth concluded his discussion of the revolutionary terror in Book 10 of *The Prelude* (1805) he affirmed characteristically, refusing to choose between Paine and Burke, that 'there is | One great society alone on earth, | The noble Living *and* the noble Dead' (10: 968–70). It is a genuinely performative sentence. Two more such sentences crystallize the brand of natural supernaturalism accomplished in *The Poem upon the Wye*. Of these the most grammatically astonishing is the one beginning 'And I have felt', while the most ontologically astonishing is that which finds 'in nature and the language of the sense ... the soul of all my moral being'. To borrow one of A. C. Bradley's remarks, if there is a way into the Wordsworth of 1798, it is 'through, and not around', that sentence.

Much of Wordsworth's writing of 1797–99, including the 'Prospectus to The Recluse', and *Peter Bell* (as read by Alan Bewell) implies that he is interested in religious history as a sort of Comtean progress from fetishism to enlightenment.[2] On 26 October 1803, five years after Wordsworth walked into Bristol composing his hymn to nature, Coleridge recorded angrily that he had experienced 'A most unpleasant Dispute with W. and

1   William Hale White, *The Autobiography of Mark Rutherford*, ed. Reuben Shapcott (London 1881), 24.

2   *Peter Bell*, in Alan Bewell's powerful reading, offers 'a history of man's religious development, from crude metaphysics to human society', 'a myth of how religion arises through (not against) superstitious imagination', and an embedded 'history of religions'. Bewell, *Wordsworth and the Enlightenment,* 120, 126, 138–9.

Hazlitt ... they spoke so irreverently so malignantly of the Divine Wisdom that it overset me'. Having already dubbed Wordsworth 'at least' a semi-atheist, Coleridge concludes on this occasion: 'O dearest William! would Ray, or Durham [both bishops], have spoken of God as you spoke of Nature?'[1] Whatever this means, it surely means that Wordsworth, when a further five years have passed, is still speaking as what the poem calls 'a worshipper of Nature'. Most people, in my experience, can meet on the ground of *The Poem upon the Wye*, to whatever strand of belief or unbelief they incline. One might conjecture that in writing it Wordsworth was attempting to construct a 'site' (for once that threadworn metaphor seems apt) where 'the noble Living and the noble Dead'—Coleridge and Hazlitt, Thelwall, Priestley and Paine, Locke, Shaftesbury, Spinoza, Cicero—might meet.[2] It worked for Hazlitt and Thelwall, and indeed for Shelley and Keats: but it didn't wash with Coleridge, who came to see in *The Wye* a dangerous heresy that he would set about eradicating in *Aids to Reflection*. But in 1798 Wordsworth was in process of repenting his long defence of revolutionary terror, and perhaps, with it, some of the philosophic baggage he carried in the early 90s, in favour of an age-less consensus. Perhaps he thought to himself that here—on a new holy ground some miles 'above' a manifestly ruined abbey—the republican diaspora might comfortably reassemble and begin what Abrams once called the process of reconstituting their grounds for hope.[3]

'For thou art with me'

That Dorothy enters the poem in line 115, as the focus of the poem's third movement, can be and has been read as anticlimax, as put-down, or as concession. It can also be read as a climax deliberately reserved, whereby the significance of the human world is restored at the end of the poem and the volume. This is not Dorothy's first appearance in *Lyrical Ballads*. She appears earlier, as Alan Grob has pertinently noted, in the guise of a compulsive *reader* (one of two readers in fact, the other being

---

1   *CN* 1: 1616. Ray or Durham being bishops.
2   For Paine's Pantheism see Jack Fruchtman, *Thomas Paine and the Religion of Nature* (Baltimore: Johns Hopkins University Press, 1993).
3   'English Romanticism: the Spirit of the Age' (1963), in *The Correspondent Breeze: Essays on Romanticism* (New York: Norton, 1984), 66.

Hazlitt, in *Expostulation and Reply*).[1] In *To My Sister*, she has to be exhorted by her brother to leave behind her book, and consent to a day of sensations rather than of thoughts, privileging 'the language of the sense'. But *Lines on the Wye* advances her partnership in the volume. Dorothy is promised that her mind will become 'a mansion for all lovely forms'. Since the mind does not, in Wordsworth, start out with its forms ready made (they are impressed by nature under conditions, for example, of 'extrinsic passion') storing or peopling the mind with *all* of nature's forms necessarily takes some years. Dorothy at this point is twenty-six to William's twenty-eight, yet she is experientially much younger: for one thing, she is much less travelled. The argument, Professor Grob has shown, depends upon an enlightenment assumption of environmental necessitarianism, and also on the assumption, shared with the contemporary feminism of Macaulay, Wollstonecraft and Hays, that the mind is without gender. It assumes that what William, being older, has experienced, Dorothy, being younger, will experience—that neither her gender, nor the fact that she has not lived in France, or been to Cambridge, will, since human experience is in the enlightenment sense of the term 'necessary', prevent this 'dear, dear Friend' from experiencing that benevolent process of maturation which applies equally to all equally endowed human minds.

It is impossible to tell whether lines 126–135, with their assurance that a sneering world will ne'er 'prevail against us', presuppose a joint career in the republic of letters. The 'us' is usually read as male, merely because it relates to experience of the 'rash judgements and the sneers of selfish men' in the public world, but is logically a brother and sister 'us' given its immediate referents (and still more logically so, since 'evil tongues, rash judgements and the sneers of selfish men' might well, by a candid reader, be recognized as applying with peculiar aptness to a brother/sister literary partnership of the kind actively envisaged by these siblings). It is clear, however, that Dorothy is recognized here as not merely the equal of her brother (such denial of difference is transparently political), but as being quite as necessary to him as that newly apotheosized sense of nature which brings the fourth movement to a close. Indeed the logic of the poem is astonishingly careless, in the sense of carefree. Having devoted four movements of the poem to asserting a strengthened faith

---

1   'William and Dorothy: a Case Study in the Hermeneutics of Disparagement', *ELH*, 65 (1998) 187–221.

in the ideology of Nature, the poet cavalierly asserts that even if he had learnt nothing of all this from his time at Cambridge and with Beaupuy ('Nor, perchance, | If I were not thus *taught*') his creative confidence would still be unimpaired. *Yea*, he implies, *though he walked through the valley of the shadow of death* he would fear no evil, *'for thou art with me'*.[1] This 'thou', however, is not the deity, but 'my dear, dear friend' and 'dear, dear sister', whose transformative power—the comparison affirms Dorothy's displacement not only of God but of some mighty poets—is equivalent to nature's own.

---

1   This allusion was noted by M. H. Abrams in 'On Political Readings of Tintern Abbey', in *Doing Things with Texts*, ed. Michael Fisher (New York: Norton, 1989).

Part 3

The Living and the Dead

There is one great society on earth
The noble living and the noble dead

—The Prelude

Chapter 7: Peopling Elysium

A CQUAINTED WITH ELYSIUM from early youth, Wordsworth claims in his homecoming poem (*Home at Grasmere*) that to healthy minds 'groves | Elysian' are but 'the growth of common day'.[1] Returning to Hawkshead in 1788 after a year at Cambridge (at least as he remembered in 1804) he was ferried across Windermere by Charon. In many a Cumbrian Springtime, his *Guide through the District of the Lakes* assures us, the soft air can be likened to 'that which gives motion to the funereal cypresses on the banks of Lethe', or might be designed 'to salute beatified spirits when expiatory fires shall have consumed the earth with all her habitations'.[2] Perhaps it is not surprising, in the light of these gracenotes, that of Wordsworth's three greatest male creations, one is dead and two others seem not altogether of this world, 'half absent' in one case, in the other 'not all alive nor dead, | Nor all asleep'.

The Discharged Soldier seems to emanate, like elements of the landscape in which he is encountered, from 'some far region' of the soul, while the Leech-Gatherer belongs partly to the Cumbrian fells, partly to 'some distant region' of the imagination. But at least these shadows can be encountered. In the poet's time, Michael, whose story begins when he has 'one foot in the grave', is a tribal memory on the point of vanishing. All three have a doubly liminal status—they are marginal to existing social structures, as well as half legendary. The Sailor and Female Vagrant of 1793–94 already had a reality that made the society that rejected them seem unreal:[3] the new figures of 1798–1802, the soldier, the shepherd and the leech-gatherer, haunt the poet (as they now haunt his readers) with an even more tutelary power.

---

1 Prospectus to *The Recluse*, 35–40, dated to late December 1799 or early 1800, not uncontentiously, by Jonathan Wordsworth, *Borders,* 389.
2 *Prose Works*, 2, 191. Wordsworth is endorsing Buchanan's 'Ode to the first of May'.
3 According to Victor Turner, an outsider may enjoy 'a statusless status…which gives him the right to criticise all structure-bound personae in terms of a moral order binding on all.' Victor Turner, *The Ritual Process: Structure and Anti-Structure* (Ithaca NY: Cornell UP, 1977) 95, 116.

The Discharged Soldier (1798–1804)

The discharged soldier, according to Book 4 of *The Prelude*, was encountered, propped on a milestone outside Hawkshead, in the course of Wordsworth's first summer vacation from Cambridge. Such is the belief in the matter-of-fact basis of anything Wordsworth wrote that modern editors tend to identify, in their notes on the poem, the ascent, the village, and even which milestone it was on which the soldier propped himself. Textually, *The Discharged Soldier* is a product of the wartime economy of the 1790s, like *The Ruined Cottage*, *The Female Vagrant* and numerous of the *Lyrical Ballads*, but it marks a considerable change of stance and strategy in Wordsworth's handling of such subjects. There are three versions of it—each shorter, and in some respects better, than the last—namely the independent and untitled text of 1798, and the two versions that close Book 4 of *The Prelude*. But the prototype of this soldier, the lens through which Wordsworth observed him, whether in 1788 when the supposed encounter took place, or in 1798 when the poem was written, was a creation of Wordsworth's in 1787 before he left Hawkshead.

Whatever Wordsworth really met in 1788 it is pretty clear what he thinks he might be meeting. The 'uncouth shape' of the soldier coalesces with another 'shape' created textually over a decade before. However assured, and however original, and however persuasive, the narrative of *The Discharged Soldier* is—and however authentic we would like it to be—it depends very heavily upon a startled encounter in a dark passage of *The Vale of Esthwaite* with a tall and ghastly figure, whose bones are apparent through his skin, who gestures with one raised hand, emits faint murmurs, accompanies the schoolboy through gloomy shades, and vouchsafes visions of forgotten battles, all amid Cumbria's 'indignant hills'. This spectral figure shaped itself textually a year *before* Wordsworth met, if indeed he ever did meet, a soldier discharged after service in the tropic isles. Imagination, in the Simplon Pass and upon Snowdon, 'usurps upon' reality. Here, the real figure, if there was one, is so cloaked by the imagined one—so overlaid by a combination of the 'wilfulness of fancy and conceit' and the 'visionary dreariness' described in *1805* (8.511–583 and 11.307–15)—that he takes some seventy lines of the 1798 text to force his way through the shadows of imagination and emerge as an independent being. Moreover, as in the childhood scenes of *The Prelude*, Wordsworth seems *led* into this encounter.

> While thus I wandered, step by step led on,
> It chanced a sudden turning of the road
> Presented to my view an uncouth shape
> So near that, slipping back into the shade
> Of a thick hawthorn, I could mark him well,
> Myself unseen. He was of stature tall,
> A foot above man's common measure tall,
> And lank, and upright. There was in his form
> A meagre stiffness. You might almost think
> That his bones wounded him. His legs were long,
> So long and shapeless that I looked at them
> Forgetful of the body they sustained.
> His arms were long and lean; his hands were bare;
> His visage, wasted though it seem'd, was large
> In feature, his cheeks sunken, and his mouth
> Shewed ghastly in the moonlight; from behind
> A milestone propped him, and his figure seemed
> Half-sitting and half-standing. I could mark
> That he was clad in military garb,
> Though faded, yet entire. (*LBOP* 36 ff)

As Hugh Sykes Davies has observed, the 'uncouth shape' recalls what Wordsworth says in *The Pedlar* of 'preternatural' tales illustrated by woodcuts: 'Strange and uncouth, dire faces, figures dire | Sharp-knee'd, sharp-elbow'd, and lean-ancled too, | With long and ghostly shanks, forms which once seen | Could never be forgotten' (*The Pedlar*, MS.E 172–5).[1] Such memories, of course, also reveal the inspiration of the fatherly spectral form in the *Vale of Esthwaite*, where the figure is ghostlier but less angular and where the grief of an orphan finds no incongruity—no inhibition of cultured taste—in perceiving his father through such forms.

The same kind of imagination—the kind that perceives nature through the 'second nature' of story—borrows from Dorothy's journal a howling mastiff, perturbed by alien presences. Nor is childhood imagination the only kind operative. Another night-time walk at Alfoxden provides a strikingly diagnostic image.[2] *The Discharged Soldier* opens with a the-

---

1   *Wordsworth and the Worth of Words* (Cambridge: CUP, 1986), 148–9.
2   On 27 January Dorothy recorded a local manufacturer's dog making 'a strange uncouth howl, which it continues many minutes after there is no noise near it but that of the brook'. On 31 January, walking with William to Holford: 'the road to the village

matic preamble addressing the issue of psychic integrity, making the land-
scape bear symbolic meanings as it will do five months later in *On revis-
iting the Wye*. In its night-time character, 'the public way | ... *assumes*
| *A character* of deeper quietness | Than pathless solitudes'. Like the
Wye hedgerows preferring to be lines of sportive wood, the public road
throws off societal constraints, and its watery surface 'seemed before
my eyes another stream | Stealing with silent lapse to join the brook |
That murmured in the valley.' Further hints of psychological context,
that will only develop into their full significance in 1804–5, are already
present. The wanderer passes along 'tranquil, | Receiving in my own
despite amusement' and 'from the stillness drinking in | A restoration
like the calm of sleep, | But sweeter far.' The landscape's 'pictures' rose

> As from *some distant region* of my soul
> And came along like dreams

—dreams that leave as their residue 'a self-possession'. Here, already,
is the germ of what the 1805 and 1850 versions of *The Prelude* will
develop as the theme of Book 4. In *1850* Wordsworth looks back on
his vacationing self as marked by self-alienation, 'an inner falling off'
(4. 278), the assumption of a false self, and tired by nothing more than
'strenuous idleness'. In both versions of Book 4, the symbolic road, for-
getting its defined function and becoming another stream, amplifies an
earlier complaint that his very garments 'Preyed upon my strength and
stopped the quiet stream of self-forgetfulness' (4. 296–7).

At the time of the supposed encounter, Wordsworth (the narrative of
Book 4 has suggested) felt guilty at having allowed Cambridge affec-
tations to tamper with his better self. By the time of *writing*, in 1798,
Wordsworth had acquired much deeper historical guilts through his still
recent identification with practitioners of terror—guilts that will shadow
his political poetry for the next forty years and be revealed only in 1842
(partially) and 1850 (with posthumous candour). Having decided in
1798 that this figure exemplifies a social alienation even deeper than his
own—

of Holford glittered like another stream'. (*Journals of Dorothy Wordsworth*, ed. Mary
Moorman, Oxford: OUP, 1971, 3). Both images are radically empowered by the context
of a poem: Dorothy's road simply glitters 'like another stream'. William's is 'stealing
with silent lapse to join the brook'. Dorothy's dog is presumably provoked into howling
by their presence. Was Dorothy or William imagining a Coleridgean 'mastiff' howling
at a spectral presence?

> he appeared
> Forlorn and desolate, a man cut off
> From all his kind.

—Wordsworth completes the configuration by developing for him a his-
tory which, like the narratives of 1793–97, implies an unwitting complic-
ity in the betrayal of humanity. The soldier, too, has been 'parted from
his better self', or in his case 'more than half detached | From his own
nature' by his trade of soldiering, which to Wordsworth (as to Godwin
and Shelley) meant being trained to murder on behalf of the state. He still
appears in 'military garb, | Though faded yet entire' as if unable to free
himself from the insignia of his trade. Knowing that he has served in 'the
Tropic islands' Wordsworth questions him about what he has endured of
'war, battle and pestilence': one associated in whatever way with slavery
will know all about fever—major outbreaks in the 1790s were perceived
by some as divine punishment for engagement on slaving.[1] In 1793–
98, while Wordsworth was busy justifying the use of terror to suppress
treason, such a soldier's duties might have included putting down slave
revolts. An estimated 40,000 British and 40,000 French died of Yellow
Fever while so engaged. So the apologist for terror confronts the vet-
eran of Caribbean wars, aware (as Marmaduke has already learned from
Oswald in *The Borderers*) that action is merely the motion of a muscle;
that in the 'after-vacancy' of action, 'we wonder at ourselves like men
betrayed'; that 'Suffering is permanent, obscure and dark | And shares
the nature of infinity' (*Borderers*, 1542–44).

At first the alienation is figured gothically: his face is turned 'Towards
the road, yet not as if he sought | For any living object', and the village
mastiff is alarmed and howls unceasingly. But Wordsworth's 1798 poetic
is committed to *harrowing* of the Gothic. The mystery is projected. For
'his shadow | Lay at his feet and moved not' we inevitably read 'at my
feet my Shadow lay and moved not'. Tokens of dread are cancelled one
by one in the simple human encounter that follows—including the fig-

---

1   Thomas Clarkson published his *Essay on the Slavery and Commerce of the Human
Species* in 1786 and founded the Society for Effecting the Abolition of the Slave Trade
in 1787, the year Wordsworth went up to Cambridge, so such associations would not
be unlikely in 1788. Joan Baum associates the 1798 poem directly with Southey's 'The
Sailor Who Had Served in the Slave Trade' and 'The Ancient Mariner' as a symbol-
ist treatment of the guilt incurred by those who worked 'the middle passage': *Mind-
Forged Manacles: Slavery and the English Romantic Poets* (North Haven, CT: Archon
Books, 1994), 53–4.

ure's touchingly counter-Gothic concern for what might ail the mastiff. Still, as they approach the village, 'every silent window to the moon | Shone with a yellow glitter.' The image subtly conveys that the soldier's fever has communicated itself to his environment, and this quiet symbol, indicative of shared guilts, goes some way to explain why it is that the soldier is enjoined, later, to claim his right to board and lodging from those on whose behalf he has suffered.

In this early version of the poem he appears thus topically dehumanised by his trade, 'cut off | From all his kind, and more than half detached | From his own nature'. In the *1850* text, which is structured so as to develop the Charon allusion at the start of Book 4—if the lakes as a whole are a kind of Elysium it makes sense to see the ferryman who introduces him to the region as 'the Charon of the flood'—he clearly appears to Wordsworth as belonging more to Hades than to Hawkshead, more to the past than the present, having strange knowledge of battles long ago. All texts retain the early remark, that 'solemn and sublime he might have seemed', but for a strange 'half-absence'. The revisions make 'seemed' an oddity. What shortens the text each time is the gradual paring away of conversation, referred to appropriately in *1850* as 'questions better spared', so that the encounter is played out in increasing silence, which revisionary strategy has the effect of intensifying the sublime, as the socialized text of 1798 is drawn back towards its 1787 point of origin. All the poet says in the 1850 text is 'Come with me', so the dominant *voice* of the final version is the soldier's solemn, sublime and self-possessed 'put down' of the poet: 'My trust is in the God of Heaven, | And in the eye of him who passes me!' The whole compositional history is a sort of history of Wordsworth's vacillations on the boundaries of 'the world which is the world of all of us' and whatever that realm is that Coleridge calls 'the ideal world' and Wordsworth more often 'the invisible world'.

Wordsworth's Discharged Soldier of 1798–1805 exemplifies the kind of encounter in which his poetry specializes, but is much the most complex such case. As a figure he marries the Godwinian social art of Wordsworth in the mid 90s (like Robert of *The Ruined Cottage*, and the Female Vagrant and her husband, and the sailor-murderer of *Adventures on Salisbury Plain*, he is a victim of national policy and social irresponsibility) with the earliest and latest instances of Wordsworth's habit of turning common people into tribal archetypes as he does in all his poetry from *The Vale of Esthwaite* to *Resolution and Independence*. The soldier is so transumed, though he manifests considerable resistance. Like other powerful Wordsworthian passages this one works simultaneously as an expression of reverence for men as they are men within themselves, *and* as an exhibition of imagination creating its own sustenance. It also leaves unanalyzed, like other spots of time, the psychological dynamics on which it is based.

The *Vale of Esthwaite* figure was part of Wordsworth's valedictory address to Hawkshead, and the encounter in that poem led to a poetic annunciation, a laying on of hands, bard to apprentice bard. To accomplish that laying on of hands the poet has first to clothe his father— who wore the Lowther livery—in bardic costume, fathering his father, as Wordsworthian children do. The final version of *The Discharged Soldier* effects a deeper therapy. But the soldier encountered in 1788 in Far Sawrey, and written up by a Jacobin poet in Alfoxden in 1798, inspires a social message. If the poem of '98 has a single extractable message it is one that remains constant in Wordsworth's work through to the 1835 'Postscript'—that a man who has served his country, in however regrettable a trade, is owed a maintenance by that country. The poet entreats that henceforth 'He would not linger in the public ways | But at the door of cottage or of inn | *Demand* the succour which his state required, | And told him, feeble as he was, 'twere fit | He asked relief or alms.' In *1805* all this somewhat garrulous welfare advice is reduced to a suggestion that he 'ask for timely furtherance and help | Such as his state required.'

The reason for this shift is clear. The debate of 1798 concerning mendicancy, like that concerning the slave trade, is no longer at the centre of Wordsworth's concerns in the passage. At the same time, however, the Discharged Soldier has been promoted from a 'feeble' recipient of the poet's interest and the cottager's charity into an Anchises / Virgil figure. With him, and suggestively with his assistance—like Dante being led by the shade of Virgil, through a *selva oscura*, or Aeneas tutored by Anchises—Wordsworth passes 'through the shades gloomy and dark' to emerge into 'an open field'.[1] In 1798 only the soldier is revived, the emphasis is on what Wordsworth does for the soldier, and with no hint of gift exchange it ends simply 'And so we parted'. But in 1805—after composition of *The Leech-Gatherer*—

---

1   Alan Bewell finds echoes of Dante's encounter with the shade of Virgil in *Inferno*, 1 60–80. Bewell, 4–5.

> Back I cast a look,
>> And lingered near the door a little space,
>> Then sought with quiet heart my distant home.

It is one of Wordsworth's greatest lines, but also one of his greatest events.

The aptness is partly architectural. The symbolism of the poem's overture, in which the public way assumes the character of another stream lapsing to join the brook that 'murmured' in the valley, does not merely anticipate the 'murmuring sounds' of the soldier, but predicts a poet freed from selfhood (his own Cambridge spectre) who can merge with, rather than remain alienated from, the soldier, be restored to authentic existence through him, and to some extent change places with him. The soldier remains of sublime stature, a survivor of unnumbered and dateless wars, but a sort of coalescence of the two is required before the poet can assume the soldier's journey to his 'native home'. At the end of the poem, as reimagined in 1805 and thereafter, the soldier is 'at rest', while the poet's journey to a 'distant home' continues. His 'quiet heart' echoes the steadiness of the soldier and his shadow. The self-possession that is only *claimed* in the preamble (there is nothing self-possessed about 'specious cowardise') is now *embodied* in the measure of the line, and is the residue of this encounter. The line 'And sought with quiet heart my distant home' echoes—rhythmically, syntactically and of course in the sense of 'something given'—the beautiful close of the Furness spot, 'and beat with thundering hoofs the level sands'. The gift is now a result of a human exchange, rather than a spot of time in nature, but it is still unequal. The poet merely places the soldier in a cottage for the night; the soldier 'places' the poet in a meaningful scheme of things, restoring him to self-possession.

One is tempted to say that whatever seems most factual about this figure is in fact most factitious, having little to do with 1788. The modern reader seizes gratefully on reference to the tropic wars and fever as situating the poem in the mid 1790s and the deaths of sailors and soldiers in French and British uniforms upholding the slave trade, which welcome 'fact' conveniently explains why the soldier seems 'more than half detached from his own nature'. It is Wordsworth's tendency in January 1798 to harrow the gothic mysteries of his imagination, and indeed the whole tendency of this narrative, in all its versions, is from the gothic towards the real. Nonetheless, in revising it, after having written *Resolution and*

Independence, in which poem the movement towards naturalism is countered by a massive increment of imagination, Wordsworth assimilates it tonally and in some respects stylistically to the achievement of the later poem, paring away much of the naturalisation implicit in the narrative. The effect is to make one wonder how many feckless youths, over how many years, in how many dark places, like dandiacal wedding guests, this archetypal figure has restored to themselves.

As with numerous of Wordsworth's revisions, one can at the same time regret the disappearance of particular lines and images, while feeling that the whole gains something from its new concentration on essentials. It is as if Wordsworth is constantly tinkering, to get the balance exactly right between sociology and mythopoeia. It is not, however, a flight from sociology to myth. The myth is grounded in the sociology. Pauperization, as Michael Friedman pointed out, was for Wordsworth both a widespread social fact and a personal anxiety, and becomes 'the conscious symbol for an inner and personal terror',[1] and in *The Ruined Cottage*, 'Many rich sank down among the poor.' The fact that the poet in the poem serves to bring the gentle reader face to face with one thrown upon distress, yet possessed of a greater strength than the writer is shown (or the reader is implied) to command, has the simultaneous effect of mythologizing the naked dignity of man, and of diminishing the implied reader's sense of difference. We are brought to recognise both our kinship, since the figure is recognisably a man, and our unlikeness, since he embodies a fortitude well beyond what is needed for a student life of 'strenuous idleness', or the implied reader's implied diet of 'routs, dinners, morning calls' (Wordsworth to Lady Beaumont, 21 May 1807). He has about him the fortitude of the ghostly British warriors *An Evening Walk* called the 'last remnant of the great and brave'.

Michael (1800)

So much for the public road. If, however, Wordsworth's pastoral masterpiece informs us,

> If from the public way you turn your steps
> Up the tumultuous brook of Greenhead Ghyll,
> You will suppose that with an upright path

---

1   Michael Friedman, *The Making of a Tory Humanist: Wordsworth and the idea of Community* (New York: Columbia University Press, 1979), 41.

> Your feet must struggle; in such bold ascent
> The pastoral mountains front you, face to face.
> But courage! for beside that boisterous Brook
> The mountains have all open'd out themselves,
> And made a hidden valley of their own.
> No habitation there is seen; but such
> As journey thither find themselves alone
> With a few sheep, with rocks and stones, and kites
> That overhead are sailing in the Sky. (*LBOP*, 252)

In a particularly fine essay in *The Unremarkable Wordsworth* Geoffrey Hartman suggests that 'The opening paragraph of "Michael" which carefully guides the reader to a strange destination, should be compared to Theocritus … and to the wayside inscription in general'. Citing one such inscription from Leonidas of Tarentum—' Not here, O thirsty traveller, stoop to drink, | The sun has warmed, and flocks disturb the brink; but climb yon upland …'—Hartman observes that Wordsworth's poem 'leads us unexpectedly to a Greek prototype' (41). It also leads to an almost visionary republic, a virtual Shangri-La. The language of these opening lines, with their seemingly strenuous invitation, belies the fact that Wordsworth is merely recommending a few minutes gentle stroll from an inn, the famous Swan. As those sonorous cadences take us into a patriarchal 'now' (no, not that kind of patriarchal) we 'journey' deep into the mountains in search of 'a hidden valley'. There, the 'pastoral' mountains not only make hidden valleys of their own, like human sheepfolds, but as in the *Guide to the Lakes*, impose a constitution on those valleys, and a legendary equality once as native to them as the (now almost equally legendary) 'kites that overhead are sailing in the sky'.

Michael is an anecdote in blank verse, and like the Discharged Soldier, Michael is an archetype, but the voice of the poem is entirely new. Although the blank verse has affinities with that of the 'Poems on the Naming of Places' (there is something of the guidebook in all of them) the narrative voice is closer to that of a retired Pedlar, than to the poet himself. It seems an idealized projection, that is to say, of Wordsworth as a genuinely rooted poet, capable of speaking of this now legendary culture as if he were a survivor of it. Inevitably, the Pedlar, whose boyhood had 'small need of books', surrounded as he was by 'many a tale | Traditionary' comes to mind as the narrator of Michael refers, as if to a point already made, to this as 'the first, | The earliest of *those Tales*' that interested him in shepherds. The patriarchal dignity of an entirely new blank verse (it is the first narrative blank verse Wordsworth published) presents the speaker as representative of a rooted and dignified culture. The speaker's declaration that he narrates his poem 'with yet fonder feeling for the sake of youthful poets who will be my second selves when I am gone'—youthful poets, I have suggested elsewhere, such as Norman Nicholson, W. S. Graham, Hughes, Hill and Heaney[1]—may seem to identify the speaker as Wordsworth himself. Yet it might equally belong to a venerable minstrel-historian imagining Wordsworth as the youthful poet who will be his heir and, in a sense, calling him to that function. So Wordsworth, far from speaking in a newly discovered voice of his own, is now anointing himself into the literary version of an oral tradition. For a young poet of thirty the speaker has an astonishing patina; he speaks like a shepherd of being, looking back to his boyhood when he learned from the patriarchs of his childhood the tale—already traditionary—of one who lives only in the memory of the elders of the tribe. These can be, and are, consulted, for it is the tribal minstrel's business to preserve the tribal memory.

Nevertheless, *Michael* is, as Don Bialostosky has argued, quite as experimental a narrative as that elusive masterpiece of 1798, *The Thorn*: it is just that 'The Michael-narrator minds his trade better than Wordsworth's other narrators, and projects the satisfaction of deliberate craftsmanship'.[2] The narrator borrows some of the Thorn-narrator's phrases and ploys. The Michael-narrator is quite as concerned that you should exercise your limbs in the ascent of Greenhead Ghyll as the earlier narrator was that you should climb the Quantocks (they do say poetry is good for the heart). His 'no habitation there is seen' recalls 'all lovely colours there are seen' in 'The Thorn'. The artfully constructed voice, in employing such phrases as ''tis not forgotten yet' and ''tis believed by all', parallel to those used by the narrator of 'The Thorn', shows the same wish for us to believe, though what is being shared is now a traditionary possession not a pathological one.

---

1 For the importance of Wordsworth's counter-metropolitan sense of regional and national history to twentieth-century poets, the discovery (after publication of the *1805* Prelude) of the youthful 'spot of time' as a late twentieth-century genre, and other aspects of Wordsworth's legacy, see my 'Wordsworth's Second Selves', *TWC* 14:4 (1983) 191–201.

2 Bialostosky, *Making Tales*, 98: *Michael* is 'the longest, the most elevated, and the last presented of a series of experiments in Lyrical Ballads', 97.

There is a distance between Wordsworth and the narrator of *Michael*, as there is between the poet and the narrator of *The Thorn*. In both cases the poet seems to be listening to, rather than writing, his narrator. In the early poem, however, there is a gap of irony, the poet watching the effect upon the reader of the story-teller's manoeuvres. In the latter case the poet seems to set aside his own perspectives to evoke a quality of life that lives so in the communal memory. The early narrator is *not* a native and his bond with the villagers is perhaps as artificial as his bond with Martha Ray. The poet of *The Thorn* is clearly sceptical about the virtues of rural community: he portrays what is clearly a dysfunctional community and dramatizes one 'offcomer' inoculating another—the auditor—with his prurient imaginings. In *Michael* there are the same appeals to testimony, but with a wholly different effect: there is a communal pride in the ancient lamp that gives the cottage its name, 'The Evening Star'.

So the voice one hears in *Michael* is closer to the Pedlar than to the Captain (and not only because of the blank verse; *The Discharged Soldier* doesn't have this same 'patina'). The Pedlar and the Michael-narrator both see about them things you cannot see; and both conjure a narrative from a heap of stones (one decayed, one never built) as the Thorn-narrator conjures one from a heap of moss. But unlike the narrator of *The Thorn* their stories are concerned to realize not reify their human subject, and they share a certain view of character. Michael's character, like Margaret's, is built through observation of the things he loves as much as through habits of speech. The observation of what he loves, and does and is, is carried out with a descriptive vividness, and a narrative skill, that Richard Clancey has detailed particularly well—a skill that seems to be informed by a lifelong apprenticeship on the part of the narrator to classical story-telling.[1] And while one is conscious of the Pedlar's tact, also, in his way of not appearing to listen to Margaret's sobs, *Michael* is justly famous for the way in which when Michael needs a little privacy the narrator turns aside to speak of other things.

Michael, though an independent shepherd, is, in the definition of the times, one of the poor, which is to say that he works for a living. One of the most telling remarks of the tale is that he and Isabel were 'a proverb in the vale | For endless industry'. The construction of a narrative

---

1   Richard W. Clancey, 'Wordsworth's Michael and Poetry Come too Late', *Charles Lamb Bulletin*, n.s. 94 (April 1996) 79–94.

voice that appears to be (like that of *The Idiot Boy*)[1] of the same social status as the character makes the voice of the poem that of honoured and independent poverty, and through this local quality—paradoxically perhaps—the poem emulates a classical objectivity quite unlike the *Prelude* voice. Virgil's *Georgics* were in all probability, as Bruce Graver argues, Wordsworth's immediate model.[2] They were, for Wordsworth himself, 'tales traditionary' at Hawkshead. But the Idylliums of Theocritus (Wordsworth's own plural) were particularly favoured by the poet in 1799, when he associated him with Burns (*EY*, 255–6), and Theocritus is favoured again in the Preface of 1815 in precisely the same conjunction (*PrW*, 2: 28). In a broader sense, however, one might offer the term Homeric.

Homer's stock rose (and stayed risen) as the cult of the primitive developed in the eighteenth century, perceived as the undegenerate original of the minstrel tradition. When James Montgomery reviewed *The Excursion* he may have had this dignified tradition in mind as he praises Wordsworth's conception of the Pedlar, and the ease with which 'the Poet lifts him above his mean estate, and invests him with that moral and intellectual dignity, which is not hereditary in the palaces of Princes, but which Nature, or rather the God of Nature, in his sovereign bounty, bestows on select individuals … scattered through every rank of life': 'Mr Wordsworth's Wanderer', Montgomery concludes, 'is a character as ideal as Homer's Achilles'.[3] But Homer himself, according to Thomas Blackwell, was 'a strolling bard', reflective, familiar with solitude in nature, and thence with himself and his own passions, accustomed to observing 'all the various situations of the human race', beholden to nobody.[4]

---

1   If I appear to compare the sublime with the ludicrous see Wordsworth's first choice of manner for this topic in the so-called 'ballad Michael' and the contextualization thereof in Stephen Parrish, 'Michael and the Pastoral ballad', *Bicentenary Wordsworth Studies*, 50–75.

2   Bruce Graver, 'Wordsworth's Georgic Pastoral: *Otium* and *Labor* in "Michael", *ERR* 1 (1991) 119–34.

3   *Eclectic Review*, n.s Vol 3, January 1815, pp 13–39, 29.

4   Thomas Blackwell, *An Enquiry into the Life and Writings of Homer* (1735), 22, 104, cited from Gary Harrison, *Wordsworth's Vagrant Muse*, 121. Gary Harrison concludes that in eighteenth-century encomiums to honoured poverty, 'The poet became a kind of Homeric wanderer, a hermit sage whose poverty always seemed to be protected from indigence and insult', 125.

The opening of the narrative proper makes it clear that Michael is both physically and spiritually, despite and because of his station, a transcendent being:

> His bodily frame had been from youth to age
> Of an unusual strength: his mind was keen,
> Intense and frugal, apt for all affairs,
> And in his Shepherd's calling he was prompt
> And watchful more than ordinary men.
> Hence had he learn'd the meaning of all winds,
> Of blasts of every tone, and often-times
> When others heeded not, he heard the South
> Make subterraneous music, like the noise
> Of Bagpipers on distant Highland Hills.
> The Shepherd, at such warning, of his flock
> Bethought him, and he to himself would say,
> 'The Winds are now devising work for me!'
> And truly at all times the storm that drives
> The Traveller to a shelter, summon'd him
> Up to the mountains: *he had been alone*
> *Amid the heart of many thousand mists*
> *That came to him and left him on the heights.*
>
> (my italics)

The peculiar quality of this passage balances naturalism—all that is said of him does indeed derive from his 'calling'—with a sense of 'summoning'. The progression from 'the meaning of all winds' through 'blasts of every tone' to 'subterraneous music' conducts one along one of those strange Wordsworthian escalators into territory where one is not quite sure what is being claimed—except that it brings Michael very close to what Wordsworth claims of the apprentice poet, who listens to sounds 'that are the ghostly language of the ancient earth'.

That Michael, having supped with the almighty, should communicate with his son through a covenant, and that the covenant should serve as a talisman, 'Thy anchor and thy shield', is only to be expected. The language of Romance has already been humanized in *The Poem upon the Wye* where it is 'nature and the language of the sense' (including the tactile and visual traces of such acts as laying stones) that together compose the poet's 'anchor', 'guide', and 'guardian'. That Michael should establish this covenant, make this declaration of faith, while foreknowing all—'whatever fate | Befall thee, I shall love thee to the last, | And bear thy memory with me to the grave'—is essential to the Abraham-transcending dignity. There may be an element of truth in the idea that Michael errs, and that his tragedy is in that sense earned, but this is surely not, as some critics would have it, a tale of a father who can relate only to things—the land—and sacrifices his only son to that obsession. He does not, that is to say—despite the poem's quite obvious equations of Michael to Abraham, Isabel to Sarah, and Luke to Isaac—*sacrifice* him. When, Richard Clancey says, Michael 'risks' Luke 'in order to save his patrimony' (83), the 'his' in 'his patrimony' necessarily implies Luke's as much as Michael's. Wordsworth, in creating a new covenant between man and nature, desirous of enlarging 'our feeling of reverence for our species' as he says to Fox, has no obvious place for God. Nevertheless, such character-equations require one to decide who or Who in this secularisation of biblical story is the villain—or, to be precise, who or what, is God? 'Gain' is the monster idol of the realm according to the Pedlar, and as far as one can see the Michael-narrator is of much the same persuasion. The notion of 'risk' is intrinsically capitalistic. As in *The Brothers*, it is the eating away of what Wordsworth prefers to see as immemorial tenure by pieces of parchment—bonds, securities, mortgages, and in this case forfeiture—that forces Michael, if he is to have anything to leave to Luke, to place his trust in Luke's capacity for enterprise.

There is a monumental quality to *Michael* that not even *The Ruined Cottage* has, an inevitability. It is partly in those repetitions. Reading *Michael* aloud beside the boisterous brook of Greenhead Ghyll, with its waters invariably 'something between a hindrance and a help', one can find the return of the italicised refrain in the quotation below almost unsayable. The narrator has tactfully turned aside from Michael's tragedy—Luke's slackening occupied the previous five and a half lines—to muse first on what applies to all of us and then on the community's perception of Michael's last years:

> There is a comfort in the strength of love;
> 'Twill make a thing endurable that else
> Would break the heart:—old Michael found it so.
> I have conversed with more than one who well
> Remember the old man and what he was
> Years after he had heard this heavy news.
> *His bodily frame had been from youth to age*
> *Of an unusual strength…*

The repetition comes with an enormous 'but'. But what can such strength avail? Such emotion is generated in the passage that in an 1820 revision Wordsworth made Michael's loss stand in for all of his own loss, personal and historical: he modified the third line quoted to read 'that else | Would overset the brain,—or break the heart'. The passage, Marjorie Levinson has rightly insisted,[1] collates Michael's endurance of Luke's breach of their covenant with Wordsworth's endurance of the perfidy of France, and perhaps, if one considers the textual moment, with his struggle to endure 'how good men on every side fall off', throughout the 1790s and the 1800s.

The last line of *Michael*, 'Beside the boisterous brook of Greenhead Ghyll', strikes with the inevitability of 'Then sought with quiet my distant home', or 'And beat with thundering hooves the level sand'. That latter line is itself used twice in *The Prelude*, the second time with enormously amplified personal and historical resonance. The *Michael* line returns us to where we began, in line 2, confronting the then 'tumultuous brook of Greenhead Ghyll' (the 'boisterousness' has since been added by Luke). It encompasses all that is laboriously—and unsuccessfully—attempted by the Pedlar's attempt to draw from speargrass a consoling sense of continuity. In any case, *The Ruined Cottage* comes nowhere near the same 'artless' incorporation of the life and buffeting inevitability of the tale into a fitting closing symbol: an unfinished covenant, beside perpetual flux (Kubla's barely finished Dome triumphantly naturalized).

When Wordsworth spoke in *Select Views* of Michael's statesman culture he spoke of it as having survived until within fifty years of the present. This needlessly gloomy fiction, as David Simpson points out, projects the end of Cumbrian self-sufficiency back in time almost a hundred years, since independent freeholder farmers of Michael's kind were still common in the 1830s, let alone in 1800 when Wordsworth was writing.[2] The process is uncannily like the memorializing of Michel Beaupuy,

---

1   The suggestive treatments of *Michael* and *Intimations* in Marjorie Levinson's *Wordsworth's Great Period Poems* deserve to be much better known.

2   According to David Simpson the *Gentleman's Magazine* of 1766 noted that although a quarter of Cumberland belonged to 30 lords and gentlemen, there were still 10,000 small landowners. Up to 40% of land was held by 'yeomen' in 1829, and there were 899 true 'statesmen freeholders' in 1829 (Simpson, 87). The death of this culture seems to have been for Wordsworth, a moveable feast: *The Prelude* claims that until he reached Cambridge in 1787 he had never encountered social inequality. See also Terry McCormick, 'Wordsworth and Shepherds', *OHWW* (2015), 629–46.

Palafox and Toussaint l'Ouverture before their deaths. In all three cases, that is to say, Wordsworth is creating a past—like Iolo Morganwg and his co-inventors of Wales—but from the lineaments of the present. The procedure seems designed to prove that the tribal days can be connected each to each in natural piety, as an originating archetype is shaped from the valued elements of what remains, rather as people make gods by projection of their own ideals—an activity Wordsworth came more and more to respect.

Michael, one need hardly say, is the final humanist dividend on that supernatural note of the 1794 revisions of *An Evening Walk*: 'So while the spirits of the virtuous rove | Haunts once their pleasure … | So have I, at the stillest watch of night, | Seen through the trees slow-gliding forms of light' and heard 'low voices die along the glade, | And echoes whispered from each hill and shade'. His voice is borne on the wind, like subterraneous music. One of the noble dead, 'apt for all affairs', his tale is now recovered. He deserves to be memorialized, at least, before passing into either legend or oblivion. But if the poem has some efficacy—if Wordsworth's commendation of it to Charles James Fox helps to revitalise the commonweal—he may become a Wordsworthian prophecy, in which the past is revealed like future.

The Leech-Gatherer (1802–07)

The encounter with the discharged soldier, if it happened at all in 1788, took its emotional charge from the death of Wordsworth's father in 1783, its textual prototype from 1787, and some of its imagery from 1798. The encounter with the Leech-Gatherer of *Resolution and Independence* took place on 26 September 1800 and his more rapid evolution from a rather peculiar roadside beggar into an archetype of independence is thoroughly documented. The meeting is narrated as a postscript to Dorothy Wordsworth's Grasmere journal for Friday 3 October, a week later, on which day Wordsworth had been discoursing on the argument of 'his Essay for the 2nd volume of LB'—which argument requires that poetry be presented with the utmost 'nakedness and simplicity'. Such conversation may have prompted Dorothy to memorialize the lineaments of the Leech-Gatherer for future restoration:

> N. B. When William and I returned from accompanying Jones, we met an old man almost double. He had on a coat thrown over his shoul-

ders above his waistcoat and coat. Under this he carried a bundle and had an apron on and a nightcap. His face was interesting. He had dark eyes and a long nose. ... He had had a wife 'and a good woman and it pleased God to bless him with ten children'. All these were dead but one of whom he had not heard for many years, a sailor. His trade was to gather leeches, but now leeches are scarce and he had not strength for it. He lived by begging and was making his way to Carlisle where he should buy a few godly books to sell. He said leeches were very scarce partly owing to this dry season, but many years they have been scarce— he supposed it owing to their being much sought after, that they did not breed fast, and were of slow growth. Leeches were formerly 2/6 [per] 100; they are now 30/-. He had been hurt in driving a cart, his legs broke his body driven over his skull fractured. He felt no pain till he recovered from his first insensibility. 'It was then late in the evening, when the light was just going away'.

Since citations of this passage tend to be accompanied by editorial remarks such as 'the following description of the old leech-gatherer was partly incorporated eighteen months later into *Resolution and Independence*', it seems useful to itemise how little is, in fact, 'incorporated'. Wordsworth's leech-gatherer has no apron, no nightcap, no Jewish nose, no children to speak of, and no cart. He does not beg, does not appear to have been in an accident, is unimaginable driving a cart, does not complain of broken bones and a fractured skull, or—after the first version of the poem—show much interest in shillings and pence. He does have, in place of dark eyes, a pair of 'sable orbs', at least he does after 1807, and he has a *tone* entirely consistent with one who might say of his wife that she was 'a good woman and it pleased God to bless him with ten children', or of his accident that 'It was then late in the evening, when the light was just going away'. That is, as in Yeats's use of Lady Gregory's researches, it is the language that resonates. He also has, though none of these terms appears in the journal, resolution, independence, and strength. Crucially, Wordsworth's figure *is* a leech-gatherer. Dorothy's figure, half beggar, half pedlar, *is not*. The particulars that matter imaginatively in the poem are largely or wholly invented in the process of composition. Dorothy, after all, had excellent eyes and ears, and lent them generously to her brother and his friend, but she kept her imagination on a close rein.

The poem as we have it, and the leech-gatherer as we know him, took a considerable time to evolve, so that there is a famous slippage between

Wordsworth's most eloquent defence of the poem (relating to its earliest and, as usual, slightly wordier version in 1802) and the received text. That defence, in any case, suggests that he expects his readers to attend to the old man not merely as already transfigured by him in 1802, but also as reported by Dorothy in 1800. In the version of the poem read by Sara and Mary Hutchinson, Wordsworth described the old man as 'like one who little saw or heard | For chimney nook, or bed, or coffin meet' yet despite this textual condescension, he still upbraids 'My dear Sara' in June 1802 for not being properly awed. His letter presents an interim figure, half way between that of the journal and that of the final poem, half his, half Dorothy's:

> I cannot conceive of a figure more impressive than that of an old Man like this, *the survivor of a Wife and ten children* [Dorothy], travelling alone among the mountains *and all lonely places* [William], carrying with him his own fortitude [William] and *the necessities which an unjust state of society has entailed upon him* [a circumlocution for Dorothy's 'bundle'].

This figure is the more impressive, Wordsworth claims, because the phrase in stanza 8, 'a leading from above' prepares us to expect something 'spiritual or supernatural', and the poem then offers '"A lonely place, a Pond", "by which an old man *was*, far from all house and home"—not stood or sat but "*was*"—the figure presented in the most naked simplicity possible.' The phrase 'naked simplicity' recalls the pugnacious defence of 'nakedness and simplicity' in the preface to *Lyrical Ballads* that Wordsworth had penned shortly before Dorothy's journal entry. So 'naked simplicity', the revolutionary poetic of Alfoxden, and a passionate concern with economic dereliction, are integral to the poem's inspiration: economic circumstances are part of the *implied* subject matter of the poem.

The result of Wordsworth's agonizing over the responses of his soon-to-be wife and sister-in-law to this transcendentally 'impressive' figure are well known. He silences the leech-gatherer, removing three or four stanzas in which the interim figure of the old man (that decrepit being, fit for chimney nook or coffin) tells of his bereavements and explains that while he spends his summers leech-gathering ('All over Cartmell fells and up to Blellan Tarn') he spends his winters hawking 'godly Books' (*PW*, 2: 541). He also removes the key phrase 'not stood or sat but was', emphasized in his epistolary defence, realizing perhaps that he had not yet done enough to create this elemental condition of 'wasness', and that once he had done so he would no longer need the phrase.

So we have, as with the discharged soldier, another imaginative amalgam: 'Imagination', Wordsworth said, 'is that chemical faculty by which elements of the most different nature and distant origin are blended together into one harmonious and homogeneous whole'.[1] His Racedown / Alfoxden imagination (concerned with the price of coal in Dorsetshire, the impact of drought and war on Margaret, or the inalienable *right* of the Discharged Soldier to relief, whatever Malthus or Martineau might think) is still one of the consciousnesses authoring 'The Leech Gatherer'. In fact he is clearly remembering the Soldier while composing his successor. One is 'the oldest man ... who ever wore gray hairs' while the other is 'a span above man's common measure tall'. One props himself upon a staff, the other, having dropped his staff, is propped on a milestone. One is bent double (despite being propped); the other, equally disconcertingly (in 1798) is both 'upright' and 'half-sitting', as if seen in a double-exposed photograph. One is motionless as a cloud, the other in 'an awful steadiness'. The leech-gatherer is overtly a cloud-man—who might move cloud-like across the moor. Both are hailed, but only after long perusal. One speaks feebly but 'in solemn order'; the other's speech is neither slow nor eager but unmoved. One houses 'with God's good help'; the other trusts in the eye of Heaven. One, however, exhibits at the outset 'a flash of mild surprise' while the other evinces 'reviving interests' only at the close. One seems to be a figure to whom the idea of suffering is almost irrelevant, while the other—repeatedly—is referred to as ghostly or ghastly and with one foot in Hades or Lethe. In 1802 the poet sentences one figure to wander about the moors alone, silently, and for ever; in 1798 he had led the other to a hospitable cottage. So much for progress in Wordsworth's way of dealing with vagrants.

If one authorial consciousness in *Resolution and Independence* remains concerned with what man has made of man, another is concerned with the state of Coleridge, who having snapped his 'squeaking baby-trumpet of sedition' as far back as 1798 is now preaching the death of nature. He (Coleridge) is as far as can be imagined from all that is symbolized by the hare in the 'one Life' celebration at the start of the poem:

1 *Prose Works of William Wordsworth*, ed. Alexander Grosart, 3 vols (London: Moxon, 1976), 3: 465, in 'Conversations and Personal Reminiscences'.

There was a roaring in the wind all night;
The rain came heavily and fell in floods;
But now the sun is rising calm and bright;
The birds are singing in the distant woods;
Over his own sweet voice the Stock-dove broods;
The Jay makes answer as the Magpie chatters;
And all the air is filled with pleasant noise of waters.[1]

All things that love the sun are out of doors;
The sky rejoices in the morning's birth;
The grass is bright with rain-drops; — on the moors
The hare is running races in her mirth;
And with her feet she from the plashy earth
Raises a mist; that, glittering in the sun,
Runs with her all the way, wherever she doth run.

The hare, as we know, comes from an altogether different experience, at another time and place: 'I was in the state of feeling described in the beginning of the poem, while crossing over Barton Fell from Mr Clarkson's at the foot of Ulswater, towards Askam. The image of the hare I then observed on a ridge of the fell' (*FN*, 14). A truly Wordsworthian utterance! 'Image' can mean a visual outline, an optical impression. It can also mean something wonderfully glossed by the great Welsh Modernist, David Jones. Describing the late 19th century 'rubicon', or the 'break' between sacramental and secular vision, Jones asks:

> If one is making a painting of daffodils what is not instantly involved. Will it make any difference whether or no we have heard of Persephone, or Flora or Blodeuedd?

He goes on: 'without having heard of Flora Dea, there are many who would paint daffodils as though they had invoked her by name.'[2] The same goes for water: 'Water is the called the "matter" of the Sacrament of Baptism. Is "two of hydrogen and one of oxygen" that "matter"?' Perhaps, but in other ways, 'in Britain, water is unavoidably very much part of the *materia poetica*' (*Anathemata*, 17). This is partly because

---

1   Fascinating rhymes. 'Waters', we know is a full rhyme for 'chatters'; but which, if any, of 'floods', 'woods' and 'broods' sets the vowel for the others is a mystery.

2   David Jones, *The Anathemata* (London: Faber & Faber, 1952), 10. Blodeuedd is glossed by Jones as 'the name given in Welsh mythology to the woman made by magical processes from various blossoms'.

of the climate, but partly (as Wordsworth observes) because of the part played by the deluge in the lore of the Druids. 'If the poet writes "wood"', Jones continues, 'what are the chances that the Wood of the Cross will be evoked? Should the answer be none, then it would seem that an impoverishment of some sort would have to be admitted' (23). And a little later 'When is a door not a door? When is a sign not a sign?' (25). When, we might ask, returning to Wordsworth, is a hare not merely a hare—a flood more than a flood?

As the companion of Aphrodite, the hare is associated with love, fertility and growth, and among the Algonquin Indians the hare figures the prime cause.[1] In Egypt, according to John Layard, a hare over water was the hieroglyph for the verb to be.[2] Because of her leaping, and wakefulness, and passage through fire, she symbolizes resurrection, and for this reason, according to Bede, the hare was the favoured form of Eostre, the Saxon Goddess of Spring. It might well appeal to Wordsworth as a way of symbolizing paradisal restoration as 'the simple produce of the common day'. Boudicca, according to Dio, would release a hare before battle, pray to Andraste, and divine success from its path. Perhaps the genealogy of the image matters little: we may no longer 'read the forms of things' with a mythological eye, and in any case, inherited mythology is supplanted in this poem by myth-making. Symbolically, with or without such dimensions, the traditionally fecund hare in this overture raises from the plashy earth a companionable form, precisely as Wordsworth's imagination is about to do with the leech-gatherer himself. Like the hare, playing in the rainwater that fell in floods, he is to be perceived on the margin of a moorish flood. One is, nevertheless, reminded of Edward Davies's remark on floods: 'The Druids represented the deluge under the figure of a lake, ... the waters of which burst forth, and overwhelmed the face of the earth. Hence they regarded a lake as a just symbol of the deluge. But the deluge itself was viewed ... as a divine lustration, which washed away the bane of corruption and purified the earth for the reception of the just ones, or of the deified patriarch [Noah] and his family'.[3] If such references seem too arcane, William Cowper's melancholia—into which Coleridge is fast descending—is of immediate moment. Perhaps

1   George Ewart Evans and David Thomson, *The Leaping Hare* (London: Faber, 1972), 133, 130.
2   John Layard. *The Lady of the Hare* (London: Faber & Faber, 1944), 151–2.
3   Davies, *Mythology and Rites*, 142.

because Robert Burton in his *Anatomy of Melancholy* 'mentions hare's ears applied to the feet among many remedies against fearful dreams', Cowper kept hares (live ones) as a cure for melancholy.[1]

The patriarch (we are, after all, expecting something 'spiritual or supernatural', as Wordsworth says in his letter to Sara) makes his appearance in a form that is compared with both vapour and the water from which it rises:

> Upon the margin of that moorish flood
> Motionless as a cloud the old Man stood,
> That heareth not the loud winds when they call;
> And moveth all together, if it move at all.
>
> At length, himself unsettling, he the pond
> Stirred with his staff, ...

In the 1807 version a further stanza had already emphasized Wordsworth's suspicion of this figure's reality status: 'A minute's space I guess | I watched him, he continuing motionless. | To the pool's further margin then I drew | *He being all the while before me in full view*'. Perhaps it was a sense that he has overdrawn his rights to mystery that led Wordsworth to cancel this stanza after 1815: its wonderful alexandrine corresponds too closely perhaps to that wonderful touch in 'Michael' about the shepherd having been 'alone | Amid the heart of many thousand mists | That came to him *and left him* on the heights'—as if they might, instead, have carried him aloft—or the similarly enigmatic emphasis in *The Discharged Soldier* on the not very unusual fact that 'at his feet his shadow lay *and moved not*', as if it might, as in folk story, have evinced an independent life.

Perhaps, too, he felt that the next stanza did this work more adequately: 'As a huge stone is sometimes seen to lie...'. In the 1815 Preface (*PrW*, 3. 33), Wordsworth took inordinate pride in the metaphorical laminations of this stanza, which in its imaginative transference of qualities from stone to sea-beast and sea-beast to man is indeed impressive in a lumbering way.[2] Its immediate impact, it seems to me, has little to do with the elaborate explanation and it survives such analysis The first figure associates the old man with the great boulders one sees in glacial land-

---

1   Layard, 188, citing Burton, Part 2, sect 5; Evans and Thomson, 242, 245.

2   Since Wordsworth's dicussion of how Imagination dissolves and diffuses in order to recreate precedes *Biographia* one wonders whose concept this is.

scapes, deposited by retreating glaciers ages before man appeared on these fells, and the second with the emergence of life from the sea. Many of the figures in Wordsworth's poems seem to emerge out of their land-scapes or merge into it, in *Lucy Gray*, but here one experiences evolu-tion, extinction, and recovery, in a single moment. Such tutelary figures as the leech-gatherer have two lives, their own and a separate existence in Wordsworth's mind as archetypes of his own psychological needs, and while the leech-gatherer is at first humanized, through discourse, he is also Elysianized.

The Elysianizing process occupies two stanzas:

> The old Man still stood talking by my side;
> But now his voice to me was like a stream
> Scarce heard; nor word from word could I divide;
> And the whole body of the Man did seem
> Like one whom I had met with in a dream;
> Or like a man from some far region sent,
> To give me human strength, by apt admonishment.

and

> While he was talking thus, the lonely place,
> The old Man's shape, and speech — all troubled me:
> In my mind's eye I seemed to see him pace
> About the weary moors continually,
> Wandering about alone and silently.

To the figure in the first of these stanzas the poet, 'Perplexed, and longing to be comforted', renews his appeal: 'How is it that you live, and what is it you do?' But to such portentous and open-ended questions the appro-priate answer might be Shelley's: 'No voice from some sublimer world hath ever | To sage or poet these responses given'.

One can, of course, emphasize that the old man remains an old man, who goes on speaking, undeterred by Wordsworth's inattention, undis-solved in this torrent of imagination, as Anthony Conran does in his ten-able 'comic' reading of the close.[1] Yet it may seem more to the point that,

---

1   Anthony E. M. Conran, 'The Dialectic of Experience: A study of Wordsworth's Resolution and Independence', *PMLA* 75:1 (1960) 66–74. Conran argues that the two stanzas of visionary dreariness are a final outburst of negative emotions, a return of the emotional spasms of stanzas 4 and 7, and he concludes that what triumphs is not the poet's transformative imagination but the leech-gatherer's habit of cheerfully popping

as in *The Prelude* spots of time, Wordsworth is celebrating imagination's exercise of visionary dreariness. Like the girl with a pitcher on her head, in the Penrith Beacon spot, who 'seem'd with difficult steps to force her way | Against the blowing wind', and who becomes spectral in the imaginative wind of the boy's emotions, Dorothy's leech-gatherer here completes his apotheosis. The process started in the first draft of the poem, when he lost his nightcap and his apron. It accelerated with the loss of most of his biography and his stock of information about the price of leeches. What remains is an icon of resilience, whose very weariness is displaced onto the 'weary moors' he paces in perpetuity.

One of Wordsworth's purposes in *Resolution and Independence* was to answer Coleridge's *Dejection: an Ode*, by presenting himself as a figure of equal vulnerability, but more receptive to whatever in daily experience can aid the mind's excursive power, its capacity for amelioration and self-healing, less inclined to live in a world of words rather than of things. Of course we receive but what we give. The Leech Gatherer is not merely *found*: he has been created by an imagination prepared to work in alliance with all that it beholds.[1] This is emphasized by the unsayability of the last line of the poem, which requires that we drop out of metre in order to say it. 'I'll think of the Leech-gatherer on the lonely Moor'. As a hexameter (ostensibly) it asks to be read by analogy with any previous hexameter in the poem, for instance, 'The oldest man he seemed that ever wore gray hairs'. But any attempt to do so casts stress upon words that won't take it. The line is an invitation to play around until one finds a satisfactory intonation that puts the stress on the right aspects of the 'resolution': metre for Wordsworth was always malleable by 'passion'. Stressing a definite article or preposition is nonsensical, and as the choice between I'll *think* (rather than *dream*, or *not* think) and *I'll* think (whatever *you* may think) is insoluble, one ends up with something like: *I'll Think* | of the *Leech-Gath* er-er | on the *Lone*-ly *Moor*—two spondees, three or four successive unstressed syllables and an amphimacer (as defined, appropriately enough, by *Co*-le-*ridge*). One candidate for the correct 'resolution' is a truculent declaration of independence from Dorothy's journal. To think of the Leech-Gatherer *on the lonely moor* and self-sufficient as a cloud, is expressly *not* to think of him a few yards

up again regardless. I think one can have it both ways.
1   For a brilliant reading of this point and of the evolution of the poem, see Robert A. Brinkley, '*The Leech-Gatherer* Revisited', *TWC* 16:2 (1985) 98–105.

from Dove Cottage dressed in an apron and a night-cap. Wordsworth is rather tartly refusing enslavement to the eye and ear. More importantly, he is also enshrining (for future restoration) an increment of the mind's creative power, a moment that not only 'shows the mind as Lord and Master' (as he defined the spots of time in 1799), but shows—rather defi-antly—that 'the hiding places of that power' have *not* closed, whatever might happen hereafter.

The poem argues, contra Coleridge—and very pertinently to the debate of 1802—that what heals the mind sometimes arises out of the mind itself interacting with what it experiences. In other words, Coleridge's *Dejection* has got its logical knickers in a twist through failure to grasp that it is not in human nature for experience to be insular. It is not, and cannot be, true that 'in our life alone does nature live', as Coleridge absurdly claims. Philosophically considered, Wordsworth might point out knowingly to this student of Fichte, 'nature' is all that is not me, including my own human nature. In Wordsworth's poetry anyway, 'me' is a field of being, it includes all that I experience. And what we 'expe-rience' is inevitably—consciously or not—in part our own creation. Equally, however, even an echo is tinctured by the echoing substance: the skating spot, with its iron echoes of joyful shouts, has already pro-vided the definitive metaphor for such exchanges. Choosing to think of the storm that closes Dejection as 'but a mountain birth' Coleridge demonstrates that he, too, is condemned to be free. The Leech-Gatherer (also, but in a rather different sense, 'a mountain birth'), is merely a more wilful exercise of that same, shared, faculty.

ALL THREE of these great poems—*The Discharged Soldier, Michael, Resolution and Independence*—are instalments in the democrati-sation of myth, or the inauguration of what later became known, in the age of James Joyce, as 'the mythic method'. They fulfil the promise to make 'Paradise and groves | Elysian, fortunate fields' the simple pro-duce of the common day—that is, to generate myth from landscape. In one poem Wordsworth encounters the shade of Anchises. In the second he represents himself as merely putting the finishing touches to a 'tale traditionary' of a local Abraham, attested by numerous vouchers of its veracity. In the third he encounters something akin to the Wandering Jew (prompted possibly by John Wordsworth's speculation, when he met him at Wythburn, that the leech-gatherer was indeed an itinerant gentleman

of that persuasion) or still more impressively a Noah newly post-dilu-
vian. The two figures met by Wordsworth (the soldier, the leech-gath-
erer) both correspond, in a sense, to the disguised magus or 'helper',
in the fundamental romance or fairy tale plot as analysed by Vladimir
Propp: they make a present of self-possession to the poet, or restore him
to himself. In return, Wordsworth immortalises both.

The three poems somehow succeed in laminating the Godwinian
Wordsworth of rationalism, to the Gothic Wordsworth of spectre, to the
Dyerian Wordsworth of benevolence, to the Coleridgean Wordsworth of
ideal imagination, and they function on all four levels simultaneously.
Just as *The Prelude* reconciles the antinomies of empiricism and ideal-
ism (its great passages can be read and understood with equal satisfac-
tion by a Lockean or a Berkeleyan) so these 'myths' of 1798/1802 belong
equally to the world of the living and of the dead, that is, to the politics
of Paine and the politics of Burke. The soldier and leech-gatherer are
anchored to the real world not merely by being propped on a milestone
or supported on a staff, but as victims of demobilisation or scarcity: they
are close cousins to the figures of the mid 1790s whose response to such
denaturing is a reflex resort to crime. *Michael* is written as, and offered
to Fox as, an exhibition of humanity being sacrificed to 'accumulation'.
These three 'Men of the North' share with the dispossessed of *Lyrical
Ballads* the fact that they are democratically conceived, though there is
clearly a step beyond naturalism. This step, however, magnifies rather
than dininishes their radical agency, certainly when read by Victorian
dissenters—the Chartists for instance. There is no getting away from the
radicalism of the *Lyrical Ballads* agenda since it finds the primary laws
of our human nature among the dispossessed: but whereas the Dorset and
Somerset figures challenge what we do (pity would be no more if we did
not make somebody poor) the Cumbrian figures challenge what we are.

From outside the obscuring structures of the everyday, they utter
words of a naked dignity, charged with extraordinary authority. They
are both archetypes, in the Jungian sense, and in the R. S. Thomas sense,
prototypes, enduring like Iago Prytherch 'under the fixed stars'. And it is
not possible to divorce the sense that they express something enduring
and essential in ourselves, from the sense that they show the way towards
the dissolution of such flimsy structures as 'mere rights of property'
(1835 Postscript) or even of class. The political lecturer W. J. Fox may
have been thinking of the naturalistic shepherd in *The last of the Flock* or

The Farmer of Tilsbury Vale, but seems likelier to have had these more commanding figures in mind when he remarks: 'Why in Wordsworth's poems, the lowliest man that ... climbs the hills of Cumberland—even the poorest of them all—is good enough not only to be a voter, but to wear a coronet.'[1] Moreover, the three poems contrive to aggrandize simultaneously both the primary laws of our human nature *and* the power of poetic imagination. They deny that the boundaries the dualistic mind creates between man and man, or between natural, human and divine, have any real foundation in the experience of man.

They may also be regarded as instances in Wordsworth's recurrent search for a father or spiritual counsellor, a naturalisation of mythological poetry. Carlyle's editorial voice in *Sartor Resartus* waxes indignant with Dr Johnson for being anxious to see a ghost. Did the good doctor not realize that *he* was a ghost? that we are *all* ghosts? Wordsworth is equally impatient with those who think that Anchises, Abraham and Noah are mere legends of an irretrievable past or 'fictions of what never was'. They are, his narrative imagination insists, the simple produce of the common day. The Discharged Soldier, Michael and the Leech Gatherer are climactic instances of Wordsworth's capacity to archetypalize his (and in Michael's case our) own experiences—to conjure out of the mundane world, figures quite as haunting as the Wandering Jew, but with the power to restore himself to himself, and ourselves to ourselves. If any poetry of Wordsworth's demonstrates the claim of the Prospectus, that his poetry will make the wonderful the simple produce of the common day, or in Emerson's terms, re-establish a direct relation to the infinite, it is these apotheoses of the marginal.

'There is little or nothing of historical or romantic interest belonging to this region' said Robert Southey.[2] For that reason he admired especially Wordsworth's tale of 'the shepherd Lord Clifford [which] gives a romantic interest to Blencathra'. When William and Dorothy made their way to Windy Brow in 1794, Southey's friend Iolo Morganwg was forging a history for his race, promoting, inter alia, the Madoc myth as one way of restoring national pride and Jacobin values at the same time, or as R. S. Thomas put such activities, 'worrying the carcase of an old song'. Perhaps, subterraneously, the example inspired Wordsworth to

---

1 *Lectures Addressed Chiefly to the Working Classes* (London, 1845), 142.
2 *Sir Thomas More*, Colloquy 12. I thank David Chandler for bringing this remark to my attention.

do something much subtler, for Cumbria, or Rheged. In any case he is less interested in the warlike qualities of a new Urien, Prince of Rheged (though Aneirin and Taliesin will be alongside Wordsworth very conspicuously, in the martial poetry of 1815–16) than in the gentler courtesies of these tutelary presences—the Discharged Soldier, Michael, the Leech-Gatherer. Historically, nevertheless, these newly minted folkheroes seem to me to possess just the shadow quality that almost always belongs to the inhabitants of the lake district Wordsworth imaginatively occupied: the world of shades, which having been must always be. *The Vale of Esthwaite* and the visionary horsemen of *An Evening Walk*, of 1787–1794, still colour the much more imaginative Discharged Soldier, Michael and the Leech-Gatherer. Like all of Wordsworth's Elysian figures, these three have about them a quality that Coleridge characteristically described in terms of exhibiting 'the height and depth of the ideal world'. What 'ideal world' Coleridge had in mind, God only knows. Perhaps it was, in reality, the height and depth of their covert classical, biblical, and Romano-British antetypes.

Michael, for all its verisimilitude, combines the stories of a feckless lad who ran away from home; a shepherd, unrelated to him, who laboured inconclusively at a sheepfold; and a cottage to do with neither, named The Evening Star: so Michael is, if anything, even more *an imagination* than the discharged soldier or the leech-gatherer. All three, however, are now among the best known inhabitants of Wordsworth's Lake District— better known even than Urien, Prince of Rheged—and very much a part of its legendary essence. Exemplars of endurance, of empowerment, and of 'a milder day', they might well meet up from time to time in a grove of Yew-Trees, in the guise of hope and fear, silence and foresight, to listen to a mountain flood murmuring from Glaramara's inmost caves. Since one of them is first encountered listening to the murmur of a stream, while the speech of another seems like a stream scarce heard, and the third is evoked by the tumultuous brook of Greenhead Ghyll, they seem to have some title to the place.

Chapter 8: 'Lucy' and her Cousins

Now ye meet in the cave,
husband sons and all
if ye've hands oh make a grave
for she dies she dies she dies.[1]

O N 4 OCTOBER 1798, Wordsworth's highly politicized assault upon
ways of seeing, and feeling, and thinking in Pitt's England was pub-
lished as *Lyrical Ballads*. Two days later, the poet and his sister arrived
in the respectable mountain resort of Goslar im Harz, and entered a state
of semi-hibernation. Those to whom a tree is a tree, and a rock is a rock,
seem to imagine that this should have been a homecoming: the poet of
Cumbria finding in the Harz mountains echoes of the landscape which
fostered his imagination. On the contrary, what Wordsworth, accustomed
to 'the sunshine of the withering fern', and the liberating fall of decid-
uous forest, found in the claustrophobic, darkly evergreen landscape
around Goslar, and its bourgeois culture, drove him into memorial recol-
lection by way of escape. He began to write poems about his childhood,
and poems about death.

The introspective Goslar oeuvre—with its poems of lost childhood,
lost children, lost spirits and lost daughters (in the *Two-Part Prelude,* the
Lucy poems, some ghostly ballads, and the Mathew poems) is in many
ways the most marvellous of Wordsworth's bursts of productivity. To
begin with the basics, what I shall treat as 'The Lucy Quintet' consists,
by a not uncontested critical consensus, of five poems, four of them writ-
ten in Goslar in the period between October 1798 and February 1799, and
one of them two years later. There is no particular authority for regard-
ing all of these, and only these, as constituting a body of 'Lucy poems':

---

1 *EPF*, 670. This previously unpublished poem of 1786 is discussed by Duncan Wu
in *Wordsworth: an Inner Life* (Oxford: Blackwell, 2002), 37–40.

Victorian reception made them so.[1] When Wordsworth himself contemplated arranging a body of poems 'about Lucy', in a letter to Coleridge of May 1809, he does not specify which they were, how many there were, or in which order he thought of printing them. Francis Palgrave and Matthew Arnold both collected them, but not in the same order. But their lifetime publishing history points to *Strange fits of passion*, *She dwelt among th'untrodden ways*, *I travelled among unknown men*, *Three years she grew*, and *A slumber did my spirit seal* as the partly-authorized and certainly logical order.[2]

The Goslar Quartet is made up of *Strange fits*, *She dwelt*, *Three years* (possibly written last) and *A slumber.* In *Lyrical Ballads* 1800 Wordsworth grouped *Strange fits*, *She dwelt* and *A slumber* together, and in that order. The more ballad-like *Three years* he placed later in the volume, after *Lucy Gray*, the 'Mathew Poems' and *Nutting*. From 1815 onwards, when Wordsworth classified his poems, *Strange fits*, *She dwelt* and *I travelled* (first published in 1807) made up a trio of 'Poems founded on the Affections', while *Three Years* and *A slumber* appeared together, in that order, as 'Poems of the Imagination', which section opens with *There was a Boy*. Read in sequence (combining Wordsworth's two 1815 sequences), the five poems make up a profound quintet on mortality. *Lucy Gray*, which Wordsworth classified as a poem about childhood, is not generally thought of as a Lucy poem although it is of course a Goslar

---

1   Two lengthy books have been devoted to this phenomenon, Brian G. Caragher's *Wordsworth's Slumber and the Problematics of Reading* (University Park PA: Pennsylvania State University Press, 1991) and Mark Jones, *The Lucy Poems: a Case Study in Literary Knowledge* (Toronto: University of Toronto Press, 1995). An early assault on the grouping was by Hugh Sykes Davies, whose anxiety to undo the Lucy Quintet seems based on the understandable but erroneous assumption that the only reason for grouping them is a Victorian desire to hypothesise a real person, and that such grouping restricts interpretive possibilities. See his 'Another new poem by Wordsworth', *Essays in Criticism* 15 (1965) 135–61, 147. It seems to me, however, that the reading community sometimes gets it right, if not necessarily for the right reasons.

2   James Scoggins in *Imagination and Fancy: Complementary Modes in the Poetry of Wordsworth* (Lincoln: University of Nebraska Press, 1966) also adopts this order in discussing Wordsworth's letter of 5 May 1809 about his scheme of classification. The letter sees *Lucy Gray* and *There was a Boy* as belonging with poems about childhood and 'such feelings as arise in the mind in direct contemplation of that state', which category would conclude with *We are Seven* and *Intimations*; but it sees 'those about Lucy' (he doesn't say which these are) as belonging to a class of poems which 'relate to the fraternal affections, to friendship and to love', leading up to *The Brothers.*

poem and the only poem with the name of Lucy in its title.[1] Her family name, for most critics—and since Lucy is a hermeneutic entity the early part of this chapter will engage in dialogue with a variety of critics—places her in a different order of reality.

The Anglo-Welsh poet Anthony Conran said in a fine essay on the Goslar poems that 'Critics who speculate on [Lucy's] death (and who she was) would surely see the problem in better perspective did they observe that in the Goslar poems almost everyone is as dead as she.' He cites the three Mathew poems, *The Danish Boy* (with its 'bloodcurdling' conclusion 'like a dead boy he is serene'), *Lucy Gray*, *Ruth*, with her promised burial, *A Poet's Epitaph* (imagining his own death), and so on. 'The poor fly, in "Written in Germany, on one of the Coldest Days of the Century", is one of the few survivors of this holocaust, and even his prospects do not seem particularly bright.'[2] Along with sixteen short poems, in a style radically different from that of Alfoxden, Goslar also produced the extension of the Tintern verse (*The Poem upon the Wye*, itself, imagines that the poet may pre-decease his sister) into 'memorials' of childhood and youth, in the Goslar drafts of the early *Prelude*. These passages include the experience of the world as 'tranquil as a dreamless sleep' in the skating passage; the ravages of *Nutting*; and the memorial to an earlier state of consciousness in *The Boy of Winander*. In each of these passages we find states of consciousness, images of tranquillity, and forms of words which make it impossible to miss the cousinship of the Lucy figure with the earlier self who was acquainted with the stars, felt that the moon he saw belonged to his own particular vale, and felt the earth move with visible motion her diurnal round.

The title of this chapter alludes faintly to L. C. Knights's 1933 essay 'How Many Children Had Lady Macbeth?' in which Knights had some

1 As a genuine ballad, with a folklore narrative, making it akin to *The Danish Boy*, *Lucy Gray* was never placed with any of the Lucy Poems. Like the 1798 poems based upon the stories of Tom Poole, *Lucy Gray* is based upon one of Dorothy's. In 1815 it was placed in 'Poems Referring to the Period of Childhood'. While I exclude it from my reading, it is treated by Alan Bewell on similar lines, as naturalizing the tale of Orpheus and Eurydice (*Wordsworth and the Enlightenment*, 202–7). Bewell's discussion of *She dwelt* in 'Wordsworth's Primal Scene', *ELH* 50 (1983) 321–46 (pp. 341–3), has the merit of seeing Lucy as arising from work on *Peter Bell* and *A Somersetshire Tragedy*, that is, as related to Wordsworth's dramatic mode rather than to biography.
2 Anthony Conran, 'The Goslar Lyrics', in *Wordsworth's Mind and Art*, ed. A. W. Thomson (London: Oliver & Boyd, 1969), 159, 160.

fun at the expense of Ellen Terry for troubling herself over such questions as how the boy in *Henry V* learnt to speak French. She asked: 'Robin's French is quite fluent. Did he learn to speak the lingo from Prince Hal, or from Falstaff in London, or did he pick it up during his few weeks in France with the army?' Knights criticizes Logan Pearsall Smith, also, for claiming that Shakespeare 'puts "living people" upon the stage, ... characters who are "independent of the work in which they appear ... and when the curtain falls ... remain as real to us as our familiar friends."' Coleridge, for his sentimental reading of Hamlet, entered the demonology. So did Hartley Coleridge, for following in his father's footsteps: 'Let us', Hartley says in *Blackwood's*, 'for a moment put Shakespeare out of the question, and consider Hamlet as a real person, a recently deceased acquaintance'.[1]

Hartley's father also carries the basic responsibility for undermining Wordsworth's sustained silence on the matter of the Lucy poems. He wrote to Poole in April 1799 enclosing what he calls 'a most sublime epitaph' (*A Slumber did my spirit seal*) and commented 'whether it had any reality I cannot say—most probably in some gloomier moment he had fancied the moment in which his sister might die'. It is an odd use of 'reality'. Coleridge seems never to have accepted that his friend, far from being wedded to the matter-of-fact, was a habitual symbolist and practitioner of a mythic art. The search in Wordsworth's biography for 'a recently deceased acquaintance' answering in general terms to the description posted in the Lucy poems has abated in recent years, though there is a periodic revival of what might be termed the strange fits of passion approach, founded by F. W. Bateson on that hint from Coleridge. Bateson gives more space to Lucy and other Goslar-work than almost anyone else. His *Wordsworth a Re-Interpretation* (1954) opens with a lengthy analysis of the Goslar verses, then offers a reading of the Lucy poems—including a subtle analysis of *She dwelt among the th'untrodden ways* which has influenced all subsequent readings—and reaches the heart of its thesis in the following terms:

> If *Tintern Abbey* shows William already half in love with Dorothy, though completely unconscious of it, the Goslar period seems to represent a determined attempt to refuse conscious recognition to the new

and explosive situation that was developing.[1]

Yet if *The Poem upon the Wye* shows William 'half in love' with Dorothy, though 'completely unconscious of it' what is one to make of *To my Sister* and 'the blessed power that rolls | About, below above'? Could a poet borrow from Donne's *Elegy on his Mistress going to Bed* the sweet sensation implied in 'About, below, above' without even noticing? Surely not. But the referent, despite the title of the poem, is attunement to 'the blessed power' of love in nature, which in *The Discharged Soldier,* too, is felt 'Above, before, behind | Around'.[2] Such erotic prepositions go back to the juvenile manuscripts. Wordsworth's primordial lake, in the *Vale of Esthwaite* (MS.3 10v) wore a 'silver zone' thrown coquettishly across her 'lovely bosom' long before her sister in *The Prelude* 'lay upon my mind even with a weight of pleasure'.

Bateson knows perfectly well that Lucy can be understood as a nature spirit, and as a distant textual cousin of Robert Anderson's *Lucy Gray of Allendale*, Langhorne's *Owen of Carron*, and 'Dulcina' in Percy's *Reliques*. But he is persuaded that she is also 'a real woman beloved by Wordsworth'. Other biographers and critics, following Coleridge and De Quincey, have also assumed that our supposedly matter-of-fact poet must have had in mind some deceased lover unknown to biography, or Mary of Esthwaite, or Mary Hutchinson, or Dorothy. Some conclude that it cannot be Dorothy, because Dorothy has not died, and because Wordsworth did not elsewhere imagine her death; and the same argument is produced to disqualify Mary Hutchinson. Margaret Hutchinson— who died of consumption in 1796—is disqualified on the grounds that Wordsworth was not in love with her. Wordsworth, it appears, is a poet of limited imagination. If he writes an epitaph, *il faut chercher le cadavre.*

The most obvious *cadavre* was canvassed vigorously in the 1930s by Hugh l'Anson Fausset, who saw Wordsworth trying to 'lay the ghost ... of a forsaken woman', but strangely, not by Herbert Read who, while reticent about 'Lucy', is most identified with the plausible thesis that Wordsworth's innumerable poems about deserted mothers and lost infants express his guilt about Annette Vallon.[3] After a headstrong affair (which

1   F. W. Bateson, *Wordsworth a Re-Interpretation* (London: Longman Green & Co, 1954), 151.
2   Wordsworth's prepositional manner of indicating 'unconscious intercourse' between the mind and nature must be borrowed from John Donne's 'license my roving hands'.
3   Hugh l'Anson Fausset, *The Lost Leader* (London: Cape, 1933), 137; Herbert Read,

some people, before publication of the love letters to Mary, believed was the only passionate moment in his life), Annette was left behind in France in 1792, with a daughter Wordsworth would not see until 1802, who was in effect dead to him, who was six when the first Lucy poems were composed, and whom he would conceive of rather oddly as already in 'Abraham's bosom' when he did see her, at last, on the beach at Calais.

Geoffrey Hartman strides from the biographical towards the mythic, seeing the mode of the Lucy poems as something in between 'ritual mourning and personal reminiscence':

> Lucy is a boundary being, nature sprite and human, yet not quite either. She reminds us of the traditional mythical person who lives, ontologically, an intermediate life, or mediates various realms of existence. Nymphs, both watery and human, are an example; heroes, insofar as both human and divine, another.[1]

Her significance in Wordsworth's mythopoeia is understood when we see her in relation to the Boy of Windermere. 'If Lucy avoids the crisis of separation, the poet does not. She dies at the threshold of humanisation' (160). From the point reached by the boy and Lucy, further growth is a kind of death—a dying out of unselfconsciousness. But not to grow is also a form of death—a dying back from full humanity, from the 'human-heartedness' which Wordsworth records in book 4 of *The Prelude*, and associates with the consciousness of human suffering. In many readings, the 'boy' stands for a former self, capable of an immediate relation to nature and to the heavens. The very act of communication with owls is an image of the paradisal state, for in Eliade's account of the primordial vision, the ability to communicate with birds and animals is a primary feature of man in a state of paradise. That the boy is buried in his native soil, is itself a moving statement, but if we bring to bear the myth of *terra*

Wordsworth (Faber, 1930).

1   Geoffrey Hartman, *Wordsworth's Poetry: 1787–1814* (New Haven & London: Yale University Press, 1964) 158. In David Ferry's similar reading, 'These girls, half goddesses, though also wholly human, are his chief … symbol for the relation with the eternal which he is always seeking'. Seeing the matter more pessimistically than Hartman, Ferry suggests that 'to grow up … is to grow away from the secret sources of one's strength (which can only be understood as one's capacity for union with the eternal) and nothing—neither the poetic imagination which searches the landscape for signs of its harmony and love, nor the mystical yearning for an immediate oneness—can prevent that separation': *The Limits of Mortality: An Essay on Wordsworth's Major Poems* (Middletown CT: Wesleyan UP, 1959), 79, 165.

genetrix, and the belief that man is earth born—and only fostered by his parents—the boy's return to his 'native soil' resonates more profoundly.[1] Yet such a self as the boy had, and the man mourns, cannot survive. None crosses the gulf between childhood and maturity intact: 'the survivor', Hartman concludes, 'contemplates his buried childhood'. We may respond to the sibling Lucy poems as transferring to a symbolic anima such a mode of being in the world.

In another major reading, Frances Ferguson considers Wordsworth's classification of *Strange fits* and *She dwelt* among the 'Poems founded on the Affections', and *Three years* and *A slumber* as 'Poems of the Imagination'. In the 'Poems founded upon the Affections', she suggests, Wordsworth presents the mind at war with the mortality which nature inflicts, and the mind loses the struggle. (In *The Brothers*, which opens the series, Leonard's discovery of the death of his brother so undermines him that now 'This vale where he had been so happy, seemed | A place in which he could not bear to live'.) But in the 'Poems of the Imagination', we find depicted 'the mind's survival of the numerous symbolic deaths which it has experienced'.[2] To Ferguson, however, as we experience the cycle, from the three love poems of the affections, to the two epitaphs of the imagination, 'both Lucy and the quest for Lucy are continually and progressively revised and attenuated'. The final epitaph has neither girl nor addressee, and ends in a grim silence (Ferguson, 174–5.). It is true that if one disregards both the voices and the life of 'rocks, and stones, and trees', one may well hear only a grim silence, but in Wordsworth's world everything speaks. There is, in the quintet, a deepening sense of loss, but Wordsworth may have categorized the last two poems as poems of imagination precisely because, in achieving a measure of transcendence, they give the quintet (in a key Wordsworthian word) a 'sanative' plot.

Goslar and the Underworld: 'Hoc erat?' / 'Was it for this?'

Underlying both the blank verse passages and the new—and more lyri-

---

1   Mircea Eliade, *Myths Dreams and Mysteries* (London: Fontana 1968) 165, 166. J. R. Watson, 'Lucy and the Earth-Mother' (*Essays in Criticism* 27 [1977] 187–202), reviews the frequent citation of Eliade's *The Sacred and the Profane* and *Myths, Dreams and Mysteries* in essays on the Lucy Poems.
2   Frances Ferguson, *Wordsworth: Language as Counter-Spirit* (New Haven: Yale UP, 1977), 69–70.

cal—Goslar poems, Anthony Conran suggested, 'is the recurrent question that summoned from the depths of his memory the electing silences of his childhood, the presences that were the ultimate guarantee of his own creative powers'. In this work 'the question "Was it for this?" tolls like a bell' (Conran, 158). Conran means, I take it, that both Mathew and the speaker of the Lucy poems have the right to ask this question, and that even when it opens the *Two-Part Prelude* the question has about it the sense of mortality and loss.

In the amplified context of the 1805 text of *The Prelude* we usually gloss 'was it for this?' as meaning, 'since nature provided for me the fair seed-time I am about to recreate, how is it that I can harvest nothing?' Jonathan Wordsworth hears the question Miltonically, as relating to Samson in his wilting phase in *Samson Agonistes*: 'For this', Manoah asks, 'did the angel twice descend, for this | Ordain thy nurture holy, as of a plant; | Select and sacred?" (361–3).[1] But 'was it for this?' happens to be the question another hero with more obvious Wordsworthian affinities asks himself at the outset of another exile. In 1798–99, Virgil is associated more deeply than Milton both with Wordsworth's earliest treatments of bereavement, and with his own belief structure. In the *Aeneid*, what Aeneas learns from Anchises in Elysium is the ultimate source— via Newton—of Wordsworth's belief that

> the sky and lands and sheets of water,
> The bright moon's globe, the Titan sun and stars,
> Are fed within by Spirit, and a mind
> Infused through all the members of the world
> Makes one great living body of the mass.[2]

And Virgil's 'hoc erat?' is where one arrives, eventually, if one traces the rhetorical tradition of 'was it for this?' back to its undoubted source. In the *Aeneid*, of course, 'hoc erat?' has a much more anguished resonance than a bad case of writer's block. Amid the ruins of Troy, Aeneas asks himself:

> Must Priam perish by the sword for this?
> Troy burn, for this? Dardania's littoral

---

1   Jonathan Wordsworth, *The Prelude: The Four Texts*, 542.

2   Virgil, *Aeneid*, tr. Robert Fitzgerald (Harmondsworth: Penguin, 1985), 185. Virgil's Cumaean sybil also provides one ancient model for the poems on the naming of places (a cape forever named for Palinurus).

Be soaked in blood, so many times for this?

Was it for this, he asks his mother, 'through spears and fire you brought me',

> To see my son, Ascanius, my father
> And near them both, Creusa,
> Butchered in one another's blood?[1]

The question leads to an encounter with the ghost of Creusa, who died, failing to follow her husband in his departure from the fallen city—because he failed to look back at the proper time.

In failing to looking back, Aeneas brings about the calamity which Orpheus achieves by fatally looking back in one of the passages Wordsworth translated at Hawkshead. Wordsworth's version of Virgil's version of the Orpheus and Eurydice legend—of the wife twice lost—is fragmentary, however excellent,[2] so I will use instead the version by Ovid, in which Wordsworth also delighted as a boy. In Ovid's tale, the naiad bride of Orpheus sinks into death on her wedding day, bitten in the ankle by a serpent. Orpheus, after a period of mourning, uses his song to charm his way past Charon and Cerberus into the underworld. There he tells Hades:

> I wished to be strong enough to endure my grief ... but love was too much for me.... If there is any truth in the story of that rape long ago [that of Proserpina] then you yourselves were brought together by Love. I beg you, by these awful regions, by this boundless chaos, ... weave again Eurydice's destiny, brought too swiftly to a close.... As he sang these words to the music of his lyre, the bloodless ghosts were in tears:... Ixion's wheel stood still in wonder, the vultures ceased to gnaw Tityus's liver ... and Sisyphus sat idle on his rock.

His suit is granted, on condition that he does not look back until they reach the daylight world. He fails, and so loses his wife a second time.

---

1   Fitzgerald, 53, 56. Fitzgerald's translation is the best and (since it is aware of the rhetorical tradition) the most effective in exploiting the 'hoc erat'. For the tradition see John A. Hodgson, 'Wordsworth's Virgilian Questionings', *Texas Studies in Literature and Language*, 33 (1991) 125–36. No doubt some Bloomian swerve must account for the odd fact that Wordsworth's own (late) translation tends to obscure the repetition of 'was it for this? ... for this?'.

2   See Duncan Wu's fine treatment of the transcreation, in *Wordsworth: an Inner Life*, 25–31.

> Up the sloping path, through the mute silence they made their way ...
> wrapped in impenetrable gloom, till they had almost reached the sur-
> face of the earth. Here, anxious in case his wife's strength be failing and
> eager to see her, the lover looked behind him, and straightway Eurydice
> slipped back into the depths.[1]

Within the Orpheus narrative there is sly reference to an earlier tale,
which of course it mirrors. It is Persephone who prevails upon Hades to
release Eurydice, and with Persephone, who was called upon to lighten
the underworld, we come closer to Lucy and her origins. In Wordsworth's
accomplished Hawkshead sonnet, a widower mourns his wife, called on
'to illume | The realms where Heaven's immortal rivers roll'.

The shadow of Persephone, or Kore, whose rites the ancients believed
to be most honoured in Britain, falls over several discussions of the iden-
tity of Lucy, but the references are fragmentary. It may be that when
critics refer to Lucy or her cousin in the Mathew poems as a nymph
or naiad, they are aware that the most appropriate Naiad is Cyane the
Sicilian nymph who was with Kore at the time of her abduction and who
turned through grief into a fountain—though as Mathew says, 'No foun-
tain from its rocky cave | E'er tripped with foot so free'. Ferguson finds
the narrative voice of 'Three Years she Grew' Plutonic (189). Danby,
using the companion myth, describes the forsaken Mathew as 'a druid
Orpheus' (*The Simple Wordsworth*, 87). But this myth of the mother and
daughter seems to me to resonate in several aspects of the Lucy poems
seen as a whole.

Demeter, also known as Ceres, the corn goddess, is the Greek Earth
Mother. She presided over the harvest, and it is in that function that we
meet her later in *The Solitary Reaper*, still singing of loss. Her sphere of
influence, says Larousse,

> reached the underworld; though her character of underworld divinity
> soon devolved on a special goddess—Persephone—who was made the
> daughter of Demeter.[2]

The only story relating to her daughter Persephone, whose terrestrial
name is Kore, is that of her abduction. Kore was gathering flowers, with

---

1   Ovid, *Metamorphoses*, tr. Mary M. Innes (Harmondsworth: Penguin, 1955, Book
10, 225–26.
2   *New Larousse Encyclopedia of Mythology*, intr. Robert Graves (London: Hamlyn,
1968), 150.

the nymph Cyane and others, when she noticed a beautiful narcissus. As she reached for it the earth gaped and Hades-Pluto (Milton's 'gloomy Dis', the Celtic Dis Pater or 'Hu') appeared and dragged her under. Demeter heard her child's cry for help and—in the words of the Homeric hymn—'bitter sorrow seized her heart' (Larousse, 152).

Archetype of the bereft mother, Demeter roams the world until she learns from Helios—whom Hecate advises her to consult—that Zeus has given Kore to Hades, otherwise known as Pluto or Dis. She disguises herself as an old woman and lives among men for some time before it occurs to her to afflict the earth with a year of croplessness. This gives her some bargaining power with Zeus who sends Mercury to negotiate Kore's return. Hades agrees, but tricks Kore into eating some Pomegranate seeds, which have the effect of reinforcing the marriage bond. So Demeter—who thought she had got her daughter back—loses her for a second time. A compromise is reached, whereby Kore spends only a third of the year in Hades. So each year in the cold season when Persephone returns to her husband there are 'neither flowers in the land nor leaves on the trees' (Larousse, 155), but Spring dresses itself in flowers to greet the return of Kore, the flower-maiden. Hence the Eleusinian mysteries—the rites of the departure of Persephone and the return of Kore, in October and February, and their intimations of immortality from the rite of the return of the child. And hence—according to Kathleen Raine—Blake's almost contemporaneous songs of innocence, concerning the little girl lost and found. Since we are concerned with the Lucy poems we should note the involvement in all of this of Hecate, who was originally a moon-goddess, as witness of Kore's disappearance, and conegotiator of her return. As Goddess of enchantment, haunter of churchyards and crossroads, spirit of the yew, Hecate is associated with the torments of mortality.

The connection between the tale of Kore and that of Eurydice is more than structural (Demeter twice loses Kore; Orpheus twice loses Eurydice) for it is Persephone the twice-lost daughter who prevails on Hades to release Euridyce so that when Orpheus looks back Eurydice becomes the twice-lost wife. Orpheus, in any case, is structurally equivalent to Aeneas, who in *The Aeneid* not only loses his wife but visits the underworld (like Wordsworth in *The Vale of Esthwaite*) in search of the shades of his father. All three of the classical tales with which Wordsworth most identified in his youth, and to which he returned in the isolation of Goslar—tantalizingly close to France, of course, but on the wrong side of the front—are myths of a double loss, and an illusory return. Whether they in any sense embody the recollections of a futile visit to Paris in October 1793, five years before, resulting in a second abandonment of a lover and daughter, Wordsworth never said.

Classical Myth and 'Radical Difference'

That the Goslar exile should return Wordsworth to where he began to practise poetry—to what Ovid calls 'the brief spring and early flowering of youth'—is not surprising. But in the case of this poet, to be returned to youth is to be reminded of a poetic apprenticeship overwhelmingly devoted to dirges and epitaphs, exercises inevitably bound up with the work of Catullus, Ovid and Virgil.[1] Recognition of Wordsworth's continuing classical undersong is obscured for many because Greek myth was part of the quarrel between Wordsworth and Coleridge in the early 1800s. This is Coleridge in *Biographia Literaria*, commenting on Gray's 'Phoebus':

> That it is part of an exploded mythology, is an objection more deeply grounded. Yet when the torch of ancient learning was rekindled, so cheering were its beams, that our eldest poets cut off by Christianity from all *accredited* machinery … were naturally induced to adopt, as a poetic language, those fabulous personages, those forms of the supernatural in nature, which had given them such dear delight in the poems of their great masters. Nay, even at this day what scholar of genial taste will not so far sympathise with them, as to read with pleasure in Petrarch, Chaucer, or Spenser, what he would perhaps condemn as puerile in a modern poet. (2: 75–76)

In such moods, Coleridge can seem, as Douglas Bush put it, 'astringently and unpoetically hostile to Greek religion and myth'.[2] In 1802 he defines the radical difference between himself and Wordsworth in terms

---

1   In addition to the dirge for a wife and mother cited as the epigraph to this chapter, there are among the juvenilia numerous translations of the poetry of loss, two formal 'dirges', and a variety of verse and prose epitaphs. The early loss of both mother and father embedded inchoate emotions which were surely reactivated by the loss of lover and child at 23, an experience which completed Wordsworth's qualification to speak, as does Tennyson's *In Memoriam*, for that loss which is 'common to the race'.

2   Douglas Bush, *Mythology and the Romantic Tradition in English Poetry* (Cambridge, MA: Harvard UP, 1969), 55.

which contrast the Hebrew Coleridge with the Greek Wordsworth. Is it because he genuinely regards Wordsworth's poetry as incorrigibly matter-of-fact, or is it (to put a more generous prision on his misprision) because he fears his friend might really be a pagan, that he starts the hare of Wordsworth's matter-of-factness? And was it for this, perhaps, that Wordsworth is silent even to Coleridge about the genesis of Lucy?

Coleridge writes intemperately to Thelwall in 1796 after Thelwall has been abusing Christianity:

> Is not Milton a *sublimer* poet than Homer or Virgil? Are not his Personages more sublimely cloathed? And do you not know that there is not perhaps *one* page in Milton's Paradise Lost in which he has not borrowed his imagery from the *Scriptures*? … I affirm that after reading Isaiah, or St Paul's epistle to the Hebrews, Homer & Virgil are disgustingly *tame* to me, & Milton himself barely tolerable.

'You and I are very differently organized', he continues, if you prefer 'the Quarrels of Jupiter and Juno' and 'the whimperings of wounded Venus' to the passage in which 'the apostle marks the difference between the Mosaic and Christian dispensations' (Griggs 1: 281).[1]

Again in 1802 Coleridge writes to Sotheby decrying 'the Genii, the Dryads, the Naiads' of Greek myth as 'poor stuff, as poor in genuine Imagination as it is mean in Intellect'. Genuine imagination 'the Hebrew Poets appear to me to have possessed beyond all others' (Griggs, 2: 458–9). Publicly, Wordsworth seems to have accepted this point of view on myth. The Preface of 1815 is strongly influenced by Coleridge. On Milton Wordsworth there says: 'however imbued the surface might be with classical literature, he was a Hebrew in soul; and all things tended in him towards the sublime' (*PrW*, 3: 35). In *The Excursion* it is the Wanderer rather than the Poet who enthuses over mythology (4.631 ff) while the Pastor (7.728 ff), following Coleridge, thinks such fables barely mentionable 'without blame' on sacred ground. More importantly, the disagreement forced Wordsworth to develop modes of evoking the invisible world which are sublime precisely because they are so couched as to be translatable into characters *either* Greek *or* Hebrew. In Book 11 of *The Prelude,* however, Wordsworth indulged in playful revenge. Coleridge is

1 Not a few readers must be 'very differently organized' in that case; in the passage in question St Paul contrasts believers whose sins 'will be remembered no more' with unbelievers who will learn what it is to affront the living God—it is the foundation of that Christian assurance of superiority so repugnant to non-believers.

in Italy, and Wordsworth imagines him a willing votary at pagan shrines in Sicily—especially among Enna's fields (where, of course, according to Milton, 'Proserpin gathering flowers | By gloomy Dis was gathered, herself a fairer flower').

Speaking to Isabella Fenwck he again plucked up courage—when speaking of the *Ode to Lycoris*—to dissent quite vigorously from Coleridge's point of view, and found arguments at last to refute several of his particular claims.

> Before I read Virgil I was so strongly attached to Ovid, whose Metamorphoses I read at school, that I was quite in a passion whenever I found him, in books of criticism, placed below Virgil. As to Homer I was never weary of travelling over the scenes through which he led me. Classical literature affected me by its own beauty. But the truths of scripture having been entrusted to the dead languages, and these fountains having recently been laid open at the reformation, an importance and a sanctity were at that period attached to classical literature that extended as is obvious in Milton's Lycidas for example, both to its spirit and form in a degree that can never be revived. No doubt the hackneyed and lifeless use into which mythology fell towards the close of the 17th century, and which continued through the 18th, disgusted the general reader with all allusion to it in modern verse. And though, in deference to this disgust, & also in a measure participating in it, I abstained in my earlier writings from all introduction of pagan fable,—surely, even in its humble form it may ally itself with real sentiment, as I can truly affirm it did in the present case. (*FN*, 121–2).

'Earlier writings' must mean the 1790s, when 'in a measure' he seems to have shared the general reader's 'disgust'. In the Esthwaite period he felt no such inhibition, and the later sonnets to Triton (*The world is too much with us*), and to Pan (*Composed by the Side of Grasmere Lake*) are among the foremost instances of explicitly mythological poetry in the nineteenth century. While Douglas Bush in *Mythology and the Romantic Tradition* says little about the more implicitly mythological work of Wordsworth, he commented sympathetically that

> though classic myth may seem remote from the Wordsworth we usually think of, it is not at all remote if we remember the animism which was for him, as it could not be for Coleridge, almost a religious faith. For one who held such conceptions of nature and of imaginative intuition, myths inevitably embodied authentic tidings of invisible things. (Bush, 62)

Hartley Coleridge seems to have agreed, as far as Greek mythology was concerned. Roman mythology may have 'fallen with Rome' but Greek myth 'stands unrivalled in the beautiful simplicity of its forms, the pregnancy of its symbols, and the plastic facility with it accommodates itself to the fancy and feelings of all mankind'. It possesses something that 'calls man out of himself and persuades him to make interest with nature', on which point Hartley calls *The Excursion* in evidence, and finds it soothing to think 'that the emotions of our hearts, the imaginations that come we know not whence, the whispers that console or awaken, flow from a higher fountain than the dark well of our own individuality'.[1] He might be writing of the Lucy poems, or those Elysian presences.

The Lucy Quintet

Strange fits of passion I have known

In its dramatic, almost jaunty measure, *Strange fits* is the most Alfoxden-like of the Lucy lyrics: though the measure is closer in some ways to *The Ancient Mariner* than to anything of Wordsworth's in that time. The theme of the Mariner verses, the fall from everyday illusion— Heidegger's sleep of *das Man* or the 'They'—into a reality which is so angst-laden, and in its moral arbitrariness so absurd, that everydayness normally takes refuge in the flight of inauthentic existence, also appears in the Lucy suite, in deepening modes as each poem proceeds. Here, in the portal poem, the poet is presented as wholly enwrapped in the poet's dream—'the lover's illusion', says Geoffrey Durrant, 'that love and its enjoyment are eternal, his forgetfulness of the immutable laws of the universe'.[2]

> In one of those sweet dreams I slept
> Kind nature's gentlest boon

but the boon is here the delusory magic of the foster-dame, whose lunar name is Hecate.

1   Hartley Coleridge, 'On the Poetical Use of Heathen Mythology' (*London Magazine*, 1822) cited from *Essays and Marginalia*, ed. Derwent Coleridge, 2 vols (London: Edward Moxon, 1851), 31–32, 38.
2   Geoffrey Durrant, *Wordsworth and the Great System: a Study of Wordsworth's Poetic Universe* (London: Cambridge UP, 1970), 144.

> And all the while my eyes I kept
> On the descending moon.

The hypnosis—for Hecate holds him with her glittering eye—is registered by that extraordinarily successful stanza about the motion of the horse.

> My horse moved on; hoof after hoof
> He raised and never stopped:
> When down behind the cottage roof,
> At once the bright moon dropped.

This remarkable ungulate (to borrow Paul Fry's term for Wordsworthian quadrupeds) keeps raising his hoofs, but never dropping them, until the rhyme is completed with the expected antithesis—'dropped'—only at the end of the stanza, and applied to a body (the moon) which can not do any such thing, cannot, that is, unless one has been in a trance of Mariner-like duration, and one is being returned to ordinary consciousness. So rapid is the drop, so abrupt the loss of the illusion of immortality, that the mortal passage into nothingness is momentarily supposed by the lover to have taken place. Love, and the beloved, are subject to the waning of the moon: but not at the remote end of some infinitely extensible natural cycle; death—to revert to the Heideggerian—is my possibility now. The task is to become 'certain' of one's death, and capable of contemplating it, of anticipating it, in resolute being-towards-death. That resolution Wordsworth makes the task of the Lucy and Mathew suites. As he plays his variations upon the images of transient humanity and intransigent mortality, each poem contrasts, to develop an insight of John Danby's concerning the Mathew Poems, 'the moment of the rose and the moment of the yew' (78–9): the moon and the rose in *Strange fits*, the violet and the star in *She dwelt*, and the dew and the yew in *The Two April Mornings* where even the oak spells mortality.

She dwelt among th'untrodden ways

If *Strange fits* is Hecate's poem, *She dwelt* belongs to Demeter, mythology's primal speaker of 'and oh the difference to me'. It renders, Swinburne said, 'the sense of absolute and actual truth, of a sorrow set to music of its own making, a sorrow hardly yet wakened out of wonder into a sense of its own reality'.[1] Bateson comments, indispensably, on the second stanza of this poem, with its puzzling similes of violet and star, that 'it looks as if the half hidden violet is intended to symbolise Lucy's insignificance in the public world, and the single star to represent her supreme importance in the private world', but that also the images superimpose in such a way that Lucy comes to occupy the whole space between them, being of sky and of earth (Bateson, 33). It is, one might add, in the nature of Kore that we should see her that way. Only John Beer has added significantly to Bateson's analysis. In *Wordsworth and the Human Heart* he glosses very beautifully the polarity between violet and star: 'at the one pole the flower, focus of human affection, and tenderness for the particular, at the other the single star, focus of the human imagination and of wondering perception. Lucy possesses the qualities of both poles.'[2] If so, she represents the poetic self as constituted in *The Prelude*, nurtured by beauty and sublimity.

As an attack on illusion, *She dwelt* continues the willing deconstruction of imaginative constructs undertaken in *Old Man Travelling*, in *The Thorn*, and in *Strange fits*. A poetry of the human heart, as Keats came to see in *The Fall of Hyperion,* must exorcise the poet's dream. *She dwelt* is part of a consistent movement in Wordsworth's poetry towards the moment in the *Elegiac Stanzas* on Peele Castle when he bids farewell to 'The light that never was, on sea or land, | The consecration, and the Poet's dream' (which delusory light Coleridge notoriously construed as imagination). Having become his own Mathew, Wordsworth announces, with the shipwrecked John in mind—

> The feeling of my loss will ne'er be old;
> This, which I know, I speak with mind serene.

And he concludes the elegiac stanzas with a re-dedication to kindly poetry:

> Farewell, farewell the Heart that lives alone,
> Housed in a dream, at distance from the Kind!

'Kindly' poetry, inevitably, has kept watch o'er man's mortality.

---

1   Algernon Swinburne, *Miscellanies*, cited Muriel Spark, ed., *Tribute to Wordsworth* (London and NY: Wingate, 1950) 114.
2   John Beer, *Wordsworth and the Human Heart* (London: Macmillan, 1978), 95.

I travelled among unknown men

In 1801, Wordsworth sent his new poem *I travelled among unknown men* to Mary Hutchinson with instructions that it was to be read after *She dwelt*, an instruction he arguably extended to the general reader, if not to all editors, by printing the poems that way after 1815. The epistolary and biographical context makes it possible to read the poem as a wedding poem, in which it makes sense to regard Mary as its subject, and to leave it at that. By echoing in the first line the first line of the previous poem—in 'She dwelt ... I travelled' syntax and metre are identical—Wordsworth at first appears to be contrasting the fixed and roving feet of a pair of connubial compasses, availing himself of Donne's *Elegy forbidding Mourning* as he had earlier availed himself of a more erotic elegy, and so offering a subdued metaphysical poem on separation.

Mary Moorman sees *I travelled* [in Germany] as proving the non-relation of Lucy to anyone French. She asserts, of the Lucy poems in general: 'One thing is certain about the Lucy poems: the woman whom Wordsworth saw in imagination and called 'Lucy' is not Caroline's mother' (Moorman, 1: 425). Geoffrey Hartman—in a more sophisticated mode—says that this poem makes the whole suite into a celebration of the spirit of place, that place being England.[1] Indeed, the poem does address 'England!' first, referring only at the close to Lucy. Whoever the Lucy figure is, she shares the poem with her country, becoming almost interchangeable with it, as perhaps its quintessence. It is not clear at what point we shift from love of England ('What love I bore to thee', line 4), to desire ('the joy of my desire', 10), or entirely clear that as we do so the object of love or desire changes. Lines 9 and 10 can, after all, be read as meaning 'among thy mountains did I feel the joy *that I desire*'. The stanza's second statement seems appositional or associative: '*And* She I cherished turned her wheel | Beside an English fire'. But if each of these lyrics is an attempt to enshrine the spirit of the past for future restoration, the spirit here enshrined is that of Goslar: this is specifically a poem of exile which one may see recalling with a kind of nostalgia the sense of England which the poet only knew when exiled. The resolve and the

---

1   'Lucy, living, is clearly a guardian spirit, not of one place, but of all English places ... while Lucy, dead, has all nature for her monument. The series is a deeply humanised version of the death of Pan, a lament on the decay of English nature feeling' (*The Unremarkable Wordsworth*, 43).

seeming of the second stanza ('Nor will I quit thy shore | A second time; for still I seem | To love thee more and more') are the only verbs in the poem which are not in the past tense until the surprising close, in which the she he returns to appears to be dead—'thine too is the last green field | Which Lucy's eyes surveyed!'. If she is dead, then love England as he may, more dear though it may be for Lucy's sake (as the Wye is for Dorothy's), it is not possible to see it, still, with Lucyan eyes. *That* England is a memory. If she is not dead—and one can read the poem as implying that his England exists because she regards it, and it exists now because she surveyed it in the moment before the moment of the poem—it becomes a poem of acute contingency, rather than of loss, and a wedding gift in that it makes Mary (later 'a Phantom of delight, … a spirit and a woman too') the moment-to-moment guarantor of that 'England'.

Three years she grew

In *Three years she grew*, the first of Wordsworth's pairing of Lucy poems in Poems of Imagination, the suite again approaches the ballad strain of 1798: the poem employs a different stanza, and one can see this Lucy poem as the inward, less obviously supernatural version of *Lucy Gray*, which folk narrative has a real—as opposed to memorial—'haunting'. Here we have the Plutonic movement of the Goslar quartet. Frances Ferguson tellingly sees the speaker in the poem as a masculine nature spirit, dwelling upon his plans for Lucy, the flower he has sown to reap for his own pleasure (Ferguson, 189). The 'Lucy' presented seems to have undergone another age shift, dying before she can become a love object to the poet. There is, again, a sense both of tragic loss and of inevitability. The poem dwells upon growth. It concerns the realization that to celebrate growth is to celebrate death: death is the goal of life, the principle of creation—as the structure of the poem—with its six stanzas of creation and its seventh of memorial peace—seems to imply. But what falls into nihilation in the seventh stanza, leaving only a conviction of irreparability in the speaker, is a spirit which is peculiarly Wordsworth-like, indeed a child singled out by Nature for just the kind of moulding which the Two-part *Prelude* narrates as his own, and expressive of just the kind of *powers* that he claims as his own. She attains such a state of reciprocity with nature that she moulds nature as nature moulds her, seemingly going beyond—or mythologizing—the poet's half-creating half-perceiving activity. Just as Lucy in *She dwelt* combines the violet and the star, with the poetic implications we have seen, Lucy in this poem represents poetic familiarity with the 'essences of things' and the capacity to draw from the silent things of nature, the calm that is theirs. Her 'election' is a macabre version of the poet's calling, and if there is any poem in the suite that might be said to imagine the death of Dorothy it is perhaps this one.

Both its beginning and its end relate it strongly to the Mathew suite: Lucy grows in 'sun and shower', as Mathew will be associated with 'tears of light, the dew of gladness'. The closing lines, which tell us that all the speaker is left with is

> The memory of what hath been
> And never more will be

connect the poem into all the poetry of loss, including a loss—in the Kierkegaardian sense—of repetition. One may hear in the lines a counter-conclusion, partly because 'never' consolingly contains 'ever', and partly because 'evermore' is the more sayable (the *n* of 'never' loses itself between the nasals of 'and' and 'more'). The *Three years* conclusion belongs with Matthew's 'Alas, that cannot be' in *The Fountain*, but later variations upon the phrase read like attempts to find something to assert. One thinks of the Demeter figure in *The Solitary Reaper* singing of things—albeit sorrows—that have been 'and may be again' and the residual trust of the *Intimations* ode in 'The primal sympathy | Which having been must ever be'.

A slumber did my spirit seal

If one doubts whether the Lucy poems are songs of Innocence or of Experience, *A slumber did my spirit seal* seems to resolve that doubt. The poem has, in some readings, the laconic irony of Experience exposing the illusions of Innocence. What Lucy seems in the first stanza she becomes in the second: she seemed a thing, she becomes a thing; his spirit slumbers, hers is still. The poem remorselessly neutralizes the expected consolations. With 'no motion' and 'no force', neither seeing nor hearing, Lucy is rolled round, a passive entity, in the Newtonian universe of death. There is no sense that—in the state of the soul here represented—one might sit beside her grave with one's little porringer: or that her grave, as in the uncensored Intimations, is 'a place of thought where we in waiting lie'. Nor, despite Mary Moorman's suggestion, can one really relate the poem to Wordsworth's 'creative sleep of the senses' in *The Poem upon the Wye* (Moorman, 426). The lines represent the nadir of Wordsworth's engagement with extinction: comparable to his meeting with the Absurd, and the sense of cosmic Abandonment, in the meeting with the Blind Beggar in *Prelude* 7, whose blindness and paper label are an emblem of 'the utmost we can know both of ourselves and of the universe'. And the most obvious identity of this Lucy, who has returned to the earth mother, is Wordsworth's natural mother: asleep in an unmarked grave in Penrith churchyard, orphanhood being the primal abandonment, and early orphanhood being the shared experience of William, Dorothy and the Hutchinson sisters, whose own parents lie in the same graveyard.

Lost wives, daughters, sisters, or mothers; the poems express all modalities of grief. But this terminal poem for all its spareness has a counter-movement again—or rather the reader is likely to bring to it one of two counter-movements. One may notice that a 'sealed' spirit is not a human spirit: it lacks either the fears or the reverence definitive of humanity. The subject of the epitaph in the second stanza is the speaker's illusion in the first—his dream. The speaker is now one who will keep watch o'er man's mortality. Or one may reject the reading of lifelessness, and find an almost pantheistic consolation in the close. Coleridge's letter to Poole called it 'a sublime epitaph', implying that it sublimates loss into peace. One may recall that Wordsworthian rocks 'mutter', and his stones speak; or that Lucy in the previous poem has felt 'the breathing balm of mute insensate things'. One may remain sceptical about the power of stones to participate in the one life, yet still hear 'and trees' as an up-beat caveat.

Wordsworth, in my reading of the quintet, is roused from the sleep of 'the They' into a resolute appropriation of being-towards-death: it is the spareness itself, and the refusal of concealment, that constitutes the triumph both of the final poem and of the series. It is an achievement he pursues in the Mathew poems, poems which arise out of such questions as 'what are the possibilities of self-renewal?' and what is 'the difference to me'? Would that difference remain (Anthony Conran asks, 167) 'like rocks and stones and trees, when the temporary shocks of sorrow were done with, and the heart had grown old in joy?' Or does the series, from rocks to trees, suggest a metamorphosis in grief? In the allusive opening of *The Two April Mornings*, Wordsworth creates a Mariner figure who has learnt to abide the shock, and has no need to compulsively repeat his own story.

> We walked along, while bright and red
> Uprose the morning sun;
> And Mathew stopped, he looked, and said,
> 'The will of God be done!'

Who then, is Lucy? or rather *what* is she? In the first place she is integral to Wordsworth's own intimations of mortality: and his thinking about what kind of immortality will suffice. 'Mathew' is to the poet speaker of the Lucy poems as 'Armytage' is to the poet in *The Ruined Cottage*. 'The aim of all life is death', said Sigmund Freud; man *is* 'Being-towards-death', says Heidegger, and authentic existence involves 'an impassioned freedom towards death—a freedom which has been released from the illusions of the "they" and which is factical, certain of itself, and anxious'.[1] Wordsworth's own difficulty in accepting the idea of death qualifies him to be its poet:

> I used to brood over the stories of Enoch & Elijah & almost to persuade myself that whatever might become of others I s^d be translated in something of the same way to heaven (*FN*, 61)

The experience of the death of others, and the consequent anticipation of one's own, is itself a border situation for each existent. Of course death engulfs life, but—as in Keats—it poses a sanative threat to the everydayness of inauthentic existence. The acceptance of death is a rite of passage for the individual, as presented in the Lucy poems.[2] And it is a cultural necessity—for which reason it becomes the permanent theme of Wordsworth's work.

In short, Lucy is not an oddity in the Wordsworth oeuvre, whose identity needs to be established, but its most appropriate icon. Her models may include Dorothy as a girl, and the lost Caroline, but they also include a little girl at Goodrich Castle, who so took possession of Wordsworth in 1793 that he revisited Goodrich in 1798 and again in 1841, hoping for news of her, and devoted much of his work in the intervening years to

---

1   Sigmund Freud, *Complete Psychological Works* (London: Hogarth Press), vol 18, 38. Martin Heidegger, *Being and Time*, tr. John Macquarrie and Edward Robinson (Blackwell: 1962), 279–304.
2   Douglas B. Wilson's 'Wordsworth and the Uncanny' (*TWC* 16:2 [1985] 92–98) makes the point psychoanalytically: 'By creating Lucy as a fictional double who stands in uncanny ambivalence between himself and other, he thus confronts death in his own right. But by mirroring his death in Lucy's he also exorcises his own fear of it', 93.

exploring her animistic imagination: she might be said to have dictated almost as much of his oeuvre as Coleridge did—and the more characteristic part. As an emblem of life perfected and beyond vicissitude, her cousins range from Toussaint L'Ouverture to the child Catherine in *Surprized by Joy*. As *genius loci* she is cousin to The Danish Boy and Lucy Gray. As an archetype, her cousins are the Discharged Soldier, himself an avatar of Anchises, who is called upon to restore to Wordsworth a quiet heart and self-possession; the Leech-gatherer, a father-figure fathered upon the mist by the urgency of Wordsworth's lack; and the Mathew who learns to distinguish between the repeatable and the unrepeatable possibilities of existence. The 'Lucy' suite also brings to perfection the precocious line in epitaphic poetry that began, for the simplest biographical reasons, in a schoolboy's earliest poetical experiments at Hawkshead. Wordsworth's art does what it says in the prospectus: it deals in paradisal recollections, and in elysian encounters with the outnumbering dead, deriving as often as not from conscious or sublimated transactions with the favoured poets of his childhood—the ancients.

Chapter 9: 'The Milder Day'; or, Manliness and Minstrelsy

SOON AFTER ARRIVING in Grasmere, Wordsworth wrote of his aesthetic programme,

> I cannot at this moment read a tale
> Of two brave vessels matched in deadly fight
> And fighting to the death, but I am pleased
> More than a wise man ought to be; I wish,
> I burn, I struggle, and in soul am there.
> But me hath Nature tamed …
> Then farewell to the Warrior's deeds, farewell
> All hope, which once and long was mine, to fill
> The heroic trumpet with the muse's breath
>
> (HG, 929–34, 953–55)

The aesthetic is confirmed in *Hart-Leap Well*'s contemporaneous renunciation—'the moving accident is not my trade'—and it is theorized, consistently with this 'farewell', at the close of *The Prelude*, where the Bard's stern tendencies are tamed by Dorothy, Coleridge, and Mary (that is, 'by all varieties of human love'). It seems to have been something of a fixity in Wordsworth's self-image. This 'farewell to the warrior's deeds' turned out to have been premature—he wrote very considerably more of warriors after 1800 than he had ever done before, even at Hawkshead—but is reaffirmed at the start of Book 7 of *The Excursion*, where the pastor's pure eloquence is deemed superior to Bardic 'strains of power', and in *Ecclesiastical Sonnet* 12, which upbraids Taliesin for his 'impetuous song' and declares that 'ours shall mourn | The unarmed host.'

Despite the prematurity, there is much corroborating evidence for this resolution. Wordsworth's muse, even at her most militant, was devoted to moral rather than to martial courage. One sees in Wordsworth's treatment of Ossian—in *Glen-Almain* (1805) and the much later *Effusion in the Pleasure Ground*—as well as in his own updates of Romance story, a marked leaning towards the pacific side of the question, whenever he modernizes legend, myth, and history. Having first banished the 'moving accident' and memorialized 'what we have been' in *Hart-Leap Well* in 1800, Wordsworth did so again, in another twice-told tale, *Brougham Castle* (1807), and he confirmed the banishment in Quarto in his most ambitious narrative poem, *The White Doe of Rylstone*, composed initially in 1808, though completed and published only in 1815—by which date national history had required him to seize 'the heroic trumpet' on several occasions. All three poems, as we shall see, are linked in place, time, and legend, and in their reconfiguration of manliness. This chapter concerns itself with two of Wordsworth's projects in the first two decades of the nineteenth century: his recreation of the minstrel mode, and his related investment in reconfiguring manliness.

Hart-Leap Well

If there is such a thing as a 'twice-told tale', *Hart-Leap Well* is that tale, even though it has the curious quality that its first telling is unheard. Part 1 presents a timeless hunting narrative, in an unidentified voice. It seems at first that Wordsworth has renounced the dramatized, problematized, psychologized tellings of 1798, in favour of the timeless minstrel-narrator, a specialist in 'moving accident', one who is in the business of rendering the joy of the hunter and the passion of the chase, quite as much as the poet of *Chevy Chase*, one aspect of whose poem Wordsworth is revising.[1] In *Chevy Chase*,

> The stout Earl of Northumberland
> A vow to God did make,
> His pleasure in the Scottish woods
> Three summer's days to take.
>
> The chiefest harts in Chevy Chase
> To kill and bear away.

In Wordsworth's poem, Sir Walter derives a 'silent joy' from driving three horses to exhaustion, his favourite hounds to death, and a hart to a suicidal leap. We are seven stanzas into Part 2 of the poem, apparently entering upon another tale altogether (though not the 'second rhyme' promised at the close of Part 1, which seemingly implies an altogether different tale concerning Sir Walter's death and burial) before we dis-

---

1   David Chandler, 'The Politics of Hartleap Well', *CLB*, ns.110 (2000) 109–19, 117.

cover that what we are now reading antedates the foregoing.[1] Part 2 introduces the shepherd from whom the poet claims to have heard the tale we have just audited, and it discloses—in arrears of the narrative— what the shepherd thinks of Sir Walter, and the hart, and the accursed spot where the hart fell. But we do not know how, and in what spirit, he told the tale itself. So who tells the first tale? We have to call it the poet's narrative, because the verses in which the poet claims to have 'rehearsed' the tale belong, clearly, to the writer, in 1800. In any case, the story has been mediated, as Don Bialostosky points out, in a manner that would not have been within the power of the shepherd—whose sympathies 'are all with "that unhappy hart"'.[2] The removal of the mask of anonymous minstrelsy at the start of Part 2 causes as much surprise as anything in the tale itself. One is therefore stimulated to discover—by going back to the start and re-reading Part 1—whether this mask is as borrowed as it appears, and *why* Wordsworth chooses to wear it. Since the shepherd himself is clearly a projection of the poet who wrote in the cancelled *Nutting* lines of 1799 that 'I would not strike a flower as many a man would strike his horse', it is unsurprising that the poet find 'small differ- ence ... between thy creed and mine'. But it is surprising that the poet's narrative has muted, if not quite erased, the shepherd's antipathy to Sir Walter.

Critics who seek to distance Wordsworth from his shepherd, who is in some respects a hero of sensibility disguised as a shepherd, seem to be chasing herrings. The poet agrees that while it may be virile it is not manly 'to blend our pleasure or our pride | With sorrow of the meanest thing that feels'. Both agree that this is 'a doleful place'. The poet-nar- rator's narrative may seem at first less antipathetic to Sir Walter, but has in fact, when we re-read it, sufficiently marked the knight's ruthlessness and brutishness. He represents a rampant masculinity defined by aggres- sion, lack of concern, and sado-eroticism (it is implied that the pleasure house built at this place of death witnessed many little deaths). His dis- dain for dogs and men alike, and his truly Ozymandian pride—

> Till the foundations of the mountains fail
> My mansion with its arbour shall endure; —

---

1   Stephen Parrish, *The Art of Lyrical Ballads*, 132–3, finds it disappointing that 'As the story is being related ... our interest focuses on its incidents, not on the speaker's psychology'. Don Bialostosky contests this view in *Making Tales*, 89–91.
2   Bialostosky, 89.

confirm the shepherd's judgement that both Sir Walter and his works were a blot on the landscape. There are, however, two essential differences.

First, the 'small difference' between the poet's creed and the shepherd's resembles that between the poet and the narrator of *The Thorn*. Like the Thorn-narrator, and the poet, this shepherd is gifted with 'strong feelings', but like the Thorn-narrator, and unlike the poet, he is burdened with superstition. In affirming (of the fountain) that 'often-times, when all are fast asleep, | This water doth send forth a dolorous groan' he exhibits 'the general laws by which superstition acts upon the mind', and his hearsay evidence ('Some say that here a murder has been done') also suggests that he has a long-lost sea-faring uncle, alive and well, and living on a small annuity in Somerset. Secondly, the poet has a truer grasp of the human genome and, given the atavistic capacities of the race, and of himself, he knows that 'lest we forget' is for the foreseeable future a necessary legend. For the poet, therefore, nature will not expunge the remains (as the mosses seek 'to bury this poor thorn forever') but allow them to be overgrown—like other relics of superstition—only when mankind no longer needs to memorialize the stages of its ascent through brutishness and fetishism:

> 'She leaves these objects to a slow decay,
> That what we are, and have been, may be known;
> But at the coming of the milder day,
> These monuments shall all be overgrown.'

I will return to the memorial impulse of *Hart-Leap Well*, and how it relates to *Brougham Castle* and *The White Doe*, after a necessary digression.

Reconfiguring Manliness

In 1597, the *Oxford English Dictionary* tells us, it was thought that the Lord placed but 'one paire of men' in Paradise; in 1752 Hume could refer to 'All men, both male and female'; and writing to the Comte de Mercy in 1793, Burke referred to French events as causing 'a deplorable havoc … in the minds of men (both sexes) …' . Having thus established that the primary meaning of 'man' is 'a human being' (the binary opposition being between 'man and beast'), and its secondary sense is 'an adult male person' (as in he has lived here 'man and boy'), the *OED* soon runs into difficulties when looking at manhood, manliness, and manly.

'Manhood', it appears, has three meanings:[1]

> 1. The state or condition of being human; human nature
> 2. The state of being a man: a. as opposed to childhood; b. as opposed to womanhood
> 3. The qualities eminently becoming a man; manliness, courage, valour. *Arch.*

Noting that it is the third of these definitions that the *OED* considers archaic, with regard to manhood, we pass on to 'Manliness', where the situation is reversed. The first meaning of manliness is 'the state or quality of being manly; the possession of manly vigour, or those virtues characteristic of a man'. And for 'manly' the entries are:

> 1. Belonging to human beings; human. *Obs.*
> 2. Possessing the virtues proper to a man as distinguished from a woman or a child; chiefly, courageous in spirit, independent, frank, upright.

If 'man' and even 'manhood' belong to the race, whereas 'manliness' and 'manly' belong to males, confusions in gender studies may be forgiven. Moreover, 'masculine', having become desynonymized from 'male' rarely means 'belonging to the male sex'. Its definition, surprisingly, is clearest when applied to a woman, that is a woman 'having the capacities, manners, appearance or tastes appropriate to the male sex'.

Anyone who writes on gender without making some inquiry as to the meaning of gender terms circa 1780–1820 may experience a shock of mild surprise when Wordsworth speaks of manly meekness. In an early-to-mid-nineteenth century text, 'manly' is most likely to mean behaviour consonant with humanity as a whole. And if manly in this sense had been '*Obs*' in Burke's time, he for one (like Emerson two generations later) seems to have been old-fashioned enough not to notice:

> The monks are lazy. Be it so…. They are as usefully employed as if they worked from dawn to dark in the innumerable servile, degrading, unseemly, *unmanly* and often most unwholesome and pestiferous occupations to which the social economy of so many wretches are inevitably doomed.[2]

---

1   *OED* citations for manhood include: 'Keep … a little Pity to distinguish Manhood lest other Men … should … judge you to be numbered with the brutes' (Rowe, 1702).
2   Burke, *Reflections*, 271, cited in David Bromwich, 'The French Revolution and Tintern Abbey', *Raritan*, 10:3 (1991) 1–23, 13.

What 'unmanly' occupations Burke has in mind is unclear from the context, except that like monkish duties they are performed by men, and unlike them are unfitted to human beings. David Bromwich takes Burke to be referring to mining, a dangerous view to articulate in parts of the North. It is clear, however, that 'unmanly' *cannot* in this passage be tortured to mean 'feminine', or 'childish' or 'effeminate': its defining other, as in most periods, is 'beastly'. In this sense the occupation of the girl Wordsworth encounters leading a heifer in Book 9 of *The Prelude* is an 'unmanly' one. Equally, it is 'unmanly' in a sense fully open to women, to lie, to evade, or to dissimulate. When Emerson uses the term it has, on about half of the occasions I can find, the same 'other': manly behaviour is behaviour distinctive of rational beings gifted with a soul, and its primary signification applies equally to persons of either sex whose behaviour is courageous, courteous, considerate, frank, and kind. Unmanliness can, of course include the 'unmanly moaning' of Childe Harold's storm-tossed shipmates in canto 1, and the 'unmanly despair' of Wordsworth's Female Vagrant or Margaret, in failing to contest their situation (unlike, say, the manlier Grace Darling or St Bega). In such instances of 'unmanly' the 'defining other' is an aspect of the manliness *required* of males but not exclusive to them. Masculinity, of course, is another matter—as Shakespeare put it, 'Man is enemie to virginitie' (*All's Well that Ends Well* 1.1.123)—which is why, at the close of the eighteenth century, marrying masculinity to manliness was perceived as a problem, not a tautology. To that problem, Wordsworth devoted numerous poems, especially in the period when he was most committed to solving the problem of reconciling domestic and public virtue.

'Manliness' is the slipperiest of terms, because although one assumes that in the binary system of language a word is defined by its *différence* from an identifiable other, one is never sure whether in this case the 'defining other' is beastliness, womanliness, childishness, or effeminacy. In any case there is no one-to-one correspondence between effeminacy and femininity: if a manly style, like Milton's, is one 'undisfigured by false or vicious ornaments' (*EY*, 379), one might fairly assume that ornamentation is a feminine quality, and that ornament in women's poetry need not be 'false or vicious', but not that Felicia Hemans is 'masculine', rather than 'manly', when not so ornamented. Peter Manning and Simon Bainbridge have shown convincingly that Wordsworth's critique of Gray in the preface to *Lyrical Ballads* is gendered in ways that concur with Hazlitt's definition of effeminacy: 'Effeminacy of character arises from a prevalence of sensibility over the will'.[1] According to Manning, Wordsworth associates Gray's poetry with 'idleness and unmanly despair' and alleges that 'Gray's grief feeds on itself and perpetuates its own condition'.[2] Grief is manly because it is common to human beings, but disablement through grief is unmanly. In Simon Bainbridge's excellent discussion of the political sonnets it is shown that sensibility is essential to manliness ('Men are we and must grieve' says Wordsworth on the fall of Venice) and that Napoleon, in 'I grieved' is 'unmanly' because unfeminized: 'wisdom does live with children round her knees'. Nonetheless, in the same sonnet, manliness must 'temper with the sternness of the brain | Thoughts motherly and meek as womanhood'.[3]

Michele Cohen, from whom Bainbridge takes a lead, argues that 'effeminacy rather than femininity or homosexuality was the defining otherness of manliness in the eighteenth century'.[4] Cohen in turn cites Kathleen Wilson on effeminacy as 'a degenerate moral political and social state that opposed and subverted the vaunted "manly" characteristics—courage, aggression, martial valour, strength—constituting patriotic virtue' and Carolyn Williams's claim that 'There can be no comprehensive definition of *manly* in Pope's day, because no universal standard of masculinity exists'.[5] There are confusions even here. Williams's slippage from 'masculinity' to 'manliness' is a suspect procedure if we attend to Samuel Richardson, who censures his virile Lovelace for 'artifices and exultations not less cruel and ungrateful, than ungenerous and unmanly', and Herbert Sussman says of Victorian manliness that it could be defined as 'the control and discipline of an essential "maleness" fantasized as a potent yet dangerous energy'.[6] And if 'no universal standard of mascu-

---

1   Hazlitt, *Complete Works*, 8: 248, cited Bainbridge, 221.

2   Peter J. Manning, *Reading Romantics*, 56.

3   Simon Bainbridge, '"Men are we": Wordsworth's "Manly" Poetic nation", *Romanticism*, 5 (1999) 216–31, 223, 226. My discussion here is broadly indebted to Bainbridge's stimulating essay.

4   Michele Cohen, *Fashioning Masculinity: national identity and language in the nineteenth century* (London: Routledge, 1996), 9.

5   Kathleen Wilson, *The Sense of the People: Politics, Culture and Imperialism in England, 1715–1785* (Cambridge: Cambridge University Press, 1995), 72; Carolyn Williams, *Pope, Homer and Manliness: Some Aspects of Eighteenth-Century Classical Learning* (London: Routledge, 1993), 9. Both cited, Cohen, 8.

6   *Clarissa*, 4.24, cited in G. J. Barker-Benfield, *The Culture of Sensibility: Sex and*

linity exists' it is rash to insist upon 'aggression' as a 'vaunted "manly" characteristic'.[1] Nevertheless, such associations were in place, and a reform of some sort does seem to have taken place. Wordsworth's poetry, along with Coleridge's *Aids to Reflection*, suffused through Thomas and Matthew Arnold,[2] has much to do with the rise of the Victorian concept of Christian manliness, in which manliness is achieved through spiritual discipline, not inherited, and is defined by the sublimation of aggression and wilfulness into tenderness and compassionate strength. As Thomas Hughes wrote, toward the end of this process, 'the more absolute the surrender of the will, the more perfect will be the temper of our courage and the strength of our manliness'.[3]

From the moment that Wordsworth decided to close *The Prelude* by using beauty to temper the sublime,[4] he could be described as embarked

Society in Eighteenth-Century Britain, Chicago & London: University of Chicago Press, 1992, 337. Herbert Sussman, *Victorian Masculinities: Manhood and Masculine Poetics in Early Victorian Literature and Art* (Cambridge: Cambridge University Press), 13.

1   Unsurprisingly, confusions abound in ths minefield. Marlon Ross claims that Nature's fostering force in Wordsworth's poetry is superseded by the assertion of masculine maturity, ignoring the more surprising fact that the maternal has usurped the place of the paternal in the first place ('Romantic Quest and Conquest: Troping Masculine Power in the Crisis of Poetic Identity', in Mellor *Romanticism and Feminism*, 26–51). Even Simon Bainbridge considers that in praising the 'manly tone' of the political sonnets in the *Annual Review*, Lucy Aikin is 'creating her own self-authorizing manly voice' (229). But it is only necessary, surely, for Aikin to be creating a 'manly voice' if manly is constructed against the female, which Bainbridge's article has placed in question.

2   *Aids to Reflection* defines 'Manhood or manliness', in seemingly gendered tropes, as 'Strength of Character in relation to the dictates of Reason; Energy of Will in preserving the Line of Rectitude tense and firm against the warping forces and treacheries of Temptation'. *Aids to Reflection*, ed. John Beer, CC Volume 9 (London & Princeton: Routledge and Princeton University Press, 1993), 195.

3   Thomas Hughes, *The Manliness of Christ* (1879; London: Macmillan, 1907). In the British Library (Boston Spa) copy of this Macmillan's Sixpenny Series reprint a reader has inscribed on the flyleaf: 'true Manhood lies in the desire of *men and women* [my emphasis] to reach the ideal'. Contrary to popular belief, Hughes contested the 'muscular' variant of Christianity in favour of the Arnoldian: 'a great athlete may be a brute or a coward, while a truly manly man can be neither' (12). See also Norman Vance, 'The Ideal of Manliness', in *The Victorian Public School*, ed. Brian Simon and Ian Bradley (Dublin: Gill and Macmillan, 1975); and J. A. Mangan and James Walvin, eds, *Manliness and Morality: Middle-Class Masculinity in Britain and America, 1800–1940* (Manchester: Manchester University Press, 1987).

4   *Prelude 1805*, 13.211–68. The lines are revised in 1850 so that Mary takes her place

on a gender-revision project. The questing hero of *The Prelude* is made imperfect in himself, the poem concludes, and requires finishing by the sororal, the fraternal, and the connubial, thus 'soften[ing] down | This oversternness' (*1805*, 13.226–7). As Hannah More, who believed in an essential feminine sensibility as strongly as Wollstonecraft derided it, wrote in 1785: 'The rough angles and asperities of male manners are imperceptibly filed and gradually worn smooth by the polishing of female conversation; while the ideas of women acquire strength and solidity by associating with sensible, intelligent and judicious men.'[1] Such strength and solidity was, for More, the point of female education; without it, lacking equal powers of analysis and reflection, their 'natural softness' might degenerate too rapidly into 'imbecility of understanding.'[2] More's filing down of 'rough angles and asperities' does suggest itself as a likely if indirect 'source' for Wordsworth's 'softening down' of a rock-like nature to make space for the flora and fauna of feminine sensibility. Such intercourse is therefore desirable, and it seems a widespread ideal at the turn of the century. Earlier in the eighteenth century there would have been rather more anxiety on the point. Cohen cites the testimony of Shaftesbury, that refinement through the society of women 'should go only so far or it would become effeminacy' and of Joseph Spence that while 'some conversation with the ladies is necessary to smooth the temper as well as the manners of men, ... too much of it is apt to effeminate or debilitate both' (the temper and the manners, presumably).[3] Even Mary Wollstonecraft agreed that given the excessive emphasis upon sen-

---

alongside Dorothy and Coleridge in the project to temper a too exclusive attachment to the Miltonic sublime. W. J. B. Owen's 'The Descent from Snowdon', *TWC* 16:2 (1985) 65–74, collected in *Understanding 'The Prelude'* (Humanities-Ebooks, 2007 [PDF only]) sees Wordsworth renouncing precisely the imaginative qualities that create the sublimities of *The Prelude*. One might argue that one revisionary aim of the *1850 Prelude* is to bring the sublime and the beautiful into optimum balance—as for instance in rephrasing the Boating spot so as magnify the sense of terror. Thus in *1850* 'with trembling *oars* I turned' amplifies 'trembling *hands*'; and 'with the din *smitten*' puts a word of power in place of the lame expression 'with the din, meanwhile'.

1   Hannah More, *Essays on Various Subjects, Principally Designed for Young Ladies* (London: 1785), 14.

2   More, *Strictures on the Modern System of Female Education* (1799), vols 7 and 8 of Works of Hannah More (London: T Cadell, 1818), 8.301–31, 7.210.

3   Shaftesbury, quoted from George Barker-Benfield, *The Culture of Sensibility*, 117; Joseph Spence, *Letters from the Grand Tour 1730–1741*, ed. S. Klima (London: McGill-Queen's University press, 1975), 9–10; both cited Cohen, 4.

sibility in the education of women they were likely to rear effeminate men. But effeminacy and excessive sensibility, in Wollstonecraft's view, are unnatural in both sexes, as they were to her admirer Mary Hays. To Hays, 'the enervating and degrading system of manners by which the understandings of women have been chained down to frivolity and trifles, have increased the general tide of effeminacy and corruption'.[1]

To choose Dorothy as the feminine principle with whom to associate is of course to step well outside the cultural norm, since her behaviour and sensibility, in De Quincey's testimony at least, are closer to the ardent ideals of Mary Hays than to those of Hannah More: perpetually at war with decorum, she seemed scandalously irregular to her relations (De Quincey, *Recollections*, 131–3). Nonetheless, to take a warning contemporaneous with the Two-part *Prelude*, one must tread carefully. If 'we' are confined to women's company, William Alexander warned, 'they infallibly stamp upon us the effeminacy, and some other of the signatures of their nature', but 'if constantly excluded from it, we contract a roughness of behaviour and slovenliness of person'.[2] William, in the last book of *The Prelude*, completed just two years before he was charged with effeminacy in *Poems, in Two Volumes*, and two years after his pursuit of a feminized manliness in the political sonnets, is playing chicken with this dangerous contagion—and doing so, presumably, because the cheerful faith of *To My Sister*, *The Poem upon the Wye* and *Nutting* have already put in question for this friend of Godwin and admirer of Wollstonecraft, the idea of gendered mind. Like *To my Sister* and *The Poem upon the Wye*, written in the previous spring and summer, *Nutting* makes no discrimination between the kinds of experience of which brothers and sisters are capable. While the published *Nutting* does not explicitly associate the female with ravishment—it merely enjoins Dorothy to widen her sense of the one life to include hazels along with butterflies—the very injunction still implies undifferentiation; that is, it questions, as did Wollstonecraft and Hays, and as Hannah More did not, whether there is some specialized area of sensibility that was gendered female.[3] Wordsworth's gender redefinition project was carried on in a

1   Mary Hays, *Letters and Essays: Moral and Miscellaneous* (London: Knott, 1793) 20. See also her cautionary 'History of Melville and Serena', 31–41.

2   William Alexander, *The History of Women from the earliest Antiquity to the Present Time*, 2 vols (London 1779), 1: 314 (Cohen, 110).

3   This departure from stereotypes has caused widespread puzzlement. For censure of

dozen of the shorter poems that gave him respite from *The Prelude*. They range from *Nutting* and *Hart-Leap Well* in 1799–1800, to *The Egyptian Maid* in 1835, and they proliferated in 1807.[1]

Poems, in Two Volumes[2]

Had Coleridge's dilatoriness not frustrated the publication in 1797 of *Salisbury Plain* and *The Ruined Cottage*, Wordsworth might have got away with the risk he took in 1807. The new experiments in extreme and provocative simplicity published in *Poems, in Two Volumes* were read with the interest due to the poet whose originality in *Lyrical Ballads* had gradually earned some recognition on both sides of the Atlantic, but with the caution and suspicion to be expected, considering the revolt against decorum practised in the ballads themselves and theorized somewhat

Wordsworth for 'confirming the socio-historical subordination of women' see Marlon B. Ross, 'Naturalizing Gender: Woman's place in Wordsworth's Ideological Landscape', *ELH*, 53:2 (1986) and Mary Jacobus, 'Behold the Parent Hen', *Romanticism, Writing and Sexual Difference* (Oxford: Clarendon, 1989). For extenuation (on the ingenious grounds that as the hazels in *Nutting* are gendered both male and female, the boy's assault destroys simultaneously father and mother figure, transferring his allegiance to the brother-sister nexus) see Rachel Crawford, 'The Structure of the Sororal in Wordsworth's "Nutting"', *SiR* 31:2 (1992) 197–211. These perspectives are discussed by Gregory Jones in 'Rude Intercourse', cited in chapter 3.

1   They include *Once in a lonely hamlet* (March 1802); *Resolution and Independence* (1802–1807); *Great men have been among us* and *I grieved for Buonaparte* (1802); *Rob Roy's Grave* (1805–1807); *The Happy Warrior* (1805–1807); *The Waggoner* (1805–1819); *The Horn of Egremont Castle* (1807, for its emphasis upon magnanimity and its exhibition of competitiveness as the antithesis of 'the happy warrior'); *Song at the Feast of Brougham Castle* (1807); *The White Doe* (1808–1815); and *Artegal and Elidure* (1815–1820). *The Waggoner* contrasts the notably gentle Benjamin with the braggart veteran of Trafalgar, whose conduct exhibits both national chauvinism after Trafalgar, and male chauvinism. This hero's true quality is attested in the way he is introduced to Benjamin, 'It is my husband', softly said | The Woman as if half afraid' (*Benjamin the Waggoner*, ed. Paul Betz [Ithaca & NY: Cornell UP, 1981], 63, lines 239–40) and is confirmed by his neglect of her when drink is to be had.

2   It was tempting to expand on this section for the 2nd edition of this book, but chapters 2 and 3 of *Wordsworth and Helen Maria Williams; or, the Perils of Sensibility* (Humanities-Ebooks, 2010) look at *Poems, in Two Volumes* as a tribute to Sensibility, and at the impact on Wordsworth of Jeffrey's sustained critique of the Sensibility element in what I call Wordsworth's 'Pansies'. Lucy Newlyn has recently treated these poems as an expression of sibling sensibilities, in *William and Dorothy Wordsworth: 'All in Each Other'* OUP, 2013).

pugnaciously, in the prefaces of 1800 and 1802. It might be the eventual destiny of these poems, as Wordsworth said to Lady Beaumont, 'to console the afflicted, to add sunshine to daylight' (very much the effect of some of the 'Moods of My Own Mind') and 'to teach the young, and the gracious of every age, to see, to think and feel' (*MY* 1, 146–7), but the immediate effect of poems devoted to kittens and falling leaves, butterflies and red-breasts, daisies, glow-worms, and the common pile wort (as more than one reviewer preferred to call the lesser celandine) was to persuade reviewers that their suspicions had been right. Wordsworth meant to degrade a manly and cultivated literature with metrically crude, ill-rhymed, namby-pamby puerility. It would be purely speculative to call this a calculated risk on Wordsworth's part. It seems not to have occurred to him that in devoting the larger part of his *Poems, in Two Volumes* to even more daringly humble topics than appeared in *Lyrical Ballads*, indulging in an unbuttoned display of 'getting in touch with his feminine side' as it were, he would invite a gendered condemnation that he would not rise above until he expiated all this naked sensibility in the ultra-stoicism of *The Excursion*. The savage reviews of *Poems, in Two Volumes* and of *The White Doe*, especially those from Edinburgh, are quite as heavily gendered as *Blackwood's* assault upon Keats: Lakers and Cockneys are found equally effeminate, and Wordsworth's sedition, like Keats's, is adjudged to be of the *'lisping'* variety.[1]

Byron, unsurprisingly, found the language of 'Moods of my Own Mind' not merely simple but 'puerile' and 'namby-pamby', although he did refrain from suggesting in public that Wordsworth, like Keats, was 'frigging his imagination'. *The Critical Review* depicted Wordsworth,

---

1   For gendered reviews of Keats see Susan J. Wolfson, 'Feminizing Keats', in *Critical Essays on John Keats*, ed. Hermione de Almeida (Boston: G. K. Hall, 1990), 317–56, Ann Mellor, *Romanticism and Gender* (New York and London: Routledge 1993), 171ff, and Wolfson and others in Nicholas Roe, ed. *Keats and History* (Cambridge: Cambridge University Press, 1995). My association of Wordsworth and Keats as poets risking emasculation runs counter to received opinion. Marlon B. Ross in *The Contours of Masculine Desire: Romanticism and the Rise of Women's Poetry* (New York and Oxford: Oxford University Press, 1989) thinks that 'the potential to have poetic foremothers, as well a forefathers, is much greater for Keats than for Wordsworth' (as if Charlotte Smith and Helen Maria Williams were not hugely significant to the young Wordsworth). Ross sees Wordsworth 'more directly linked to the male tradition of Dryden and Pope both in terms of time and class status [?]' and as returning poetry 'to its roots in manly action' and away from the 'emasculation' threatened by 'sickly German tales or presumptuous female romancers' (156).

with the sodomite version of effeminacy in mind, as 'the capricious minion of a debasing affectation'. *Le Beau Monde* thought his muse must have entered her second childhood to spend two volumes drivelling out such 'puerilities'. This London wit and witling accused Wordsworth of imitating 'the lisp of children'. Francis Jeffrey, on cue, complained of 'namby-pamby' poems, 'babyish absurdity', 'silliness and affectation', 'childishness and insipidity' and plain 'trash'. *The Cabinet*, the *British Critic* and the *Poetical Register* found, respectively, 'puerile affectation', 'flimsy, puerile thoughts', and 'drivelling nonsense'. Lord Chesterfield who bought the volume on Sir George Beaumont's recommendation expressed surprise at the quantity of 'puerile nonsense' it contained.[1]

In Volume 1, neither the staunch dignity of Alice Fell nor the exemplary manliness of the Leech Gatherer made much impression, though both *The Character of the Happy Warrior* and *The Horn of Egremont Castle* were recognized by some critics as presaging what Lucy Aikin called the 'manly tone' of the political sonnets. In Volume 2 the subtle contrasting of male and female principles in the first six poems went unnoticed: in *Rob Roy's Grave* and *The Solitary Reaper*, *Stepping Westward* and *Glen-Almain*, *The Matron of Jedborough* and *The Highland Girl*, the noble dead may be male but the noble living are all female.[2] The namby-pamby suite of poems entitled 'Moods of my Own Mind' (joyful, vigorous and sometimes startling creations of Wordsworth's most playful mode) created a mood of intolerance further aggravated by the provocative household tub of *The Blind Highland Boy*, which Lamb alone had the manliness to defend from Coleridge, Byron and Jeffrey. Interestingly, however, Francis Jeffrey did like the most overtly Annette-related poem in Wordsworth's oeuvre, *Once in a lonely hamlet*. He refers approvingly to the 'sweet and amiable verses on a French lady separated from her own children' (Woof 192), presumably because it dramatizes (ostensibly) the feelings of a woman. It pursues the exploration of maternal feelings begun in 1798 in *The Complaint* and *Her Eyes are Wild*. With *The Affliction of Margaret*, these make up a quartet of poems in which Wordsworth's loss of Caroline is translated into motherly loss.[3]

---

1   Woof, 170, 173, 182, 185, 191–201, 222, 230, 231, 254.
2   The Matron's husband, her 'helpless charge', is alive, but 'utterly dead' to fear and hope.
3   The richest of all Wordsworth's expressions of empathy with motherhood, *Once in a lonely hamlet* combines the dependency of *The Mad Mother* with the desire of the

Song at the Feast of Brougham Castle

Persuaded by Scott to admire a poem 'which I like exceedingly myself' (Woof 235), Francis Jeffrey gave his least qualified (if somewhat barbed) approval to *Song at the Feast of Brougham Castle*. In Jeffrey's opinion what saves the poem is the fact that the poet has, for once, been forced by his material to live up to what is expected of a minstrel. It is, duly, the only one that 'scapes whipping in his review. Composed and published in 1807, *Brougham Castle* is in several respects a rehearsal for *The White Doe* begun in that year, though not published until 1815, and is historically its necessary prelude. And it has subterranean links with *Hart-Leap Well* and even with *Yew-Trees*, which belong to the same immemorial landscape.

Hart-Leap Well is just off the road from Richmond, Yorkshire, to Askrigg. Using Richmond, Askrigg, and Catterick a little to the East, as triangulation points one would be enclosing the generally accepted site of the battle at which 300 Men of the North died in the great poem of the North, Aneirin's *The Gododdin*. That link, however, is exceedingly immemorial and I am not suggesting that Wordsworth is conscious of it. What he is clearly conscious of, given the sequence of *Hart-Leap Well*, *Brougham Castle*, and *The White Doe*, is the intertwined history of border warfare, the Hundred Years' War, and the Wars of the Roses. The Sir Walter of *Hart-Leap Well* is based on Sir Walter de Barden, a veteran of the Scottish wars of the late 13th century.[1] Barden's name links him with Barden Hall, the favourite refuge of Wordsworth's 'Shepherd Lord', the 16th century Lord Clifford, whose restoration is celebrated in *Brougham Castle*, and whose alchemical pursuits are alluded to in *The White Doe*. The white doe herself, who haunts Barden Fell, is conjectured by one bystander in her poem to have been one of Lord Clifford's familiars. There are of course several Barden Fells (as there are several rivers Dove, beside which 'Lucy' might have dwelt). The Barden Fell

Forsaken Indian Woman to hold her child once more. The emigrant mother's desire to pretend 'one little hour' that this English child is hers is contrasted with the aged Mathew's courage, in 'and did not wish her mine'. In her whispered dialogue with a borrowed child, the mother is troubled by inability to visualise the smiles of her own child. She knows that her tears burden and perplex the borrowed infant, yet needs 'to call thee by my darling's name' so that for a while, at least 'My heart again is in its place'. It is impossible not to suppose that the poet knew all about such temptations.

1   David Chandler, 'The Politics of Hart-Leap Well', 110.

near Hart-Leap Well is perhaps a day's walk from another near Bolton
Priory, the resting place of both Francis and the Shepherd Lord (buried
there, by repute, in 1523).[1] This Lord Clifford's ancestor (the first Lord
Clifford, Robert de Clifford, Lord of Westmorland), was created the first
lord warden of the marches in 1296, and was slain at Bannockburn in
1314,[2] having gone there in all probability with one of the Umfravilles
of Cockermouth, alluded to in *Yew-Trees*. *Yew-Trees* itself evokes every
battle between Bannockburn and Agincourt simply by waving the name
of Umfraville. Sir Gilbert Umfraville, a Northumbrian, became Earl of
Angus in 1243. The third of his line supported Edward II at Bannockburn
in 1314. Another fought with Edward III at Halidon Hill in 1333, when
the English avenged Bannockburn by slaying 4000 Scots, for the loss—
it is said—of 14 men. A later Sir Gilbert landed at Harfleur in 1415,
commanded the right flank at Agincourt, and became Marshal of France.
Edward's victory at Crecy in 1346, that of the Black Prince at Poitiers in
1356, Harry Hotspur's rout of the Scots at Homildon Hill in 1402, and
Henry V's victory at Agincourt in 1415, when 30,000 French confronted
a tattered English army of 6000 and lost 10,000 dead, repeated the pat-
tern. In all of these engagements with the Scots, French, or both at once,
longbows provided by the yew were decisive.

Brougham Castle picks up the story a generation later in the Wars
of the Roses, which provide the decisive reason why the Rising of the
North, deplored by Francis in *The White Doe*, was a rank bad idea—the
revolt of what we have been against what we are and might be. The poem
sets out, in the hero Clifford, who is notably pacific in this poem, and
quite immune to the call of the warlike harp, something of the character
of Francis Norton, and something of the reason for Francis's position.
The poem's Lord Clifford was deprived of his estates after the Battle
of Towton, in 1461, and restored to them after the battle of Bosworth
Field in 1485, which established Henry VII. At the age of 60 this same
Clifford will fight with distinction at Flodden Field, the closing event of
Scott's *Marmion*, and thus take part in cementing Henry VIII's position,
while (by occasion) avenging the death of his ancestor at Bannockburn.
In *The White Doe*, Francis's loyalty to the Tudor dynasty, and to the
Protestantism established by Edward IV, is contrasted with his father's
participation in the Rising of the North, 1569, which of course threatened

---

1   Wordsworth attributes this information to Dr Whitaker, *PW*, 3: 550.
2   Nicolson and Burns, xxxviii.

both Protestantism and Elizabeth I.

Clifford spent twenty-four years as a shepherd in Yorkshire and Cumberland, protected by his father-in-law Sir Lancelot Threlkeld, until restored to his estates by Henry VII. That is, *Song at the Feast* celebrates indirectly the fulfilment of the prophecy of Merlin. Did Wordsworth know this? Yes. *Brougham Castle* is unprecedentedly annotated in Wordsworth's oeuvre, being accorded eight pages of notes in *Poems, in Two Volumes*, notes which sustain comparison with Geoffrey Hill's similar notes to the related poem *Funeral Music*—a sequence of eight intense sonnets 'dedicated' (after a fashion) to the Duke of Suffolk, beheaded 1450; the Earl of Worcester, beheaded 1470; and the Earl Rivers, beheaded 1483. Henry Clifford, Wordsworth's note informs us in almost impenetrably baroque style, is the son of the Lord Clifford who was slain at Towton Field, aged 25, on Palm Sunday 1461. This Clifford (the shepherd lord's father) had slain the 16 year old Earl of Rutland in the bloody pursuit that followed the prior battle of Wakefield, in order to avenge the death of the previous Lord Clifford (Henry's grandfather) by the Duke of York. As Wordsworth points out, Henry lost not only his father and grandfather in the field, but his *four immediate progenitors.* As for Clifford's slaying of Rutland, Wordsworth himself cites Speed's history in partial palliation: 'who dare promise anything temperate of himself in the heat of martial fury?' (*P2V*, 163). But one notes that in *The White Doe*, Francis is slain in similarly vengeful pursuit by 'cruel Sussex' after his father's 'rash levy'.

The Battle of Towton (1461), which dispossessed the Shepherd Lord, was, in the words of a modern military historian cited by Geoffrey Hill, 'a holocaust': some 26,000 men died in this battle, and 'the scene must have beggared description'.[1] The battle that restored him was little better. The minstrel's line 'earth helped him with the cry of blood' is cited, Wordsworth's note points out, from Sir John Beaumont's *Bosworth Field*; it is almost the only *enigmatic* line in Beaumont's lengthy narration.[2] Both poems open with celebration of the end of the wars of the roses, but while Wordsworth's unreconstructed minstrel wishes joy on both parties, 'but most to her | Who is the flower of Lancaster!', Beaumont's voice is considerably less partisan:

1   Col. A. H. Burne, cited by Geoffrey Hill, *Collected Poems,* 201.

2   John Beaumont, *Bosworth-field: With a Taste of the Variety of Other Poems, Left by Sir John Beaumont ... Set Forth by his Sonne, Sir Iohn Beaumont* (London, 1629).

> The Winters storme of Ciuill warre I sing,
> Whose end is crown'd with our eternall Spring,
> Where Roses ioyn'd, their colours mix in one. (1–3)

In Beaumont's poem, the future King, 'just scourge of murder, virtue's light', is assured in a vision that

> The combate, which thou shalt this day endure,
> Makes Englands peace for many ages sure,
> Thy strong inuasion cannot be withstood,
> The earth assists thee with the cry of blood,

Richard, naturally, thinks otherwise:

> And shall this Welshman with his ragged troupe,
> Subdue the Norman, and the Saxon line,
> That onely Merlin may be thought diuine? (220–22)

In the battle itself (lines 373 ff), stout Rice and Herbert 'leade the power of Wales' making such slaughter 'That carefull Bardes may fill their precious bookes | With prayses, which from warlike actions spring, | And take new themes, when to their Harpes they sing'.

Wordsworth detaches Beaumont's haunting 'cry of blood' from its particular application to Bosworth, as does Geoffrey Hill in *Funeral Music*:

> They bespoke doomsday and they meant it by
> God, their curved metal rimming the low ridge.
> But few appearances are like this. Once
> Every five hundred years a comet's
> Over-riding stillness might reveal men
> In such array, livid and featureless,
> With England crouched beastwise beneath it all.
> 'Oh, that old northern business…'. A field
> After battle utters its own sound
> Which is like nothing on earth, but is earth....[1]

Given Geoffrey Hill's homage to Wordsworth's sense of responsible tristia, one might imagine that this adaptation of Beaumont, in the last two lines quoted, is tutored by Wordsworth's own variation on Beaumont in his sonnet on the battlefield at Waterloo:

1   Geoffrey Hill, *Funeral Music, 3* (*Collected Poems*, 72).

> We felt as men should feel
> With such vast hoards of hidden carnage near,
> And horror breathing from the silent ground (*CWRT,* 3: 429)

('Men' here, includes Mary and Dorothy, and their immediate Beaumont-like response is recorded in Dorothy's *Continental Journal*). In *Song at the Feast*, however, martial bardism, as envisaged by Beaumont, is given the first word. The speaker is a minstrel bard of British lineage, whose impetuous song seeks to restore Lord Clifford not merely to the estates but to the instincts of his ancestors. The Minstrel breaks into a trochaic, unnaturally accented stomp (as illustrated by my italics in the first five lines) as his imagination warms to the theme of battle:

> *Arm*our *rust*ing *in* his *Halls*
> *On* the *blood* of *Cliff*ord *calls*;—
> "*Quell* the *Scot*", ex*claims* the *lance*,
> *Bear* me *to* the *heart* of *France*,
> *Is* the *long*ing *of* the *Shield*—
> Tell thy name, thou trembling Field;
> Field of death where'er thou be,
> Groan thou with our victory!
> Happy day, and mighty hour,
> When our Shepherd, in his power,
> Mail'd and hors'd, with lance and sword,
> To his ancestors restored,
> Like a reappearing Star,
> Like a glory from afar,
> First shall head the Flock of War!

Sir Philip Sidney, we are told, confessed that 'the ballad of Chevy Chase, when chanted by "a blind crowder," stirred his blood like the sound of trumpets.'[1] Wordsworth's catalectic tetrameters clearly attempt the same effect. It is, to borrow Geoffrey Hill's comment on his own *Funeral Music*, 'a florid grim music broken by grunts and shrieks'. The summons to 'a reappearing Star' is uncannily close enough to Wordsworth's own invocation of Milton ('Thy soul was like a Star and dwelt apart') to have an authentically Wordsworthian ring, but may remind us that Milton, too, 'dwelt apart'.

But like *Hart-Leap Well*, this is a twice-told, or at least twice-authored,

---

1   Online http://24.1911encyclopedia.org/B/BA/BALLADS.htm.

tale. In its lyrical close, intervening directly on this martial utterance, the 'milder day' promised in *Hart-Leap Well* is actuated (conspicuously so, in a shift to the stanza and tone of *Hart-Leap Well*). What the shepherd shares with the Shepherd Lord is defined in a companion poem in *Poems, in Two Volumes*, a poem at first associated with Nelson as well as with John Wordsworth, namely *The Happy Warrior*. The 'happy warrior' is 'the generous spirit', loyal to 'the plan that pleased his childish thought', 'placable', 'alive to tenderness', who rises 'by open means', does not lust for 'Wealth, or honors, or for worldly state' (appropriately, the American spelling of 'honors' causes Washington to rise in memory). He is one who—unlike the antagonists of the wars of the Roses—'through the heat of conflict keeps the law | In calmness made'. Clifford will eventually head the flock of war and 'Quell the Scot', but his 'master bias', like the Happy Warrior's, 'leans | To home-felt pleasures and to gentle scenes'. The poet's voice in *Brougham Castle* supersedes on the minstrel's 'florid grim music':

> Love had he found in huts where poor Men lie,
> His daily teachers had been Woods and Rills,
> The silence that is in the starry sky,
> The sleep that is among the lonely hills
>
> In him the savage Virtue of the Race,
> Revenge, and all ferocious thoughts were dead:
> Nor did he change...

Clifford seems to have discovered a secular version of what one *OED* citation defines as 'That real Manhood of Christ our lord, which binds him ... to collective humanity'.[1]

The desires of the actual shepherd of *Hart-Leap Well* and those of the Shepherd Lord in *Brougham Castle* gloss the shepherd trope applied in *The Prelude* to Beaupuy, and in the political sonnets to the heroes of Saragossa and the Tyrol, as shepherds of their kind. The later poem is placed conspicuously toward the close of *Poems, in Two Volumes*, preceding only the elegies for Fox and John Wordsworth, and the 'illegible and unintelligible' (*pace* Jeffrey) *Intimations*. When both poems are transferred to *Poetical Works*, we find them in very distinguished company: the sequence runs *The Thorn, Hart-Leap Well, Brougham Castle, The Poem upon the Wye*. Pairing *Hart-Leap Well* with *The Thorn* invites

---

1   *OED*, citing Bishop Wilberforce, 1848.

us to recognize the shared narrative sophistication, the problematization of imagination. Pairing *Hart-Leap Well* with *Brougham Castle* calls attention to the 'twice-told tale' technique pioneered in one and resumed in the other. *Brougham Castle*'s proximity to *The Poem upon the Wye*, perhaps, invites one to perceive Wordsworth's own 'philosophy' as bred in natural piety to the shepherd lord who was, like Wordsworth, tutored beneath Cumbria's 'Indignant Hills'. Both shepherds share with Francis, in *The White Doe*, a scepticism about ineluctable maleness that is personally mythologized in *Nutting*—especially the early version in which it is Dorothy's merciless ravage of the woods that puts Wordsworth in mind of his own hormone-driven contestations with nature—and both share the animism of *The Two-Part Prelude*.

The White Doe of Rylstone

Wordsworth's anti-militaristic poem, *The White Doe of Rylstone*, originally composed in 1807–8, and set aside for *Concerning the Convention of Cintra*, was revised and published in 1815. Announcements of the poem mingled, somewhat incongruously, with notices of Napoleon's return to Paris. Number 126 of John Scott's *The Champion*, Sunday June 4, 1815, announced: 'This day is published ... THE WHITE DOE OF RYLSTONE'. No 127, Sunday June 11, 1815, carried a three column report from Paris on the acclamation of Napoleon, at his restoration. In No 128, Sunday June 18, 1815, Scott announced 'The important news of the week is, that Buonaparte is generally believed to have left Paris, and to have joined his troops: the awful blow may therefore be hourly expected.'

The poem's coincidence with the final act of this great drama, may have accentuated a general sense of its insipidity, and no doubt helped to elicit Jeffrey's remark that: 'This, we think, has the merit of being the very worst poem we ever saw printed in a quarto volume ... a happy union of all the faults, without any of the beauties, which belong to his school of poetry.'[1] To be fair to Jeffrey, one could find *The White Doe* a very fine poem and still think it undeserving of 'quarto'. Jeffrey, how-

---

1 *The Edinburgh Review*, Vol 25, October 1815 (No. L), 355. 'In the Lyrical Ballads, he was exhibited, on the whole, in a vein of very pretty deliration [sic]; but in the poem before us, he appears in a state of low and maudlin imbecility... It may be that he has dashed his Hippocrene with too large an infusion of lake water, or assisted its operation too exclusively by the study of the ... ballads of "the north countrie".'

ever, finds it a work 'of low and maudlin imbecility' and insupportably dull compared with what Scott or Byron might have done with the subject. Begun in mourning for the death of John Wordsworth and completed when the Wordsworths were slowly recovering from the deaths of Thomas and Catherine, *The White Doe*, like *Salisbury Plain*'s divided families, reflected personal anguish. Its verse preface speaks of the need for poetry to encourage the fortitude 'needful among life's ordinary woes'. Like *Salisbury Plain* it assumes a Spenserian mode, while dealing with a naturalistically conceived world of events. The form promises a realm of traditional values and romance superstitions, but as Geoffrey Hartman says, 'Wordsworth enters the realm of Romance to harrow its Christian mysteries, and to naturalise them.'[1]

Wordsworth's own remark, that in *The White Doe* 'everything that is attempted by the principal personages ... fails, so far as its object is external and substantial; so far as it is moral and spiritual it succeeds' (*PW*, 3: 543), sufficiently explains the general consensus that it lacked action, plot and pace, indulged in too reflective a conclusion, and generally failed to rival Scott—which a poem in seven Cantos (one more than Scott's usual six), on historical matter (nothing less than the death-agonies of Catholic feudalism), and published in quarto, seemed designed to do.[2] But why anyone, in 1815, would still expect a poem by the author of *Lyrical Ballads* to do what its generic frame implied, is itself a bit of a puzzle. In any case, expectations of narrative having evolved somewhat in the last two hundred years, and Scott having disappeared from college reading lists along with Byron's tales, it is no longer inevitable that anyone making a comparison between the three poets would share the contemporary verdict. As a handling of Coleridge's verse medium (Wordsworth, like Scott, is adapting the accentual verse of *Christabel*) Wordsworth's is considerably superior to Scott's *Lay of the Last Minstrel*,

---

1   Hartman, *Wordsworth's Poetry*, 328. For another major reading see John F. Danby, *The Simple Wordsworth*, 128–45. For reception, see W. J. B. Owen, 'The White Doe of Rylstone in its Time', *TWC* 29: 1 (1998) 20–25, and Peter J. Manning, *Reading Romantics: Text and Context* (New York and Oxford: OUP, 1990).

2   I borrow from W. J. B. Owen two of Wordsworth's remarks to Scott. Wordsworth wrote to Scott in 1805: 'High as our expectations were, I have the pleasure to say that the Poem [*The Lay*] has surpassed them much. We think you have completely achieved your object" (*EY*, 553). How high were those expectations? Of *Marmion* he wrote: 'I think your end has been attained; that it is not in every respect the end which I should wish you to propose to yourself, you will be well aware (*MY*, 1: 264). Owen, 22.

with its blatant plagiarisms—of the 'Jesu Maria shield us well' level of blatancy.[1] As story it is much less congested and much more comprehensible than *Marmion*, and it is mercifully free of Scott's stock characters—manly suitor, would-be ravisher, and heroine 'so witching fair'. If one expects a poem to offer some subtlety of symbolic expression, especially when dealing with the human generation of values—that is, to exhibit not merely poetic imagination, but a grasp of the imaginative acts upon which action is founded—it is on an altogether different plane from *The Lay* or *The Corsair*. There is justice in Wordsworth's claim to Wrangham, in January 1816, that the poem 'starts from a high point of imagination, and comes round ... to a still higher', and the genuine quality of the poem's continuous exhibition of mental acts is well described in the same letter's further elaboration:

> Throughout, objects (the Banner for instance) derive their influence, not from properties inherent in themselves ... but from such as are bestowed upon them by the minds of those who are conversant with or affected by those objects. Thus the Poetry, if there be any in the work [not the most persuasive piece of diffidence], proceeds as it ought to do, from the soul of Man [of both sexes, clearly], communicating its creative energies to the images of the external world,

which communication effects what he called the poem's climactic 'apotheosis of the animal'.

Wordsworth felt that the true action of the poem 'was spiritual—the subduing of the will, and all inferior passions, to the perfect purifying and spiritualising of the intellectual nature' (*PW*, 3: 548). That part of it which is 'external and substantial', concerns the involvement of a divided family in 'The Rising of the North', that is, the rebellion of the Northern earls against Elizabeth's new polity. On one side is Norton and his six warlike (and briefly differentiated) sons, who join in the rising

1   See de Selincourt's judgement that 'whereas Scott never achieved or, indeed, attempted those subtler melodies on which Coleridge based his claim to metrical originality, W. equalled if he did not surpass them' (*PW*, 3: 546). *The White Doe* is written in iambic tetrameters, with the usual allowance of trochaic and occasional anapaestic substitutions, yet its supple music sounds as free and various as *Christabel*. Coleridge quotes Wordsworth to Wordsworth on this music: 'the metre being—as you [WW] observed—rather dramatic than lyric, i.e. not such an arrangement of syllables, not such a metre, as acts a priori and with complete self-subsistence (as the simple anapaestic in its smoothest form ...) but depending for its beauty always, and often even for its metrical existence, on the sense and passion' (*CL* 3:112).

in the belief that they are serving the cause of traditional Catholic piety, and who bear a standard on which are emblazoned the wounds of Christ. On the other side are a compromised sibling pair made up of Emily and Francis. Emily, who represents a Wordsworthian version of the new Protestant faith, nevertheless embroiders the banner her father raises, which becomes in Romance terms, Francis's bane. Her brother Francis, as Wordsworth's more obvious representative in the poem, is torn between family loyalties and political ideals. He opposes his father's cause, yet he dies attempting to obey his father's last wish that the talismanic banner be returned to the altar of Bolton Priory. Not only do the good guys—and Francis and Emily are undoubtedly the good guys—lose. It is not even immediately apparent *why* they are adjudged to succeed in the 'moral and spiritual' sphere. But if 'success' involves subduing the will to spiritual and intellectual nature, this judgement applies equally and exactly to the brother and sister, albeit in their separate spheres.

As for Wordsworth's authorial stance towards the historical events, some critics assume that the poem castigates treason because Wordsworth has now renounced opposition politics, while some find a nostalgic preference for regional values as opposed to metropolitan ones.[1] Neither assumption really works for the poem. It is clear, however, that the narrative voice indicts the private motives of the Earls: Percy and Neville are 'two Earls leagued fast in discontent', who merely disguise their ambition as a 'general plea' (370). That voice also deplores a religious ata-

---

1   Peter J. Manning argues that 'At the core of both the materials of *The White Doe* and the political situation on the Peninsula is the struggle of a native Catholic population against a powerful central authority.... The Rising of the North of 1569 was the last battle of feudal England against the modern state .... All Wordsworth's local and nostalgic sympathies should have been with the rebels, as they were with the oppressed Spaniards and Portuguese' (*Reading Romantics*, 180–1). Aligning Elizabeth with Napoleon seems odd to me, and the idea of Wordsworth as a Catholic apologist even odder, but Manning's reading of Wordsworth is premised on the idea that Napoleon represented progress. Marlon B. Ross, whose treatment stays safely distant from the text, finds it robustly Tory: 'through the voice of Francis, Wordsworth issues a warning to jacobin sympathisers or other disgruntled factions threatening civil discord'. Both *The White Doe* and Scott's *Rokeby*, Ross claims, are about 'the potential loss of property' and incitements to British imperialism. 'Romancing the Nation-State: The Poetics of Romantic Nationalism', in Jonathan Arac and Harriet Ritvo, ed., *Macropolitics of Nineteenth-century Literature: Nationalism, Exoticism, Imperialism* (Philadelphia: University of Pennsylvania Press, 1991), 82, 73, 75. It is true that property is a concern of Wordsworth's sources, but this is nowhere manifested in the poem.

vism that stamps upon bible and prayer book and converts the emblems of redemption into a military fetish. Under the unhallowed banner:

> Horsemen and Foot of each degree,
> Unbound by pledge of fealty,
> Appeared, with free and open hate
> Of novelties in Church and State
> … And in Saint Cuthbert's ancient seat
> Sang Mass,—and tore the book of prayer—
> And trod the bible beneath their feet (702–14)

Wordsworth may have told Wrangham (*MY*, 842) that 'As to the Nortons the Ballad is my authority and I require no more', but in fact his poem eschews the ballad's version of Percy, 'the noblest earle in the north countrie', its vengeful portrait of Elizabeth, and its exculpation of Westmorland and Northumberland for declining the field: 'The Erles, though they were brave and bold | Against so many could not stay' (cited, *PW*, 3: 538–40). Wordsworth's Earls are clearly 'frit'. Moreover, although the Yew of Lorton Vale may have been 'not loth' to furnish arms for Umfraville or Percy, one detects little sympathy in the poem for warriors who in the twelfth year of 'great Eliza's golden time' are *still* 'Not loth the sleepy lance to wield | And greet the old *paternal* shield' (700–1).

When the poem opens, in the shattered heart of Bolton Priory, some years after the events about to be narrated, it is still 'the sunrise of zeal'. The first event of the poem is visionary, but its symbol is natural rather than liturgical. Like the Leech-Gatherer of 1802, the eponymous doe materializes through syntactical delays in some of Wordsworth's most beautiful lines. They are not in fact truly accentual, as sometimes thought, but they do employ frequent anapaestic leaps, some brought about by caesurae or inversions, or both, so that the metre, as Coleridge put it, is not 'a priori' but depends upon the passion:

> When soft!—the dusky trees between,
> And down the path through the open green,
> Where is no living thing to be seen;
> And through yon archway, where is found,
> Beneath the arch with ivy bound,
> Free entrance to the churchyard ground…
> —Comes gliding in with lovely gleam,

> Comes gliding in serene and slow,
> Soft and silent as a dream,[1]
> A solitary Doe!
> White she is as lily of June,
> And beauteous as the silver moon... (49–62)

The doe, celebrated for over a hundred similarly cadenced lines, is both a natural doe and a legendary being. She belongs in the present of the onlookers in the poem, in which nature is healing the effects of Henry's dissolution, and the still recent past of the Nortons, when such actions still rankled; but she also belongs, in legend, to the time of the good Lord Clifford in the Tudor dawn. Her reality status, as she ranges among the parishioners, is made the subject of conjectures not unlike those of the villagers in *The Thorn*. Like the pond in that poem she is a mirror for the fears and fantasies of the doubting crowd. Their 'strange delusion', 'conjecture vague, and idle fear | And superstitious fancies strong' may 'do the gentle Creature wrong' but they also exemplify the mind's compulsive search for meanings, its creation of values, and its search for symbols.

At the close of the narrative, the doe achieves an apotheosis, which mysterious event is glossed in the poem's epigraph from Bacon: as human being is raised by belief in divinity, so the creature's being is raised by society with Emily, becoming capable of intuiting Emily's moods, and needs. She is capable of 'a thoughtful pause', is blessed with 'unclouded memory', and has the familiar canine skills of 'pleading look' and learning 'when to approach or to retire'. But in Emily's mind she is also 'This lovely Chronicler of things | Long past, delights and sorrowings', a living part of the landscape of mankind. Between the two, a field is created, in which they can live, by virtue of their relationship, even though beyond that 'field' there is only despair, or 'a dearth of love' (344). What dictates the doe's apparently mysterious behaviour at the start of the poem (soon after the close of the narrative) is simply memory: she 'Loves what Emily loved most'. At last, Francis Jeffrey commented, 'the old Priory itself takes [the doe] for a daughter of the Eternal prime—which we have no doubt is very great compliment, though we have not the good luck to understand what it means' (353). We, more familiar with what Shelley

---

1 'Tis line with its trochaic opening ('Soft and silent'), a marked caesura, and the anapaestic 'as a dream' (brought about by that caesura) illustrates the freedom of the poem's metre, and its manner of approximating to that of *Christabel*.

called 'the human mind's imaginings', are better placed to understand what a hoary pile 'subdued by outrage and decay', might admire in a doe who remains unmoved by adversity, and seems 'not a Child of Time'. Like Keats's Nightingale, whose song is perhaps the same as found its way to the sad heart of Ruth, or Ted Hughes's predatory thrushes with their 'single-mind-sized skulls', the doe knows no falling away, and no self-division.

As nature's creature she is polarized with the poem's secondary symbol, the banner: an 'unblessed work', a personal testament of the faith of the Nortons, an embodiment of Norton's 'headstrong will' (353), a talisman for the 'potent vassalage' of the Northern Earls, and Francis's bane. Made by Emily against her will, it comes to symbolize for Norton the supposed treachery of Emily and Francis, subverted by their Protestant mother. In the hands of its enemies it becomes an object of superstitious fear. For Francis it is merely 'a piteous object', a 'sad burden' and an 'unhappy freight'. He returns it to Rylstone, to rest among decaying pieties, only because he honours his fathers and his brothers. The contrast between the fetish of archaic belief and the living doe configures Wordsworth's own replacement of woven pieties by natural ones—his substitution of a living spirit for inherited dogma.

One of those dogmas, conspicuously, is patriarchal authority. The narrative of the departure of Norton and his eight loyal sons, which occupies canto 2, is given to Emily by Francis (frequent change of point of view is one of the poem's subtleties) who is well aware of the pain his narrative must cause. He bares his tragic consciousness to her alone, recognizing 'the awful sympathy of sire and sons'—wondering whether one day a son might command a sire, recognizing the pain that his sister has borne, in loyally making a disloyal banner, yet imposing upon her further pain, in carrying out his own despairing instructions. The same self-contradiction is further symbolized by the fact that after lancing patriarchal wisdom he finds in his hand a lance 'Which he had grasped unknowingly'. The gesture prefigures his equally reflexive seizure later on of the very banner he reprobates (as in *Hart-Leap Well*, one cannot wholly sunder what we are from what we have been). He sets this lance aside before setting out, unarmed, to watch over his father and his brothers. Francis's speech to his sister, requiring her to renounce 'All prayers for this cause or for that', has remarkable emotional force. This, with his later agonizings over motives and sanction, mark him as Wordsworth's closest projection of his own moral crisis in 1794–98:

> now believing,
> Now disbelieving; endlessly perplexed,
> With impulse, motive, right and wrong, the ground
> Of obligation, what the rule and whence
> The sanction... (*1850*, 11.295f) [1]

He is the last of a series of surrogate Wordsworths, including the remorse-laden Marmaduke, the misanthrope in *Lines left upon a Seat in Yew-Tree*, and the Solitary.

That Francis's prophecies for Emily will be disproved, and his motives are unclear even to himself, does not lessen his 'triumph' in Canto 3 and Canto 5. The gathering of the Northern forces is far better done than has been granted, but the first and greatest high point in the poem, comes after the representation of Norton in battle array with his sons:

> Who sees him?—many see, and One
> With unparticipated gaze;
> Who 'mong these thousands Friend hath none,
> And treads in solitary ways

Its structural point is to associate Francis both with the Doe and with Emily (the doe's return to the poem in Canto 6 is likewise as 'a single One' and Emily's is a chosen solitude), but its ethical point is to mark Francis as one of *The Prelude*'s 'higher minds' who grasp that 'points have we all of us within our souls where all stand single'. He somehow maintains this autonomous stance—'With breast unmailed, unweaponed hand'—without scorning 'the awful sympathy of sire and sons'. In Canto 5 he is acclaimed by the crowd at York for his 'natural Piety' (1246) in joining his brothers, and again for claiming the banner. He sees a soldier bearing it to the scene of execution

> And with a look of calm command
> Inspiring universal awe,
> He took it from the Soldier's hand;
> And all the people that were round
> Confirmed the deed in peace profound. (1346–51)

---

1   James Mulvihill, 'History and nationhood in Wordsworth's *White Doe of Rylstone*', *CLIO* 18:2 (1989) 135–151 also makes the point that Francis experiences the poet's 'conflict of sensations without name', 148.

We may wonder whether Francis finds himself in joining his father and brothers, or loses himself, or simply demonstrates that one man's atavism is another man's natural piety. But, as Mulvihill argues, he does find his 'sanction' in the people—the same 'people' appealed to and vindicated in *The Convention of Cintra*—and is adjudged by them to have acted well, both in opposing and in aiding his family, as Wordsworth still adjudges himself to have acted well in opposing and in applauding his country (Mulvihill, 150).

The narrator here, however, is Emily's comforter, once the elder Norton's rival hunter and fellow warrior, a noble remnant of what we have been. His version of events is both moving—it is designed to comfort—and unreliable, because it sees only the externals. But the event is twice-told. At the start of Canto 6, a stroke of Romantic irony reveals that Francis is as unaware of having seized the banner as he was of having seized a lance in Canto 2. Even an action 'inspiring universal awe' is no better, no worse, than the murder committed by the sailor in *Salisbury Plain*. The heroic act was merely, in the lines from *The Borderers* prefixed to the poem, 'The motion of a muscle—this way or that', the kind of action after which 'We wonder at ourselves like men betrayed'. The 'triumph' is that alone and in despair, knowing how it incriminates him, he chooses the deed—he tells himself he has no choice, which is not the case—and acts 'for their sakes, come weal or woe'. Bearing what for him is not merely loathed but in effect a counter-talisman (as he tells his pursuers, 'it weakens me') he is slain by followers of cruel Sussex, and the banner is 'borne exultingly away', transmogrified one last time, atrophied indeed, into a trophy.

One dogma questioned in the poem is the authority of fathers. Another is that of well-intentioned brothers: Francis's last conduct towards Emily takes the form of a lengthy speech mapping out her future, taking it on himself to tell Emily how to live, and to 'depend | Upon no help of outward friend' (546). The Doe will decide otherwise, and under this sororal solicitude the fate which befalls Emily is not that prophesied by Francis. She comes to inhabit a new world. In Canto 4, in moonlight and amid the fragrance of the breathing flowers, Emily questions her brother's interpretation of their doom. The imaginative time brings a sense of alternatives. Instructed by her brother to abandon hope, Emily prays instead (in the 1836 revision) that he will 'beware | Of that most lamentable snare, | The self-reliance of despair'. Nonetheless, bound, as she sees it, to abide in resignation 'and secure o'er pain and grief a triumph pure' (1073) she becomes a wanderer.

The temptation that besets Emily is to remain in the role allotted by her brother, which passive condition is very hard to distinguish from the 'unmanly' despair of the Female Vagrant or of Margaret in *The Ruined Cottage*. Like the Female Vagrant, Emily has 'wandered , long and far … | Yea like a ship at random blown | To distant places and unknown' (1630–32). At the start of Canto 7, returned to Rylstone, she resembles Margaret:

> The walks and pools neglect has sown
> With weeds, the bowers are overthrown…
> And with the silent gloom agreeing
> There is a joyless human being,
> Of aspect such as if the waste
> Were under her dominion placed   (1588–1600)

She has, unaided, followed her brother's prescription and brought her feelings to 'the subjection of a holy, | Though stern and rigorous melancholy' (1615–16) but such sternness seems not 'native' to a face

> which cannot lose the gleams,
> Lose utterly the tender gleams
> Of gentleness and meek delight
> And loving-kindness ever bright.   (1621–24)

In solitude she has become 'Undaunted, lofty, calm and stable, / And awfully impenetrable' (1646–7). That this triumph is not what Wordsworth means by 'success'—though it is asserted to be so by one critic—is helpfully signalled by that dreadful rhyme. While the poem may not succeed in making these gradations plain, it is clear from the reading instruction in the prefatory poem, that to be 'thoroughly forlorn' and 'awfully impenetrable', immured within the fastness of the self—a metaphor implied in 'Her soul does in itself stand fast' (1642)—is not Emily's destiny. We are to look for something similar to Mary Wordsworth's hard-won triumph over 'lamentable change', and her learning 'How nearly joy and sorrow are allied'.[1]

---

1   In one of the touches of the poem that bear on personal sorrow, Francis is buried—by communal tact—at the priory, not at the hall, so that Emily will not have it constantly before her. Emily's transfiguration towards the point when she can return to the burial place and receive 'the memory of old Loves, | Undisturbed and undistressed' is

But unlike Mary, Emily is a tragic heroine, and her brother's sibling. Had the poem been by Shelley, Emily would have followed her instincts (she does think of following Francis to the front): she would have mounted a charger, seized a broadsword and rescued her father from his enemies or Francis from cruel Sussex. It isn't, and she doesn't. But one can think of *Laon and Cythna* as rewriting the less conspicuously revolutionary behaviour of Wordsworth's sibling pair, who also make their own values, challenge atavistic behaviour (rather more consistently in some ways) and replace patriarchal authority by equality.

The barely perceptible difference between mere obedience and Emily's disciplined triumph lies in the change from the deep frost of 'holy … stern and rigorous melancholy' to the 'soft spring-day of holy, | Mild, delicious melancholy |… by tender fancies brightened' (1776–9) and the agency of this recovery, as in *The Poem upon the Wye*, is nature. As in *The Prelude*, and as in the encounter poems, solitude needs an appropriate centre, an agent whereby the self can be returned to itself. Emily is healed by her brother's milder representative, the doe, who manifests his love yet also 'disproves his words' (1808–9). The return of this childhood companion, after Emily's wanderings, is subtly keyed to Francis's own high-point in the narrative, as if the doe were the brother's anima: 'For, of that band of rushing deer, | *A single One* in mid career hath stopped' (1662–3). This 'lovely chronicler of things', like other agents of restoration in Wordsworth's poetry or relationship, restores Emily to herself. Wordsworthian positives abound. The doe engages Emily's affections, opens the passages through which the ear speaks to the heart, awakens the 'natural piety' of memories, and repairs the mind's excursive power. Emily, it is true, chooses a neighbourly and almost monastic solitude, for her meditative discipline, but as another 'single One', she echoes her sibling's conduct rather than obeys his injunction: 'her sanction inwardly she bore, | … | But to the world returned no more'. To confirm the symbolic equivalence of Francis and Emily, it is in fact his grave, not hers, that the doe haunts at the opening of the poem. Nature's affection for what man may become thus occasions the poem's 'mystery'.

not unlike Mary Wordsworth's. Remaining in Grasmere, overlooking the churchyard where the bodies of Thomas and Catherine lay, would, Wordsworth wrote in 1813, 'grievously retard our progress towards that tranquillity of mind which it is our duty to aim at' (MY, 2.66). As W. J. B. Owen argues, Mary attained her 'triumph pure' only slowly and with great difficulty, and Wordsworth's poem honours her for it.

'Let us have the old Poets and Robin Hood'

Wordsworth is unlikely to have known that, in writing to John Hamilton Reynolds on 3 February 1818, Keats expressed a preference for 'Robin Hood' over 'Wordsworth's grandeur and Hunt's merit',[1] but he nonetheless obliged in returning to 'the old poets' and something as folkloric as Robin Hood. *Artegal and Elidure* (composed 1815; published 1820) takes off from a prose work of Milton, and *The Egyptian Maid* (composed 1828; published 1835) derives in the loosest possible manner, from Geoffrey of Monmouth and from Malory. Neither is quite 'Robin Hood', because Keats wanted his poems 'uncontaminated and unobtrusive' and both poems provide something of a moral; but one moral is founded in tradition and is as old as Holinshed; the other is manifestly ironized, framed almost as impertinent to the tale. Written in 1815 as 'a token of affectionate respect for the memory of Milton' (*FN*, 8) and published in 1820, *Artegal and Elidure* is the last and least inspired of this series of bardic revisions, being little more than a versification of Milton's version of Geoffrey of Monmouth's tale. Milton's affection for the tale is itself an instance of that magnanimous meekness Wordsworth identifies as the quality of the Commonwealthmen, and Wordsworth's treatment offers a further gloss on such 'magnanimity'. Elidure, whose triumph over the lust for kingship—'that so often dazzled and vitiates mortal men', says Milton—makes him epitomize the happy warrior.[2]

There is, however, a further fruit of Wordsworth's belated engagement with the Matter of Britain, though not quite as in Geoffrey or in Malory. Wordsworth, I pointed out earlier, grew up on Arthurian tales. He was informed in schooldays by Bishop Percy (in *The Reliques*) that 'In Carleile dwelt king Arthur, | A Prince of passing might; | And there maintained his table round, | Beset with many a knight' (*Reliques*, 3: 340). The ballad cited here is a bawdy account of how a lad shows up all the incontinent wives and cuckolds of Arthur's court with a mantle the women cannot wear and a horn cuckolds cannot drink from, but, Percy assures us, it was asserted by Evan Evans to be based on an old Welsh ms

---

1   *Letters of John Keats*, ed. Maurice Buxton Forman, 4th edn (London: Oxford University Press, 1960), 96.

2   Milton, *Prose Works*, 5.34. In Milton, but not in Wordsworth, Elidure is subsequently deposed by his two younger brothers, who divide the kingdom, but pre-decease him, whereupon Elidure becomes king for the third time, 'finishing the interrupted course of his mild, and just reign, as full of virtuous deeds, as daies to his end' (5.35).

tale of a mantle owned by one of King Arthur's mistresses. Percy affirms that Carleile is one and the same with Carlisle, and that the round table was, as local topography insists, situated near Penrith. Wordsworth's piece of Arthuriana is equally apocryphal if less bawdy.

The Egyptian Maid; or, The Romance of the Water Lily (1828) narrates the triumph of Nina, Lady of the Lake, and 'a gentle sorceress, and benign', over Merlin, in delivering the Egyptian Maid to the spousal of Sir Galahad in the Court of King Arthur. It has no source in Geoffrey, beyond 'the names and persons', and arose we are told in the Fenwick Notes from an entirely chance association. Listening to his nephew Henry Hutchinson giving an animated description of the motions of a vessel called *The Water Lily* (*FN*, 97) Wordsworth remembered his own boyhood delight in water lilies and the poem, he says, 'rose out of my mind like an exhalation' (*PW*, 3: 502; *LY*, 1: 667). The poem presents Merlin as envying the beauty of the boat's movement, and through 'envious spleen' raising a storm that puts the Egyptian Maid at risk. This motiveless malignance implies perhaps that the 'mechanist' magician is fearful of the threat such a mysterious otherness offers to his pride. One wonders, given the date, whether Wordsworth constructs Merlin as one who cannot emulate Keats's magnanimous pleasure in the nightingale ("'tis not through envy of thy happy lot') and himself as one who can.

Like *Hart-Leap Well* and *Brougham Castle*, *The Egyptian Maid* is a twice-told tale—the poem in this case is told first in a manner engaged with the triumph of feminine sorcery over male magic, and then subjected (in the manner of 1798) to a lame and pointedly unpersuasive afterword, which seems to echo, structurally, Coleridge's gloss to *The Ancient Mariner*. This afterword (lines 355–86) is allegedly sung by a choir of 'angels', who, following Merlin's failure to sink the vessel, seek to circumscribe the dangerous implications of the tale itself in terms of a safer moralism. In the poem, the boat is 'a Pinnace bright', 'supreme in loveliness and grace | Of motion':

> Behold, how wantonly she laves
> Her sides, the Wizard's craft confounding;
> Like something out of Ocean sprung
> To be forever fresh and young. (ll. 43–6)[1]

The craft-defying craft has a figurehead, cast up upon the beach, in the

---

1   *CWRT*, 3: 630–41.

form of 'a carved lotus':

> Sad relique, but how fair the while!
> For gently each from each retreating
> With backward curve, the leaves revealed
> The bosom half, and half concealed,
> Of a divinity, that seemed to smile... (ll. 127–31)

That the angels articulate the baptised Wordsworthian superego of 1828 is immediately, almost naively, manifest: they dismiss the beautiful figurehead as 'an idol'. Less angelic readers may think of Blake's lotos-lily in *Jerusalem* (Plate 28), and Nina herself describes the 'Goddess with a lily flower' as 'The old Egyptian's emblematic mark of | Of joy immortal and of pure affection' (ll. 76–77). Wordsworth's headnote, in any case, has already alerted the reader to the symbolic status of this flower-goddess: 'the Lotus, with the bust of the Goddess appearing to rise out of the full-blown flower, was suggested by the beautiful work of ancient art, once included among the Towneley Marbles, and now in the British Museum'. This unexpectedly Keatsian appreciation of the warm south, allied to *un*envious contemplation of perfect beauty, combines with boyhood fascination with the erotic motion of water-lilies, and the surprising hint, in the motion of the boat, of the birth of Venus (the pinnace is 'Like something out of ocean sprung | To be forever fresh and young). All this leads into another curiously retrospective image. The sleeping maid is conveyed to Carleon in an ebon chariot drawn by two mute Swans provided by a repentant and chastened Merlin. There Arthur's knights approach this sleeping beauty, attempting to wake her, but with mixed anticipations and apprehensions:

> Next, disencumbered of his harp,
> Sir Tristram, dear to thousands as a brother,
> Came to the proof, nor grieved that there ensued
> No change; — the fair Izonda he had wooed
> With love too true, a love with pangs too sharp,
> From hope too distant, not to dread another.

> Not so Sir Launcelot; — from Heaven's grace
> A sign he craved, tired slave of vain contrition;
> The royal Guinever looked passing glad
> When his touch failed. — Next came Sir Galahad;
> He paused, and stood entranced by that still face

> Whose features he had seen in noontide vision.

But as she wakes at the touch of Sir Galahad—a parfit gentle knight whose potency had, as in Malory, survived the Perilous Seat—

> The Swans in triumph clap their wings;
> And their necks play involved in rings,
> Like sinless snakes in Eden's happy land   (ll. 321–3)

Nothing quite so erotic has taken place in Wordsworth's poetry since the Swans of *An Evening Walk*. These, in the 1794 revisions, were seen as an image of connubial bliss, and encouraged voyeuristically to 'Involve your serpent necks in changeful rings, | Rolled wantonly between your slippery wings'. Since this revision remained unpublished in 1794, the erotic metaphor makes a very unexpected debut in 1835.

Some will find the poem consonant with Wordsworth's alleged marginalization of the feminine—the Egyptian maid remains nameless, though she claims the title of the poem, and like Lucy, she remains speechless. But it is abundantly clear that the dominant voice of the poem, and its commanding presence—overshadowing a worried Arthur, the wily Merlin, and even bold Sir Galahad, who is permitted just two lines of grief over the body of the maid—is that of Nina, the spirit of the waters. The poem is undoubtedly, as Judith Page, has suggested, a mildly feminist addendum to and revision of Geoffrey—a restoration of the voice and power of woman to a male-authored version of legendary history.[1]

It is also an instance of what can happen when a sudden impulse, from hiding places forty years deep, leads Wordsworth back (as the seductive piano music in Lawrence's great poem *Piano* 'betrays me back') towards the preoccupations of adolescence. His use of the twice-told tale may be less effective than in his previous revisions of minstrelsy, but it does dramatize a vigorous conflict between his pagan inspiration and his tutored conscience, a conflict he usually managed to persuade himself did not exist. Nina, the lady of the lake, is effectively a genius loci, a newly mythologized version of one of those 'presences' who displace divinity in *The Prelude*. Forty years before, on the banks of Ullswater, she had seduced him into commandeering an 'elfin pinnace'. Now she

---

1   See Judith W. Page, *Wordsworth and the Cultivation of Women* (Berkeley: University of California Press, 1994), 133–42. Without this discussion I doubt if I would have considered this poem in these terms, or indeed been responsive to its merits.

dictates his first and only revision of Arthurian lore, just two years before Tennyson's *The Lady of Shalott*.

Keats, Shelley, Tennyson: Wordsworth in his forties and fifties is more often abreast of his young contemporaries than readers of selected Wordsworths, with their emphasis on the 'great decade' may suspect.

Part 4

Wordsworth and Kindliness

I hope you'll kindly take it
 —'Simon Lee', 1798

Kindly emotion tending to console
And reconcile
 —'Prelude', 1842

Chapter 10: Making *The Excursion* Do[1]

MARY SHELLEY's celebrated response to *The Excursion* might have softened if she had persisted to the end of the poem, as Shelley's was, but the shock of the lost leader's self-exposure on the first page of his book was ne'er so well expressed: 'he is a slave'.[2] The dedicatory sonnet 'To the Right Honourable William, Earl of Lonsdale, K.G. etc. etc' makes this instalment of *The Recluse* almost as much the poem to Lord Lonsdale as *The Prelude* was the poem to Coleridge, and it seems a gross instance of self-abasement that the author of *The Prelude*—the definitive celebration of a child's upbringing through interaction with the rocks and trees and fells and waters that are every child's birthright—could write these lines:

> Oft, through thy fair domains, illustrious Peer!
> In youth I roamed, on youthful pleasures bent;
> And mused in rocky cell or sylvan tent,
> Beside swift-flowing Lowther's current clear.[3]

---

1   Since writing this chapter I have benefited from numerous other readings, including Sally Bushell's indispensable *Re-Reading The Excursion* (Ashgate, 2002); Judith Thompson's chapter on the poem in *John Thelwall in the Wordsworth Circle: The Silenced Partner* (New York: Palgrave Macmillan, 2012), Adam Potkay's *Wordsworth's Ethics* (Baltimore, MD: Johns Hopkins Uniovsrity Press, 2012); and Jacob Risinger, 'The Excursion as Dialogic Poem', in *The Oxford Handbook of William Wordworth* (2015). I have also, with considerable overlap, looked further at its writerly qualities in 'Is *The Excursion* a metrical Novel?', *Grasmere 2010: Selected Papers from the Wordsworth Summer Conference* (Humanities-Ebooks 2010), 195–217; examined Thelwall's unique approach to its metrics in 'Mr Thelwall's Ear; or Hearing *The Excursion*', *Grasmere 2011* (Humanities-Ebooks 2011), 171–203; and considered Wordsworth's claims for its musicality in 'Does *The Excursion* demonstrate an unparalleled 'variety of musical effect'? *The Wordsworth Circle*, 45.2 (Spring 2014).
2   Woof, *Critical Heritage*, 499.
3   Similar self-abasement appears in Wordsworth letter to Lonsdale, 6 May 1815, thanking him for the Collectorship at Whitehaven. 'My Lord, | I take the liberty of informing your Lordship that in consequence of your letter of the 28th Inst I have

Wordsworth's childhood was mortgaged to the Lowthers, and he grew up 'a determined enemy to aristocracy'. Perhaps one should celebrate the magnanimity of a poet who can come to terms with the present Lowther. One can certainly grasp the romantic as well as pecuniary attractions to a once itinerant Bard of finding a niche at the fireside of a cultured patron (if Lonsdale was at all 'illustrious' it was as a patron). As Anthony Conran writes, in Welsh [i.e. British] poetry 'the over-riding symbol of [the] good life, is always the hospitality extended by the great to the small ... the relationship of tribal king to tribal bard, or poet-priest.... This was [the poet's] "office" in the world—to praise the great lords'.[1] Moreover, the title of this great lord was created in the last days of the Welsh Bards, by Henry II, whose interest in Taliesin is said to have led to the discovery of Arthur's tomb. Nevertheless, the opening lines of this sonnet can only jar (for modern readers) with Wordsworth's earlier representation of himself as a naked savage sporting in the thunder shower, against the backdrop of Skiddaw bronzed in the radiance of the setting sun. As we read the sonnet, a cage descends upon that child.

What Francis Jeffrey deplores, however, in his famous review of *The Excursion* (beginning 'This will never do...') is not apostasy or inconsistency but incorrigibility. In 1802 the Edinburgh despot had denounced the Lakers for their 'splenetic and idle discontent with the existing institutions of society', and for failing to grasp that the standards of poetry 'were fixed long ago, by certain inspired writers, whose authority it is no longer lawful to call into question'.[2] In 1814 he sees *The Excursion* as more of the same: as reaffirming the poet's class hostility, his lack of decorum, his defiant prosaism and—worst of all for this Caledonian positivist—his uncorrected flights of mysticism. In this, Lamb's response confirms Jeffrey. Prior to *Prometheus Unbound* or *The Prelude*, however difficult this may be to grasp, *The Excursion* was Romanticism's primary thesis statement. 'Its leading moral', says Lamb, 'is to abate the pride of the calculating understanding, and to reinstate the imagination and the

thought it right to communicate to you my sentiments in person upon this signal mark of your Lordship's consideration. | If I do not hear from your Lordship that you are otherwise engaged, I purpose doing myself the Honour of calling in Charles Street tomorrow morning at ten o'clock.| I have the honour to remain | my Lord | your Lordship's | most obliged and faithful servant | Wm Wordsworth' (*MY*, 2: 235).

1   Anthony Conran, *The Penguin Book of Welsh Verse* (Harmondsworth, 1967), Introduction, 15.
2   *Edinburgh Review*, No 1, October 1802, 63.

affections in those seats from which modern philosophy has laboured too successfully to expel them'.[1]

It was also controversially democratic. According to Jeffrey in 1802, the author of *Lyrical Ballads* had failed to grasp that 'the love, or grief, or indignation of an enlightened and refined character, is not only expressed in a different language, but *is in itself a different emotion* from the love, or grief, or anger of a clown, a tradesman, or a market wench. The things themselves are radically and obviously distinct...'.[2] We do *not* 'have all of us one human heart'. Consistently with this class consciousness he now complains that, though the tale of Margaret has considerable pathos, one has first to get over 'the repugnance excited by the triteness of its incidents and the lowness of its objects', not to mention that is narrated by *a Pedlar*. What most now admire and many have come to prize as one of the great tragic poems in the language, and powerful in its reliance on naturalistic detail and its entire avoidance of sentimentality, Jeffrey criticized for its 'Mawkish sentiments' and for 'detail of preposterous minuteness'.[3]

On this point, especially, it ought to be notorious that Coleridge's public verdict in *Biographia Literaria* will not only back Jeffrey, but will do so by plagiarizing him. First, however, he makes a feint of solidarity with the poet. Where Jeffrey asks 'Did Mr Wordsworth really imagine, that his favourite doctrines were likely to gain anything in point of effect or authority by being put into the mouth of a person accustomed to higgle about tape, or brass sleeve-buttons?' Coleridge points out, properly enough, that the tape and buttons come from Jeffrey's imagination, not the poet's. Nevertheless, it is one thing, Coleridge says, to rejoice in a ploughman poet, but quite another to 'read a poem where the author, having occasion for the character of a poet and a philosopher in the fable of his narration, had chosen to make him a chimney-sweeper; and then in order to remove all doubts on the subject, had invented an account of his birth, parentage and education, with all the strange and fortunate accidents which had concurred in making him at once poet, philosopher and

---

1   *Quarterly Review*, Vol 12, October 1814, 107.

2   *Edinburgh Review*, No 1, 66, my emphasis.

3   *Edinburgh Review*, Vol 24, November 1814, 7. See Chapter 3 of *Sensibility* for a dicussion of Jeffrey's treatment of Wordsworth, informed by Russell Noyes, *Wordsworth and Jeffrey in Controversy,* Humanities Series No 5 (Bloomington: Indiana University, 1941) and Philip Flynn, *Francis Jeffrey* (Newark: University of Delaware Press; Associated University Presses, 1978).

sweep.' Is there, Coleridge asks, after another page on Wordsworth's failure of decorum, 'one word, ... attributed to the pedlar in *The Excursion* characteristic of a pedlar? One sentiment that might not more plausibly ... have proceeded from any wise and beneficent old man of a rank or profession in which the language of learning and refinement are *natural* [my emphasis] and to be expected?' The choice of profession involves Wordsworth, Coleridge says, in 'minute matters of fact, not unlike those furnished for the obituary of a magazine by the friends of some obscure ornament of society lately deceased in some obscure town'. Then he quotes the very passage selected by Jeffrey to ridicule such matter of factness: beginning 'Among the hills of Athol he was born. | There on a small hereditary farm' and ending 'From his sixth year, the boy of whom I speak, | In summer tended cattle on the hills'. And he makes this unholy alliance all the more hurtful by twining into Jeffrey's analysis strands from Wordsworth's pained letter to himself—asking for concrete illustration of his failures—as he converts the substance of an ephemeral review into a canonical text of allegedly philosophic criticism.[1] The motive is plain: on the business of whether there is 'one human heart', or whether a pedlar can have such 'language, feelings, sentiments and information' as this pedlar possesses, Coleridge and Jeffrey are as one. A pedlar, Jeffrey and Coleridge are agreed, could not have the same *feelings* as a man of culture.

Were it not that Jeffrey also deplores twaddle, incomprehensibility, and acres of tedium we might take his review as a eulogy to Wordsworth's consistency.

> This will never do. It bears no doubt the stamp of the author's heart and fancy; but unfortunately not half so visibly as that of his peculiar system. ... His first essays we looked upon in a good degree as poetical paradoxes,—maintained experimentally, in order to display talent and court notoriety... But ... we find that he has been for twenty years exclusively employed upon articles of this very fabric. (*Edinburgh Review*, 1815, 1, 4)

---

1 *BL*, 2: 134–5. For analyses of Coleridge's forensic treatment of Wordsworth's faults see my 'Coleridge's Wordsworth', *TWC* 15:2 (1984) 38–46, and Bialostosky, passim. The waywardness of the *BL* critique is confirmed by William Whewell's remark in July 1817: 'Even yet I doubt whether Wordsworth would allow that man to understand his poems who talks of them as Coleridge does.... How the man who wrote the critique on Wordsworth could write 'Christabel' I cannot conceive'. Woof, 984.

And Jeffrey is right; on both counts. *The Excursion* is far more consistent with early Wordsworth than we tend to suppose. And it does have acres of tedium. Jeffrey is both funny and exact about the sense of vertigo that accompanies the struggle with some of this poem's interminable sentences, a style that too often 'eludes all comprehension, and fills the despairing reader with painful giddiness and terror' (10). For all its superb music in sustained passages, it is a radical fault in a conversation poem for many of its sentences to be literally *unsayable*—incapable of auditory communication. Nor can he be blamed for not quite grasping what *The Excursion* actually was—Wordsworth's preface describes it as 'only a portion of a poem' which '*belongs to* the second part of a long and laborious Work, which is to consist of three parts'—or how long it threatened to become. Wordsworth himself seems confused: he attributes the decision to undertake a review of his own mind to Grasmere ('Several years ago, when the Author retired to his native mountains'). The poem on his own mind, i.e. *The Prelude*, he says, has long been finished, and 'the result of the investigation which gave rise to it was a determination to compose a philosophical poem, containing views of Man, Nature, and Society; and to be entitled, the Recluse; as having for its principal subject the sensations and opinions of a poet living in retirement.' As we all know, 'The Recluse' was conceived in Alfoxden, not Grasmere, and the writing of *The Prelude* was the result of, not the cause of, his determination to compose a philosophical poem. Moreover, if the projected poem is to be called 'The Recluse', 'as having for its principal subject the sensations and opinions of a poet living in retirement', it is unhelpful for the poet-narrator of this instalment to distinguish himself as one *not* living in retirement, from 'the pale Recluse', who is. Furthermore, since *The Excursion* raids *Home at Grasmere* for much of its celebration of retirement, and some of its lengthier anecdotes of rural life, the effect of publishing *The Excursion* was to rob 'the poem, to be intitled the Recluse' of its only substantive existence. *The Excursion* is indeed not an expectoration for, but the death-song of, *The Recluse*.

Three of the poem's four characters (the Pastor is the odd man out) are, as readers have to feel, somewhat hard to distinguish (even Lamb's review at one point appears to confuse the Solitary and the Wanderer). Coleridge made the point most persuasively in *Biographia*, where he listed as third of Wordsworth's five characteristic defects, an 'undue predilection for the dramatic form'. From this predilection, Coleridge

Dealmar Banner's painting at the Old Dungeon Ghyll Hotel, Great Langdale

argues, there must arise one of two evils:

> Either the thoughts and diction are different from that of the poet, and then there arises an incongruity of style; or they are the same and indistinguishable, and then it presents a species of ventriloquism, where two are represented talking while in truth one man only speaks.

Few have disagreed. Coleridge buried some of the finest poems in *Lyrical Ballads* for almost a century and a half by his lampooning of the first of these two evils, and he invited a similar dismissal of *The Excursion* by exaggerating the second. A painting by Delmar Banner, probably inspired by Coleridge's remark, shows three figures in conversation at Blea Tarn: a white haired Wanderer, more weather-beaten than the others, and with rock-like solidity; a rather inert, seated poet; the Solitary somewhat twisted, his face turned away; but, arguably, three versions of Wordsworth. This, too, may exaggerate the case. Minimally, Wordsworth apportions his experiences differently and fairly consistently between the three. The Wanderer has been for the most part self-educated among his native hills: one could say that he is given the education of Wordsworth, though it would be truer, chronologically, to say that when Wordsworth writes *The Prelude* he ignores his actual education in Hawkshead and borrows instead, as more poetical, the education he imagined for the Pedlar. The Wanderer is also gifted with a stoicism the poet neither possesses nor is quite sure he wants: I concur with Susan Wolfson that the Poet's silence at the end of Book 1 implies less than total reconcilement to the Wanderer's view of Margaret's tale, and with Regina Hewitt that the Poet's greater sensitivity to the inappropriateness and inefficacy of the Wanderer's moral discourse throughout Book 4 significantly qualifies the authority of that figure.[1] What makes the Wanderer interesting is not his moralistic view of duty and faith but his uncanny ability to alternate between the humanistic vision of *The Poem upon the Wye* and the transcendentalism of *Intimations*: he shares both kinds of experience with Wordsworth but synchronically rather than diachronically. In some respects, indeed he moves away from the quasi-Christian stoicism of the *Ode to Duty* and *Intimations*, which is most apparent in the first half of the poem, towards the animism of *Lyrical Ballads* and *The Two-Part Prelude*, as the poem progresses. This happens in correspondence with two tendencies in Wordsworth's composition. One is that he does not notice that he has aged, so that lines written fifteen years back do not easily dovetail with the new. The other is that:

> Poetry … takes its origin from emotion recollected in tranquillity. The emotion is contemplated till, by a species of reaction, the tranquillity gradually disappears, and an emotion kindred to that which was before the subject of contemplation is gradually produced, and does itself actually exist in the mind. In this mood successful composition generally begins… (*PrW* 1: 148)

In *The Prelude* Wordsworth's childhood is not merely remembered in Books 1 and 2, but reanimated. The same happens to his Jacobin self in Books 9, 10 and 11.[2] Such selves are co-present and co-authoring, as

---

1   Susan J. Wolfson, *The Questioning Presence: Wordsworth, Keats, and the Interrogative Mode in Romantic Poetry* (Ithaca and London: Cornell University Press, 1986), 115. The poet, Wolfson says, 'is keenly alert', here and later in *The Excursion*, to what Keats would call '"Negative Capability"'. Regina Hewitt, '*The Excursion* and the Progress of Poetic Sociology' in *The Possibilities of Society*.

2   Wordsworth's 'France' is partly his own, but is also a cultural construction, derived from Louvet's *Narrative*, and from his revolutionary anima, Helen Maria Williams's in her *Letters from France*. His account also shares Mary Wollstonecraft's view of the devastation wrought by 'upstart theory'. Because 'vanity had made every Frenchman a theorist', Wollstonecraft says, it took the French unconscionably longer than it took the Americans to arrive at a constitution: 'Such is the difference between men acting from practical knowledge, and men who are governed entirely by theory, or by no principle whatever'. Mary Wollstonecraft, *An Historical and Moral View of the French*

'some other being'. In *The Excursion*, too, Wordsworth's buried and only partially exorcised selves are from time to time exhumed or reborn.

In the notes he dictated to the pious Isabella Fenwick, the septuagenarian Wordsworth confides that the Wanderer 'is chiefly an idea of what I fancied my own character might have become in his circumstances' (195), though combined with observations of actual pedlars. The Solitary, he said to Miss Fenwick, was based in part on 'Mr Fawcett, author of The Art of War, which had a great deal of merit'.[1] What he does not say, is that—like the self presented in *The Prelude*—the Solitary offers a very close match for his own experience. He is imagined as old enough to have lost a wife and two children *before* being radicalised by the French revolution—so that in a sense Wordsworth's own loss of two children in 1812 (which he explores more fully in the Solitary than in any first-person writing), is fused with his loss of Annette and of Caroline. Already bereaved, he goes through the euphoria and the disillusion of the French revolution—disillusioned, like Wordsworth, as much by the fickleness of its supporters as by the terror. Horrified by the 'panic dread of change' that ruled in England, he turns his back on Europe's 'blasted hopes, her fields of carnage and polluted air' and sets sail for America. There, even further disillusioned by the sight of 'big passions strutting on the petty stage' of that 'unknit republic' (it has not yet been 'knit' by the civil war Wordsworth himself believed would be necessary), he steps Westward in search of 'primeval nature's child', only to experience still more disillusionment. The Solitary, then, has

Revolution (1795), 299, 399–400. For kindred studies of Wordsworth in France see my '"Some Other Being": Wordsworth in *The Prelude*', in The *French Revolution in Art and Literature*, ed. J. R. Watson, *The Year's Work in English Studies* 19 (1989), 127–43, and Brooke Hopkins, 'Representing Robespierre' in Stephen Behrendt, ed., *History and Myth: Essays in English Romantic Literature* (Detroit: Wayne State University Press, 1990) 116–29.

1   *FN*, 197. Arthur Beatty cites Hazlitt on Fawcett: 'the disappointment of the hopes he cherished of the freedom and happiness of mankind, preyed upon his mind and hastened his death' (Beatty, *Joseph Fawcett, The Art of War: Its relation to the early development of William Wordsworth*, reprinted from University of Wisconsin Studies in Language and Literature, 2, 1918, 225–270, 234). It is, to be candid, hard to see how *The Art of War* has 'a great deal of merit', other than in its rational onslaught on the practice of war, and its emphasis on the effect of war on those left at home—as in *The Ruined Cottage*.. The poem is devoid of people, and almost devoid of scene or incident. Moreover, according to Godwin, Fawcett was inclined to denounce 'the domestic affections' (Beatty, 232) unlike Wordsworth or his Solitary.

experienced in even greater measure Wordsworth's own crisis (compounded by an infusion of the imagined fate of the Pantisocrats), but has done so without the support the poet had, in the love of Dorothy and Coleridge, in Racedown and Alfoxden. Given that the Solitary is the only character referred to in the poem as the Recluse, it seems legitimate to see him, not the Poet, as the eponymous *hero-designate* of the unwritten, unwritable epic of the mind.

Having distributed these experiences between the Wanderer and the Solitary there is, you may think, rather little left for the Poet, apart from describing some scenery. Partly, perhaps, to keep his powder dry for *The Recluse*, and partly, perhaps, because Wordsworth *needs* to listen to the debate between his Alfoxden and Grasmere selves, unsure as yet which of these is the real him, the 'Poet' in *The Excursion* is indeed something of a cipher. Nevertheless, he voices the reader's own scepticism about whether the Wanderer's response to the story of Margaret is desirable. He expresses occasional shock at the sentiments of the Solitary. He notes clearly when the Wanderer's moralism seems strident and counterproductive in his debate with the Solitary—undermining the Wanderer's thesis that a belief in providence, healthy exercise, and strict observance of a moral rulebook is the golden way. And he delivers a remarkably un-Wordsworthian eulogy on church and state.

The Poet's most important contribution to the poem, however, is that he first builds up the Wanderer, and then plays a role in underwriting some of the Solitary's perceptions. For instance, in Book 3 we learn of the circumstances surrounding the death of a pensioner, who has been sent out on the fells by a grasping and unfeeling landlady who treats him as 'her vassal of all labour'. When the old man is brought back alive (but only just) from a night of exposure on the fells, the Solitary remarks that she puts on 'a great show of joy'. This remark ends Book 2 on a note of cynicism which one might feel demonstrates the misanthropy which is to be corrected, and one therefore reads the whole of books 3 and 4 trying to decide whether the Solitary manifests cynicism or rational scepticism. At the end of book 4, however, the Poet finally meets this 'matron' and finds in her 'aspect'

> A plain assurance that the words which told
> How that neglected pensioner was sent,
> Before his time, into a quiet grave,
> Had done to her humanity no wrong.

In short, the Solitary can be trusted.[1] Elizabeth Gaskell used the same tactic to underwrite the authority of John Barton, who in chapter 5 of *Mary Barton* opines that the employers, being well insured, will welcome a factory fire that puts their employees out of work. First she presents this cynicism without comment, and contrasts it with the heroism of others at the scene of the fire. In chapter 6, however, the narrator comments that John Barton 'was not far wrong' and then shows him to be precisely right.

To return to Banner's painting: the Solitary, contorted in anguish, has his back to the viewer. Were it not so, we might know whether he is truly the poet's double. The Poet's inexpressive countenance expresses the relatively passive role of the poet in the poem. In one draft of many attempts to conclude the tale of the ruined cottage Wordsworth gave the Poet these powerful lines:

> I looked around, the cottage and the elms,
> The road, the pathway and the garden wall
> Which old and loose and mossy o'er the road
> Hung bellying, all appeared, I know not how
> But to some eye within me all appeared
> Colours and forms of a strange discipline.
> The trouble which they sent into my thought
> Was sweet, I looked and looked again… (*PW* 5: 400)

Perhaps because these lines derive so clearly from the same lode as the spots of time (Penrith Beacon's visionary dreariness; the Boating spot's troubling forms), they never made it into *The Excursion*, and while *The Excursion* has numerous passages of great descriptive beauty, no moment in the finished poem gives 'the Poet' himself that kind of depth.

The Solitary struck Jeffrey as the liveliest character in the poem. He will strike most readers as guilty only of a rational scepticism, a welcome tendency to interrupt the Wanderer's longer flights, an understandable tendency to fidget while the Pastor is speaking, and as being the only character in the poem who is at any point *shown* to be, rather than said to be, an engaged member of a community—comforting the bereaved child of Book 2 and energetically engaged in the search for the pauper. The Wanderer finds him guilty of 'An infidel contempt of holy writ', and

---

1   Tellingly, this aspect of the Solitary's experience is borrowed from the author. In the Fenwick note Wordsworth says of the 'matron' that 'her name was Ruth Jackson, & she was exactly such a person as I describe' (*FN*, 201).

judges him dead to all personal and social concerns, but the Wanderer's pious enthusiasm for providence, rules, and piety, as 'the only support' for mortal life, makes him a prejudiced witness on the first point, and it is amply evident that the latter is also a mistaken judgement. He is, then, not merely the voice of the heckler in the poem, but the only figure that gives this 'conversation poem' as Lamb called it, a plausible element of the dialogic.[1]

The main evidence for the Solitary's misanthropy is his retirement from the world, and the poem's handling of this theme is very ambivalent indeed, for obvious reasons. On his first sight of the Solitary's chosen retreat the Poet's heart leaps up: the vale is uplifted by the mountains 'even as if the spot | Had been from eldest time by wish of theirs | So placed, to be shut out from all the world!' Moreover,

> Urn-like it was in shape, deep as an urn;
> With rocks encompassed,... (2: 328 ff).

The simile compresses *Home at Grasmere*'s no less morbid desire to be 'Entrenched, say rather peacefully embowered' and its sequel:

> Ay think on that my heart and cease to stir
> Pause upon that and let the breathing frame
> No longer breathe but all be satisfied.

The end of desire is one definition of death. When the Poet throws himself down 'Upon a bed of heath' and continues to rhapsodize on this 'hidden beauty' ('So lonesome and so perfectly secure: | Not melancholy—no, for it is green, | And bright, and fertile, furnished in itself | With the few needful things which life requires | —In rugged arms how soft it seems to lie, | How tenderly protected') one notes immediately the same ecstatic (and headily gendered) eroticism with which Wordsworth celebrates his retirement in *Home at Grasmere* in the rapturous opening of that poem.[2]

All unconscious, it seems, of this self-revelatory passage, with its blend of Eros and Thanatos, the Poet insists at the start of Book 5 that

---

1   Adam Potkay, in *Wordsworth's Ethics,* 165, 152–3, points to the Solitary's real deficiency, from a stoic point of view, his dependency on outward circumstance. Indeed, the Solitary diagnoses this fault in himself. The death of his wife, he says, left him 'Infirm, dependant, and now destitute!' (3. 694).

2   Wordsworth's retreat to Grasmere may have been a self-destructive act, but the preamble to *Home at Grasmere* is nevertheless, as Thomas McFarland has written, 'the great mother lode of Wordsworthian joy' (McFarland, 80).

his own retirement is quite different, choice having 'fixed me in *a still retreat* | Sheltered, but not to social duties lost, | Secluded but *not buried*; and with song | Cheering my days, and with *industrious thought…*'. This is special pleading of a rare order, pressing a distinction wholly without difference, and it makes nonsense of the poem's singling out of the Solitary as the one to be cured. The plot, I began by saying, concerns the attempt of the Wanderer, aided by the Pastor and Poet, to convert or 'save' the Solitary. If the poem leaves most readers unconvinced that he needs saving, the reason is that Wordsworth is equally unconvinced. We are reminded at the close of the poem that the Solitary is alleged to be 'a wounded spirit, | Dejected, and habitually disposed to seek in degradation of the kind, | Excuse and solace for his own defects' but since at that point the Pastor has engaged in degradation of the kind for a hundred lines or more, and the Solitary has been shown in acts of practical benevolence, the charge misses its mark. Imaginatively, it seems, Wordsworth simply cannot join the general conspiracy to reconfigure his Solitary.

The confusion may owe not a little to the role of John Thelwall in inspiring both the figure of the Solitary and Wordsworth's poetics. Any reader of the Fenwick notes must find it odd that Wordsworth makes no mention of Thelwall. Thelwall is not only a signal case of one whose best hopes for mankind were 'blasted' by the rise of Napoleon. He had also, in *The Peripatetic* (1793), explored something of the terrain of *Lyrical Ballads*, and his *Poems Chiefly Written in Retirement* (1801) configured the kind of imaginatively engaged reclusiveness aimed in *The Recluse*:

> Yet not for aye
> In hermit-like seclusion would I dwell
> (My soul estranging from my brother Man)
> Forgetful and forgotten: rather oft,
> With some few minds congenial, let me stray
> Among the muse's haunts, where converse, meet
> For intellectual beings, may arouse
> The soul's sublimer energies… [1]

---

1   *Lines, Written at Bridgewater on the 27th July, 1797*, in *Poems Chiefly Written in Retirement*, (1801; Woodstock Books, 1989), 128. The full title of Thelwall's poem tells its own intertextual story: 'Lines written at Bridgewater, in Somersetshire, on the 27th of July, 1797; during a Long Excursion, in Quest of a Peaceful Retreat'. Wordsworth merely glanced at the Bridgwater lines in the title and date of *The Poem upon the Wye* but he palpably emulates them in the argument of *Home at Grasmere*—both poems share the attempt to justify hermit-like retreat by the creation of an intellectual com-

This 'conversation poem' closes by imagining a state of 'philosophic amity' with Coleridge and 'Thy Sara, and my Susan, and perchance, | Alfoxden's musing tenant, and the maid of ardent eye'—whose eye functions similarly in *The Poem upon the Wye*. It is hardly surprising that *The Poem upon the Wye* glances covertly at Thelwall's *Lines* both in its title and in its conjectured 'hermit', or that *Home at Grasmere* emulates quite precisely its concept of sublime reclusiveness. On a larger scale, *The Prelude* closes by conceiving a similar philosophic amity between brother poets as a necessary strategic withdrawal from a world in which, as Thelwall says, 'the Trump of Truth ... but wakes The Ruffian Crew of Power | To deeds of maddest anarchy and blood'.[1]

A Day in (Quaker) Heaven

Jeffrey thought *The Excursion* offered a kind of mystical Methodism, Lamb contentedly observed its liberal Quakerism; Montgomery objected severely on its natural religion or Pelagianism (he doesn't call it that, but that was Wordsworth's lifelong heresy, as it was of the ancient Britons). All three point to the poem's great failure as Coleridge saw it; its failure to illustrate 'a scheme of redemption'. Montgomery, in the *Eclectic Review*, opened with a rapturous question: 'Who can behold this beautiful world, and imagine, for a moment, that it was designed to be the abode of miserable beings' (13). He concludes that in man's heart there is 'something which incapacitates him from the full fruition of the blessings thus abundantly dealt around him'. 'What is it? It is sin!' (14). The author of *The Excursion*, however, is far from sound on sin. He fails to make it clear that 'Every system of ethics which insists not on the extinction of sin in the human soul, by the only means through which sin can be extinguished, and everlasting righteousness substituted, is radically defective; and ... a snare to him who receives it as sufficient (19). Montgomery returns to this nagging problem at the end of the review: 'The Sceptic twice asks questions concerning the way of salvation revealed in the Scriptures, *and in neither case does he receive a direct answer'* (30; my emphasis).

munity conquering mental mountains. For Thelwall's influence on Wordsworth and Coleridge, see Gravil, 'The Somerset Sound; or, the Darling Child of Speech', *The Coleridge Bulletin* 26 ns (Winter 2005) 1-21 and for his exemplary auditory analysis of *The Excursion* see my 'Mr Thelwall's Ear; or Hearing *The Excursion*', cited earlier.
1   Thelwall, 129; c.f. *Prelude 1805*, 13: 431–5, with its grim vision of a world 'too weak to tread the ways of truth' falling back on 'old idolatry'.

That did not prevent Lamb telling Wordsworth: 'I cannot tell you how pleased I am with the great Armful of Poetry which you have sent me ... It is the noblest conversational poem I ever read. A day in heaven.' One has only to imagine a Catherine Earnshaw making that remark to realise that it is susceptible of irony. One would not put it *quite* past Lamb to be implying that Wordsworth's attempt at 'something of a dramatic form' has all the cut and thrust of exchanges between God and Christ, or Adam and the Archangel in *Paradise Lost*: his exchanges bear quite as little relation to any conversation ever heard on earth. But then, the same charge could be levelled at Plato, at Cicero, at Shaftesbury, at the whole tradition of dialogic philosophizing to which Wordsworth is adding.

Keats, too, saw *The Excursion* is one of 'the three things superior in this age'.[1] What Lamb and Keats were responding to is first the thumbnailing of *The Prelude*. Book 1 contains what is, in fact, an ur-*Prelude*, in its minimally revised version of *The Pedlar* of February 1798. There is, for instance the Wanderer's ecstasy at dawn, structurally and tonally contrasted to the Pastor's sunset at the poem's close:

> Ocean and earth, the solid frame of earth
> And ocean's liquid mass, in gladness lay
> Beneath him: — Far and wide the clouds were touched,
> And in their silent faces could he read
> Unutterable love. Sound needed none,
> Nor any voice of joy; his spirit drank
> The spectacle: sensation, soul, and form,
> All melted into him; they swallowed up
> His animal being; in them did he live,
> And by them did he live; they were his life.

Logical positivism this may not be, but Jeffrey's description of it as an example of moral and devotional ravings seems as little to the point as his malicious and self-indulgent description of Emily in *The White Doe* as running about 'in a very disconsolate way in a worsted gown and flannel nightcap'.

Like Wordsworth in part 2 of *The Two-Part Prelude,* the Wanderer learns to enjoy the interaction of nature, mind and imagination, and he does so in a way that brings out the latent theme of 'nature's education of man', here a more obviously scientific education in Newton's universe

---

1   The others being Haydon's pictures and 'Hazlitt's depth of taste' *Letters*, 19 Jan 1818.

than we may be conscious of when reading the Part 1 'spots of time'.[1] Like Wordsworth, he loved the midnight storm, seeking out 'the sounds that live in darkness'. And as Wordsworth found solace in geometry, the Wanderer is an amateur physicist who 'scanned the laws of light | Amid the roar of torrents, where they send | From hollow clefts up to the clearer air | A cloud of mist, that smitten by the sun | Varies its rainbow hues.' Such compression (and scientific amplification) of key passages of *The Prelude* may explain why Keats and others, including Emerson, aided by the few passages actually published, seem at times to have intuited that poem's argument.

Second, there is the unparalleled power of the *Ruined Cottage*, introduced by a narrator who knows how honest families can be 'o'erthrown | By passion or mischance, or such misrule | Among the unthinking masters of the earth | As makes the nations groan' and thus exhibits the historicizing grain of Wordsworth's imagination. Third, there is the birth of Romantic Hellenism in Book 4, in a speech which, while it inspired Keats and Shelley, would—as the Solitary rather cannily points out—have outraged the elders of the Wanderer's native church in Athol. Fourth, the Book 8 attack on industrial alienation, in which Ruskin, Carlyle and Marx are all anticipated, allows the Wanderer and the Solitary, between them, to construct a joint critique of the condition of the urban and the rural poor, making this poem, in Mary Moorman's words, 'the poetic charter of the poor, the ignorant, and the underprivileged, in a way that no English poem has been before or since'.[2] Fifth, the appeal in Book 9 for universal literacy is powerful not only in its urgency, but in its theoretical underpinning, exploding Coleridge's and Jeffrey's essentialism as regards both class and gender. Adding these elements together—from the tragedy of Margaret as an exemplary instance of indifferent government, to the social arguments of books 8 and 9—*The Excursion* is the most extended treatment of liberty, equality and fraternity in Wordsworth's oeuvre, if not in any Romantic oeuvre. Sixth, its numerous disturbances make one wonder whether *The Excursion* embodies a conscious attempt to develop from the ironic instabilities of the ballads, a counter-authori-

1   For a reading of the spots of time cognizant of their interest in physics, optics, and geophysics, see my '"Knowledge not purchased with the loss of Power": Pestalozzi and the Spots of Time', *European Romantic Review*, 8:3 (1997): 231–61.
2   Moorman, 2: 182. See also Mary Wedd's meditation on 'Industrialization and the Moral law in Books 8 and 9 of *The Excursion*', *CLB*, ns 81 (1993) 5–25.

tarian epic form. The poem has just sufficient differentiation of voice to deny the reader any sure landing place from which to sift the poem's ironies, giving it, in a lumbering way, an almost postmodern instability. All in all, and for all his distaste, when Jeffrey diagnosed in *The Excursion* the poetic DNA of *Lyrical Ballads* he was exactly right.

In failing to find in it any serious ideological shift from *Lyrical Ballads*, Jeffrey and Hazlitt were responding to what is indeed there. The poem is, to a degree that Jeffrey and Coleridge found wearisome, founded in common life, and in a perception of the poor as victims. In Book 1 the heroine is a victim, without doubt, of war and famine. In Book 2 the character whose funeral is the first event in the narrative time of the poem, is recorded is a victim of greed—his landlady is a sort of social security rentier, one who siphons off welfare payments into her own purse. The one character in Book 6 who all readers find as compelling as Margaret, is an unmarried and deserted mother treated unfeelingly by her employers. And nowhere is the Wanderer's piety ironised more than in his *second* failure to comment appropriately on a tale of female suffering:

> 'Blest are they
> Whose sorrow rather is to suffer wrong
> Than to do wrong, albeit themselves have erred.
> This tale gives proof that Heaven most gently deals
> With such, in their affliction.'

'Such', here, means repentant sinners, like Ellen, as opposed to undeserving ones such as the next character about whom the Wanderer importunes a narrative. Ellen's faith and contrite heart, the Wanderer says:

> 'Call to my mind dark hints which I have heard
> Of one who died within this vale, by doom
> Heavier, as his offence was heavier far.
> Where, Sir, I pray you, where are laid the bones
> Of Wilfred Armathwaite?' (6.1018–1079)

Both the clumsy verse and the callous transition question the Wanderer's authority.

The problem with *The Excursion* is that it is, for the most part, sedentary, a posture conducive to constipation and deep vein thrombosis. Without the caustic quality of the Solitary it would be unendurable. Seated in the churchyard the Solitary utters the opinion that if these mute graves could speak,

> We should recoil, stricken with sorrow and shame,
> To see disclosed, by such dread proof, how ill
> That which is done accords with what is known
> To reason, and by conscience is enjoined.

In book 6 he generalises more grimly still, in what seems an appropriate epitaph for Margaret and Ellen:

> Amid the groves, under the shadowy hills,
> The generations are prepared; the pangs,
> The internal pangs, are ready; the dread strife
> Of poor humanity's afflicted will
> Struggling in vain with ruthless destiny.

Fundamentally the purpose of the poem is, or may be, to persuade the reader, as the Wanderer puts it, that one can still learn 'To prize the breath we share with human kind; | And look upon the dust of man with awe.' What both Wanderer and Solitary want from the Pastor, as they survey Grasmere's necropolis, is an authentic appraisal of those whose great virtue for the researcher is (in the Pastor's curiously Sartrean line) that 'with these | The future cannot contradict the past' (5.664). Their existence over, their essence is perfected.

These are serious questions, addressed on serious ground, by serious minded men, the grim work of a man who, with his wife Mary, has spent too long (until the move to Rydal) overlooking the graves of his children, and who bestows that experience in the Solitary in the deeply moving autobiographical elements of Book 3. The Wanderer wants an answer to this question: 'Are we a creature in whom good | Preponderates, or evil?' and the answer is to arise from a sociological appraisal of the buried life of Grasmere: 'Give us, for our abstractions, solid facts; | For our disputes, plain pictures.' If one can get past the sense that Wordsworth's real forte, from which he should not have been deflected, is the dramatic ballad, and that his more experimental mode of writing is here reduced—at Coleridge's insistence—to a monotone inventory, what remains is authentic enough. The concern for a genuinely sociological rather than *a priori* investigation, and the desire to treat actual lives as exempla of what *The Prelude* calls 'human nature faithful to itself under worst trials', are both moving and—in precisely the way that discomforted Jeffrey—bound by natural piety to the agenda of *Lyrical Ballads*.

There is, moreover, welcome evidence at the start of Book 5 that the Wordsworth in whom Hazlitt found 'a convulsive inclination to laugh about the mouth, a good deal at various with the solemn, stately expression of the rest of his face' is still capable of resurgence. Entering the churchyard the party disturbs a sexton at his work, described by the Solitary as 'that self-solaced, easy-hearted churl, | Death's hireling, who scoops out his neighbour's grave, | Or wraps an old acquaintance up in clay, | All unconcerned as he would bind a sheaf, | Or plant a tree.' Standing in a graveyard, above 'A subterraneous magazine of bones, | In whose dark vaults my own shall soon be laid,' the Solitary wonders what religion and philosophy have done for the village dead:

> Where are your triumphs? your dominion where?
> ... whom, I ask, of individual Souls,
> Have ye withdrawn from passion's crooked ways,
> Inspired, and thoroughly fortified? — (5.331–54)

The Poet's innocent reply, that 'from this pregnant spot of ground, such thoughts | Rise to the notice of a serious mind | By natural *exhalation*' puts one in mind of one of the more mordantly humorous stanzas in *Expostulation and Reply* and the wisdom '*breathed* by dead men to their kind'. He agrees, in part, with his sceptical alter ego, that for all the 'smooth and solemnized complacencies' of Christian lands, 'Earth is sick, | And Heaven is weary, of the hollow words | Which States and Kingdoms utter when they talk | Of truth and justice' (5.369–81). And far from stabilizing the tone, the entry of the Pastor into the poem deepens the instability.

As the Pastor converses apart with the Wanderer, the Solitary looks as if he would have vanished 'if a wish | Could have transferred him to the flying clouds, | Or the least penetrable hiding-place | In his own valley's rocky guardianship.' The Poet, however, pronounces himself 'well pleased' to contemplate the two in conversation, the one comparable to 'a weather-beaten oak, | Fresh in the strength and majesty of age', and the other

> like a stately sycamore,
> That spreads, in gentle pomp, its honied shade.

The prospect of 'gentle pomp' and 'honeyed shade' recalls the satirized preacher (borrowed from Cowper) in *The Prelude*, guiding his captivated flock, and lurking somewhere in the background, surely, is Thomson's 'little, round, fat, oily man of God' (*The Castle of Indolence*, 1: lxix). The Pastor's answer to the Wanderer's urgent question about the preponderance of good and evil only confirms this satiric undertow. Like that celestial traveller Emanuel Swedenborg, our Pastor is an authority on angels:

> 'Our nature,' said the Priest, in mild reply,
> 'Angels may weigh and fathom: they perceive,
> With undistempered and unclouded spirit,
> The object as it is; but, for ourselves,
> That speculative height we may not reach.'

A satirist seeking a model for honeyed vacuousness could do worse than take *Excursion* 5.440–549, especially the thirty stately lines that the Pastor requires to explain that things looks very different in different lights, just as the churchyard looks different in the Spring sunshine and under winter snow:

> We safely may affirm that human life
> Is either fair and tempting, a soft scene
> Grateful to sight, refreshing to the soul,
> Or a forbidden tract of cheerless view;
> Even as the same is looked at, or approached.
> Thus, when in changeful April fields are white
> With new-fallen snow, if from the sullen north
> Your walk conduct you hither, ere the sun
> Hath gained his noontide height, this churchyard, filled
> With mounds transversely lying side by side
> From east to west, before you will appear
> An unillumined, blank, and dreary, plain,
> With more than wintry cheerlessness and gloom
> Saddening the heart....

'Go forward, and look back' however, and (in similarly expansive lines, labouring the epic simile) all is 'green and bright'. Given his distaste for sermons one would not put it past Wordsworth to be revenging himself, through this trite and leadenly elaborated analogy, on a hundred Sunday torments. What the Pastor labours to say, Wordsworth himself says in just two lines of the prefatory poem to *The White Doe*, a year later, when treating Mary's grief: 'soft gales dissolve the dreary snow | And give the timid herbage leave to shoot' (*WD*, 78).

　　'This subterraneous magazine of souls' (it is a remarkable line from a poet two of whose children lie in this 'magazine') contains some genu-inely interesting portraits, praised by the reviewers: a case of unrequited love, a miner sustained by his unfulfilled quest for riches, the life of a man deaf from birth. Among them is a remorseless forester (7.590–631), very possibly the archetype of James Fenimore Cooper's mad lumber-jack in *The Pioneers* whose ambition is to deforestate New York State before he dies. He is closely followed by another Cooperesque character (739–816) whose shooting prowess with regard to eagles, swallows and sea-gulls, puts one in mind of the thoughtless youth of Hawkeye himself. What is wrong with these portraits, each of which is a potential addition to the lyrical ballads corpus, is that as intoned by the Pastor, they lack the quality that made *Lyrical Ballads* so vital. With each and every ballad, in 1800 quite as much as in 1798, the reader starts in the same place, need-ing to ascertain by trial and error, what kind of speaker the poem deploys, what that speaker's relation is to the subject, with what degree of irony the speaker is treated in the poem. The implicit authority of the Pastor—however much we feel licensed to question it—neuters the dialogic and often fails in human reverence towards the lives he appropriates.

Nevertheless, the task of the reader is the same as in *Lyrical Ballads*. It is to learn how to find a standpoint from which to appraise the appraiser. What finally undercuts the Pastor is not Wordsworth's inability to refrain from ironising him a little on first introduction, or the Solitary's impa-tience to be off, or even the rather too challenging suggestion (Book 7, 25) that we should prefer the Pastor's 'pure eloquence' to the 'strains of power' in Bardic 'pastoral melody or warlike air'. It is that his the-ology—along with the Wanderer's fitful Calvinism—is undermined in Wordsworth's own 'Prospectus'.

The Return of the Repressed

Of course, reading *The Excursion* is, as Geoffrey Hartman says, 'a mas-sively depressing experience' (*Wordsworth's Poetry,* 292). Indications that the poem may be designedly ironic, intended to lead to a subse-quent work in which the probing mind of the Solitary turns the tables on his pompous tutors, are fleeting and perhaps delusive. And Jeffrey has a point: the leaden harangues and effusions *do* suggest that Wordsworth had spent too long 'in retirement' from the daily contest of ideas. If Wordsworth really intended the lengthy dialogue in Grasmere churchyard, surrounded by the Pastor's buried flock, to redeem his promise to make 'Paradise, and groves Elysian, fortunate fields' appear 'the simple produce of the common day' (and the Pastor's epitaphs are, if very distantly, evocative of Aeneas visiting Anchises in the Underworld) one may feel one has been sold a false prospectus.

Yet it remains a mildly subversive monument, quietly but tellingly deconstructive of the marriage of Platonism and Christianity it is supposed to celebrate. Wordsworth's first disobedience takes the form of devoting a considerable part of the poem to a celebration of the lives of ordinary people, and the rest to a philosophic pedlar. This working man is conceived rather along the lines of Gaskell's Job Legh, who is representative of the kind of weaver who works with Newton's *Principia* open beside his loom. The question to which Books 6 and 7 are in fact addressed is not whether creation is awaiting redemption, but whether, on the whole, there are grounds for recovering a faith in what the work calls 'social man'. Do the gravestones hide a history of human failure, as the solitary has come to believe? Is man helpless without divine intervention, as the Pastor believes? Or is there ground for believing in 'human nature faithful to itself under worst trials'? To determine the balance of good and evil in human life, the wanderer says, we need not idealisms, but 'facts', and the place to look for them is the last place Coleridge would be inclined to look: in the same territory as lyrical ballads, the short and simple annals of the poor—the actual poor, neither idealized nor generalized, as Coleridge thought people in poems should be. The way the question is formulated sets aside Coleridge's agenda. The way it is answered, by enumerating individual lives rooted in local particularities, seems almost designed to scandalize him.

The poem is a debate in which the prize for victory is the soul of the Solitary. The Solitary plays the part—ostensibly—of his own evil angel, and he is offered a choice, peculiarly polarized, of good angels. Book 9 concludes this debate, but becomes also a debate, one may feel, for the soul of the Poet. It is constructed in a curiously binary fashion. The Wanderer and the Pastor, supposedly allies, come to express contrary views of human life and possibilities, polarized between the natural Quakerism of the one and the abject Pietism of the other. Put briefly, the Wanderer—suddenly rejuvenated—preaches by and large an Alfoxden vision of 'the one Life', and of how we have all of us 'one human heart'. He invokes that active principle which circulates through all things and is 'the Soul of all the worlds', which nameless 'something far more deeply interfused' (inspired by Lucretius, Virgil, Newton and the *philosophes*) underwrites the humanist faith of *The Poem upon the Wye* and the ascent of Snowdon. In this faith, all man needs to listen to is what emerges from himself, and the only law he needs to obey is 'the law of life, and hope and action'. From this premise the Wanderer develops a view of human life as progressive, offering a sort of vision of permanent revolution: a programme based on the idea that our real home is 'the world which is the world of all of us', and that our desire is for 'something ever-more about to be'. The Pastor, contrariwise, sees all progress as given by heaven, and human being as weak, bewildered, dark, and able to hope for nothing better than law and order, peace and quiet. The emotional curve of Book 9 parodies that of *The Eolian Harp*: we begin in transcendence and end on our knees.

The conclusion drawn from the Pastor's histories by the Wanderer in Book 9, specifically critiques Burke's top-down notion of social progress, and denies Coleridge's belief in the 'known and abiding' essentials of class.[1] What matters about the Wanderer's famous plea for education in Book 9 is not simply that it is an appeal for the war cabinet to act *now*, even in wartime, to implement universal literacy—

> Transfer not to futurity a work
> Of urgent need. — Your Country must complete
> Her glorious destiny. Begin even now, ...
> Now, when destruction is a prime pursuit,
> Show to the wretched nations for what end
> The powers of civil polity were given. (9.415ff)

—but that the appeal is based on a dynamic model of human being, consistent with the depiction of the Pedlar himself. In David Simpson's admirable formulation, the Wanderer's speech on education 'argues that until everyone is educated we will not know what human nature can become'.[2] That, basically, is what John and Harriet Mill would be argu-

---

1   As Don Bialostosky says, 'Wordsworth ... does not recognize the essentiality of the empirical classes which the Aristotelian ideal accurately represents [and which Coleridge adopts in full faith], nor does he concede the generality of the fallen condition which makes it necessary to respect them'. *Making Tales*, 33.

2   Simpson, *Wordsworth's Historical Imagination*, 194. A tendency in recent criticism to confuse this passage with 'imperial rant' seems to me highly anachronistic, though it would be interesting to investigate first, whether anybody was not 'imperialist', from

ing almost fifty years later with reference to 'the nature of women'. Alas, he asks:

> Alas! what differs more than man from man!
> And whence that difference? Whence but from himself?

And the answer to this *Lyrical Ballads* question, concerning 'what man has made of man', is that when we contemplate true equality we find ourselves

> Lamenting ancient virtues overthrown,
> And for the injustice grieving, that hath *made*
> So wide a difference between man and man. (9.206ff)

Class and racial differences (the implication is equally plain) are made not found, they are social constructs not natural essences. That is why education is a 'sacred right, the lisping babe proclaims | To be inherent in him'. Wordsworth never wrote a more serious attempt to challenge the kind of class bias on which Coleridge, Jeffrey, and Byron would judge his poem. To Coleridge and Jeffrey, shepherds were clowns (yes, I know why one might object to that point). To Byron, whose readers rarely question his radical pretensions, pedlars and waggoners were scum:

> 'Pedlars' and 'Boats' and 'Wagons'! Oh ye shades
> O Pope and Dryden, are we come to this?

'Trash of such sort' he continues, 'from bathos' vast abyss | Floats scum-like uppermost, and these Jack Cades | Of sense and song above your graves may hiss' (*Don Juan*, 3.889–94).

To the Pedlar, human nature is, by implication, no more fixed than political territories. The point is made in a brilliant metaphor, based on the political map of Europe, and how from Spain to the Baltic the age has seen:

> Laws overturned; and territory split,
> Like fields of ice rent by the polar wind,
> And forced to join in less obnoxious shapes
> Which, ere they gain consistence, by a gust
> Of the same breath are shattered and destroyed.

a modern perspective, at this date, and second, how one might compare the stances of Wordsworth, Coleridge, DeQuincey, Southey, Keats and Hunt towards the Anglo-Saxon diaspora.

Being a necessitarian, the Pedlar is in this respect a Marxist: those who profess a belief in historical materialism yet quarrel sentimentally with empire as a process whereby society evolves are of course hopelessly mixed up. Wordsworth, as a citizen of British, then Norse, Saxon, Scottish, Danish, Norman and finally Tudor Rheged, who shared Matthew Arnold's lack of sentiment for the disappearance of minor principalities and tongues, knew a little about the ineluctable processes of cultural transmission.

Dreams of human evolution may be visionary, and the climax of the poem is marked by the Wanderer's designation as a prophet. The Pastor's wife delivers this backhanded compliment to his almost Emersonian eloquence:

> While he is speaking I have power to see
> Even as he sees; but when his voice hath ceased
> Then, with a sigh, sometimes I feel, as now,
> That combinations so serene and bright
> Cannot be lasting in a world like ours

and so saying she ushers in the poem's second finale, its belated attempt to reach the Coleridge-ordained conclusion that human endeavour avails nothing without divine intervention.

According to Coleridge, in the shorter and marginally less preposterous of the two versions we have of what was allegedly 'agreed on' for Wordsworth's career-long homework, the poet was to 'assume the station of a man in mental repose, one whose principles were made up, and so prepared to deliver upon authority a system of philosophy' (*Table Talk,* 21 July 1832). That system, in the longer account of 1815, was to have

> affirmed a Fall in some sense, as a fact ... attested by Experience & Con-science ... and not disguising the sore evils under which the whole Creation groans, to point out however a manifest Scheme of Redemption from this Slavery ... and to conclude by a grand didactic swell on the necessary identity of a true Philosophy with true Religion. (Griggs, 4: 574–5)

Believing neither in the fall nor in the necessity for grace, Wordsworth was almost the last person who could have offered such an argument, except in the conspicuously compromised form in which it appears, namely the Pastor's grovelling (and possibly ironised) response to the

Book 9 sunset. Here especially, it seems safe to insist the work is structured so as to deny authority to any single figure or any single speech—to end, as lyrical ballads so often do, in a way that sends one back into poem in search of firmer ground.

The conclusion of the work seems peculiarly haunted by dissent. Grasmere, which materialised mysteriously in Book 5 just a few steps from Blea Tarn, now dissolves into Ullswater, as the Poet and his comrades, take to a 'pinnace' and cruise the waters in search of sublime experience. Their destination, via the island, is a lofty fellside path known as Loughrigg Terrace, where the sunset is first described by 'the Poet'. In the rays of light 'multitudes of little floating clouds' become

> Vivid as fire; clouds separately poized,
> Innumerable multitude of Forms
> Scattered through half the circle of the sky;
> And giving back, and shedding each on each,
> With prodigal communion, the bright hues
> Which from the unapparent Fount of glory
> They had imbibed, and ceased not to receive.
> That which the heavens displayed, the liquid deep
> Repeated; but with unity sublime!

Clearly the passage is symbolic of imaginative transformation, perhaps of the kind that 'higher minds' achieve in the *Prelude*'s climactic ascent of Snowdon, in which such unity derives in a double sense from 'the liquid deep'. It seems, however, more immediately expressive of 'the poetry of nature', as wrought by the moonlight in that same ascent, or by Coleridge's imaginative clouds in *Frost at Midnight* (those clouds 'which *image* in their bulk both lakes and clouds, and mountain crags'). The most imaginative touch is the quietly disruptive communion metaphor (the bright hues which they *imbibed*) which takes one back sixteen years to the metaphysical play of *Lines written in Early Spring*, when the 'pores' of the mind *drink* the 'spirit' of the season. Either way, a disruptive animism is infused into a scene on which the Pastor is about to sermonise, seeing the radiance merely as an image of 'thy paternal splendors and the pomp of those who fill thy courts in highest heaven, the radiant cherubim'.

The introduction of the Pastor's disruptive meditation may or may not censure that disruption, but while 'We gazed, in silence hushed' the Priest's 'holy transport' is profoundly depressing. More than any outburst of the Solitary, it converts a personal sense of defeat into a libel on the species, and into something very hard to distinguish from idolatry:

> 'Eternal Spirit! universal God!
> Power inaccessible to human thought,
> Save by degrees and steps which Thou hast deigned
> To furnish; *for this Image of thyself,*
> *To the infirmity of mortal sense*
> *Vouchsafed;* this local transitory type
> Of thy paternal splendors, and *the pomp*
> *Of those who fill thy courts in highest heaven,*
> *The radiant Cherubim;* — accept the thanks
> *Which we, thy humble Creatures, here convened,*
> *Presume to offer'*

What 'We, thy humble Creatures' are enjoined to be thankful for is that we may eventually join 'the elect', 'divested at the appointed hour | Of all dishonour, cleansed from mortal stain.'[1] Let our days end, he prays. 'Conclude | Time's weary course!'; remove 'The sting of human nature' out of mercy to 'thy wretched sons'; let humanity reach its quietus. 'The way is marked | The guide appointed, and the ransom paid....'. He thus converts the natural beauty of the sunset into a dubious typology of his Calvinist creed, denigrates human being, and, crucially, denies every humanist postulate the Wanderer has advanced throughout Book 9.

Only the manner in which Wordsworth concludes the book enables some purchase on a stance from which the ambivalence might be resolved. He now rewrites the *Salisbury Plain* and *Prelude* vision from a clerical standpoint:

> 'Once,' and with wild demeanour, as he spake,
> On us the venerable Pastor turned
> His beaming eye that had been raised to Heaven,
> 'Once, while the Name, Jehovah, was a sound
> Within the circuit of this sea-girt isle

---

1   Here the poem alludes to the Solitary's sardonic account of baptismal laundering in 5.280–85: 'And when the pure | And consecrating element hath cleansed | The original stain, the child is there received | Into the second ark, Christ's church, with trust | That he, from wrath redeemed, therein shall float | Over the billows of this troublesome world | To the fair land of everlasting life'. The Pastor's typologically interpreted sunset seems designed, also, to be compared to the Solitary's more eloquent, more impassioned, cloudscape in Book 2. 860–911.

> Unheard, the savage nations bowed the head
> To Gods delighting in remorseless deeds;
> Gods which themselves had fashioned, to promote
> Ill purposes, and flatter foul desires.'

Even here, 'Mysterious rites were solemnised' and the sounding cataracts were too weak to drown 'the groans and shrieks | Of human victims, offered up to appease | Or to propitiate.' Sacrifice was made to Taranis, the Celtic Jove,

> Or to Andates, Female Power! who gave
> (For so they fancied) glorious Victory.

The Priest, who seems especially troubled by female power, has clearly not read the two-part *Prelude*, where deity, such as it is, invariably *is* female power. And certainly he is unaware of Wordsworth's last major treatment of this theme, in the 1805 *Prelude*, which presents the imaginative poet standing by nature's side among the men of old. There, in a passage discussed in chapter 1, Wordsworth relates his own vision of a ritual whose 'pomp | Is for both worlds, the living and the dead', and another vision, unavailable to the Pastor, of druids as long-bearded teachers, moving in time to music while 'the waste | rejoiced with them *and me* in those sweet sounds'.

   In the *Sonnet composed by the Side of Grasmere Lake* (possibly composed in 1814), as in *The World is too much with us* (1802), and in the Wanderer's Book 4 hymn to pagan imagination, we meet recurrent intimations that in worship of the Universal Pan, or under Triton's wreathed horn, are to be found 'the [poetically palatable] hiding places of man's power'. To the Pastor, innocent of the poet's bond with what he himself deplores,

> — A few rude Monuments of mountain-stone
> Survive; all else is swept away. —

More than once in this work, however—the theme was started with the Yewdale family, who are seen implicitly as the genetic remnants of the ancient Britons, the Cymri who gave their name to Cumberland—the sense is offered that if anything consecrates this place it is continuity rather than disruption; the recognition in the rites of the present of the mysterious rites of the past. Everything the Pastor says in his constant rhetoric of polarities, seems designed to present his *priestly* function, his offerings, his way of accommodating the dead, as acceptable to the poet not because it is what the Pastor calls 'this marvellous advance | Of good from evil; as if one extreme | Were left, the other gained' but precisely because it accommodates the past to the present. Shortly after *The Excursion*, Wordsworth will present Waterloo as an event worthy of the God of battles, the father of Carnage.

In any case, what the close of the poem returns us to is the strident challenge to orthodoxy represented by the *Prospectus* to 'The Recluse'. To respond to the sunset (the trigger of this effusion) the pastor has to figure the divine spirit anthropomorphically, creating a severely patriarchal 'father figure' as his own way of figuring 'power put forth in personal form'. Yet Wordsworth's *Prospectus* had promised that its Satan-emulating poet will

> tread on shadowy ground, [and] sink
> Deep — and, aloft ascending, breathe in worlds
> To which the heaven of heavens is but a veil.
> All strength — all terror, single or in bands,
> *That ever was put forth in personal form* —
> Jehovah — with his thunder, and the choir
> Of shouting Angels, and the empyreal thrones —
> I pass them unalarmed.

The Pastor's belief that only pagans worship 'gods which themselves had fashioned' is clearly not the poet's. Supreme fictions in 'personal form', even Hebraic ones, cannot compare with their creator, namely 'The *sense* of God or whatsoe'er is dim | Or vast' in the human mind itself, or what Blake called, in *Jerusalem*, 'the bosom of God, the human imagination'.

Ironically, then, *The Excursion* closes with an ostensible attempt to forestall the revolution wrought by Wordsworth's oeuvre: we all know that in the words of William Hale White (in *The Autobiography of Mark Rutherford*, 1881), 'Wordsworth unconsciously did for me what ever ygreat religious reformer has done; he recreated my Supreme Divinity, substituting a new and living spirit for the old deity, once alive but gradually hardened into an idol'. Against that reformist pressure, inaugurated by Wordsworth himself in his 'Poem upon the Wye', the Pastor is powerless.[1] As James Montgomery noticed in his review, Wordsworth's invo-

---

1   The danger of writing a dialogic poem, however ponderous, is that it can be used to

cation, in the Prospectus, of a 'dread power that inspires the human soul of universal earth' and possesses 'a metropolitan temple in the heart of poets'—is suspiciously heterodox:

> we do not clearly comprehend who is 'the prophetic spirit', and who 'the dread power'; whether they are two or one;—a creature of the imagination, or the Creator himself; or whether the first be not the creature of imagination, and the second the Creator. If 'the 'dread power' means not God, it is difficult to imagine how the Author can justify the language which immediately follows that phrase, as addressed to any other being.[1]

As much as any of Wordsworth's early texts, *The Excursion* is surprisingly writerly, likely to deconstruct itself, shaped by disruptive energies. It is not possible to entertain a fixed view either of the Poet, or of the Wanderer or of the Solitary in this poem, not least because each of them is, in a sense, The Recluse, who may be its hero. It is a fitting climax that Wordsworth not only wonders at the close of Book 9 whether seven books of moral discourse have effected any renovation whatever of the Solitary (implying rather mischievously that they haven't) but does so in a climactic scene that brings into focus his ineradicable scepticism about the very theme that, on Coleridge's behalf, he is attempting to make thematically central. 'The Recluse' was meant (by Coleridge) to demonstrate a redemptive process in operation; a redemption based upon a trinitarian theology. Nothing in Wordsworth's biography suggests that he gave much thought to either. He did believe in immortality of some kind, in female power, and in a kind of pantheistic world-soul to which he knew he belonged. But so did those ancient Britons and 'wise druides' to whom he gives so vivid a last word. By ending with a scene of re-enactment *The Excursion* inaugurates a curiously prominent theme in Wordsworth's long anti-climax: that of natural piety to the men of old and to the recalcitrant element in himself that they came to symbolize. Perhaps his dedication to His Lordship of a poem whose primary voice is an erstwhile Pedlar, whether accustomed or not to 'higgle about tape and brass buttons', itself symbolizes that recalcitrance.

---

bolster quite antithetical tendencies. For the varieties of Victorian believer and sceptic who found it possible to enlist Wordsworth—*Excursion* and 'Tintern' alike—in quite polarized causes, see Stephen Gill, *Wordsworth and the Victorians* (Oxford: Clarendon Press, 1998) chapter 2.

1   *Eclectic Review*, n.s 3 (January 1815) 23.

Chapter 11: National Pieties; or, the Road to Waterloo

> The genuine dignity of the nation grows as its history gathers, and there is a moral power in the mere memory of an heroic age. The spirit of a people must be fed with its historic associations; its natural food is the story of the good and great men of their blood; deprived of that it languishes and dies.
>
> —Henry Reed, *Lectures on English History* [1]

IN 1804 WILLIAM PITT commissioned an impressive series of squat Martello towers along the south coast to guard against invasion. Wordsworth's contributions to national defence, in the political sonnets of 1802–3, were similarly rounded, and like some of Pitt's, they addressed vulnerable points to landward as well as seaward. Daniel Stuart, who published some of the sonnets in the *Morning Post*, described them as each forming 'a little Political Essay, on some recent proceeding' (Moorman, 1: 571) and Wordsworth himself told Lady Beaumont, when he published the *Poems, in Two Volumes*, that the sonnets made up a collective poem 'on the subject of civil liberty and national independence'—a poem 'likely to have few parallels in the Poetry of the present day' (*MY* 1: 147).

This public Wordsworth who emerged in somewhat different guises in 1802–3, 1806–10, and 1815–16 was in some ways an aberration, in others a throwback. One thinks of Shelley's splendidly pompous remark in *A Philosophical View of Reform*, that although 'no friend of mankind and his country' could desire a revolutionary crisis, if the moment were to arrive one could not 'hesitate under what banner to array his person and his power'.[2] Unlike the destined baronet or his lordly companion,

---

1 *Shelley's Prose: The Trumpet of a Prophecy*, ed. David Lee Clark (London: Fourth Estate, 1988), 255.

2 I have avoided detailed discussion of the political alignment of the sonnets, taking

Wordsworth had no 'power' to array under any of his favoured banners—whether that of France in 1793, of Spain in 1809, or of England in 1815—but he did have a sense of bardic lineage. The presiding genius of the political sonnets is, of course Milton, author of *Areopagitica*, a model of 'manners' and of 'cheerful faith', and advocate of Cromwell and Fairfax. Their politics is pure Commonwealthman, and frequently founded in positions well to the 'left' of those then prevailing in Consular France. But the language of the sonnets, with their frequent 'banners', the 1802 lament for

> altar, sword, and pen,
> Fireside, the heroic wealth of hall and bower

CWRT, 1: 646

the invocation in 1803 of the prose of Daniel, with its reference to 'the flood of British freedom' flowing from 'dark antiquity' and the armoury of 'invincible Knights of old' and the climactic 'countenance of grim war', reaches back through to Shakespeare and Malory to *The Gododdin* and the men who marched to Cattraeth. Freedom in these sonnets is conspicuously *British*; rapine, avarice, and emasculation are *English*. It took little to swell the 1802 trickle of lamentation over the ruined hearth of 'the good old cause' into the 1803 torrent of still more Bardic exhortation to valiant deeds. A trip in August to the Burns country in Scottish Rheged, where Robert Burns had collected taxes for Pitt the Elder, alarms over

---

the 'old historicist' case for granted. E. P. Thompson's 'Disenchantment or Default: a Lay Sermon', in *Power and Consciousness*, ed. C. C. O'Brien and W. D. Vanich (London and New York, 1969), 149–81 remains the most interesting treatment (a subsubsequent 'lay sermon' developing the theme was delivered from a Methodist pulpit in Grasmere). I share Thompson's view that Wordsworth's turning away from 'deraciné Godwinist intelligentsia' was at the same time a turning 'toward the common people' (150); that the Wordsworth who wrote the political sonnets in 1802 is still the same man who offered to house John Thelwall at Alfoxden in 1798 (161); that one can understand someone who, after a decade or more as an inner emigré, opts to 'rejoin' his nation (172); and that Wordsworth's post 1815 apostasy is less remarkable than his keeping the faith at least until the Cintra tract. Ultimately, 'If the social context makes all insertion seem impossible—if all objective referents for these hopes are cruelly obliterated ... if *fraternité* produces fratricide, *égalité* produces empire, *liberté* produces liberticide—then aspirations can only become a transposed interior faith'. (174). One is, however, entitled to complain that Wordsworth did not follow up the passionate critique of *The Convention of Cintra* with a similar public critique of *The Congress of Vienna* (176), of which he was, in fact, privately critical.

an expected invasion, and a meeting with the warlike Sir Walter Scott, released in Wordsworth the tethered bard and all his border-minstrel heritage and cause him to enlist in the Grasmere volunteers as, according to Dorothy, 'a determined hater of the French' (*EY*, 403)

Nor was this splicing of Commonwealthman and Warlike Patriot unique. William Frend, who was sacked from Jesus College in 1793 for sedition, published in 1804 a lengthy work on *Patriotism: or, the Love of Our Country* dedicated to 'the Volunteers of the United Kingdom'. Adopting 'the immortal Alfred' as the patron saint of English liberty, and casting aspersions on subsequent kings, courtiers, and sycophants, Frend's true Whig interpretation of history saw continental despotism threatening English liberty. 'Lost as it is to honour and virtue', England might now be doomed

> to run the same career with other nations; to see arbitrary power placed on its throne; its institutions trampled under foot; vexatious tyranny dragging the peasant from his cot; arbitrary impositions, emanating from a tyrant or a corrupted aristocracy.[1]

Despite old corruption, Frend assumes, as do Wordsworth's sonnets, and with similar self-contradictions, that Napoleon 'sees no obstacle to his vast pre-eminence, but the liberty, the spirit, the independence of Britain' (210). Compared with the spirit prevailing in France, however, England is 'a nation enervated by luxury, unused to the labours of warfare, incapable of facing danger in the field; whose strength is worn out in manufactures; whose mind is absorbed in the mean calculations of counting-houses; a nation of hucksters; fit only for the tricks of bargain and sale' (211). Like Wordsworth, Frend looks back to 1793 with unchanged ardour. When the 'confederate despots' threatened Paris, 'who did not rejoice that their schemes were baffled: who did not applaud the French for standing up for their rights and bravely defending their country against foreign intrusion?' (218). But, he asks, 'if Frenchmen then, upon the very dawn of liberty, could thus act, how much more must the inhabitants of this island be inflamed with ardour, to preserve their rights and independence! Liberty is not here a novelty' (219). His practical advice to the Volunteers ends up, like Wordsworth's sonnet *Anticipation*, by predicting victory for 'The Men of Kent'.

---

1   William Frend, *Patriotism: or, the Love of Our Country; an Essay ... dedicated to the Volunteers of the United Kingdom* (London: J. Mawman, 1804), 86.

David Williams had made the same journey much earlier. Williams had been among the most distinguished of the British in Paris, an honorary Citizen, and a counsellor to the Constitutional Convention, applying a talent for administration for which he is commended by Mme Roland.[1] He left Paris, however, on the day of the execution of the King. His 1797 pamphlet urging mobilisation against terror sets out a position anticipatory of Wordsworth's *Lines on the Expected Invasion*. Wordsworth's 1803 poem invites Royalists and Commonwealthmen to unite; Williams urges a tactical alliance of those 'who would preserve [Europe's] ancient institutions, even in their worst abuses—of those who would gradually assimilate them to the gradual improvements of man—and of those who would rapidly exchange them for the forms of fancy, or the faultless monsters of unexperienced philosophy'.[2] In 1793, he reflects, the assault of the Combined Powers had caused four million Frenchmen to enlist, and this, he argues, produced anarchy. 'When Armies, formed of the best Citizens in the lower classes, marched to the frontiers, the idle, the lazy, the vicious were drawn, like floating particles towards a vacuum, into the general centre; and Paris, after she had furnished forty thousand soldiers found her population prodigiously increased', mainly by 'incendiaries and depredators' (including fifty thousand unemployed tax collectors for the ancien régime), and the prolific class of unemployed servants discarded by the fallen nobility (15–17). If there is an invasion, says the knowing legislator, 'The same causes will produce the same effects in London; and the monster ... will rise spontaneously, like a pestilential

---

1 'Paine throws light upon a revolution better than he concurs in the making of a constitution... for cool discussion in a committee, or the regular labours of a legislator, I conceive David Williams infinitely more proper than he ... A deep thinker, and a real friend to mankind, he appeared to me to combine their means of happiness, as well as Paine feels and describes the abuses which constitute their misery.... How is it possible, said he, for men to debate a question, who are incapable of listening to each other?' Marie Jeanne Roland de la Platiere, *An Appeal to Impartial Posterity by Citizenness Roland* (London: J. Johnson, 1795), 42. Excellent pages on this remarkable man can be found in Damian Walford Davies, *Presences that Disturb* (Cardiff: University of Wales Press, 2002) 21–55.

2 David Williams, *Regulations of Parochial Police, Combined with the Military and Naval Armaments to produce the Energy and Security of the Whole Nation, Roused from its general Torpor by the Prospects of the Disorder, Pillage, Crimes and all the Desolation and Horror which, without such regulations, may be the Consequences of the determined and repeated Efforts of France to Invade Great Britain and Ireland* (London: J. Owen, 1797), 5.

vapour, from the amalgamated masses of the idle, unemployed, profligate and desperate inhabitants of the Capital' (21). His solution is a nationwide system of security and surveillance by Parochial Committees empowered to expel vagrants, prevent 'clubs of domestics' (perpetrators of the worst Parisian excesses) and form an armed householder police.[1] Wordsworth's continuing trust of the people in 1802 (he would feel very differently in 1832) is placed in a remarkable light by this early recipe for the combat of terror by surveillance.

The best way to read the composite poem on 'National Independence and Liberty' is to start with the twenty-six sonnets as laid out in *Poems, in Two Volumes* (1807), and then turn to *Poetical Works*, volume 3. In 1807 the sonnets are seen to their best advantage, two by two. The two sonnets written in Calais face each other, as do the two written in a valley near Dover. The laments for Toussaint and for the deported Negro Woman, for the subjugation of Switzerland and the degradation of England, the broadsides on 'blasted' France and 'fettered souls', the appeals to 'Milton!' and 'Great men' are paired on facing pages. The Men of Killikranky still stand between the Saxon Men of Kent and their modern descendants. The Bard calls upon the Men of Kent to prove their 'hardiment', and imagines their foes (the poem has the function of shamanic ritual) 'lying in the silent sun, | Never to rise again'. But the final note of the volume is provided by *November 1806*, which queries whether the land's rulers be 'Wise, upright, valiant' or merely 'a venal band'—sentiments, Byron said, 'which we hope are common to every Briton at the present crisis'.[2] Surprisingly, the *Lines on the Expected Invasion* are added to the sequence as late as 1842, when Wordsworth chooses to remind the country that some still think 'a state would live in sounder health | If Kingship bowed its head to Commonwealth'. Part Two of the series has the merit of integrating the Iberian and Tyrolean sonnets with the outpouring on Waterloo. Its close, in the final arrangement, balances epochal atonement, through the blood-sacrifice at Waterloo, with a prayer for 'equity

---

1   According to David Williams, every Parish, or in London boroughs, every large street and square, should 'be charged with its own Security; and be empowered to register its inhabitants; to confine [or] expel all vagabonds; to take cognizance of the characters and conduct of domestics...; to visit all public and lodging houses [registering occupants]' and to involve all householders in forming a police. (28) Clubs of domestics should be proscribed (33–35), and Parochial committees should ensure that arms are removed from those who are not required to bear them by the Committee (38).

2   *Monthly Literary Revelations*, July 1807; Woof 169.

renewed … and peace restored'.

The heroes of Part 1 are Milton, Sidney, Harrington, Toussaint and those warlike Men of Kent whose ancestors, in legend, wrested recognition for their charters from William the Conqueror. In Part 2 they include Clarkson, Arminius, Sobieski, Hofer & Tell, Palafox and Mina, 'Brave Schill', and the peasants of the Tyrol and Iberia. These, like Sertorius, Mithridates, Dominique de Gourges, Gustavus, and Wallace —the liberators celebrated in *The Prelude* (*1805*, 1.186–219)—illustrate magnanimity and devotion to human liberty. The villains of Part 1 are 'rapine, avarice, expense', the heartless Napoleon, 'Pope, Consul or King', and monied worldlings, joined in Part 2 by imperial Rome.

In the thematically pivotal sonnets of Part 1, in line with the gender narrative that occupied Wordsworth throughout the first decade of the new century, 'manliness' is at issue. Sonnet 4, *I grieved for Buonaparté* (May 1802) finds Napoleon lacking in tenderness.

> 'Tis not in battles that from youth we train
> The Governor who must be wise and good,
> And temper with the sternness of the brain
> Thoughts motherly, and meek as womanhood.
> Wisdom doth live with children round her knees.[1]

In sonnet 15, the wisdom of 'The later Sydney, Marvel, Harrington, | Young Vane and others who called Milton friend' is that they had the strength of magnanimity. They

> Taught us how rightfully a nation shone
> In splendour: what strength was that would not bend
> But in magnanimous weakness.

And in sonnet 21 (1803)

> England! The time is come when thou should'st wean
> Thy heart from its emasculating food;

England's weakness, under Pitt, is her penchant for despotism

> If for Greece, Egypt, India, Africa,
> Aught good were destined, thou would'st step between.

---

1 At about the moment Wordsworth wrote this sonnet Napoleon was refusing to meet the educationist Pestalozzi on the grounds that he could have no interest in a man who taught children. See my '"Knowledge not purchased with the Loss of Power': Pestalozzi and the spots of time', *European Romantic Review*, 8:3 (1997) 231–61.

'O Grief!', the sonnet concludes, 'that Earth's best hopes rest all with Thee.' One link between emasculation and despotism is that in the eyes of sober Commonwealthmen and libertine Wilkeites alike, though with differing connotations, effeminacy was, throughout the eighteenth century, the besetting vice of aristocratic ministries. The differing connotation is that for the libertarian left manliness and phallocentrism were virtually synonymous.[1] Wordsworth's sonnets, by invoking Milton and Sidney, distance themselves from both effeminate ministers and licentious 'democrats'. But a further refinement is provided by John Scott in *The Champion* in 1815:

> There is a peculiar kind of cruelty in vicious and effeminate minds, by which, though they do not imbrue their own hands in blood, they avoid interposing any good offices to repress the vindictive spirit of others... Those persons content themselves with that negative virtue which consists in being silent when great oppressions are committed.[2]

The persuasion that in 1815 made reconciliation impossible between Wordsworth and Brougham, and prevented him from adulating either Nelson (who betrayed liberty in Naples and hanged 'the patriot Caracciolo from the yard-arm of the Minerva')[3] or Wellington (who betrayed liberty at the Convention of Cintra) is precisely defined in John Scott's understanding of 'effeminacy', or Wordsworth's of 'emasculation'. That persuasion goes back to the multiform varieties of unmanliness found in Napoleon, in those 'monied worldlings' (XX) who wear his fetters 'in their souls' (XIX), and in public heroes who fail in their duty to liberty.

1   See Kathleen Wilson, *The Sense of the People: Politics, Culture and Imperialism in England, 1715–1785*, 219–23 and *passim*. Wilson summarises the Reverend John Brown of Newcastle, in his Estimate of the Manners and Principles of the Time, as attributing military defeats to 'the luxurious and effeminate Manners in the higher ranks, together with a general defect of principle', 187 n.

2   From a review published in John Scott's *The Champion*, in May 1815, of *Memoirs of Lady Hamilton* (Coburn, 1815). Scott (1783–1821), a schoolfellow of Byron, was later editor of *The London Magazine*, to which Lamb and Hazlitt contributed. He died in 1821 from wounds received in a pistol duel. Wordsworth said of his book *Paris Revisited in 1815 by way of Brussels* (1816) 'every one of your words tells'.

3   Moorman, 2: 63. See Eric C. Walker, 'Wordsworth, Wellington, and Myth', in *History and Myth: Essays on English Romantic Literature*, ed. Stephen C. Behrendt (Detroit: Wayne State University Press, 1990) 100–115, for Wordsworth's refusal to engage in panegyric for Wellington, and for his 'antonomastic strategies' whereby Wellington's name is suppressed in every poem he wrote on Waterloo.

The Convention of Cintra

In August 1808 Sir Huw Dalrymple and Sir Arthur Wellesley negotiated a Convention whereby a defeated French army was enabled not only to make its way back to France unimpeded but to do so with all its arms, and its plunder, intact. Wordsworth found himself, for the first time since the invasion scare of 1803, thoroughly in tune with outraged public opinion about this betrayal of the Spanish and the Portuguese struggle for liberty, and he attempted with Southey and Spedding to set up a public meeting of protest and a petition. Frustrated by Lord Lonsdale, who seems to have threatened to break up any such meeting with a latter day equivalent of the 'church and king' mob that burned Priestley's laboratory, Wordsworth devoted the better part of the next six months to his longest prose work: *Concerning the Relations of Great Britain, Spain and Portugal, to Each Other and to the Common Enemy, at this Crisis; and specifically as affected by the Convention of Cintra: the whole brought to the test of those Principles by which alone the Independence and Freedom of Nations can be Preserved or Recovered.* In short, he theorises the 'Sonnets Dedicated to Liberty' while redefining in a national context what he means by 'natural piety'.

In Spain, it seems, among a people roused by love of country and of liberty, the 'higher minds' recently defined in *The Prelude* are legion: their conduct exemplifies a life sustained 'by self-support and self-sufficing endeavours; by anticipations, apprehensions and active remembrances; by elasticity under insult, and firm resistance to injury; by joy, and by love; by patience…; by admiration; by gratitude…' (*Cintra*, 204; *WPW*, 211). The *Cintra* tract is Wordsworth's fullest development of a statement of faith in 'the hearts of the many', in the elasticity of human imagination and 'the dignity and intensity of human desires', and his belief that in every form and station of life, in every town and village, one can trust the instincts of humanity, because just as the human mind grows more beautiful than the earth on which it dwells (*1850*, 14.449), so do 'the passions of men … immeasurably transcend their objects' (*WPW*, 1: 228–9; *Cintra*, 218).

Certain phrases and arguments in *Concerning the Convention of Cintra* seem Burkean in form and substance but it requires considerable sophistry to interpret the work as Burkean in the common acceptance of that term. Such common acceptance tends, in any case, to forget that

Burke came to prominence as an advocate of cultural diversity (India's for example) and of national independence and liberty (America's most notably). When Wordsworth attacks 'the pestilential philosophism of France' exemplified in d'Holbach, Condillac, Voltaire and Rousseau as 'plants which will not naturalise in the country of Calderon and Cervantes' (*WPW*, 219), there is certainly an echo, if hardly the 'extended echo' James K. Chandler finds, of Burke's declaration that thanks to the 'natural entrails' and 'inbred sentiments' of Englishmen, 'We are not the converts of Rousseau; we are not the disciples of Voltaire; Helvetius has made no progress among us' (*Reflections* 181–2).[1] Since Wordsworth is now denying the powerful influence of Rousseau and Baron d'Holbach on his own Frenchified psyche, Burke's leverage does seem probable.[2] It is also conceivable, if less likely, that Burke's vision of society as 'a partnership ... between those who are living, those who are dead, and those who are to be born', which partnership is itself a component of the primal partnership 'connecting the visible and invisible world' (*Reflections*, 194–5), stimulates Wordsworth's thought that 'there is a spiritual community binding together the living and the dead; the good, the brave, and the wise of all ages' (*WPW*, 229). The same thought, which both Burke and Wordsworth derive from the liturgy, is paralleled in *The Prelude* and in numerous other places in the oeuvre, from very early to very late—as it is in Walt Whitman, whom nobody labels a Burkean.

What weakens Chandler's case is that on matters most immediately germane to the argument of the *Cintra*, as in arguments concerning mendicancy in 1798 and in 1835, Wordsworth's position in 1809 is diametrically opposed to Burke's.[3] He does not accept (as both *The Prelude* and the *Cintra* make clear) that the war against France was either just or necessary, until at least 1798, possibly 1800. What Burke had termed a just and necessary war in 1793 'had, some time before the treaty of Amiens, viz. *after the subjugation of Switzerland, and not till then*, begun to be regarded by the body of the people, as indeed both just and necessary' (*WPW*, 73 my italics). When Wordsworth complains in the *Cintra* that Britain's war for liberty in the peninsula is governed by 'the same pre-

1   James K. Chandler, *Wordsworth's Second Nature*, 43–44.
2   Wordsworth not unnaturally borrows from the great orator, and as Chandler shows, he was undoubtedly studying Paine, Rousseau and Burke, side by side, when penning the *Letter to the Bishop of Llandaff* in 1793 (Chandler, 20–25).
3   On mendicancy see David Simpson, *Wordsworth's Historical Imagination*, 167–74.

sumptuous irreverence of the principles of justice, and blank insensitiv-
ity to the affections of human nature' which determined its conduct in
the war against liberty in 1793 (*WPW*, 188) that 'presumptuous irrev-
erence' and 'blank insensitivity' clearly belong as much to Edmund
Burke as to Pitt: in 1793–94, after all, Wordsworth's sympathies were
with those whose acquittal in the treason trials Burke considered trea-
sonable.[1] Wordsworth does, however, raid Burke's *Letters on a Regicide
Peace* for arguments impertinent in 1796 but highly pertinent in 1808,
by when total war against France, in aid of the 'whole people' of Spain,
has become both just and imperative. In Spain the spirit of 1790 seems
born again, and Wordsworth expresses a mixture of elation, anxiety (lest
'the people' be once again betrayed by their leaders), and a sense of
vindication. The mood is remarkably close to that of Nature's 'interreg-
num' after the execution of Robespierre: 'To Nature, then [along with
Louvet] | Power had reverted' (*1805*, 10.609–11). Wordsworth finds him-
self believing once again that with the revolutionary spirit 'new-born'
the people's triumphs would be 'Great, universal, irresistible' (10.585).
'From the moment of the rising of the people of the Pyrenean peninsula,'
he writes, 'there was a mighty change; we were instantly animated.'

> We looked backward upon the records of the human race with pride,
> and, instead of being afraid, we delighted to look forward into futu-
> rity. It was imagined that *this new-born spirit of resistance,* rising
> from the most sacred feelings of the human heart, *would diffuse itself
> through many countries*; and not merely for the distant future, but *for
> the present*, hopes were entertained as bold as they were disinterested
> and generous. (*WPW*, 75, 76, my emphases)

'For the present'. The present, one recollects, is where 'we find our hap-
piness or not at all'. Bliss was it then; bliss could it be, once again, in
this new dawn to be alive, but for a perennially perfidious Albion. The
hour needs a man of iron who will not lay down the sword until liberty is
achieved. The author of *Character of the Happy Warrior*, with its praise
of meekness and magnanimity, now emphasizes more martial *virtu*. 'The
French army was not broken?'—this was Sir Huw Dalrymple's paltry
excuse for the Convention—'Break it then—wither it—pursue it with

---

1   See Deirdre Coleman, 'Re-living Jacobinism: Wordsworth and the Convention of
Cintra', *The Yearbook of English Studies*, Volume 19, 1989, *The French Revolution in
English Literature and Art*, ed. J. R. Watson, 144–61, 151.

unrelenting warfare—hunt it out of its holds ... never for a moment forget who the foe is and that he is in your power' (*WPW*, 178). Wordsworth, who in *The Prelude* saw himself as a Dion manqué, was still regretting in 1812 that he had not entered 'that Profession to which I was most inclined and for which I was perhaps best qualified', namely soldiering (*MY*, 2: 2).

Since the Iron Duke (a later sobriquet) was not yet sufficiently iron towards his adversary or sufficiently magnanimous to his allies, Wordsworth produced more Martello towers in 1810–11 in the form of fifteen sonnets on 'the struggles of the Peninsula' (*MY*, 1: 460) which—together with the Waterloo poetry—make up Part 2 of the 'Poems Dedicated to National Independence and Liberty'. The sonnets celebrated, Gordon Thomas says, 'the same two categories [of hero] named in Book 10 of the *1805 Prelude*: "The noble Living and the noble Dead"', namely, classical heroes like Sertorius and Viriathus, along with two captives analogous to Toussaint L'Ouverture (Palafox and Mina, the heroes of Saragossa), both 'missing and presumed dead':

> The noble Living of Iberia in 1810 were of a downright democratic sort. They were the anonymous members of 'roving Spanish bands' (Sonnet 30); they were the 'Spaniards of every rank' (sonnet 29), the mingled 'Peasant and lord' (26), nameless defenders of home and family and liberty ... representatives of popular power and right.[1]

The sonnets retain the premise of the *Cintra*, that the cause of the people would be safe only as long as it remained 'not only in the bosom but in the hands of the people' (*WPW*, 202). Spain's strength lies not in 'fleets and armies, and external wealth', and certainly not in the 'regular armies and well-bred officers' relied upon by the ostensibly democratic Henry Lord Brougham,[2] but in 'forests' of 'men of low degree', ordinary Spaniards, 'blunt', and 'self-respecting' and possessed of precisely that love of country that Hazlitt, at his most theoretical, thought to be 'an artificial idea', the product of 'reason and reflection, rather than the offspring of physical or local attachment'. Overlooking Wordsworth's sense that story and legend, literature and history, are as real to the imagination and the affections as physical attachments, Hazlitt deemed 'patriotism'

---

1   Gordon K. Thomas, 'Wordsworth's Iberian Sonnets: Turncoats Creed', *TWC* 131 (1982) 31–34, 33.
2   Cited Coleman, 159.

a confection wherever 'our country is no longer contained within the narrow circle of the same walls', or is not visible from 'from the top of our native mountains'.[1] In the *Cintra* Wordsworth says that the strength of a people's army lies in 'a texture of life which, though cut through (as hath been feigned of the bodies of the Angels) unites again' (*WPW*, 85). In sonnet 30, less transcendentally, they have the power of scattering and reuniting like 'a flight | Of scattered quails'. In sonnet 31 their knowing by instinct when to open or to close 'The ridges of grim war' (*Paradise Lost* 6.234–6) invokes, as Gordon Thomas points out, the democratic host of angels in the war in heaven, among whom (like the Gypsies in *Salisbury Plain*) 'each is Chief'.

Concerning the Convention of Cintra argues that 'the true army of Spain ... is the whole people' and adds the melancholy yet consolatory rider that 'when a people are called suddenly to fight for liberty ... their best field of battle is the floors upon which their children have played; the chambers where the family of each man has slept ... and among their congregated dwellings—blazing, or up-rooted' (*WPW*, 224). Imaginatively, Spain has been annexed to that visionary republic of Cumbria, and her peasant heroes seem to have the capacity to operate in both worlds: melting from the French, 'gone are they, viewless as the buried dead' (sonnet 30). But the inspiration for these ethereal guerrillas is not merely Cumbrian legend. Wordsworth's material precedent for conflict between 'gross—tangible' military force on the one side and a 'spirit of resistance...subtle—ethereal—mighty—and incalculable' (*WPW*, 188) provoked by the mere presence of such force, is the memorable triumph of American patriots over Hessian mercenaries, a formative moment of his schooldays at Hawkshead.

'Governments ... newly issued from the people', Wordsworth has commented earlier, 'could not but act from the spirit of the people—be organs of their life' (*WPW*, 174–5). He was already suspicious of the elevation of the Spanish Cortes, and became more so.[2] What threatens Spain is the premature removal of power from the People, the giving of 'an undue preponderance to birth, station, rank, and fortune', and the

1   William Hazlitt, 'On Patriotism', *The Round Table*, ed. Catherine M. Maclan, London: Dent, 1964, 67.
2   Wordsworth to John Scott: 'The Cortes were what Lord Castlereay describes them, and worse. They thirsted after the independence of their country, and many of them nobly laboured to effect it; but as to civil liberty and religious institutions, their notions were as wild as the most headstrong Jacobins of France' (*MY*, 2: 280).

election of 'men whose very virtue would incline them superstitiously to respect established things, and to mistrust *the People*' (319). Similarly, 'There are promptings of wisdom from the penetralia of human nature, which *a people* can hear, though the wisest of their practical statesmen be deaf towards them … This authentic voice, *the people* of England had heard and obeyed' (*WPW,* 74–5). In neither of these utterances is the phrase 'the People' used in the routine Burkean sense of referring to a select group of propertied persons. 'I have often endeavoured to class those who, in any political view', says Burke in 1796, 'are to be called the people':

> In England and Scotland, I compute … about four hundred thousand. … Of these four hundred thousand political citizens, I look upon one fifth, or about eighty thousand, to be pure Jacobins; utterly incapable of amendment; objects of eternal vigilance, and when they break out, of legal constraint.[1]

On this fundamental point Wordsworth's language is thoroughly counter-Burkean throughout the *Cintra*, and outside it: 'We are here all in a rage about the Convention in Portugal; if Sir Hew were to show his face among us, or that other doughty Knight, Sir Arthur, *the very boys* would hiss them out of the Vale' (*MY*, 1: 269).[2] When he speaks in the *Cintra* of the condemnation 'which the People did with one voice pronounce upon the Convention' (*WPW, 103*) these Cumbrian boys are hissing for 'the People'.

In the *Cintra* Wordsworth writes as a poet of 'the people' in all its senses—the peasantry, the nation, and the 'noble dead' (including those who once spoke a common tongue from the Solway Firth to the land of the Basques). These three senses seem more integrated in this passionate prose than at any time in Wordsworth's career. It is hard to imagine historical circumstance more favourable to speaking simultaneously as Republican, a one-nation agrarian, a Briton, and an internationalist. Perhaps this spending of pent-up frustrations (the *Cintra* is a work of eros: it deploys swelling rhythms and artfully delayed climaxes) is itself what relaxed the poet's defences against apostasy. Over the next

---

1 Burke, *Thoughts on the Prospect of a Regicide Peace* (London: 1796), 16–17.
2 'Wordsworth's championing of the voice of the common people as the inspiration of a nation's true greatness runs directly counter to Burke's belief that this greatness can only ever devolve "from above"', Coleman, 152.

few years he identifies increasingly with land, with titles, with blood (in senses far from the use of 'Earth's first blood' and 'titles manifold' in the sonnet of 1803, when Milton still stood guard), with tradition, and even with old corruption. His privileging of universal benevolence in the mid-1790s, along with Richard Price and Joseph Fawcett, had led similarly to a pronounced reaction-formation in the late 1790s in favour of local personal and familial ties—along with Dyer, Mackintosh, and a repentant Godwin—of which the address to Dorothy in 'The Poem upon the Wye' is perhaps the major symbol.[1] To Burke, universal benevolence was a fatal abstraction; to Hazlitt, nationhood was. Wordsworth, as he does with all such antinomies, comes to refuse the choice.

Wordsworth, John Scott and Waterloo

> Then Peter wrote odes to the Devil;—
> In one of which he meekly said:
> 'May Carnage and Slaughter,
> Thy niece and thy daughter
> May Rapine and Famine,
> Thy gorge ever cramming,
> Glut Thee with living and dead!'
> —Shelley, *Peter Bell the Third*

On Sunday 25 June 1815, under the headline 'The Victorious Commencement of the War against Napoleon', *The Champion* took up the line of argument pursued in William Frend's *Patriotism*: 'The countrymen of Alfred continue to prove their legitimacy.… The allies have committed many faults, their intentions are suspicious, their measures often require to be resisted and exposed by friends of liberal principles … but … they are within the pale of social confidence.' 'No battle in the annals of the world', Scott said, 'is superior in splendour and interest to that of Waterloo.'

Wordsworth's somewhat tardy response, fascinatingly entangled with Scott's, was a slim volume of poems containing almost 700 lines on Waterloo, including three sonnets first published in *The Champion* (very promptly for Wordsworth) on the initiative of Benjamin Robert

---

1   See Evan Radcliffe, 'Revolutionary Writing, Moral Philosophy, and universal benevolence in the Eighteenth Century', *Journal of the History of Ideas*, 54: 2 (1993) 221–240, and Nicholas Roe, *The Politics of Nature*, passim.

Haydon. Henry Crabb Robinson sent the volume to Wordsworth's revolutionary anima, Helen Maria Williams, and read its centre-piece, *The Thanksgiving Ode,* to Mrs Thornthwaite:

> It has heavy passages [Robinson noted], but the commencement and conclusion are both fine indeed. His assertion that the great calamities of life are the instruments of providence, though very trite, was never expressed with more force and beauty. 'He puts the earthquake on its still design' deserves to pass into proverb. The verses on the Russian Winter are, perhaps, the most delightful in the volume.[1]

Wordsworth's 'advertisement' advised the reader that 'this publication may be considered as a sequel to the Author's "Sonnets, dedicated to Liberty"' and that it was 'printed uniform' with the *Poems* (1815) 'to admit of their being conveniently bound up together.' Volume one of the *Poems* ended with *Glen-Almain*—so its last poetic lines are: 'That Ossian, last of all his race | Lies buried in this lonely place', which lines are followed by the pugnacious 'Essay, Supplementary to the Preface', which essay concludes with an appeal to the judgement and the wisdom of the people (and the famous assault on Macpherson). Volume 2, which includes the sonnets to liberty, opens with *To a Highland Girl* and *The Solitary Reaper* and ends with another manifesto, concerning poetic diction and the language really used by men. Binding *1816* into this collection represents Wordsworth as the voice of 'the people'—especially northern people—and the nation.

Two sonnets from the collections of 1807 and 1815, in particular, set the tone for the 1816 volume. The first, *October 1803* praises the 'shepherds and herdsmen' who in 1689 defeated six thousand veteran soldiers enslaved by 'precept and the pedantry | Of cold mechanic battle'.[2] The

---

1   *Henry Crabb Robinson on Book and their Writers*, ed. Edith J. Morley, 3 vols., Dent 1938, 1, 182.

2   Titled *October, 1803* in the 'Sonnets to Liberty', but later removed to 'Memorials of a Tour in Scotland, 1803' as *Sonnet in the Pass of Killikranky* (*PW*, 3: 85). Peter Manning's comment on this poem that it 'transforms the [Jacobite] Highlanders from the dangerous enemies of English order into the epitome of English courage' (*Reading Romantics*, 263) seems unusually wide of the mark. Their irregular *Scottish* courage is a markedly tribal challenge—tribal on Wordsworth's part—to England's 'mechanic battle'. Wordsworth moderated his irresponsibly romantic opinion in 1816 when recommending military colleges: 'Admirable officers, indeed, have been formed in the field, but at how deplorable an expense of the lives of their surrounding brethren in arms, a history of the military operations in Spain … would irresistibly demonstrate'.

second, *Spanish Guerillas, 1811*, lauds Spain's 'self-supported chiefs—like those | Whom hardy Rome was fearful to oppose'.[1] It compares one unnamed shepherd warrior to Viriatus of Lusitania (who defeated several Roman commanders), and compares the scholarly guerilla Francisco Espoz y Mina to Quintus Sertorius, who held Spain against several Roman armies. Sertorius, according to Plutarch, strongly wished to go and live in the fortunate isles as an escape from 'tyranny and never-ending wars'.[2] In 1809 Wordsworth had imagined 'Brave Schill! By death delivered' also finding solace 'With heroes 'mid the islands of the Blest, | Or in the fields of empyrean light'. 'Paradise, and Groves Elysian, and Fortunate Fields' are still, for imaginative minds, 'the simple produce of the common day' but in the work of 1810–15 it is not titled commanders but folk heroes who invoke most often those fortunate fields, somewhere in 'the western main'.

The preface of 1816 is quietly optimistic. The nation may be bankrupt, but 'On the wisdom of a very large majority of the British nation, rested that generosity which poured out the treasures of this country for the deliverance of Europe' and if the same wisdom and energy preside in time of peace 'the cup of our wealth will be gradually replenished.' And it is cautious. It would be wrong if a scrupulous dread of standing armies (associated with despotism in Commonwealthman utterance) were to discourage expressions of proper gratitude for the services of the British army. Nonetheless, Wordsworth expresses some satisfaction that the country's defence rests basically on 'a form of armed force [the navy] from which her liberties have nothing to fear' (vi).

The bardic association with blood, which the poet encounters with fascinated dread in *The Vale of Esthwaite*, again in daring sympathies with power in 1793–94, and again in the early phase of the Napoleonic Wars, manifests itself powerfully in 1815. Waterloo appeared to Wordsworth an event which only the true bard ('if such breathe'), the bard 'whose soul is meek as dawning day | Yet trained to judgements righteously severe', could rightly comprehend and worthily rehearse (*Sonnet: occasioned by the battle of Waterloo*). Another sonnet praises 'Heroes!—for instant sacrifice prepared'. What Wilfred Owen called 'the cess of war'

Thanksgiving Ode, January 18, 1816, viii.

1   Sonnet 29 of 'Sonnets dedicated to Liberty, Part Second' (P2V, 1815, 2: 255)—sonnet 31 in *PW*, 3.

2   *SPK*, 511. See also *Prelude, 1805*, 1.189–201.

is mourned, also. In the quasi-Shelleyan, quasi-Blakean *Invocation to the Earth*—Shelleyan in its desire for Discord to be 'chained for ever to the black abyss', Blakean in that the spirit is asking Earth 'why wilt thou turn away?'—a celestial spirit mourns the 'tens of thousands rent from off the tree | Of hopeful life' and promises 'Thy cherished fetters to unbind | And open thy sad eyes upon a milder day'.[1] Here the promise of *Hart-Leap Well* seems overshadowed by the brooding battlefield plates of Blake's *America*. But these shorter pieces are merely ancillary to the outpouring of odes which marks the extraordinary zenith of Wordsworth's Bardic career.

The 1816 volume includes four odes, of which one, subsequently divided into two separate odes, is the notorious *Thanksgiving Ode.*[2] While Carl Ketcham's Cornell edition of *Shorter Poems, 1807–1820* somewhat dissipates the impact of this collection, by dispersing the poems chronologically in accordance with Cornell ideology, it does of course restore the original text of the ode, a poem of which John Scott wrote:

> I read your Ode with delight,—and acknowledge its gift from the author, with a truly proud pleasure.... It is the hymn of a high & well-tuned soul, the poetic harmonies of which have been called into play by the ardour of patriotic affections.... the other Poets who have taken Waterloo for their theme have totally failed: a gentleman wrote favourably of Mr Southey's Pilgrimage in The Champion but I confess it appears to me poor.[3]

William and Dorothy had watched the vacillating conduct of the Allies with much misgiving, Dorothy especially. She wrote to Catherine Clarkson on 28 June 1815 about the abdication of Napoleon exhibiting

---

1 The image of leaves 'rent from the tree' looks back to Wordsworth's figuring of himself in 1793, at the start of the war, as 'a green leaf on the blessed tree | Of my beloved country... cut off, | And tossed about in whirlwinds' (*1805*, 10.254–8).

2 The odes include an *Ode on the Disinterment of the Remains of the Duke d'Enghien*, the *Ode, Composed in January 1816*, in which St George descends to bless the triumphant isle and compares her deeds with Marathon (later called *Ode 1814* as if written to welcome Napoleon's earlier setbacks), and a further visionary *Ode* ('Who risesd on the banks of Seine') which rewrites *France: an Ode*. Again Shelleyan in manner (it is odd how much Shelley's style of 1819 resembles Wordsworth's in 1815/16) this Ode relates how the spirit of 1789 'rises on the banks of Seine' only to become 'a terror to the earth'.

3 Dove Cottage: DC WLMS a / Scott, John / 3, 29 May 1816, my italics. This and subsequent quotations from Scott are cited by kind permission of the Wordsworth Trust.

half a dozen different emotions in as many lines:

> I do not like the word abdication, What right has he to abdicate?, or
> to have a word to say in the business? I am only afraid that the armies
> have stopped too soon, as they did before. A few hours will explain all,
> but I confess I dare not hope that matters will not again be mismanaged.
> The particulars of the battle of the 18th are dreadful. The joy of victory
> is indeed an awful thing, and I had no patience with the tinkling of our
> Ambleside bells upon the occasion; nor with the Prince Regents mes-
> sage—recommending remuneration of the Duke of Wellington instead
> of mourning the gallant Duke of Brunswick. (*MY*, 2: 242)

Dorothy snubs Wellington again on 15 August: 'Would that all the
English had Prussian hearts and that our Generals and Councillors had
the will of Blucher. Then we should not have seen the Jacobins lift up
their audacious heads' (*MY*, 2: 244). Her frustration arises from the delay
of Caroline's marriage, which she was supposed to attend once Europe's
affairs were settled (much of Dorothy's information about French
affairs came in letters from Annette Vallon). In April she had written to
Catherine Clarkson in an especially pugnacious spirit: 'God grant that if
[the Allies] have once again the Sword and the Victory in their hands no
puny relentings of mercy may stop the slaughter till the Tyrant is taken
and his wicked followers completely subdued.'

Although William shared most of these sentiments, his Ode is, as Scott
says in his letter, 'professedly contemplative and abstracted': its keynote
is the meditative 'say not that we have vanquished—but that we survive'
(*PW* 3.158). For once Wordsworth really is contemplating *ab extra*. He
shares Dorothy's sense that 'the joy of victory is indeed an awful thing',
and resists the 'rejoice!' mentality of the Rt. Hon. Margaret Thatcher,
MP, on the sinking of *The Belgrano*. It is, as he said to Southey, not so
much a formal component of the day ordained for national thanksgiving
as 'a poem ... uttering the sentiments of an *individual* upon that occasion
(*MY*, 2: 324)'. One thinks of Francis in *The White Doe*: 'Thousands see,
and One | With unparticipated gaze'.

The ode begins at dawn, meditating quietly on the meaning of victory.
As it is now among Wordsworth's least familiar works, and as it mani-
fests the responsible Bardic vocation as fully as any other work, I shall
quote it at some length:

> Have we not conquered?—by the vengeful sword?

Ah no, by dint of magnanimity;
That curbed the baser passions, and left free
A loyal band to follow their liege Lord
Clear-sighted Honour, and his staid Compeers,
Along a track of most unnatural years

The battle, when it finally arrives in the 1816 poem (there is merit in Wordsworth's later decision to separate the battle poem from the thanksgiving poem), is presented as a double atonement, atoning for guilt and error, and making 'at one' a long divided people.

Waterloo, the Ode claims, satiates as no prior heroic feat can do, the poetic Imagination. Though 'ne'er before content | But aye ascending … | From all that martial feats could yield | To her desires', Imagination 'stoops' to this victory.[1] She need yearn no longer, as in the Simplon Pass, for 'something evermore about to be'. In Taliesinic spasms, italicized as are the direct allusions to Taliesin and Aneirin in staccato half lines of *Ecclesiastical Sonnets*, Wordsworth alludes as briefly as can be to the battle itself:

> —*The shock is given— the Adversaries bleed—*
> *Lo, Justice triumphs! Earth is freed!* (*SPK*, 185, ll.177–8)

Waterloo announces itself as refreshing incense to a grateful world, or as a ritual oblation ('where'er the upturned soil receives the hopeful seed'). In London, Wordsworth argues, a new temple should be erected to house 'the sacred wealth of time', the 'heroic dust'. If not, Westminster Abbey will have to do. Heroes belong 'Where their serene progenitors are laid; | Kings, warriors, high-soul'd poets, saintlike sages' and solemn rites should be performed within those Gothic walls:

> Commemoration holy that unites
> The living generations with the dead;
> (*SPK*, 187, lines 233–40)

Wordsworth's God, perhaps appropriately, has a considerable amount of

---

1   *SPK*, 185, *Thanksgiving Ode* lines 163 ff; *PW*, 3: 151, *Ode 1815*, line 1.Compare Helen Maria Williams, who wrote of France's victories in the Pyrenees, in Holland and over the Austrians in Crevecoeur, Coblentz, etc, in 1793–94, that 'Imagination toils after victories like these'. *Letters from France* (8 vols, 1790–96), 2.4.217. See *Sensibility*, 111–21 for ten pages of parallels in the writings of Williams and Wordsworth, and 16–40 for a discussion of Wordsworth's use of the *Letters*.

the Old Testament about him, not to mention traces of Taranis:

> Nor will the God of peace and love
> Such martial service disapprove.
> He guides the Pestilence—the cloud
> Of locusts travels on his breath;
> The region that in hope was ploughed
> His drought consumes, his mildew taints with death;
>
> ...
>
> We bow our heads before Thee, and we laud
> And magnify Thy name, Almighty God!
> But thy most dreaded instrument
> In working out a pure intent
> Is Man—arrayed for mutual slaughter,—
> Yea, carnage is thy daughter.
> Thou cloth'st the wicked in their dazzling mail,
> And for Thy righteous purpose they prevail;
>
> ...
>
> Thy presence turns the scale of doubtful fight,
> Tremendous God of battles, Lord of Hosts! (*SPK*, 187–8)

'God', Geoffrey Hill agrees in *Ovid in the Third Reich*, 'is distant, difficult': 'Too near the ancient troughs of blood, | Innocence is no earthly weapon.' Milton's God, too, is of course a Lord of Hosts; Tennyson's a God of Battles. Blake's God designs Tygers to devour Lambs, and Coleridge's allows the fate of a crew of Christian Souls to rest upon a game of dice. But such analogies pale before the four indented lines above, which public opinion caused Wordsworth to soften in 1820. Shelley's response we have seen, in the epigraph to this section. Crabb Robinson deflects attention to the rather subtler message: 'He puts the earthquake on its still design', which reminds one quietly of the metaphor applied to revolutionary terror, that 'the earthquake is not satisfied at once' and seems to hint (in the ominous 'still') of Shelley's contemporaneous Mont Blanc glaciers 'watching their prey'.

It is not that Wordsworth has become indifferent to human outcomes. Visiting the battlefield in 1820, which Lord Byron had scoured for souvenirs, Wordsworth seems to have recalled Towton Field and Bosworth, as referred to in *Song at the Feast of Brougham Castle*. His sentiments on the field of battle were sombre enough:

> We felt as men should feel
> With such vast hoards of hidden carnage near,
> And horror breathing from the silent ground. (CWRT, 3: 429)

In any case, 'carnage' is not where the Ode terminates. The sacrifice has been made; the people have wielded the 'exterminating sword'. The hope, now, is that even those who, like Wordsworth in 1793–96, once sat silent in village churches like 'an uninvited guest' feeding on 'vengeance yet to come', while the '*simple* worshippers' bent all to '*their* great father' and offered praise for victories (*1805*, 10.268–74), may now be reconciled in communion. The Great Father 'has brought our warfare to an end' so 'let all who do this land inherit'—all factions and all tribes—'Be conscious of the moving spirit':

> Bless Thou the hour, or ere the hour arrive,
> When a whole people shall kneel down in prayer,
> And at one moment, in one rapture, strive
> With lip and heart to tell their gratitude.
> > For thy protecting care,
> Their solemn joy—praising the Eternal Lord
> > For tyranny subdued,
> And for the sway of equity renewed,
> For liberty confirmed, and peace restored!

'Or *ere* the hour arrive'? It is an odd reservation, surely, since the bells are already ringing. Wordsworth's headnote says he composed the poem on his garden mount, and his stance in the poem is that of one who has no real intention of being summoned by those bells. If one imagines St Oswald's, he mght be looking down on it from Arthur's Seat (that favourite eminence) somewhat like the Bard imagined by Gray, and pictured by John Martin and De Loutherberg:

> On a rock, whose haughty brow
> Frowns o'er old Conway's foaming flood
> Robed in the sable garb of woe
> With haggard eyes the Poet stood...
> And with a Master's hand and Prophet's fire
> Struck the deep sorrows of his lyre.

Wordsworth's bardic persona views imagined congregations from a distance, in parish chapels and minsters, counselling *them* to 'Go ... present your prayers' (as he once described village worshippers bowing to *their* great Father) and 'rejoice aloud.' They perhaps have less reason than he to remember the double moral of the last of the Iberian sonnets: first, 'That an accursed thing it is to gaze | On prosperous tyrants with a dazzled eye'; and second, never 'Forget thy weakness, upon which is built, | O wretched man, the throne of tyranny (sonnet 33 in *PW*, 3, Part 2). The *accursedness* belongs to Hazlitt, Brougham and the Whig establishment at large. The *weakness* is of the kind only half expiated in the depiction of Mortimer in the yet unpublished *Borderers*, on whose remorseful isolation from society the conclusion of *Thanksgiving* seems half-modelled. The note of penitential self-exclusion goes back to 1803 and the anguished sonnet *When looking on the present face of things*:

> But, great God!
> I measure back the steps which I have trod;
> And tremble, seeing whence proceeds the strength
> Of such poor Instruments, with thoughts sublime
> I tremble at the sorrow of the time.

In lines 125–8 of the ode:

> —the guilt is banished,
> And, with the Guilt, the Shame is fled;
> And with the Guilt and Shame, the Woe hath vanished,
> Shaking the dust and ashes from her head!

Ostensibly, the guilt is that of 'prostrate lands', but the lines also confess what it means to be an 'ungrateful son' (line 143). Publication of *Thanksgiving* may have assuaged his sense of guilt, but the spirit of reconciliation did not last. It was a family joke that Wordsworth wrote an *Ode to Duty* and then had done with the matter; so perhaps with reconciliation.

The Excursion imagines, in Book 6, magnanimous reconciliation between 'flaming Jacobite and sullen Hanoverian'. But what reconciliation can there be with those who flattered the Corsican between 1802 and 1815, even for one who 'fed on vengeance' in 1794? Blake had much difficulty with forgiveness; Wordsworth too.

The Making of a Tory Apologist

'These sort of people are so taken up with their theories about the rights of man, that they have totally forgot his nature. Without opening one new avenue to the understanding, they have succeeded in stopping up those that lead to the heart'.[1] Burke's famous critique of French theory finds its way into *The Excursion* as a vicarious confession that 'false conclusions of the reasoning power' may close 'the passages | Through which the ear converses with the heart' (4.1154), as happened to the poet in 1794 and to Oswald in *The Borderers*. Such confession does not, in itself, make the poet of 1809 either a Burkean Whig or an ideological Tory. Wordsworth, after all, was famously described by Farington on 17 June 1806 as still 'strongly disposed towards Republicanism',[2] as is amply clear from the sonnets of that time, and by Sir George Beaumont in 1809 as holding 'terrific democratic notions' (amply shown in the Cintra tract). Neither remark (making all due allowance for Sir George's politics) suggests conspicuous devotion to Burkean sentiments. Whatever made Wordsworth a Tory had not done so, ostensibly, by 1809.[3] Shelley still praised his independence in 1811, and both Dorothy and William deplored Coleridge's 'servile adulation of the Wellesleys' and his 'party spirit' in *The Courier*.[4] By August 1813, however, Wordsworth was already writing to Francis Wrangham, defending his employment as distributor of stamps and explaining succinctly his view of Tory ministers:

> I very much prefer the course of their policy to that of the Opposition, especially on two points most near my heart,—resistance of Buonaparte by force of arms, and their adherence to the principles of the British constitution in withholding Political Power from Roman Catholics. My most determined hostility shall always be directed against those statesmen who, like Whitbread, Grenville and others, would crouch to a sanguinary Tyrant; and I cannot act with those who see no danger to the constitution in introducing Papists into Parliament. There are other points of policy in which I deem the Opposition grievously mistaken,

1   *Reflections on the Revolution in France*, ed. Conor Cruise O'Brien (Harmondsworth: Penguin, 1968), 156.

2   *The Diary of Joseph Farington* 7: 2785, cited Gill, 274.

3   The Torifying factors may include critical derision for his poetic experiments from Napoleon's fellow-travellers; principled contempt for the Whigs; a belief that Whig magnanimity had been assumed by the Tories; ideological assimilation by Mary, Dorothy and his Rydal neighbours; the example of Coleridge; and appreciation of the decency of Southey, the patronage of Lord Lonsdale, and the culture of Sir George— at whose home some of the earliest political sonnets were written. Altogether, a huge weight of personal pressure on a man geographically severed from the radicals.

4   F. M. Todd, *Politics and the Poet* (London: Methuen 1957), 157.

> and therefore, I am at present, *and long have been by principle*, a sup-
> porter of the Ministry, as far as my little influence extends. (*MY*, 2:
> 108)[1]

Wordsworth's alliance with the Tories was initially tactical, and it seems
to have dated, quietly enough, from about 1806. In that year Grenville
(the 'onion head' in Wordsworth's imitation of Juvenal) succeeded Pitt,
and this succession led the poet to speak of the plight of a state ruled by
a servile band 'Who are to judge of danger which they fear | And honour
which they do not understand'. The two lines were adapted, Wordsworth
noted, from 'Lord Brooke's Life of Sir Philip Sidney' (*P2V*, 1: 158).

Wordsworth's correspondence with John Scott in 1815–16 differs on
two points in which Scott had reasonably assumed agreement. The first
was the role of Wellington, whom Scott eulogized in *Paris Revisited*
almost as manifesting Wordsworth's happy warrior, in his 'unexam-
pled justice, forbearance and humanity'.[2] Wordsworth has still not for-
given him for the Convention of Cintra. Wellington goes unmentioned in
Wordsworth's six or seven hundred lines about Waterloo, and a remark
to Scott explains why: 'I am convinced there is no magnanimity in his
nature' (MY, 2: 280). That is, Wellington has none of the quality of a
deliverer, those whose military exploits 'assert ... the rights of human
nature', whose conduct teaches nations to 'mutually to abstain from inju-
ries', and who add to the sum of human liberty.[3] That kind of 'magnanim-
ity', typified in 1802 in the heroes of the Commonwealth, Wordsworth
in 1816 attributes to the People, or to 'Britain'. As Eric Walker points
out, even in the late sonnet inspired by Haydon's portrait of Wellington,
Wordsworth names Wellington 'by a series of four epithets—Warrior,
master, Chieftain, Conqueror' but neither by his proper name nor by
the sublime epithet 'Deliverer'.[4] That epithet he bestowed in the *Cintra*
upon Alfred, 'the elder Sidney', the Cid, and 'the honour of our own

1   Compare his more detailed letter to James Losh, 4 December 1821.
2   John Scott, *Paris Revisited in 1815 by way of Brussels: including a Walk on the
Field of Battle at Waterloo* (London, 1816), 197. Helen Maria Williams was another
adulator: see *Sensibility*, 38 and Williams's *Narrative of the Events Which Have Taken
Place in France ... 1815* (2nd edn John Murray, 1816).
3   *WPW*, 1: 108, 121. 'I have found nothing more mortifying in the course of my life
than those peeps behind the curtain, that have shown me how low in point of moral
elevation stand some of those men who have been the most efficient instruments and
machines for public benefit that our age had produced' (*MY*, 2: 280).
4   Walker, 111–12, 104.

age, Washington' (*WPW*, 117, 161, 229). Nor did Wordsworth accord a much higher station to the victor of Trafalgar.[1] He might have agreed with *The Champion*, in its review of *Memoirs of Lady Hamilton*, that: 'Lady Hamilton …was the Dalilah who turned to shame and weakness the glory and strength of our British Samson.' More importantly, however, as evidence of both emasculation and lack of magnanimity, the *Memoirs* criticized Nelson's weakness in accepting 'a ducal title from the court of Naples—a court which "like all vicious governments, was [as] sanguinary in prosperity [as] it had been abject and cowardly in affliction".'[2]

Scott had also assumed, however, from the *Cintra*'s Jeremiad against corrupt rulers divorced from the people, that Wordsworth would grasp the need for vigorous opposition politics, and told him so on 7 February 1816.[3] On 22 February, however, Wordsworth replied that while he held to the principles explored in the *Cintra*,

> It is the duty of an English Opposition to be rigorously hostile to the Ministry, but never let their endeavours to accomplish the downfall of their political antagonists excite in them a favourable aspiration for the enemies of their country. The English opposition party were unable to discern that a time of war and a time of peace required very different modes of proceeding on their part; that a style of hostility, which would have been very laudable in the one, became detestable in the other. (*MY*, 2: 281)

On 18 April, in a friendly letter, opening with a warm expression of concern for Mrs Scott, Wordsworth insists that he cannot think 'without trembling' of such as 'Romilly, Lord Holland, the Grenvilles, the Wellesleys, the Foxites, the Burdettites in office' (*MY*, 2: 302–5). His tone is markedly tetchy. In March he had said of Brougham that a man who scribbles in praise of 'the Corsican' and begs Parliament to treat

1   The note of 1807 which temporarily associated Nelson with the Character of the Happy Warrior was never reprinted, and his appearance alongside Epaminondas, Sidney and Washington in the *Cintra* (256) is strikingly qualified.

2   *The Champion*, No 123, May 12, 1815, reviewing *Memoirs of Lady Hamilton*. No 127, Sunday June 11, 1815, echoes Wordsworth's opinion of the restoration of Ferdinand: 'It was at a former restoration of this court, that Nelson assisted in a manner so infamously unjust and cruel, that its shame will live in the latest records of history…. If the abominations of the foulest corruption, and the lowest superstition are also to be restored in Naples … will not England be deeply and heavily responsible?'

3   DC WLMS a / Scott, John / 1, 7 February 1816.

him kindly in his insular prison has 'no intellectual sanity'. In February he had made a gratuitous reference to Scott's friend 'the bold bad Bard Baron B'. Now he adds of Byron that 'the man is insane; and will probably end his career in the madhouse': *The Farewell*, he says, is 'disgusting in sentiment, and in execution contemptible'.

Scott replies to this series of animadversions on his opposition allies by citing the *Cintra*'s striking anticipation of Lord Acton's famous adage— 'there is an unconquerable tendency in all power, save that of knowledge … to injure the mind of him who exercises that power' (*WPW*, 187). This 'profound & universally applicable maxim', Scott says, animates 'my labours as a Political Writer'. 'It is this truth, and a conviction that our superiority as a nation has arisen almost solely from the exercise of *opposition*, that gives me a general bias to what are called opposition politics.' Although Brougham and other Whigs were wrong throughout the Napoleonic war, Scott says, mankind still 'have a better property in the minds of such men' than in the Tories. Their fault is that 'Out of power they saw too acutely & closely the errors of their domestic adversaries to catch a view of the formidable mischiefs which were hanging over them & us from France.'[1] But to Wordsworth, the posture of an ungrateful son has become the one unforgivable sin, and he begins to adopt towards the oppositionists of 1815 the attitude Burke had maintained against treasonable Jacobins in 1794–96, including Wordsworth himself.

Wordsworth's long Striptease

After Coleridge's numbing response to *The Excursion* in the famous letter of 30 May 1815 (*Griggs*, 4: 574–5)—numbing as a simply awful prospectus for a poem; numbing as a misreading of Wordsworth; numbing in its intellectual conservatism; numbing to Wordsworth as sublime ingratitude for his fifteen years hard labour as a dutiful amanuensis— and his complicity, in *Biographia*, with Jeffrey's attack, Wordsworth began to clear his desk. Brought up as we are on *The Prelude* and *Lyrical Ballads*, what we notice about Wordsworths's later years is his galloping 'dessication', to use Thomas McFarland's term.[2] Yet from 1814 to 1842 Wordsworth's public appearances, if we set aside the innumerable tours and memorials, are increasingly youthful and redolent of the 1790s. He

1   DC WLMS a / Scott, John / 3, 29 May 1816
2   McFarland, chapter 4.

appeared in 1814 masked as the disillusioned 'Solitary'; in 1820 as the maddened 'Vaudracour'; in 1835 as acerbic critic of political economy and prophet of the welfare state; and in 1842 he spoke to his country-men through the masks of a Godwinian sailor and the Jacobin 'Oswald'. Wordsworth's last thirty odd years of publication see him repeatedly appearing before his increasing (and increasingly Victorian) public in a provocative state of undress, as if conforming to Haydon's open-necked portrait, and at times almost *sans-culottes*. It is hard to interpret this strat-egy. It may be that underneath the post-Waterloo Wordsworth, whose political convictions so often manifest the 'panic dread of change' his Solitary found in Britain's rulers, there is a poet whose self-image is unchanged. It may be that he is engaged in a very long confession.

The major landmarks of his later years are recovered—and increas-ingly provocative—works of his youth. In 1819 came *Peter Bell* and the *Waggoner*, poems of 1798 and 1806, both published rather pugnaciously as self-sufficient volumes. One offers (according to Alan Bewell's mas-terful reading) a sceptical review of the religious history of mankind; the other (according to John Williams) exhibiting the downfall of the gentle Benjamin by association with a vainglorious militaristic braggart.[1] In 1820, sandwiched between two lake District works—the sonnet sequence on *The River Duddon*, and his nostalgic dream of 'perfect equality' in his prose guide to that 'almost visionary republic'—he revealed the fic-tionalized confessional poem, *Vaudracour and Julia* (1805), prefaced by the rather tantalizing remark that 'the facts are true; no invention as to these has been exercised'. (One cannot help wondering what contempo-rary readers could have made of that.) The facts, such as they were (and as, by and large, he found them in Helen Maria Williams's *Letters from France*), have little or nothing to do with critiquing juvenile amatory excesses in a revolutionary atmosphere. They concern the vicious disre-gard for human life under the *ancien régime*. *Vaudracour and Julia* is not merely an oblique confession; it is also the *1805 Prelude*'s major instance of the 'that' against which, in Beaupuy's phrase, 'we are fighting'.

In 1835, in *Yarrow Revisited*, a volume devoid of poetic offence, except in the question 'shall man assume a property in man?', the famous 'Postscript' launched an impassioned attack on the heartless political

---

1   See Alan Bewell, *Wordsworth and the Enlightenment*, 109–4, and John Williams, 'Salisbury Plain: Politics in Wordsworth's Poetry', *Literature and History* 9:2 (1983) 164–93, 185–9.

economy of such laissez-faire proponents as his future neighbour Harriet Martineau. Martineau had completed her fatuous *Illustrations of Political Economy* (in 9 volumes) in the previous year. The Poor Law Amendment Act (1824)—the inhumane monument of a supposedly reformed parliament—partly justified his opposition to reform. But in his passionate opposition to this measure, Wordsworth once again finds himself making strange alliances. Opposition to Napoleon made him a reluctant fellow-traveller with the Tories long before he became one. On the Poor Law, travelling in a reverse direction, he unconsciously allies himself with the Chartists, who cut their teeth on this issue. Such figures as Joseph Rayner Stephens, the Methodist preacher and incendiary, and Robert Lowery and Henry Vincent, later prominent in the temperance movement, were first energized by the perception, as Stephens put it, that the Poor Law Amendment Act was 'unchristian and unconstitutional'.[1] The Postscript, with its citation of *The Female Vagrant* as evidence of his consistent opposition to Malthusian doctrines, may have had something to do with Wordsworth's decision a few years later to prepare the poems of 1793–97, written while he was still 'feeding on vengeance yet to come', for publication in 1842. My last chapter, therefore, reads the authorized but now unfashionable texts of *Guilt and Sorrow* and *The Borderers* in their proper context, as works addressed to a land 'mournfully cast down'.

---

1   Stephen Roberts and Dorothy Thompson, *Images of Chartism* (London: Merlin Press, 1998), 32.

Chapter 12: 'The Steps which I have Trod'

> as far as the people are capable of governing themselves,
> I am a Democrat
> —WW to Henry Reed, 10 November 1843.[1]

IN JUNE 1842 *Tait's Edinburgh Magazine* reviewed Wordsworth's *Poems Chiefly of Early and Late Years*, in which it found little of interest. Its next issue carried the following sample of the regional press, under the headline 'ALARMING STATE OF THE MANUFACTURING DISTRICTS':

> —This part of the country is in a deplorable state, for hundreds and thousands have neither work nor meat. They are daily begging in the streets of Haslingden, twenty or thirty together, crying for bread. Meetings are held every Sunday, on the neighbouring hills, attended by thousands of poor, haggard, hungry people, wishing for any change, even though it should be death. ...The people say they are determined to have their just rights, or die in the attempt, and say they will neither support delegates nor conventions,—for present relief they want, and present relief they will have before another winter makes its appearance. They say they might as well die by the sword as by hunger.
>
> *—Correspondent of the Liverpool Mercury.*[2]

The People's Charter of May 1838 was presented to parliament in 1839, in 1842 (with 3,317,752 signatures) and again in 1848. In 1840, John Frost, William Jones and Zephaniah Williams were sentenced to death for their part in leading the thousands of colliers and iron workers who marched in the Newport Rising of November 1839. When their sentences were commuted to transportation in a politic act of clemency, Thomas Cooper said in his prison poem, *The Purgatory of Suicides*, 'fear | Of Labour's vengeance, stayed the hangman's hand'.[3] In August 1841, Feargus O'Connor,

---

1   *LY*, 4.496.
2   *Tait's Edinburgh Magazine*, 9 (July 1842), 423.
3   *The Purgatory of Suicides*, 1845, Book 5.

editor of *The Northern Star*, was released from imprisonment in York Castle to general acclamation, and Cooper wrote 'the lion of freedom comes from his den | We'll rally around him again and again'. In March 1842, as Wordsworth addressed his *Poems, Chiefly of Early and Late Years* to a land where 'unforeseen distress spreads far and wide | Among a People mournfully cast down',[1] a Chartist Convention assembled in London, prior to presentation of the second Petition on 10 April. Rejection of that petition, dramatized by Elizabeth Gaskell in *Mary Barton*, and the decision of various employers to reduce wages, led to the great strikes of the Summer of 1842, and *inter alia*, to the arrest of Thomas Cooper, for 'seditious conspiracy' in the Potteries. In August that year, soldiers opened fire on Chartists protesters in Preston. Strangely, on all such matters—the Merthyr Rising of 1831, the agitation to save the Tolpuddle Martyrs in 1834, the petitions of 1839 and 1842, and the strikes of that summer, the Newport Rising of 1840, and the imprisonment of such figures as O'Connor and Cooper—Wordsworth's letters, preoccupied with Popery and the copyright campaign, are entirely silent. As one visitor, the American feminist Margaret Fuller, reported to the *New York Daily Tribune*, 29 September 1846, 'Living in this region … where there is little poverty, vice or misery, he hears not the voice which cries so loudly from other parts of England.'

The essence of Chartism was encapsulated in the famous six points of the Charter: universal male suffrage, the secret ballot, annual elections, abolition of property qualifications for MPs, salaried MPs, and equal constituencies. Wordsworth's letters provide evidence of sympathy for only the last of these points: one of his arguments against reform in 1832 was that the Whig measures were unprincipled, and that equal representation of Whitehaven and Manchester was an absurdity that could not survive.[2] Chartist complaints in the 1842 petition included, also, the effects of the new Poor Law, the excessive hours of factory employment, starvation wages, and restrictions on the press, and on these points, gener-

---

1   The words are from the collection's prefatory poem, dated 26 March 1842.
2   'Will not Manchester and Birmingham, etc., point on the one hand to the increased representation of London and its neighbourhood, and on the other to the small places which, for their paltry numbers, are allowed to retain one or two votes in the House; and to towns of the size of Kendal and Whitehaven, which for the first time are to send each a member? Will Manchester and Birmingham be content? Is it reasonable that they should be content with the principle of numbers so unjustly and absurdly applied?' (to Lord Lonsdale, 24 February 1832, *LY*, 2: 500).

ally speaking, Wordsworth agreed with them. To judge from his remarks in the 1835 Postscript, not to mention *Michael*, he would, or should, have supported one of the great Chartist enterprises of the mid 1840s, the Chartist Land Plan, in which O'Connor's objective was to foster independent production and a viable smallholder way of life.[1] Chartists also wanted disestablishment of the Church of England, and (most, though not all of them) repeal of the Act of Union with Ireland, matters on which Wordsworth—persuaded that as Popery, intolerance, reaction and repression were synonymous, an autonomous Ireland would represent the greatest possible threat to liberty—was profoundly opposed.[2] Daniel O'Connell the anti-Unionist MP is a frequent reference point in the letters; Feargus O'Connor the Chartist goes unmentioned.

The Chartist Land Company, with its implicit 'back to Michael' ideology, was founded a year before Thomas Cooper's famous visit to Rydal Mount in 1846, a poignant encounter, described (identically) in *Cooper's Journal* (1850) and in his autobiography. Cooper had recently been released from a two-year spell in prison for seditious conspiracy. In his case seditious conspiracy meant rousing people to fury by arguing that each and every aspect of industrial poverty was a violation of the precept 'thou shalt do no murder', which argument Engels adopted in 1844 for his *Condition of the English Working Class*.[3] In September 1846, Cooper—who had been commissioned by Douglas Jerrold to write articles on 'The Condition of the People of England' for his new paper—was touring the Lake District. Arriving at Rydal mount poorly dressed, and 'covered with dust', he was eyed suspiciously by a servant maid. So:

---

1   John K. Walton, *Chartism* (London: Routledge, 1999) 30–31 and Dorothy Thompson, *The Chartists: Popular Politics in the Industrial Revolution* (Aldershot: Wildwood House, 1984), 299–306.

2   See *LY*, 1: 363 (June 1825) for a passionate and passional Wordsworth: 'How far it is possible for legislation to interfere for the punishment of those who abuse the power of inflicting spiritual terrors I do not enquire.... But the grosser parts of their discipline are surely fit subjects for public investigation. The Popish priesthood ought to be prevented from punishing such of their Flock as they may find possessed of the Holy Scriptures. ... If Nunneries are to be allowed at all, no one ought to be received under the age of 21...; nothing can be more cruel than to take advantage of the inexperience of a child, to entrap her into a course of life by which Nature is counteracted and religion distorted.' On wider issues see F. M. Todd, *Politics and the Poet*.

3   *The Life of Thomas Cooper: Written by Himself* (London: Hodder & Stoughton, 1872), 187–99.

'Stop a moment!' I said,—took off my hat, drew a slip of paper from my pocket, and resting it on my hat crown, I wrote instantly 'Thomas Cooper, author of "The Purgatory of Suicides", desires to pay his devout regards to Mr. Wordsworth.'

In another half minute I was in the presence of that majestic old man, and I was bowing with a deep and heartfelt homage for his intellectual grandeur … when he seized my hand, and welcomed me with a smile so paternal, and such a hearty 'How do you do? I am happy to see you'— that the tears stood in my eyes for joy. (*Life*, 288)

While this was, as far as we know, Cooper's only meeting with Wordsworth, the famous Chartist was a friend of William and Mary Howitt, W. J. Fox, Thomas Noone Talfourd, Douglas Jerrold, etc—i.e. with that part of the dissenting culture with which Wordsworth remained in contact throughout his Tory years, just as he had kept up with Godwin, Losh and Thelwall. Stranded in Nottingham in June 1831, overcome by sciatica, Mary Wordsworth availed herself of the Howitts' hospitality, along with Dora, for ten days or so (*LY*, 2: 402), and *Howitt's Journal*, like William Thompson's *The Chartist Circular*, and John Saunders's *The People's Journal*, espoused both Chartism and Wordsworth's poetry. Wordsworth might have been reputed 'a grand old conservative', but Howitt saw him as 'at the same time the greatest of levellers' (*The People's Journal*, 24 January 1846).

What Wordsworth said about Cooper's prison rhyme we are not told, except that it consoled him for the *Quarterly*, the *Edinburgh* and even the *Westminster* not having condescended to mention it, but:

Nothing struck me so much in Wordsworth's conversation as his remarks concerning Chartism—after the subject of my imprisonment had been touched upon.

'You were right,' he said; 'I have always said the people were right in what they asked; but you went the wrong way to get it.'

I almost doubted my ears—being in the presence of the 'Tory' Wordsworth. He read the inquiring expression of my look in a moment,—and immediately repeated what he had said.

'You were quite right: there is nothing unreasonable in your Charter: it is the foolish attempt at physical force, for which many of you have been blameable.' (*Life*, 290)

The last ostensibly direct quotation in Cooper's report of his lengthy visit (which included tea with Mrs Arnold and Mrs Wordsworth, an exchange of views on Byron, Southey and Tennyson, and a treasured introduction to Dorothy as 'a poet'),[1] expands significantly on this theme:

> 'The people are sure to have the franchise', he said, with emphasis, 'as knowledge increases; but you will not get all you seek at once—and you must never seek it again with physical force,' he added, turning to me with a smile: 'it will only make you longer about it'....
>   When I hastened to depart—fearing that I had already wearied him— he walked with me to the gate, pressing my hand repeatedly, smiling on me so benevolently, and uttering so many good wishes for my happiness and usefulness, that I felt almost unable to thank him. I left him with a more intense feeling of having been in the presence of a good and great intelligence than I had ever felt in any other moments of my life.[2]

The most intriguing detail of Cooper's report is the remark that Wordsworth not only took similar views of the spread of freedom in Europe and in Britain, but 'descanted with animation on the growth of Mechanics' and similar institutions'. If 'animation' is taken to imply enthusiasm, the *Letters* offer directly contrary indications. Seventeen years earlier, in his overtly Tory period, which seems to have moderated in his late sixties and seventies, Wordsworth had endorsed James Watt's suspicion that Mechanics Institutes encouraged 'discontented spirits and insubordinate and presumptuous workmen' (*LY*, 2: 22–24).

Guilt, Sorrow, and Extreme Distress

In 1842, the year of the main action of Gaskell's *Mary Barton*, Wordsworth addressed to a land wracked by Chartism, the startling combination of the much revised but still profoundly Godwinian *Guilt and Sorrow*, his reconsideration of Godwin in the 'Sonnets upon the Punishment of Death', some miscellaneous sonnets including three under the collective title 'In Allusion to Various Recent Histories and notices of the French Revolution', and the guilt-laden analysis of his Jacobin alter ego in *The*

---

1   Cooper would have relished such conversation, as well as inclusion in the brotherhood of poets. His *Cooper's Journal: or, Unfettered Thinker and Plain Speaker for Truth, Freedom and progress* (London: 1850; repr. NY: Kelley, 1970) included one or two page synopses of the wisdom of Milton, Locke, Hume, James Burgh, Paine, Burke, Bentham, Godwin, Shelley, Landor, Carlyle, and Emerson, along with lengthy articles eulogising Newton, Pope and Robert Owen.

2   *Life*, 294–5. The account was first published in *Cooper's* Journal (May, 1850), 291–2, 324–5.

Borderers. The collection included a title page enabling the purchaser to bind the new volume as Volume 7 of the *Poetical Works*—as an adjunct to volume 6, *The Excursion*.

The first substantive moment of *Poems Chiefly of Early and Late Years* (1842) is a description of Wordsworth's feelings about impending war in the Summer of 1794, based upon 'having been a witness, during a long residence in revolutionary France, of the spirit which prevailed in that country' ('long', one might feel, is needlessly ominous; it might imply as long as that of the revered Helen Maria Williams, whose *Letters from France* are conspicuously plagiarized in the still hidden *Prelude*). Its last is a note on *The Borderers*, concerning how that same residence enabled him to witness how, 'as sin and crime are apt to start from their very opposite qualities, so are there no limits to the hardening of the heart, and the perversion of the understanding to which they may carry their slaves': such 'hardening of the heart' and 'perversion of understanding' constitute the personal 'fall' from which the latter part of *The Prelude* records his redemption. Worked over these almost posthumous texts may have been, but Wordsworth's message to his countrymen in 1842 remains essentially the work of the poet of 1794–1796 witnessing how people can be ground between economic disaster and political theory. Or rather, it is the work of 'two consciousnesses': one witnessing such events in the hungry 90s, the other resurrecting that witness in the newly hungry 40s. That the sacrificial altars of antiquity, fed with living men, are said to remind Wordsworth of 'certain aspects of *modern* society' ('Advertisement', 1842) seems no less pertinent in 1842 than in 1793.

In the poetry of 1793–97, including *The Borderers*, organized society is shunned as an unreal element, inexpressive of human values and realities. The bounds of human life seem to be marked by the village, the inn, the family, the commune: these are natural institutions, built upon primary human values and needs which become abstracted, generalized and devalued in organized society. In *Guilt and Sorrow*, society can only be related to through the organism of family or friendship—those 'bonds of nature' without which neither society nor the individual is authentic. Values, in Wordsworth's universe, are social but extra-societal, expressed in 'meeting'. The whole plot of *Guilt and Sorrow* concerns a meeting between two victims of war and government indifference, victims of a society which does not recognize the state's responsibility for the welfare of its citizens. This principle was theorized by Wordsworth in the 1835 Postscript: 'that all persons who cannot find employment, or procure wages sufficient to support the body in health and strength, are entitled to a maintenance by law', which right 'is one of the most precious rights of the English people' (*WPW*, 386). Welfare places a value upon life 'which can belong to it only where the laws have placed men who are willing to work, and yet cannot find employment, above the necessity of looking for protection against hunger and other natural evils, either to individual and casual charity, to despair and death, or to the breach of law by theft or violence' (387). It is a principle of the social compact that 'the right of the state to require the services of its members, even to the jeopardising of their lives in the common defence [not, presumably, via the press-gang], establishes a right in the people (not to be gainsaid by utilitarians and economists) to public support when, from any cause, they may be unable to support themselves' (388).

Wordsworth pugnaciously presents the indigent as victims of 'theories of political economy that whether right or wrong in the abstract, have proved a scourge to tens of thousands' (391) and argues, contra Harriet Martineau, that 'it is better for the interests of humanity among the people at large that ten undeserving should partake of the funds thus provided, than that one morally good man, through want of relief, should either have his principles corrupted or his energies destroyed; that such a one should either be driven to do wrong, or cast to the earth in utter hopelessness' (395). The Sailor and the Female Vagrant come immediately to mind as exemplars of the last two consequences (he cites *The Female Vagrant* on p. 390), and with reference to destruction through want of relief, *The Last of the Flock* remains as pertinent in 1842 as it was in 1798.

Between *Salisbury Plain* and *Guilt and Sorrow* much has changed, but social responsibility for the creation of scarcity has not. His sailor has been 'betrayed' into murder, to use the phrase upon the transitoriness of action that belongs to *The Borderers*:

> Action is transitory—a step, a blow,
> The motion of a muscle—this way or that—
> 'Tis done; and in the after vacancy
> We wonder at ourselves like men betrayed;
> Suffering is permanent, obscure and dark,
> And has the nature of infinity.

Ripped from domesticity, trained for war, and defrauded of his rightful pay, the sailor will be sentenced for an involuntary act of murder for which he is not fully responsible. The volume includes Wordsworth's *Sonnets on the Punishment of Death*, lambasted for illogicality and low morality by *The City of London Magazine*, which subscribed fully to abolition arguments, and which praised *Guilt and Sorrow* for its inward account of the sailor.[1] Yet the sailor, as another reviewer put it, is 'guilty of a barbarous murder, *of which the poet seems to perceive the atrocity less strongly than might be expected.*'[2] At this date, for the reviewer as for society in general (if not for the young Friedrich Engels, already at work in Manchester), Godwin's sense of necessitarianism is clearly in abeyance.

The Female Vagrant has suffered from the actions of an unfeeling landowner, and from the government's war against American liberty. A reader of her tale in 1798 would have interpreted her sufferings in terms of the 1790s, thus bridging the gap between what Wordsworth much later (in the *Cintra* tract) called Britain's 'two wars against liberty'. The phantasmagorical aspect of her tale (stanza 39) would have evoked the fearful losses in the West Indies campaigns of the mid-nineties, already alluded to in chapter 7. As many have complained, the revisionary process whereby *Adventures on Salisbury Plain* became *Guilt and Sorrow* lessens the poem's focus on particular issues of the 1790s, so that such matters as rural expropriation and the evils of enlistment or of official fraud become less prominent than, and perhaps less dissonant with, the poem's extraordinary depiction of alienation and social exclusion. Both figures, the Vagrant especially, are too mired in despair to contemplate class action—as mired, say, as Gaskell's Davenports in their Manchester cellar—but they are capable of that socially foundational act, meeting and responding. At the outset of the (already) hungry forties one would have expected reviewers to find the depiction of social exclusion, and of consequent violence, especially apt to the reading moment. Within a few years Kingsley would be telling readers who wished to understand why people were marching, protesting, and preparing for action, to read *Mary Barton*. At about the same time, Charles Dickens would depict an industrialized world in which humane values seem to exist only in the carnivalesque world of the circus—dramatizing, as it were, the praise of

1   *City of London Magazine*, 1 (1842), 111–115.
2   *The British and Foreign Review* 14 (1843) 1–28, 4. My italics.

anarchy (gipsy anarchy in this case) cut from the Female Vagrant's story in 1805. Yet nobody told readers who wanted to know what it feels like to be deprived of employment, denied food, defrauded of pay, cast as a criminal, betrayed into violence, and to find humane treatment only on the outermost fringes of organized society, to read *Guilt and Sorrow*. This is partly, of course, because Gaskell and Dickens wrote about the urban nightmares of Manchester and Preston, while Wordsworth wrote about Salisbury Plain, where his own experience of alienation was most acutely felt. Although he admitted in one of his Iberian sonnets that human nature must be as resilient among the Burghers of Saragossa as among the shepherds of Cumbria, the admission that city life is as human as country life rarely realized itself in his poetry outside Book 7 of *The Prelude*, with its blind beggar and child-minding artificer.

Perhaps more pertinently, Wordsworth's voice is already, in reviewers' minds, associated with a time almost half a century back. His introductory notes licence them to read *Guilt and Sorrow* and *The Borderers* solely as revelations of how the now venerable poet responded to what *The British and Foreign Review* describes as 'the time when all Europe was lighted up with the most fearful eruption of evil which history has witnessed' and the faces 'even of the healthiest men [i.e. Wordsworth] looked pale and livid in the blaze'. *The Christian Remembrancer* while praising the poem's simplicity and power, quite ignores the poem's depiction of the plight of have-nots in a world of haves. Even *The Gentleman's Magazine*[1] pays no attention to the contemporary relevance of *Guilt and Sorrow,* or of *The Borderers,* despite including among its extracts from the volume a sonnet that might have been written precisely to point this relevance, a sonnet in which the spital on Salisbury Plain seems to coalesce with the Davenport cellar in *Mary Barton:*

> Feel for the wrongs to universal ken
> Daily exposed, woe that unshrouded lies,
> And seek the sufferer in his darkest den,
> Whether conducted to the spot by sighs
> And moanings...

The sonnet argues (in a manner unnoticed then or since) that private charity can only supplement, not supplant, statutory relief and statutory redistribution:

---

1   *The Gentleman's Magazine* ns 24 (December 1845), 555–575.

> Feel for the poor, but not to still your qualms
> By formal charity, or dole of alms...
> Far as ye may[,] erect and equalize;
> And what ye cannot reach by statute, draw
> Each from his fountain of self-sacrifice.

Aesthetic qualities fared better. *The Christian Remembrancer* saw *Guilt and Sorrow* as revealing Wordsworth's strengths as a poet in a remarkable degree: 'the whole poem ... forms the finest specimen of the severe graces of our author's earlier style.... What a proof ... it affords of the deep-seated originality of his mind! and how innate are the peculiar characteristics of his genius'. It is impressed by Wordsworth's ability to write—when no good models existed, and before the friendship with Coleridge—'a poem so pure from all tinsel and conventionality, so majestic in its simplicity'.[1] Some of that majestic simplicity, in reality, arises from decades of reconsideration, during which the poem loses the artificial diction of *Salisbury Plain*, the farcical moments of *Adventures*, and the strident rhetoric of both, while the poet balances the stories of the Sailor and the Vagrant, and finally clarifies the scenes praised by *The British and Foreign Review*—the brilliantly sustained desolation effect of the opening stanzas, and the purest account of the Sailor's encounter with the Female Vagrant 'whom [because she appeared in *Lyrical Ballads*] we have so long known' (5).

'Majestic simplicity' would flatter *Salisbury Plain*, but it is not a bad description of the aesthetic quality released in *Guilt and Sorrow* by its artful revisions. The vehicle of the poem, its Spenserian stanza, invites one to bring to bear on a tale of contemporary suffering, the world of Christian allegory in which images become emblems: from time to time its language invokes, as it did in 1798, the values of pastoral, perhaps specifically in that Shakespearean mode of pastoral where Arcadian retreats—here in the form of a rural inn where milking pail o'erbrims and the table groans with plenty—mock the realities of day-to-day existence, whether of the wartime economy of the 1790s or those of the 1840s. The first thirteen stanzas, now simplified to a Hardyesque presentation of a man adrift on the heath, present an experience—the terms seem appropriate—of both alienation and nausea. As he treks across the plain there is no welcome at the inn (stanza 2), the distant spire is 'lost' (3), he seems beyond human habitation, and even the cornfields 'stretched and

---

1   *The Christian Remembrancer*, ns 3 (June 1842) 655–71, 663.

stretching' (3), the whistling grain (4), crows rushing by 'in eddies' (5), the spreading waste, the stones rolling at his back (10), the gibbet-circling raven (11), and the affrighted bustard (12), emphasize the Sailor's burden of rejection and alienation. This is explained in stanzas 6–7 as the product of having been impressed, trained to kill in the state's behalf, defrauded, denied the ability to feed his wife and children, and become in 'the motion of a muscle', a murderer: 'He met a traveller, robbed him, shed his blood' (8). The depiction of his state throughout the poem is precisely that which in *Mary Barton* the author funks: the state of an involuntary murderer as he encounters emblems of guilt and slowly comes to terms with the inevitability of choosing his guilt. He is, objectively, a murderer, even though he, the reader and the poet know that subjectively he is not. The poem intuits the structure of what Sartre calls *mauvaise foi*. Because of the structure of human consciousness, as *not being what it is*, the sailor is not, *for* himself, or even for others, what he is *in* himself. In Sartre's way of putting it, he really *is not* a murderer in the sense in which an inkwell *is* an inkwell. On the other hand, as he recognizes, he cannot claim *not* to be a murderer in the sense in which an inkwell *is not* a pen. The poet who *was*, and *was not*, a terrorist in 1793–94, knows very well what it is to take responsibility for oneself. The 1842 volume is a confession; but it is delivered, very poignantly, at a time when that confession links him with those who are similarly tempted to physical force on whatever justifications.

The first social action in the poem comes after the Sailor leaves Stonehenge and encounters the Female Vagrant, sighing in her sleep at the mysterious abandoned spital. Each, knowingly or unknowingly, becomes responsible for the equanimity of the other. She has the tact to keep to herself the tale she has heard of a 'late murdered corse': instead, he listens to a tale almost but not quite like his own. From her beginnings in a life of rural virtue and self-education, her father is made destitute and she is made homeless by 'severe mischance and cruel wrong': in 1842, when Wordsworth softened the reference to naval fraud, he decided also not to reinstate the reference to cannibalistic landowners and the enclosure of fishing rights deleted earlier.[1] But he does retain the equation between Britain's two wars on liberty, that on America and that on France. Her 'happy' father—happy in the Davenport sense—dies before

---

1 The *British and Foreign Review* noted alertly that the sailor is 'cheated of his gains, by whom it does not appear', 4.

he has to witness again a cold hearth and silent loom, but when 'the noisy drum | Beat round to clear the streets of want and pain' her husband enlists for the American War. They suffer pestilence, from official negligence, even before setting sail. They reach the new world 'devoted' to sacrifice, and like the victims of revolutionary terror (Wordsworth uses identical phrasing of both events) 'All perished—all in one remorseless year'.[1] The Vagrant of 1842, however, is neither a precocious philosophy sophomore nor a veteran of rather too many demonstrations. She no longer laments, as she did until 1802, that it is a 'dreadful price of being to resign | All that is dear *in* being'. Nor does she portray her husband and his friends as 'dog-like, wading at the heels of war' willing to 'lap (their very nourishment) their brothers blood'.[2] She has, however, come to exemplify the theory of relief developed by Wordsworth in the 1830s.

She feels the need to escape from too much trauma by perpetual wandering. Cast reluctantly upon shore she finds herself in her homeland where there is neither home nor succour, 'And near a thousand tables pined and wanted food'. More deeply than the sailor, she evinces the destruction of spirit by want. As Wordsworth warned his readers in 1835: 'Despondency and distraction are no friends to prudence: the springs of industry will relax, if cheerfulness be destroyed by anxiety; without hope men become reckless, and have a sullen pride in adding to the heap of their own wretchedness' (*PrW*, 3: 245). 'Unsought for was the help that did my life recall', is her melancholy recollection, and she has about her a consistent listlessness. She remains too full of grief, or perhaps of stable virtues, to befriend the gipsy 'travellers' who befriend her. It may be a failure of courage on Wordsworth's part not to restore the stanza praising this anarchic challenge to the social order (it was deleted some time after 1805) as a world where 'all belonged to all, and each was chief'. Nevertheless, the subversive point of their kindliness remains: it is from them, not from the wealthy, or the well housed, that she receives food and rest. The Vagrant still indicts reliance upon 'chance bounty', and decries the notion of leaving family support to families ('kindred of dead husband,' she comments tartly, 'are at best | Small help') and she thus supports implicitly the 1835 Postscript's stance on state relief. But her topical role in the poem is to show the destructive effect of poverty,

---

1   In the Terror, Wordsworth says of the Directory's victims (*1805*, 10.333), '—all perished, all—'.

2   *PW*, 1: 111; this phrasing was dropped in 1802 at the time of the war sonnets.

not to associate the poor with threats to the social order: 'In open air forgetful would I sit | Whole hours in moping sorrow knit'. She still has no destination in view, after three years of wandering, and after performing compassionate service for the sailor's dying wife the last thing we are told is that 'she lingered'. The focus of the poem is upon her decay, the tenderness of the sailor, and upon his wife's progress from extreme indigence to a merciful release: like the death of the pauperized Davenport in *Mary Barton*, and of the Female Vagrant's own father, such release is envied by the survivor.

Salisbury Plain focused upon the Annette-surrogate, the female vagrant. *Guilt and Sorrow*, like *Adventures* but more effectively, begins and ends with the Sailor. Clearly forgiven by the narrator—the sailor is depicted rescuing one child from abuse and at the hospitable cottage he has children playing about his knees—he cannot forgive himself. Like Raskolnikov in *Crime and Punishment* (1866), and as Mortimer in the manuscript of *The Borderers* intends to do, he delivers himself up to judgement.[1] His manner of doing so, however, invites the reader to conclude that (as in the 'Sonnets upon the Punishment of Death') he will at the moment of his self-chosen execution, in expiation of man's law, be 'wafted' to bliss. His every action, from comforting of the Vagrant to protecting a child, has substantiated his wife's words: 'He was mild and good. | Never on earth was gentler creature seen; | He'd not have robbed the raven of its food' (a macabre touch, in the light of the gibbet-circling raven of stanza 9); 'My husband's loving kindness stood between | Me and all worldy harms and wrongs however keen.' The Sailor has become Browning's 'tender murderer', and his wife has been made as destitute as the Female Vagrant. Both reductions are as clearly the state's doing in *Guilt and Sorrow* as they were in earlier texts. But the fact that the sailor renders himself up to justice is now, clearly, his own doing: in *Adventures* it is implied that the cottagers betray him.

Part of the revised *Adventures on Salisbury Plain*, the encounter with the gibbet in stanzas 13–14, goes back to Hawkshead Grammar School and a vivid image by John Bernard Farish, the brother of Wordsworth's

---

1 In 1842 Wordsworth cut from the concluding Act of his drama a passage of the early text which (in the context of a combined publication) would have associated Mortimer too closely with the sailor, and which, in any case, since Mortimer does not follow through his resolution, adds to the early text's numerous confusions. Mortimer commands the cottager; 'Thou must conduct me hence. The executioner | Must do this business' (*Borderers*, 282).

schoolfriend Charles Farish, who treated the topos in three precocious Spenserian stanzas:

> Beside us stood the Murtherer's gibbet high,
> And hovering round it often did a raven fly.
>
> Eftsoons we heard the ghastly carcase shake
> His iron chains; up-born upon ye blast,
> While with his weight ye rusty chain did creek,
> Oft swinging he did beat the gibbet mast.
> Before our eyes a griesly terror past,—
> We stood, ne durst approachen for dismay;
> The raven croaked full sore, and himself cast
> On's wing, and fled, for it did him affray:
> The wind did cease, and darksome wox ye face of day.[1]

In this Gothic performance, Farish's 'griesly terror', the ghost of the murdered man, takes his place at the foot of the gibbet and shows the fatal wound. In Wordsworth's poem, the raven circles a gibbet in similarly portentous fashion, but it is the murderer who beholds this token, and who at the close of his poem, after too many such reminders of his guilt, hands himself over to the law to be punished. In all versions hereafter (critics often allege, misleadingly, that *Guilt and Sorrow* is revised so as to imply a wholly different stance) the reader is invited to entertain the Godwinian thesis that it is irrational for society to behave in such a way as to (a) train a man to kill, (b) place him in a situation where he has (almost) no option but to do so, and (c) punish him for what is the (almost) inevitable consequence of 'the system'. Equally, no version of the poem represents the sailor *as exculpating himself* by this logic. In his capacity for right thinking, and for decent feeling, he is almost—and given Wordsworth's sniffiness about Dickensian popularity this is something of an irony—a sort of Magwitch (serialized 1860–61).

As in *Mary Barton*, where John Barton, the child-solacer and chance-chosen agent of class-murder, delivers (before he becomes a murderer) most of the work's moral argument, it is the sailor who in stanza 47 delivers the poem's 'moral'. *The British and Foreign Review* found it 'short and we fear not very intelligible'. That 'not very intelligible'

---

1 T. W. Thompson, *Wordsworth's Hawkshead*, ed. Robert Woof (London: OUP, 1970), 319.

lesson, complete with an allusion to *Paradise Lost*,[1] is this:

> Much need have ye that time more closely draw
> The bond of nature, all unkindness cease,
> And that among so few there still be peace.

The Murderer's moral stature, moreover, rebukes the poet's. To confess one's implication in the fever of the times, and to take responsibility for the blood one has shed, or the blood-letting one has been prepared to exculpate, is an action the poet feels only tangentially able to measure up to.

Guilt and Sorrow is accompanied by a brief series of sonnets under the collective title 'In Allusion to Various Recent Histories and notices of the French Revolution'. Wordsworth confesses in sonnets 9 and 10 of this series—which constitute a sort of trailer to the still unpublished Books 9 and 10 of *The Prelude*—that 'monstrous theories of alien growth' can persuade one to set conscience aside on the grounds that one is assisting historical necessity, or Providence,

> ...But woe for him
> That, thus deceived, shall lend an eager hand
> To social havoc!

Such remarks were unlikely to be read in 1842 as the confessions of an erstwhile terrorist, but Wordsworths's identification with Oswald, in *The Borderers*, comes much closer to self-unmasking.

The Ministry of Pain

> Ay, we are coupled in a chain of adamant:
> Let us be fellow-labourers, then, to enlarge
> Man's intellectual empire. We subsist
> In slavery; all is slavery; we receive
> Laws, but we ask not whence those laws have come;
> We need an inward sting to goad us on.[2]

The first three of these lines, as nobody outside Rydal Mount knew in 1842, are a dark parody of Wordsworth's final address to Coleridge in

---

1   Adam says to Eve in *Paradise Lost*, 9.955–96: 'So forcible within my heart I feel | The Bond of Nature draw me to my owne...'.
2   *Borderers*, 4.1854f. I cite the play from *Poetical Works*, vol 1.

The Prelude, where he speaks of himself and Coleridge as fellow-labourers. Because the author of Books 10 and 11 of *The Prelude* knows all too well the temptation to transgress Heaven's perpetual ban on 'All principles of action that transcend | The sacred limits of humanity' (*PELY*, sonnet 7) he identifies in *The Borderers* most closely not with the tenderhearted Marmaduke but with the villain named in 1842 after the Jacobin John Oswald, but cloaked in the manuscript as Rivers (a name more suggestive of the Wars of the Roses).[1] Captain John Oswald was described by Tom Paine as having 'a most voracious appetite for blood': he planned to do for Britain what Oswald does for Marmaduke in the play—namely attempt to regenerate it through violence—and he was also, by way of Romantic consistency, an impassioned vegetarian.[2] Oswald appears in *The Borderers* as Wordsworth's necessitarian 'Spectre'.

'Necessity', says Friedrich Engels, 'will force the working men to abandon the remnants of [religious] belief which, as they will more and more clearly perceive, serves only to make them weak and resigned to their fate, obedient and faithful to the vampire property-holding class'.[3] England is diseased, Engels argues, and the disease while chronic in the country is acute in the towns. As a result of the concentration of men in cities, the 'patriarchal relation' (148) of ruler to ruled has been destroyed:

> Only when estranged from his employer, when convinced that the sole bond between employer and employee is the bond of pecuniary profit, when the sentimental bond between them, which stood not the slightest test, had wholly fallen away, then only did the worker begin to recognise his own interests and develop independently; then only did he cease to be the slave of the bourgoisie in his thoughts, feelings, and the expression of his will.

1   Earl Rivers was beheaded in 1483.

2   For the Scottish Jacobin, John Oswald, see David Erdman, 'Wordsworth as Heartsworth; or, Was Regicide the Prophetic Ground of Those "Moral Questions"?', in *The Evidence of the Imagination*, ed. Donald H. Reiman, et. al. (New York, 1978), 12–41 and 'The Man Who Was Not Napoloen', *TWC* 12: 1 (1981) 92–97. In *The Cry of Nature; Or, an Appeal to Mercy and to Justice, on behalf of the Persecuted Animals* (London: J. Johnson, 1791) Oswald appeals histrionically on behalf of animals 'to these bowels, fraught with mercy, and entwined with compassion; to these bowels which nature hath sanctified to the sentiments of pity and gratitude; to the yearnings of kindred, to the melting tenderness of love! (33).

3   Friedrich Engels, *The Condition of the Working Class in England* [1845], ed. Victor Kiernan (Harmondsworth: Penguin, 1987), 243.

Engels, of course, welcomes this: 'And as the English nation cannot succumb under the final crisis, but must come forth from it, born again, rejuvenated, we can but rejoice over everything which accelerates the course of the disease'. Now, Engels observes with satisfaction, even with relish, 'social war is under full headway' in that 'every one sees in his neighbour an enemy to be got out of the way, or, at best, a tool to be used for his own advantage. And this war grows from year to year, as the criminal tables show, more violent, passionate, irreconcilable' (156). It is a historical irony that *The Borderers* appeared just three years before this parallel analysis of sentiment undermined by revolutionary consciousness.

The setting of the play, upon the Borders in the time of Henry III, is also a moral frontier. When Oswald says of Marmaduke's band, 'Happy are we … that own | No law but what each makes for himself', he knows he is overstepping the mark. What unites these outlaws is, rather, a Romantic rebellion of the kind theorized by Albert Camus, a rebellion against anarchic greed and power, on behalf of order. The gypsy world of benign self-rule, dropped from *Guilt and Sorrow*, is still present in *The Borderers*, where it constitutes the frame of the moral action. Marmaduke leads a somewhat anarchic band of well-intentioned redistributors and avengers, in a sort of borders version of Sherwood Forest. His men are self-appointed guardians of the peace—as were the Chartists when they briefly assumed the functions of a militia in parts of the north in 1842 and 1848—and they deal out what they see as natural justice. Here, on the turf of ancient Rheged, Oswald's leader Marmaduke 'Stand[s] like an isthmus 'twixt two stormy seas | That oft have checked their fury at your bidding,' and so

> Your single virtue has transformed a Band
> Of fierce barbarians into Ministers
> Of peace and order (2.607–12)

That 'single virtue' of one 'higher mind' is, as in the Snowdon meditation, twinned with love: thanks to Marmaduke, aged men have learned to bless the steps of these tamed barbarians, and 'the fatherless retire | For shelter to their banners'. But Oswald is no Robin Hood, standing in for the absent King. He makes war not merely on Norman sheriffs but on all 'fathers'. In his creed, the obstacle to progress is Marmaduke's belief that compassion 'to our kind is natural as life' (627). Such beliefs Oswald decries as 'highways of dreaming passion', and he will 'shatter the delusion, break it up | And set him free' (2.931, 934–5). He despises Marmaduke for his generous construction of others' motives (including Oswald's own), and above all his subscription to the illusion of brotherhood. Oswald's purpose is to persuade Marmaduke to pass beyond good and evil, because as Madame Roland wrote in her manuscript defence in 1793, 'Liberty is for those lofty minds, that despise death, and can inflict it when necessary'.[1] Or as Oswald puts it:

> Benevolence that has not heart to use
> The wholesome ministry of pain and evil,
> Becomes at last weak and contemptible. (2.618–20)

The Borderers is one of the definitive expressions of Romantic immoralism and Oswald is Wordsworth's closest approach to Byron's nay-saying Lucifer in *Cain*.[2] The play's analysis of revolutionary consciousness is comparable, Thomas McFarland has shown, to Plato's 'Callicles' in *The Republic* or Nietzsche's *The Genealogy of Morals*.[3] But it is also—not that anybody seems to have noticed in 1842—the most straightforwardly topical of Wordsworth's publications. The story concerns the deliberate plot of Oswald, a sublimely self-applauding intellectual, against the tender scruples of Marmaduke, who is still like his earlier self, 'one of love's simple bondsmen' (4.1841). Oswald, who in his youth was betrayed into a ghastly crime against his captain, has argued himself into gratitude for the moral liberation thus accidentally accomplished, liberation from the 'soft chain' (4.1841) of bourgeois morality. Alone, like the Jacobin Wordsworth, in 'a region of futurity' (4.1816) he obeys the urge to make a creature like himself, by liberating the sentiment-ridden Marmaduke from his bondage to bourgeois morality, or the illusion that 'we have all of us one human heart' (*Old*

---

1   From the manuscript defence of Mme Roland, assassinated by the revolutionary tribunal, Brumaire 19, 2 (November 9, 1793), cited from Louvet's *Narrative* (1795). Wordsworth read the *Narrative* in 1795.

2   He preaches 'self-affirmation in evil … the achievement of suffering which hath the nature of infinity' (Lascelles Abercrombie, *The Art of Wordsworth* [London: Hamden, 1965], 132); he is 'a metaphysical villain who forces the hero to pass from a naïve to a new and isolating consciousness' (Hartman, *Wordsworth's Poetry*, 126); and what he argues is 'the dark version of [Romanticism's] creative psychology' (P. M. Ball, *The Central Self* [London: Athlone Press, 1968], 28). r areent treatment, see Freridk Burwick, '*The Borderers* (1796–1842)', *Oxford Handbook of William Wordsworth* (2015).

3   McFarland, *William Wordsworth: Intensity and Achievement,* 147–58.

Cumberland Beggar). To do so, Oswald feeds Marmaduke with disinformation. He reifies Herbert, Idonea's blind, frail father, as the perpetrator of (imagined) villainies, a lap-dog of the class enemy, Clifford, and so persuades Marmaduke to assassinate him. Real 'manliness' in Oswald's ideology ignores the 'wiles' of women and the 'craft' of age, and 'spares not the worm' (2.1079–81). When he believes that his plan is fulfilled, that Marmaduke has murdered his prospective father-in-law, he eases Marmaduke into the higher awareness that he lives in a world of material interests not of ideal boundaries. His 'chain of adamant' speech continues: 'we receive | Laws but we do not ask whence those laws have come; | We need an inward sting to drive us on (4.1854–59).

We need to grasp, Engels argues, that the bourgeois can 'tyrannise … and plunder … to his heart's content, and yet receive obedience, gratitude, and assent from these stupid people by bestowing a trifle of patronizing friendliness which cost him nothing, and perhaps some paltry present, all apparently out of pure, self-sacrificing, uncalled for goodness of heart, but really not one tenth of his duty' (Engels 149). To Oswald, only 'the torpid acquiescence of our emasculated souls', makes us endure 'the tyranny | Of the world's masters, with the musty rules | By which they uphold their craft from age to age' (3.1489–92). We are slaves only because we allow the cunning authors of slave morality to banish the 'institutes | Of Nature' from 'human intercourse':

> If a snake
> Crawl from beneath our feet we do not ask
> A license to destroy him: our good governors
> Hedge in the life of every pest and plague
> That bears the shape of man; and for what purpose,
> But to protect themselves from extirpation? (3.1575–84)

Wordsworth not only shared Engels's view that social war was indeed in train, but was exceptionally well qualified (perhaps as well qualified as Engels) to explore the kind of passion that would commit itself to this war. Wordsworth, too, had felt, like Oswald, 'daring sympathies with power' (10.457), and had stood, in imagination, beside the sacrificers of men. There is an enormous element of confessionalism in Oswald, who lacks only two elements of the poet's world-view, self-doubt, and an ontology of love. He is, simply, an enormous Shadow. *The Borderers*, McFarland says, relates to 'what Wordsworth was not and could not let himself become': Rivers is 'a rejected version of Wordsworth's own self ... a mind actuated by pride and feelings of superiority, by contempt of society and its mores: he has [in Wordsworth's prefatory essay] "shaken off the obligations of religion and morality"'(McFarland, 139–40).

No reader of 1842 could have suspected that like Oswald, Wordsworth had known the intellectual pride that felt able to 'look through all the frailties of the world' and 'to the blind restraints of general laws | Superior, magisterially adopts | One guide, the light of circumstances, flashed upon an independent intellect' (*Prelude* 1850, 11.237–44). When this light failed he had known, like Marmaduke, 'a sense | Death-like, of treacherous desertion, felt | In the last place of refuge—my own soul' (10.413–5), and been close to the despair in which both Marmaduke and the Solitary are mired—

> Roaming at large, to observe and not to feel,
> And therefore not to act—convinced that all
> Which bears the name of action, howsoe'er
> Beginning ends in servitude (*Excursion* 2.89ff).

The question whether 'the clear light of circumstances flashed upon an independent intellect' is or is not Godwinian has been the major theme of critical debate on the play. The play's point appears to be that both 'clear light' and 'independent intellect' are delusions, just as the ideal of purely rational perfectibility is 'a composition of the brain' (*1850*, 13.82). Oswald's ostensibly independent intellect is, in reality, driven by malevolent passions, injured pride (925), vain self-delusions (2245), and pitiable loneliness. As a Crusader in Palestine, he has been trained to wage sectarian war on unbelievers. His belief that superior insight gives him a licence to kill is, in the end, as socially conditioned—as unfree— as the reflex action of the sailor in *Guilt and Sorrow*. Unlike the Sailor, but like Wordsworth in 1794, Oswald resorts to casuistry. Marmaduke, betrayed into crime, succumbs to remorse, in voluntary self-sacrifice to the furies. Oswald keeps them at bay by plotting fresh accumulations of guilt to keep remorse forever in the future.

Oswald's narrative of the after-vacancy of action, once he discovers that he has been betrayed into crime, is a dark variation both on the *Prelude* breakdown, and on the Solitary's 'dim and perilous way' (*Excursion*, 3.701):

> Three sleepless nights I passed in sounding on,

> Through words and things, a dim and perilous way;
> And, whereso'er I turned me, I beheld
> A slavery compared to which the dungeon
> And clanking chains are perfect liberty. (*Bord*, 1774 ff)

Oswald emerges from his nightmare 'Thirsting for some of those exploits that fill | The earth for sure redemption of lost peace'. What he sees as redemption, however, is merely, as Wordsworth's prefatory essay says, a sterile cycle of fresh accumulations of 'uneasiness' (*CWRT,* 1: 765). Both Oswald and Wordsworth have to deal with a despair within themselves occasioned by the fatal gap between dream and reality. Oswald deals with his by a violent and antinomian self-assertiveness. He concludes that for him everything is permitted, and lays claim, in Gabriel Marcel's terms, 'to a kind of cosmic governance', his mind becoming 'less and less capable of examining its own credentials to the exercise of such dominion'.[1]

If Oswald's wholesome 'ministry of pain' sounds like another dark parody, this time of Nature's pedagogy in *The Prelude* ('fostered alike by beauty and by fear') it is because Oswald shares Wordsworth's theory of growth. Knowing, as the poet's alter ego, 'What mighty objects do impress their forms | To elevate our intellectual being', and that a man must not be doomed 'to perish self-consumed' (1808 ff), he embraces nature's gift: he seemed to himself 'a Being who had passed alone | Into a region of futurity, | Whose natural element was freedom'. In short, he sings all of the play's best tunes, and comes very close to articulating the great Wordsworthian positives. Like the poet of the Peele Castle stanzas, he knows that 'The wise abjure | All thoughts whose idle composition lives | In the entire forgetfulness of pain' (3.1549–51). He knows that he lives; he has found the power 'to thaw the deepest sleep that time can lay upon us', and he seeks out those eminences where the winds blow keener and will not let him sleep. The prefatory essay reveals how much of himself Wordsworth invested in Oswald. When 'dormant associations are awakened' in Oswald, the essay says, 'in tracing the revolutions through which his character has passed, in painting his former self, he really is great' (*PW*, 1: 347). Oswald, however, cannot convert these 'associations' into 'natural piety'. He cannot allow his unfallen self to communicate its innocent energies to the present—as in the therapy

---

1   Gabriel Marcel, *The Philosophy of Existence* (London: 1948), 19.

of Books 1 and 2 of *The Prelude*—and reconnect him to himself. He has, like the poet, a powerful imagination—he is especially adept, for instance, 'in imagining a future world where his crimes would not be crimes'—but, crucially, he has not read *The Prelude*. He does not know that Imagination and Love 'cannot stand | Dividually'.

'Genuine Liberty'

In the moonlit scene described in Book 14 of *The Prelude*, an imaginary sea, created by vapours ascending from unseen abysses, usurps upon the real sea. It thus balances, and reverses, the material Mont Blanc which, in Book 6, to Wordsworth's disappointment, had 'usurped upon a living thought | That never more could be'. Snowdon's 'dark abyss' (*1850*) or 'blue chasm' (*1805*) is naturalistically described as

> A deep and gloomy breathing place through which
> Mounted the roar of waters, torrents, streams
>
> > (*1805*, 13.57–58),

In that abyss Nature had lodged 'The Soul, the Imagination of the whole' (65) and it is this transmuting factor that Wordsworth sees as emblematizing one aspect of the freedom of 'higher minds', those not 'enthralled' by sensible impressions (such as the actual sea) but capable of sending abroad 'like transformations'. In their imaginative power, such minds include, pre-eminently, minds like Oswald or like Robespierre, who was a ministering angel of mercy to some in Tom Poole's circle, in part because he was capable of imagining 'a world how different from this'.

Wordsworth, however, beholds in the moon-and-mist-scape a second mode of freedom from enthralment. It is

> the emblem of a mind
> That feeds upon infinity, that broods
> Over the dark abyss, intent to hear
> Its voices issuing forth to silent light
> In one continuous stream (*1850*, 14.70–74)

or, in the early version, a mind that is exalted by

> an under-presence,
> The sense of God, or whatso'er is dim
> Or vast in its own being (*1805*, 13.71–73)

Here Wordsworth is at his closest to Blake, who desired in *Jerusalem* 'To open the eternal worlds, to open the immortal eyes | Of man inwards into the bosom of God, the human imagination'. Such a mind, like Martin Buber's 'free man' in *I and Thou*, 'listens to what is emerging from himself, to the course of being in the world; … to bring it to reality as it desires'.[1] In Wordsworth's subsequent commentary, only such minds possess 'genuine liberty'.

The meditation that follows defines the higher minds' capacity (perhaps the capacity of all beings in their 'higher minds') for counter-usurpation, for thawing the deepest sleep that time can lay upon us, as grounded in 'the consciousness | Of whom they are' infusing 'every image' and 'every thought'. This riddlesome 'consciousness' is diffused throughout existence, and is opposed to the inertia of matter.[2] In the philosophy of nature to which Wordsworth subscribed, both *natura naturans* and *natura naturata* (the organic system and its living components) enjoy consciousness. Because of 'the one life within us and abroad', because there is a realm in which 'all beings live with God, themselves are God',[3] such appositional phrases as 'the sense of God' or 'whatsoe'er is dim or vast' will do alike for what Wordsworth calls 'the Soul of things' (*Prelude*, p. 6). Higher minds are not merely conscious; they are *of* 'consciousness'. They see into 'the life of things', and share in the conscious life of what philosophers call the Absolute, believers call God, and Wordsworth called 'the one life'.

> Oh! Who is he that hath his whole life long
> Preserved, enlarged, this freedom in himself?
> For this alone is genuine liberty (14.130–2)

This 'genuine liberty' belongs to those who live 'by sensible impressions not enthralled', and who enjoy their kinship with the 'consciousness' of the world or the soul of things; those whose natural piety assures them of 'Emotions which best foresight need not fear, | Most worthy then of trust when most intense', and who are sustained by 'delight | That fails not in the external universe' (*1805*, 13.103–119). An apt commentary on

1 Martin Buber, *I and Thou*, tr. Ronald Gregor Smith, 2nd edn (Edinburgh: T. & T. Clark, 1958), 81–2.
2 For Coleridge on consciousness in this sense see Anthony Harding, 'Coleridge, the Afterlife and the Meaning of "Hades"', *Studies in Philology* 96:2 (1999) 204–23, 217, 218–9.
3 From the Peter Bell MS, De Selincourt *Prelude*, p. 525.

this passage, though it was not written as such, was penned by Thomas Carlyle, in one of the essays which inspired what is known as American Transcendentalism:

> According to Fichte, there is indeed a 'Divine Idea' pervading the visible Universe; which visible Universe is indeed but its symbol and sensible manifestation, having in itself no meaning, or even true existence independent of it. To the mass of men this Divine Idea of the world lies hidden: yet to discern it, to seize it, and live wholly in it, is the condition of all genuine virtue, knowledge, freedom; and the end therefore of all spiritual effort in every age.[1]

Wordsworth's version of this 'genuine virtue, knowledge, freedom', however, far from dismissing nature, is presented as the gift of material Nature. In Book 14 Nature is still capable of inspiring insights into that 'Soul of all the worlds' which to Wordsworth—nurtured in empirical intercourse with rocks, water, stones and trees—is the common ground of Nature and of Man.

Wordsworthian Imagination is, in the first instance, a power that 'dissolves, diffuses, dissipates', in short, a solvent. Wordsworth has the good sense to call Coleridge's *primary* imagination, the power that constitutes our world, by another name—'the first poetic spirit of our human life'.[2] Imagination, as such, in Wordsworth's explorations, is prone to wilfulness and waywardness. His poetry recognizes that secondary imagination, the power of the mind to obliterate or suspend what is presented to it, in favour of its own constructs, is both existentially definitive, *and* constitutive of anxiety.[3] There is, that is to say, no essential differ-

---

1   Thomas Carlyle, 'The State of German Literature', *Edinburgh Review*, 1827. The next sentence foreshadows Emerson's mission as outlined in 'The American Scholar': 'Literary men are the appointed interpreters of this Divine Idea; a perpetual priesthood, we might say, standing forth generation after generation, as the dispensers and living types of God's everlasting wisdom.'

2   Coleridge's unsatisfactory defnitions of Imagination in *Biographia* are probably an attempt to put Wordsworthian theory and practice into what Coleridge sees as philosophic terms. The coincidences between (a) the 'infant babe' lines in *The Prelude* and Coleridge's primary imagination, and (b) Wordsworth's commentary on Imagination in 1815 and Coleridge's secondary imagination, are too close to be accidental, but I am inclined to agree with Mary Warnock that Wordsworth is the more cogent on the subject. See Mary Warnock, *Imagination* (Faber & Faber, 1976) 72–130.

3   Wordsworth, like Sartre, associates imagination with consciousness itself: 'Imagination is not an empirical and superadded power of consciousness, it is the

ence between the wilful imagination of the Captain in 'The Thorn' who associates natural imagery with infanticide, and that of the poet in *The Prelude* who associates a similar image cluster with unconscious parricide. Imagination is morally neutral. That is why *The Prelude*'s climactic discussion of Imagination insists that while Imagination is one constituent of 'genuine liberty', it must be completed, as it is not for Oswald, by Love. Wordsworth's discussion throughout *The Prelude* is sceptical of imaginings which refuse to be anchored to empirical realities, and critical of imaginations which abuse the lordship and mastery of mind, especially when they exercise what Coleridge called 'the instinct of all fine minds to totalize' (*CN*, 1: 1606).

In the crisis of Books 10 and 11 of *The Prelude*, Wordsworth, like Oswald, is all too able to imagine the man of the future 'parted as by a gulph from him who had been'; what he needs is the power to cherish 'men as they are men within themselves'. The power of love

> Provokes to no quick turns
> Of self-applauding intellect, but lifts
> The Being into magnanimity. (*1805*, 12.30–32)

In love is grounded that sight 'in everyday appearances' of a new world, not Oswald's affectionless and unmagnanimous 'region of futurity' but 'a world ... fit | To be transmitted' (13.368–71). The succinct and unequivocal statement in the *Cintra*, that 'love and admiration must push themselves out toward some quarter: otherwise the moral man is killed' (*WPW*, 213) explain why Wordsworth's moral crisis led to the writing of *Salisbury Plain* and *The Ruined Cottage*, while Oswald's led to the murder of Herbert and the moral assassination of Marmaduke.

That the public exposure of Oswald's casuistry, drafted in the era of the guillotine, coincides with the era of physical force Chartism is one of those intriguing coincidences, illustrative, perhaps, of the fact that the earthquake is not satisfied at once. Joseph Rayner Stephens, a Methodist minister, was arrested in December 1838 for exhorting his Manchester audience to confront the military with petrol bombs: 'You have only to take a couple of matches and a bundle of straw dipped in pitch, and I will see what the Government and its hundreds of thousands of soldiers will do against this one weapon if it is used boldly': after all, 'a child of

whole of consciousness as it realises its freedom'. Jean-Paul Sartre, *The Psychology of Imagination* (New York: Citadel, 1963), 279.

ten can wield it' (Engels, 237). For some critics (incendiary day-dreams enjoyed something of a vogue in late twentieth-century common-rooms) Wordsworth, and Elizabeth Gaskell, too, should have grasped the need for an epoch of fire-bombs and blood-letting. Surely, it is argued by arm-chair revolutionists, a generation or so of government by revolutionary tribunals would have been worth while, *if* at the end of it, in Professor Teufelsdröckh's words, we were to find ourselves 'once more in a living society'. But Wordsworth had been there, done that, got the T-shirt. He had contemplated serving the revolution; dreamed of being the 'paramount mind' required to oversee the work of renovation; shared the desire to see human being remade, on new principles; he had 'spun' the Terrorists' lust for the guillotine (in the modern sense of 'spin') as comparable to a child's delight in the motion of a windmill; and he had scorned the timid, who failed to see that the revolution could not be the season of true liberty but was its necessary prelude. In his nightmares he had become a prosecutor of the innocent. So he had earned the right to preach temperance. Engels, who confidently predicted that the English revolution would take place in 1847, predicted equally confidently that through it society would be 'born again'. Wordsworth shared Thomas Jefferson's belated recognition that the false dawn of the French revolution had cost the lives of 'eight or ten millions of human beings' over a generation.[1] He wrote to Edward Moxon in 1835 that once an English revolution got under way it would be a generation or more before 'liberty' was established again:

> I have been in the midst of one Revolution in France, and recoil with horror from the thought of a second at home. The Radicals and foolish Whigs are driving the nation rapidly to that point—Soon, alas! It is likely to be found that power will pass from the audacious and wicked to the more audacious and wicked, and so to the still more and more, till military despotism comes in as a quietus; and then after a time the struggle for liberty will recommence, and you, young as you are, should your life be prolonged to the 70 years of the psalmist, will not live to see her cause crowned with success.   (*LY*, 3: 7)

It requires 'jacobinical infatuation' he told the Freeholders of Westmorland in 1818—with a profoundly personal authority wholly unsuspected by those he addressed— to sacrifice 'the near to the remote' (*WPW*, 321).

---

1   *The Portable Jefferson*, ed. Merrill D. Peterson (Harmondsworth: Penguin, 1977), 551.

In July 1844 the *North American Review*, as was still American practice, reprinted entire from the British *Foreign Quarterly Review* of January 1844, an article on Britain as the heart of darkness. It included this harrowing paragraph on mining conditions in Halifax and Bradford where 4000 boys and girls, between 4 and 12 years old, were employed not to tend donkeys, but *as* donkeys, drawing wagons of coal, hewn by naked miners, along lengthy galleries to the foot of the shaft:

> The necessity of employing very young children for this work arises from the low and narrow dimensions of the passage, which is often but twenty, and seldom more than thirty-two, inches high. The poor child … is fitted with a girdle to which a chain is attached that passes between its legs, and is fastened to the wagon behind. Slowly then, through the long gallery, over the broken and sharp surface … the poor wretch creeps on its hands and knees [while] the heavy chain strikes against the legs and excoriates them. And to these sufferings, half-naked girls, from six to twelve years of age, are exposed for twelve hours in the day.[1]

The reporter asks: 'could no sharp cry of anguish, or dull groan under stupefying pain, reach even from the depths of these dreadful pits to the ears of philanthropists of Christian and enlightened England?'

It is salutary to remember that just as the Pinney's Racedown (like Jane Austen's Mansfield Park) had been built on West Indian sugar, My Lord Lowther's money came from the labour of 14,000 miners in the pits of Whitehaven,[2] and Sir George Beaumont's from those of Coleorton. When one considers the tortured state of Wordsworth's relation to his land in the last thirty years of his life, and wonders what impelled him to publish his carefully even-handed assault on class violence in 1842, the titles of both *Guilt and Sorrow* and *The Borderers* seem not inapt. In 1803 he had alluded in a wartime sonnet to his own casuistical justifications of terror in the 1790s:

> I measure back the steps which I have trod,
> And tremble …
> > at the sorrow of the time.

The remark applies as forcibly to his equally casuistical justifications of

---

1   *North American Review*, 59 (July 1844) 17–20, p. 17.
2   Michael Friedman, *The Making of a Tory Humanist*, 79.

aristocratic power in the 1820s and 30s.

One wonders, also, what went through Wordsworth's mind in 1818 when penning his *Addresses to Freeholders of Westmorland*, in which anomalous work he commends an opulent patriarchy and the virtues of old corruption. He had seen the British Constitution vindicated in the outcome of the treason trials of 1794, and he came to accept its privileging of property and aristocracy as preferable to dictatorship. Republicans like John Adams and the Swiss theorist De Lolme had long taught that the British Constitution was, in its essentials, a virtual republic with a titular monarch. Most Commonwealthmen and True Whigs merely wanted to remove its corruptions. But by 1818 Wordsworth had come to admire its 'mellowed feudality' (*WPW*, 328), and to accept that a liberal dosage of 'influence' was required to lubricate the system and to compensate the declining power of the Lords (339–40). For this reason, while it is technically improper under standing orders of the house, for a Peer to 'concern himself in the election of members to serve for the Commons', he supports the practice whereby Lord Lonsdale nominates the candidates for Westmorland. Tom Paine had argued that it is the living, not the dead, who must decide constitutional issues. Wordsworth argues that a corrupt practice found useful '*to the living*' should not be 'rendered useless ... *by the formal repetition of a voice from the tombs*' (326–7, my emphases). Thus, though surely not without a twinge, Wordsworth deploys in the Tory interest Tom Paine's most powerful trope.

Wordsworth still suffered, in 1842, from what his Solitary called 'a panic dread of change'. He had not softened in his view that universal suffrage, prior to universal education, meant government by the worst, and would lead to the intimidation of the worst by the even worse. He imagined a rabble of thousands intimidating the Commons, as the *sans culottes* had led the National Convention, abetted by a licentious press (*WPW*, 335). He may still have believed, as he wrote to H. J. Rose in 1829, that

> The revolutions among which we have lived have unsettled the value of all kinds of property, *and of labour, the most precious of all*, to the degree that misery and privation are frightfully prevalent. We must bear the sight of this, and endure its pressure, till we have by reflection discovered the cause, and not till then can we hope even to palliate the evil. *It is a thousand to one but that the means resorted to will aggravate*

it. (*LY* 2: 25, my italics)

The tumbrils rumbled on. But the uneasy balance, in *Poems Chiefly of Early and Late Years*, between compassion for 'a People mournfully cast down' and rejection of 'social havoc' as likely to multiply their sufferings, suggests that Wordsworth's habitual 'two consciousnesses' were, as happened each time he undertook a major revision, still in harness. In 1835, one of those consciousnesses had produced the poem *Humanity* with its generous anger at the people's 'slavish toil', while another consciousness had issued *The Warning* with its alarmist dread of 'marshalled thousands darkening street and moor'. In 1842, forty-four years after asking the 'gentle reader' to identify with Simon Lee, despite his one eye, his faded jacket and his swollen ankles, Wordsworth was still inviting his audience to see things 'kindly'.

Epilogue

Intimations of Immortality from Recollections of Zeno, Virgil and Ossian

> Thrice with my arms I strove her neck to clasp,
> Thrice had my hands succeeded in the grasp,
> From which the Image slipped away, as light
> As the swift winds, or sleep when taking flight.
> —Wordsworth's *Aeneid* (1823)

> Well sang the Bard who called the grave, in strains
> Thoughtful and sad, the 'narrow house.'
> —*Yarrow Revisited* XII (1831)[1]

> Such ebb and flow must ever be
> —*Lines Composed at Grasmere* (1806)

Shall we 'see them face to face'?

An epitaphic art often implies that 'we shall see them face to face'. But Wordsworth's expressions of such a faith are almost wholly classical, which is to say, knowingly fictive. For the poet who once described earth as the 'the place where, in the end, | We find our happiness or not at all', what follows mortal life is uncertain. Numerous of his critics intuited, even in *The Excursion*, a lack of the confidence one should expect of a Christian writer, and the bolder of them denied that he was a Christian at all. Henry Crabb Robinson cites Richard Cargill to the effect

---

1 Poem 12 of *Yarrow Revisited* is a wry piece on 'The Earl of Breadalbane's Ruined Mansion', 1831. Burns has been identified as co-progenitor of this phrase, but Ossian has priority. The phrase occurs in the first book of *Fingal*; Fingal, Malvina and 'the heroic age' are invoked in poem 15 of the sequence.

that if Christianity means 'faith in redemption by Christ' *The Excursion* is 'no better than atheism'.[1] Nothing in his poetry, at any date, despite Coleridge's plans for *The Recluse*, suggests 'a scheme of redemption' or a system of qualification for the afterlife. After *Intimations*, which (I shall argue later) avoids giving any particular characteristics to its ostensible subject, immortality, the death of John seems to have led him slowly towards the quasi-Christian stance of the *Essays upon Epitaphs* (1810). Eventually, Wordsworth's loss of Thomas and Catherine seems to have brought him into communion with the church, and to such reconciliation with its creed as he ever attained, but the outcome is never radiant, and is sometimes surprisingly shadowed by a mordant humour such as that permitted to his *alter ego* (the Solitary) in *The Excursion*.

For some decades, in his early poetry, Wordsworth's poetic representations of death fluctuated between a Roman sense of Elysian fields, an Enlightenment sense of returning to the elements of nature, and—which is much the same thing—an Ossianic sense of death as joining the numerous 'souls of lonely places'.[2] From *The Vale of Esthwaite*, through *An Evening Walk, A slumber did my spirit seal*, *Lucy Gray* and the Christmas 'spot of time', one meets with passages in Wordsworth that recall Werther's considerably more excessive allegiance to Ossian:

> What a world that exalted soul leads me into! To wander across the heath in the pale moonlight, with the gale howling and the spirits of his forefathers in the vaporous mists! To hear amidst the roar of a forest torrent the faint moans of the spirits in their mountainside caves.[3]

This Ossianic version of the afterlife lingered in Wordsworth's poetry long after he relinquished any formal allegiance to Enlightenment thought—in which death was thought of as returning at a molecular level to the mineral and vegetable world. 'The only difference I know of between life and death' Diderot wrote to Sophie Volland, 'is that at present you live *en masse*, and that twenty years hence you will live minutely, dissolved and dispersed in molecules.' Since molecules are capable of sensibility, this implies little diminution in her capacity to enjoy, and none

1   *Henry Crabb Robinson on Books and Their Writers* (ed. Edith Morley, 1938) 1: 65.
2   The appeal of 'Ossian', according to Ted Underwood's impressive 'Romantic Historicism and the Afterlife', *PMLA* 117:2 (2002) 237–51, was that its vision of death concurred with Enlightenment notions of elemental survival.
3   J. W. von Goethe, *The Sorrows of Young Werther*, tr. Michael Hulse (Penguin Classics 1989), 95.

at all in her capacity to be. 'What lives has always lived and will always live.'[1] It is not entirely clear, even in Wordsworth's most extended considerations of the afterlife in the Fenwick Notes and the 'Essays upon Epitaphs', that he dissents from this view.

If, eventually, Virgil and Ovid, with their vividly realized Elysian presences, rather than 'Ossian' with his vaporous ones, reigned in Wordsworth's poetics of death, they did so in part because of his own experience of the death of John Wordsworth in 1805 and of his children Thomas and Catherine in 1812. Even after the death of John, Wordsworth was able to write in the first of his 'Essays upon Epitaphs', in 1809, that 'a grave is a tranquillizing object: resignation springs up from it as naturally as the wild flowers', but 1812 changed all that. Bereavement helped to bring Wordsworth into communion with the church, and partly reconciled him to its creed, but 'resignation' proved not at all natural. Nothing in the numbed poems he wrote about his double loss expresses hope and even in 1825, the fear 'That friends, by death disjoined, may meet no more' was very real to him.[2]

One Victorian bench-mark of what it means to 'look through death' is Robert Browning's *Prospice*. This rapturous vision of the moment of reunion with Elizabeth imagines the knight of faith approaching death. Browning's knightly speaker knows that if he faces the 'arch-fear' manfully, with unbandaged eyes,

> The fiend-voices that rave,
>   Shall dwindle, shall blend,
> Shall change, shall become first a peace out of pain,
>   Then a light, then thy breast,
>   O thou soul of my soul! I shall clasp thee again …

In Wordsworth, the poems inspired by personal loss achieve no such radiance. His first public treatment of the loss of Catherine is ventriloquized in the most harrowing lines of *The Excursion,* in an extended passage (3.639–705) which accounts for the fact that of all four characters in that poem—Pastor, Pedlar, Poet and Solitary—the one Wordsworth identified with most passionately is the last. For the Solitary, like Wordsworth (and unlike the somewhat featureless 'Poet' in the poem) has lost a daughter.

---

1   Diderot, Letter to Sophie Volland, 15 October 1759 (my translation).
2   From 'O dearer far than light and life are dear', addressed to Mary Wordsworth in 1824.

'Caught in the gripe of death' she was

> conveyed
> From us to inaccessible worlds, to regions
> Where height, or depth, admits not the approach
> Of living man, though longing to pursue. (3.641–4)

Despite the ambivalence over 'height, or depth' the classical arche-types for this longing, in the tales of Virgil and Ovid that possessed Wordsworth in schooldays, are apparent enough. The Elysian exercises of Hawkshead, inspired by the loss of both parents, now return to haunt him as a father.

The *Fenwick Notes* speak simply, and 'for private notice', of how the poem *Maternal Grief,* composed in 1811–13 but not published until 1842, was 'in part an overflow from the Solitary's description of his own and his wife's feelings upon the decease of their children' (174). Wordsworth points out with touching naiveté—speaking as if the Solitary were a real neighbour with whom they sympathized—that Wordsworth and Mary, too, 'lost two of our children within half a year of each other'. *Maternal Grief* expresses Mary's state of feelings between the death of Catherine and that of Thomas, feelings that informed, also the treatment of resig-nation in *The White Doe*. 'Shall I admit', the Mother asks, 'that nothing can restore | What one short sigh so easily removed?' All that remains of Catherine is:

> A shadow, never, never to be displaced
> By the returning Substance, seen or touched,
> Seen by my eyes or clasped in my embrace.
>
> $\qquad$ (*PW*, 2: 51 and *app. crit.*)

'Clasped'. In Browning's *Prospice* and in Wordsworth's *Maternal Grief* and *Laodamia* the word expresses what alone will suffice.

In 1812 Wordsworth's six-line epitaph for Thomas is similarly ter-minal. It begs, in the not altogether persuasive vein of the *Ode to Duty* (which speaks of submitting to 'a new control'), that he and Mary may be taught 'calmly to resign | What we possessed, and now is *wholly* thine'. And in 1814 he wrote that wrenchingly beautiful sonnet to Catherine, *Surprized by joy*. Having achieved sufficient forgetfulness of her death to experience a moment of unaccustomed joy, the poet turns to share that joy with his daughter—'with whom but thee | Deep buried in the silent tomb!' and grieves anew:

> Through what power,
> Even | for the least | division | of an hour,

—the line articulates in its bald and unpoetical diction a pained deliberateness—

> Have I been so beguiled as to be blind
> To my most grievous loss!

Renouncing such 'beguilement', the sonnet closes with the grim recollection that nothing, 'neither present time nor years unborn' will 'to my sight that heavenly face restore'.[1] Heaven, it seems, is not where Catherine is, but what she was.

In *Ecclesiastical Sonnets* (1821–22) Wordsworth writes of another daughter. This time he writes of seeing Dora in a dream ('exactly as here represented') and he records how

> The bright corporeal presence – form and face –
> Remaining still distinct grew thin and rare,
> Like sunny mist; – at length the golden hair,
> Shape, limbs, and heavenly features, keeping pace
> Each with the other in a lingering race
> Of dissolution, melted into air.

The vision is contemplated with the sceptical intelligence appropriate to illusion. Although she was 'no spirit' but 'one I loved exceedingly' the apparition 'spake [only] Fear to my soul' and left him in sadness, rather than joy, as that 'dissolution' already implies. More surprising, perhaps, is the trace in the sonnet of Wordsworth's still Ossianic sense of death. Dora is figured as a *corporeal* presence, yet one that is as capable of dissolution, as was Charles James Fox, and as was the parting Cathmor at the close of *Temora*—'Gradual vanish his limbs of smoak, and mix with the mountain-wind'.[2] Many years before, in the Christmas spot of time in the 1805 *Prelude*, Wordsworth had borrowed from *Fingal* and *Temora* to record a (retrospectively) premonitory encounter with the spirit of

---

1 Intriguingly, this beautiful poem is hidden away in 'Miscellaneous Sonnets' rather than given pride of place among the 'Elegiac Pieces'.
2 *Poems of Ossian*, ed. Howard Gaskill, with an introduction by Fiona Stafford (Edinburgh: Edinburgh University Press, 1996), 291.

his dying father. As the boy Wordsworth looks forward impatiently to the arrival of the horses to take him home for Christmas, waiting at the intersection of two roads, he is surrounded by intermittent mists through which he peers, in hope of seeing the horses that will take him home. In Ossianic retrospect, however, the scene recomposes itself in terms of guilt and admonition. Knowing that he had, however unwittingly, wished away some of his dying father's last mortal moments, he imagines those mists advancing 'on the line of each of those two Roads / ... in such indísputable shapes' (1805 *Prelude*, 11: 355–81)—which shapes allude transparently enough to the 'questionable shape' in which Hamlet's father appears to his son in Act 4 of Shakespeare's play.

Intimations of Elysium

If anything could rouse Wordsworth after the deaths of Thomas and Catherine, it was intimations of Elysium from recollections of Virgil and Ovid. The closest he ever gets to affirming the notion of recognizable personal survival is in his numerous anxiety-laden versions of the failure of Virgilian and Ovidian heroes and heroines to 'clasp' their deceased spouses, versions which begin in childhood and climax in the remarkable 'Laodamia'. The seriousness of Wordsworth's endeavour in this poem of 1814, inspired by the sixth book of the *Aeneid*, is conveyed by his comment that he desired to treat the subject in 'a loftier tone than ... has been given to it by any of the Ancients' and that he bestowed upon it considerable pains (*FN*, 67).

In it Wordsworth returns to the story told by Ovid and by Virgil of how by Jove's consent, Laodamía[1] is granted three hours with 'her slaughtered Lord'. As her lord appears, accompanied by Hermes, the early *Vale of Esthwaite* motifs derived from Orpheus and Aeneas achieve their final expression in Wordsworth's poetry:

> Forth sprang the impassioned Queen her Lord to clasp;
> Again that consummation she essayed;
> But unsubstantial Form eludes her grasp
> As often as that eager grasp was made.
> The phantom parts—but parts to re-unite,
> And reassume his place before her sight

---

1   In Wordsworth's Englished Latin, husband and wife are both pronounced as a trochee followed by an amphibrach, or Léo-damáya and Próte-siléus.

The grieving Wordsworth sides, quite transparently, with the resistance mounted by Laodamía to the pious instructions of her immaterial husband that she reconcile herself to his dissolution.[1] Protesiláus's Olympian advice to his widow is to 'control rebellious passion' because 'the Gods approve | The depth and not the tumult of the soul' (rather as the Wanderer counsels the Poet in *The Ruined Cottage*). When Laodamía pleads that if Hercules retrieved Alcestis from death, and Medea's spells restored Aeson, surely the gods might also indulge their love, the plea is met with the stern injunction 'Peace'. For a moment she is pacified, but only because

> In his deportment, shape, and mien, appeared
> Elysian beauty, melancholy grace,
> Brought from a pensive though a happy place.

He comes, he says, from a place without fears or strife, where 'The past [is] unsighed for and the future sure'. He speaks

> Of all that is most beauteous, imaged there
> In happier beauty; more pellucid streams,
> An ampler ether, a diviner air,
> And fields invested with purpureal gleams;
> Climes which the sun, who sheds the brightest day
> Earth knows, is all unworthy to survey.

But as Protesiláus departs, the lesson of resignation unlearned, Laodamia shrieks and dies. For thus exhibiting the weakness also shown by Orpheus and Persephone in their respective trials, she is sentenced by 'the just Gods whom no weak pity moved' to dwell for an appointed time apart from the 'happy Ghosts that gather flowers | Of blissful quiet 'mid unfading bowers' (*PW*, 4, 267–72).

'No poet', says Douglas Bush, 'has absorbed with finer understanding, or rendered with more wistful beauty, the spirit of Virgil's picture of

---

1   For Wordsworth's identification with Laodamia see the extended reading of this poem in Judith W. Page, *Wordsworth and the Cultivation of Women* (Berkeley: University of California Press, 1994): 'Why does Wordsworth feel so strongly for this character? Laodamia's tragic resistance to the consolations of religion and the afterlife attracts Wordsworth more than the un-Wordsworthian heroism of Protesilaus because he himself has known the power of the passions associated with his experiences in France and those of his mourning for his brother and children'. Moreover, where Protesilaus is 'abstract' his wife speaks '"the genuine language of passion"', i.e. in figures (Page, 83).

Elysium.'[1] Equally, it seems to me, only the Virgilian inspiration allows him to write this positively of 'heaven'. Elsewhere, Wordsworth's sense of an afterlife seems to evolve from a somewhat heterodox Judaeo-Christian position in childhood, through adolescent Ossianism, towards a quasi-pantheist content with sharing in the life of things, of which one of his greatest expressions is *A slumber did my spirit seal*. When Wordsworth is at his most impressive on the subject, as in the Lucy and Mathew suites of 1798–99, he betrays little assurance of *individual* survival.

The obsession with contacting 'the other side' began early, in the Hawkshead period, and its major expression is Wordsworth's implied desire (in *The Vale of Esthwaite*) to visit the Cumbrian underworld to speak with his father—like some latter day Aeneas—in 'dark Helvellyn's inmost womb'. Along with numerous attempts at epitaphs, two shorter poems are also of some interest. One is the sentimental imitation of Catullus, entitled 'The death of a Starling' of which the second stanza—published by Coleridge in the *Morning Post* in 1798—reads:

> Yet art thou happier far than she
> Who felt a mother's love for thee.
> For while her days are days of weeping
> Thou, in peace, in silence sleeping
> *In some still world, unknown, remote*
> The mighty Parent's care hast found,
> Without whose tender guardian thought
> No sparrow falleth to the ground.

'Still', 'unknown, remote'; the tones already anticipate the 'sunless land' of *Extempore Effusion* and the 'eternal silence' of *Intimations*.

The specific question of Elysian illumination—as in the 'purpureal gleams' of *Laodamia*—is raised first in the highly accomplished Hawkshead poem, 'Sonnet written by Mr— Immediately after the death of his wife' (1787). Here death is associated with the image in which Wordsworth will later summarise the betrayal of the French revolution, the death of the sun, and the sonnet betrays an uncertain balancing of earthly sunlight, religion's moonlight and a (sunless) 'bright morn':

> The sun is dead—ye heard the curfew toll,

---

1   Douglas Bush, *Mythology and the Renaissance Tradition in English Poetry* (New York: Norton, 1963), 63.

> Come, Nature let us mourn our kindred doom;
> My sun like thine is dead—and o'er my soul
> Despair's dark midnight spreads her raven gloom,
> Yes, she is gone—he called her to illume
> The realms where Heaven's immortal rivers roll.

From this Eurydicean moment, the widower recoils in the sestet to call upon 'Religion's moonlight ray | To cheer me through my long and lonely night | Till Heaven's bright morn leads on the Eternal day'. Scholarship, often most assiduous in answering irrelevant questions, informs us that the parish registers have not yielded the name of the widower. One would be more interested to discover where it is supposed that 'Heaven's immortal rivers roll', why its realms should need to be 'illumed', and what sort of perplexity and obscurity concerning our notions of death leads the schoolboy to the contradiction between the dark heaven of line 6, which needs the widower's wife to 'illume' it, and the 'bright morn' promised in the conventional closing line.

Just as much perplexity and obscurity, perhaps, led to the astonishing stanza of Intimations (prior to Coleridge's public protest in *Biographia*) in which the six-year-old 'mighty prophet! Seer blest!' who knows the truth we toil 'all of our lives to find' also knows that the grave 'is but a lonely bed without the sense or sight | Of day or the warm light, | A place of thought where we in waiting lie' (*PW* 4, 282). In some moods, William and Dorothy found this heterodox thought congenial enough. In April 1802 Dorothy records lying in a trench in 'John's grove' while Wordsworth speculated on lying thus in the grave listening to 'the *peaceful* sounds of the earth' knowing 'that our dear friends were near'. The heroine of *We are Seven* in 1798, the speaker of *To a Sexton* in 1800, the man of 1802, and the poet of *Intimations* in 1804 are all agreed: our graves are green, our hearing unimpaired, and we wait in peace. What we wait for, presumably, is expressed in a well-known song to do with articulation of bones ('dem bones, dem bones, dem *dry* bones…'). After which, in *Intimations*, comes 'the eternal Silence'. But we might equally be awaiting molecular or misty re-emergence into the life of the fells.

Heaven, as far as Wordsworth can envisage the state, is 'still', 'unknown, remote', 'sunless' and 'silent'. On the whole, Elysium is more inviting. Its climes, we are told, are sunless because their light transcends the sun's. So, logically, must heaven's be, if God is light. But poetry does not function through mathematical equations and it is counter-intuitive to read 'sunless' as meaning 'sun-surpassing'. Neither 'sunless' in the *Extempore Effusion*—'How soon has brother followed brother | into the sunless land'—nor the 'the eternal silence' of *Intimations* makes Heaven much more inviting than the 'still world, unknown, remote' to which starlings are consigned in that early imitation of Catullus. Nor is the afterlife made a lot more inviting, or more personal, in any of the cluster of poems that precedes the *Intimations* Ode in Wordsworth's arrangement of his collected works—the *Epitaphs and Elegiac Pieces*.

In *The Prelude* Wordsworth makes two possibly contrary affirmations. One is that 'our home | Is with infinitude' (*1805* 6.539). The other is that this 'very world' is the place 'where, in the end, | We find our happiness or not at all'. There is of course no reason to assume that the 'invisible world', the world referred to in the Simplon Pass lines as revealed 'when the light of sense | Goes out', means 'the beyond'. It makes more sense if the entire passage is read as a declaration that in acts of imagination an imagined world, grounded in the mind, usurps on the material world that is imaged by our senses. But one can hesitate over the meaning of 'home' and 'infinitude' in the continuation:

> Our destiny, our nature, and our home,
> Is with infinitude, and only there—
> With hope it is, hope that can never die,
> Effort and expectation and desire,
> And something ever more about to be.

Those who choose to interpret this reference to a Romantic programme of endless becoming as referring instead, or as well, to immortality, can cite, in corroboration, Wordsworth's argument for immortality in the first of the *Essays upon Epitaphs*, which were designed to support Coleridge's labours in *The Friend*, and which argument may be germane to *Intimations*. One of the major arguments in the first essay is based upon the veneration for death found in the pre-Christian Simonides (*PrW* 2, 52). It echoes another poem for John, *The Daisy*, which records the comfort the Wordsworths found in the discovery and respectful formal burial of John's drowned body after six weeks 'beneath the moving sea'. Much of the first essay rehearses the implied argument of *Intimations* that the sense of immortality is strong in childhood, co-eval with the birth of reason: the child grasps, intuitively, Wordsworth says, that if a running stream has a source it must also have a destination, which destination can only be 'a receptacle without bounds or dimensions;—nothing less than infinity' (*PrW* 2, 51). Here, it would seem, the 'receptacle' is God, our point of origin, and our eternal home, but whether God is more than a Spinozistic 'source' and 'receptacle' remains obscure.[1]

Wordsworth clearly did believe in some kind of immortality for some part of us. Yet the Fenwick note on *Intimations*, dictated in 1843, actually avoids comment on Wordsworth's mature beliefs. Instead he affirms that when he was '*impelled* to write this poem on "the Immortality of the Soul"' he decided to make what use he could of the doctrine of pre-existence. There is something shifty about claiming that he by no means 'meant to inculcate such a belief' while pointing out, nevertheless, that 'in revelation there is nothing to contradict it'. He confides to Miss Fenwick that he found it difficult *in childhood* 'to admit the notion of death as a state applicable to my own being' because of 'the indomitableness of the spirit within me' and that, brooding on the stories of Enoch and Elijah, he used *almost* to persuade himself 'that whatever might become of others I s^d be translated in something of the same way to heaven'.[2] Both manoeuvres—the pre-existence hare and the ascension rabbit—successfully deflect attention from the question of whether he still believes what he believed then, or whether he believes now in the resurrection of the body, and if so, in what sense. It is the same in each of Wordsworth's utterances on the matter: the belief takes the form of an inability to apply the notion of death to one's own being, and it is strongest in childhood. In Christopher Wordsworth's *Memoirs* Wordsworth is quoted as saying that 'I could not believe that *I* should lie down quietly in the grave' and speaks of his infantine sense of 'absolute spirituality, my "all-soulness", if I may so speak'.[3] In the *Essays on Epitaphs* (1810) he says that 'If we look back upon the days of childhood, we shall find the time is not in remembrance when, with respect to our own Being, the mind was without this assurance.' A letter to Mrs Clarkson in 1815 refers to 'an *indisposition* [in youth] to bend to the law of death, as applying to

---

1   I am reminded of Tom McFarland's use of that term in his discussion of Spinoza in *Coleridge and the Pantheist Tradition*.

2   *The Fenwick Notes*, 160. Coleridge makes a comparable point more philosophically in a notebook entry of c. 1826 [Notebook 39 f. 36^v]: 'What is [the assurance of immortality] but the impossibility of believing the contrary? ... The moment that the Soul affirms, I am, it asserts, I cannot cease to be'. Cited in J. Robert Barth, SJ, *Coleridge and Christian Doctrine* (New York: Fordham University Press, 1987), 187.

3   *Memoirs*, 2: 476

our particular case'. None of these passages contains an overt commendation of this position as a viable one for maturity. One might, on this evidence, and in the light of the body of great poetry devoted to coming to terms with mortality, conclude that Wordsworth focuses on his childhood beliefs so as to avoid offending Miss Fenwick with his maturer scepticism, having put away childish things, not least when he wrote the 'Lucy' poems.

And yet. The first *Essay on Epitaphs* describes as 'forlorn, and cut off from communication with the best part of his nature' a man who should ascribe a child's faith in immortality to either 'blank ignorance' or 'unreflecting acquiescence' in what s/he has been taught. Moreover, the same essay makes the (to me) astonishing remark that 'it is to me inconceivable, that the sympathies of love towards each other, which grow with our growth, could ever attain any new strength, or even preserve the old, after we had received from the outward senses the impression of death' if that impression were not counteracted by what he earlier referred to as 'an intimation or assurance within us, that *some part of our nature is imperishable.*'[1] Again, if that were not enough, 'with me the conviction is absolute, that, if the impression and sense of death were not thus counterbalanced, such a hollowness would pervade the whole system of things, such a want of correspondence and consistency … that there could be no repose, no joy' (52). Strong language. Could someone as pantheistically inclined as Wordsworth think that a belief in personal survival was either viable, or necessary to the growth of love or to the moral life? The implication is so astonishing that one forgets to ask the obvious questions: what is meant by '*some part of our nature*' (other than what Diderot meant) and by '*imperishable*' (likewise). Just what Wordsworth did believe on these two points is impossible to say.[2]

1   *PrW*, 2: 50, 51, my emphases. He is, at that point paraphrasing Weever's *Ancient Funerall Monuments within the United Monarchie of Great Britaine. Ireland and the Islands adiacent* (1631) which work (according to Owen and Smyser) is in turn quoting, without acknowledgement, from Camden's *Remaines Concerning Britain.* What Camden calls 'the presage or fore-feeling of immortality, implanted in all men naturally', Coleridge, in *Aids to Reflection*, will call a 'pre-assurance'. Strangely, Coleridge seems not to have written of such 'pre-assurance'—as opposed to a more routine belief in reward and punishment after death—before the *Ode* or the *Essay*, which may account for his veneration of the *Ode* as tantamount to revelation.

2   Anthony Harding in 'Coleridge, the Afterlife, and the Meaning of "Hades"', *Studies in Philology*, 96:2 (Spring 99) 204–223, quotes a notebook entry of surprising indefiniteness—'the Soul may & probably must survive the Body; but in what state and con-

Elegies and Epitaphs

As Wordsworth conceded at the start of his second *Essay upon Epitaphs*, in a churchyard brimful of 'faithful Wives, tender Husbands, dutiful Children, and good Men of all classes' one may wonder 'Where are all the *bad* People buried?' It is the duty of epitaphs, he goes on, to create a 'picture ... of lasting ease | Elysian quiet, without toil or strife' in which all one is conscious of is 'silent Nature's breathing life'. I am, of course, paraphrasing the argument of the *Essay* in phrases from *Elegiac Stanzas Suggested by a picture of Peele Castle*, written in 1805 after the death of John. The 'Essay' does not cite this poem overtly, yet the poem informs the *Essay*. Contemplating Peele Castle for four 'summer weeks', the poem begins, the Form of the Castle was every day 'sleeping on a glassy sea'. It 'trembled' a little but 'it never passed away'. In *fancy* even 'the mighty deep' seemed 'the gentlest of all gentle Things'. To peruse a series of epitaphs, he says in the *Essay*, creates 'sensations akin to those which have risen in my mind while I have been standing by the side of a smooth sea, on a Summer's day'; one is pleased by the absence of detraction, though conscious of the anxieties and vices and rancour which must have agitated the hearts of 'those who lie under so smooth a surface'. One may retain the consoling image of 'an unruffled sea' while one's fancy penetrates into the depths, with accompanying thoughts of shipwreck, and even of 'monsters of the deep' (*PrW* 2, 63–4).

Epitaphs soften and idealize, but as Wordsworth had claimed more generally in the first essay, the character of the deceased *ought* to be seen 'as a tree through a tender haze or a luminous mist, that spiritualises and beautifies it'. The mist 'takes away' whatever is discordant, but the image nonetheless 'is truth, and of the highest order' because only then does one see what before 'had been only imperfectly or unconsciously seen'. So the truth offered by the idealising epigraph 'is 'truth hallowed by love—the joint offspring of the worth of the dead and the affections of the living!'. The test of this truth is for one 'whose eyes have been sharpened [into the faults of a good man] by personal hostility' to observe the transformation that takes place on 'tidings of his death': the 'charac-

---

dition is another question... Shall its Life meet with Life? or shall it be Life in Death and in a World of Death?'—and comments: 'the issue for Coleridge' was not whether there was an afterlife, but 'whether anything peculiar to the individual human being, to the person we know in this life, survived' (210).

ter' idealised in such a moment by filtering of inessentials approximates to what the deceased may be assumed to be, in reality, 'as a Spirit in heaven'. This lower case reference to heaven is, even in the essays, about as close as Wordsworth comes to considering the Christian meaning of death.

Although the opening of the second *Essay upon Epitaphs* of February 1810, five years after the death of Captain John Wordsworth, draws deeply upon personal associations, Wordsworth claims to be inspired mainly by working on his nine translations of the Epitaphs of Chiabrera. These compose the first of 17 items in the *Epitaphs and Elegiac Pieces*, which category of poems precedes, in all collected editions after 1815, the *Ode: Intimations of Immortality from Recollections of early Childhood*. His interests in the *Essays* seem to be theoretical and technical, and the second and long third essays take the form of practical criticism on a variety of epitaphs from the age of Chaucer to the corruptions of the age of Pope. The most powerful sentiments are those which gloss the uncanny recurrence on his poetry of that credal phrase 'the living and the dead' his career-long point of contact with Christian terminology. A parish church-yard, with its reminder of the 'general home' towards which we are travelling, is he says 'a visible centre of a community of *the living and the dead*' (56); its best epitaphs are 'the joint offspring of the worth of *the dead* and the affections of *the living*' (58); a grave (which is itself 'a tranquillising object', from which 'resignation … springs up … as naturally as wild flowers'), is much enhanced by an epitaph in which the deceased, through what Wordsworth calls a 'tender fiction', appears to address the living, so as to unite 'the two worlds of *the living and the dead*' (60); and the desire even of the migrant poor to be buried among their forefathers exemplifies 'the wholesome influence of that communion between *the living and the dead* which combining the place of burial and that of worship tends to promote'. Indeed it is the *dead*, throughout the essays, rather than their saviour or their priest, who have the most to say to the living, and the place of worship is manifestly secondary to the place of burial—the former being significant mainly for bringing the living to commune with their dead.

The Elegiac Stanzas suggested by a Picture of Peele Castle in a Storm (1805) have all the enigmatic quality of Wordsworth's mourning poetry at its best. They communicate the stoicism the poet has not yet arrived at in *The Ruined Cottage* (in which he is overborne by Margaret's tale), which he tries to realize in the Lucy poems, and which he dramatises, with benefit of distance, in *Michael*. As Morris Dickstein says, 'What comes out in the Lucy poems … is that Wordsworth is the man of feeling who desperately longs for the condition of not-feeling, the insensibility that might free him from the distinctly human trials which are his subject'.[1] But for one anonymous reference to 'Him whom I deplore'—Captain John Wordsworth—one could take *Peele Castle* to be a purely theoretical meditation on the passage from an illusioned to an unillusioned state of existence. The primary motif of the early part of the poem is borrowed from *Intimations*, the loss of 'the gleam | The light that never was on sea or land'—a light projected from the youthful mind. The year in which Wordsworth was Peele Castle's 'neighbour' was 1794, when he still saw the plated shield of human life from 'the golden side', as he puts it in *The Prelude*, and would have fought to attest the quality of metal that he saw. One is therefore at liberty to associate this gleam with utopian illusions. *Had he* painted Peele Castle at that time he *would have* 'planted it' he says

> Beside a sea that could not cease to smile;
> On tranquil land, beneath a sky of bliss.
>
> Thou shouldst have seemed a treasure-house divine
> Of peaceful years; a chronicle of heaven;
> …
>
> A Picture had it been of lasting ease,
> Elysian quiet, without toil or strife

Now, however, 'humanised' by 'a deep distress', the loss of 'him who I deplore',

> Not for a moment could I now behold
> A smiling sea, and be what I have been;
> The feeling of my loss will ne'er be old;
> This, which I know, I speak with mind serene.

Sir George's painted castle 'cased in the unfeeling armour of old time' exemplifies what one needs if one is to brave 'The lightning, the fierce

---

1   Morris Dickstein, '"The Very Culture of the Feelings": Wordsworth and Solitude', in Johnston, Kenneth R. and Gene W. Ruoff, eds. *The Age of William Wordsworth: Critical Essays on the Romantic Tradition*. New Brunswick and London: Rutgers University Press, 1987, 315–43, 323.

wind, and trampling waves'. So adamant is the poet's apparent stoicism that one may admire the imaginative force of 'trampling', without thinking of the particular circumstances—the loss of the *Abergavenny* and its trampled commander—that inform it. The condition of being housed in 'a dream at distance from the Kind', is now formally and experientially renounced. Blindness will not suffice:

> But welcome fortitude, and patient cheer,
> And frequent sights of what is to be borne!
> Such sights, or worse, as are before me here.—
> Not without hope we suffer and we mourn.

But what hope exactly?

The maritime imagery returns a year later in a more distant elegy for Charles James Fox, or *Lines composed at Grasmere ... having just read ... that the dissolution of Mr Fox was hourly expected* (1806). 'Dissolution': the same disconcerting term that is applied to Dora's imagined death in *Ecclesiastical Sonnets*. Here, the apparent pun on parliamentary dissolution is compensated for in the grandeur of the six stanzas commemorating the Whig leader, one of 'the great and good':[1]

> A Power is passing from the earth
> To breathless Nature's dark abyss.

What do such passings mean?

> That man, who is from God sent forth,
> Doth yet again to God return?—
> Such ebb and flow must ever be,
> Then wherefore should we mourn?

Written two years after *Intimations* (though helpfully preceding the Ode when it appeared in *Poems, in Two Volumes*) the lines appear to gloss and underwrite the Ode's sense of the soul's journey from and back to that 'God who is our home'. Here, though, remembering the 'something' that 'rolls through all things' in *The Poem upon the Wye*, the metaphor of 'ebb and flow' seems barely to concern itself with the survival of individuated souls. The lines also provoke an overwhelming question: is 'breathless Nature's dark abyss', in the poem's stoic logic, another expression for

---

1   A note to *Excursion* 7:1002 (*CWRT*, 2., 523.), citing the foundation charter of Furness Abbey, associates the term 'dissolution' with the 'Transit Gloria mundi'.

'God who is our home'? [1]

There is no 'mourning' as such in the deeply personal elegy *Written after the Death of Charles Lamb* (1835), though there is the intensest possible feeling as the poem builds from its opening address 'To a good man of most dear memory' to its exclamation, 'O, he was good, if e'er a good man lived!' The words Christian and Heaven make an appearance in this 1830 poem. It also bows to God as the author of wedlock and siblinghood, 'Without whose blissful influence Paradise | Had been no Paradise; and earth were now | A waste where creatures bearing human form, | Direst of savage beasts, would roam in fear, | Joyless and comfortless.' Just as Wordsworth in *The Poem upon the Wye* moves through the valley of the shadow of death fearing no evil 'for Thou are with me'—thou being Dorothy, not the Holy Ghost—so in Lamb's case, though in phrases sufficiently separated to camouflage a related sacrilege: 'Unto thee … Was given … a Sister'. Such poems underwrite Arnold's 'Ah, love, let us be true | To one another! for the world … | Hath really neither joy, nor love, nor light, | Nor certitude, nor peace, nor help for pain'. The desire that this brother and sister should know no separation leads to what may be Wordsworth's most positive reference to an afterlife in the conventional sense. He comforts Mary in the last line of the poem, with the thought of that 'blest world where parting is unknown', a blessing that may—or may not—imply that such a 'world' exists.

Five years later, Wordsworth read in a newspaper of the death of 'the Ettrick Shepherd' James Hogg, a man for whom he felt no particular regard, except perhaps in his association with the 'Border-Minstrel', Sir Walter Scott. He went up to his room and emerged half an hour later, we are told, having written an eleven-stanza elegy for Hogg, Scott, Coleridge, Lamb, himself, George Crabbe and Felicia Hemans. It is a poem, Bill Ruddick argued, in which there occurs 'a spontaneous, almost instantaneous filtering and selecting process' of the kind recommended in the Essays upon Epitaphs.[2] No filtering was required in the case of Lamb, but in the case of Coleridge an enormous repression of years of estrangement, and accumulated resentments, produced these astonishing lines:

---

1   My enigmatic speculation on the stoicism of Wordsworth's elegies is carried very slightly further in my 'Mr Bryant's Wordsworth,' *TWC*, 46 (Summer, 2015).

2   William Ruddick, 'Subdued Passion and Controlled Emotion: Wordsworth's Extempore Effusion upon the Death of James Hogg', *CLB* n.s. 87 (July 1994) 98–110, 99.

> Nor has the rolling year twice measured,
> From sign to sign its stedfast course,
> Since every mortal power of Coleridge
> Was frozen at its marvellous source;
>
> The rapt one of the godlike forehead,
> The heaven-eyed creature sleeps in earth:

'Stedfast'? As contrasted with Coleridge's 'moral delinquency' (Ruddick, 104) the epithet licenses a question whether some scepticism might be present in the lines. No rancour is present, but there is perhaps a gentle questioning of transcendental idealism. Is there an implication that Coleridge's powers were indeed 'mortal', and marvellous because they were wholly human, 'godlike' though his forehead may have been? The heaven-regarding creature now 'sleeps in earth' and wears, like any Shropshire lad, the turning globe.

Coleridge and Lamb and Hemans, in her 'breathless sleep', attract the poem's most feeling epithets. Honesty forbids Wordsworth to speak more than neutrally of the fact that death 'has closed the Shepherd-poet's eyes', or that Crabbe, too has 'gone before'. Crabbe does get six lines of the poem (or seven including 'ripe fruit, seasonably gathered'), as many as do Scott, Hogg, and Coleridge. But they run, with stoical gloom:

> Our haughty life is crowned with darkness,
> Like London, with its own black wreath,
> On which with thee, O Crabbe! forth-looking,
> I gazed from Hampstead's breezy heath.
>
> As if but yesterday departed,
> Thou too art gone before …

Crabbe, the naturalist, is knowingly evoked as one concerned with London's 'black wreath', rather as Ruskin watched the storm-cloud of the nineteenth century darken over Coniston, but he hardly looms as a companionable being. Wordsworth's detachment comes out in the Fenwick note, where he scorns Crabbe's need for the spur of public acclaim, and carelessness about his art—an acerbity which attracts from Dora the delightful riposte: 'daddy dear, I don't like this—think how many reasons there were to depress his Muse; to say nothing of his duties of a priest'; perhaps, she offers sweetly, public praise merely 'put it into his heart to try again' (*PW*, 4: 460–61). Nonetheless, that crown of darkness crystallising into a 'black wreath' is one of the poem's most telling images. It recalls antithetically the 'coronal' of *Intimations*, and the brightness of the sleeping city in *Westminster Bridge*. It draws its dark, arrested energy from the imagery of flux and annihilation that follows the first quartet of deaths in the poem:

> Like clouds that rake the mountain-summits,
> Or waves that own no curbing hand,
> How fast has brother followed brother,
> From sunshine to the sunless land!

Such clouds might, of course, reflect the radiance of the setting sun in *Intimations*, but they derive in the first instance from Ossian, and hark back to the peopled mists of *An Evening Walk*.

The high water-mark of intellect in this age

So Emerson called the *Ode: Intimations of Immortality from Recollections of Early Childhood*.[1] Francis Jeffrey, of course, thought the (then untitled) ode the most 'illegible and unintelligible' of the Poems of 1807, and in terms of intelligibility he has a point. Anna Seward thought it a 'manifest imitation' of Coleridge's *Dejection*, and an excursion into 'the dark profound of mysticism'.[2] Thomas Noon Talfourd's 1820 essay 'On the Genius and Writings of Wordsworth' declared it the 'the noblest piece of lyric poetry in the world'.[3] Gerard Manley Hopkins was inspired by the ode to class Wordsworth among those 'very few men', Plato pre-eminently, whom common repute adjudges to 'have *seen something*': it may even come to be the opinion of the world at large 'that in Wordsworth when he wrote that ode human nature got another of those shocks, and the tremble from it is spreading. This opinion I do strongly share; I am, ever since I knew the ode, in that tremble.'[4] What that *something* is, he does not say.

---

1   *The Collected Works of Ralph Waldo Emerson*, ed. Alfred R Ferguson, et. al. (Cambridge, Mass.: The Belknap Press of Harvard University Press, 1971 ff), Volume 5, English Traits, 168. His exact words are: 'The high-water mark which the intellect has reached in this age'.
2   Robert Woof, *William Wordsworth: The Critical Heritage* (London and NY: Routledge) 251.
3   Woof, 870, 852.
4   *The Correspondence of Gerard Manley Hopkins and Richard Watson Dixon*, ed. Claude Colleer Abbott, 2nd edn (London: OUP, 1955) 148. Letter XXXVII, pp. 145–

For Coleridge, Emerson, Poe, Peabody, Melville, Whitman, Thoreau and Hopkins the Great Ode was the inescapable text: its phrases echo in their writings, taking on the colouring of the echoing substance—spiritual, transcendental, macabre, sceptical. Coleridge began the canonization in a celebrated passage of *The Friend*. The climactic eleventh essay of the series 'On the Grounds of Morals and Religion' takes as its starting point the ninth stanza of the ode, with its mysterious thanks and praise for

> Those shadowy recollections,
>   Which, be they what they may,
> Are yet the fountain light or all our day.

Coleridge's soaring commentary on those 'shadowy recollections' leads to the suggestion that 'enlightening enquiry' will lead man at last 'to comprehend gradually and progressively the relation of each to the other, of each to all, and of all to each' (*Friend*, 1: 511). His essay finds in the notion of a 'world of spirit' nothing less than 'the substantiating principle of all true wisdom, the satisfactory solution of all the contradictions of human nature, of the whole riddle of the world' (524). Poe's rather clearer but more Pantheist solution to 'the riddle of the world', in *Eureka!*, is that deity spends eternity, like a cosmic Emerson, in 'perpetual variation of Concentrated Self and almost infinite Self-Diffusion', and that what are called his creatures 'are really but infinite individualisations of himself' and are, by faint indeterminate glimpses, conscious 'of an identity with God'.[1]

Thomas Noone Talfourd's reasons for celebrating the ode make a comparable point rather less philosophically. On the one hand, he argued in 1820, the ode celebrates all those innate qualities of childhood that 'it is the first object of Calvinism to extinguish'.[2] It therefore appeals to the modernising intelligence desirous of being rid of all that baggage. On the other, it expresses the desire—perhaps the single most pervasive of desires in the coming Victorian age—that around the peaks of modernity there should still cluster some clouds of spirituality. 'What a gift did we then inherit!' says Talfourd,

159, 32 October 1886.
1   For more on Poe's use of Coleridge's use of Wordsworth see 'Intimations in America', *OHWW* (2015) 767–85.
2   *New Monthly Magazine*, November 1820 (Woof, 852).

> To have the best and most imperishable of intellectual treasures—the mighty world of reminiscences of the days of infancy—set before us in a new and holier light; to find objects of the deepest veneration where we had only been accustomed to love; to feel in all the touching mysteries of our past being the symbols and assurances of our immortal destiny! The poet has here spanned our mortal life as with a glorious rainbow, terminating on one side in infancy, and on the other in the realms of blessedness beyond the grave, and shedding even upon the middle of that course sweet tints of unearthly colouring. (Woof 870)

Those 'realms of blessedness beyond the grave', surely, come from Talfourd's desires, not from the poem. He then quotes stanzas V and IX, those parts of the ode that Coleridge implies in *Biographia* could only be found intelligible by a small class of readers, those who have 'been accustomed to watch the flux and reflux of their inmost nature, to venture at times into the twilight realms of consciousness, and to feel a deep interest in modes of inmost being, to which they know that the attributes of time and space are inapplicable and alien, but which cannot be conveyed, save in symbols of time and space'.[1] The latter of these two stanzas, says Talfourd, constitute 'such a piece of inspired philosophy—we do not believe exists elsewhere *in language*' (Woof, 870, my emphasis). What they mean, he does not say.

That 'inspired philosophy' relates to the 'something that doth live' (IX) in the embers of remembered childhood—some gleam beneath the 'freight', 'weight' and 'frost' of custom that survives our descent from 'being's height' (VIII) and it occupies in the main one giant sentence. 'The thought of *our* past years in *me* doth breed | Perpetual benediction' not for the hope delight and liberty of childhood but for a less predictable assortment of experiences. These include 'those obstinate questionings | Of sense and outward things, | Fallings from us, vanishings' of which Wordsworth speaks in the Fenwick note—the sense he had in childhood that apparently external things were 'inherent in my own immaterial nature'—and occasional 'Blank misgivings of a Creature | Moving about in worlds not realized', experiencing a vertiginous attraction to the 'abyss of idealism' to which the Fenwick note also refers. Other gifts for which he raises thanks are more positively toned, namely 'those first affections, | Those shadowy recollections, | Which, be they what they

---

1   *BL* 2: 147, 154. To be more exact, Coleridge says this of the ode in general, in page 147, but quotes these stanzas only on pages 153–4.

may, | Are yet the fountain light of all our day, | Are yet a master light of all our seeing; | Uphold us, cherish and have power to make | Our noisy years seem moments in the being | Of the eternal Silence'.

Francis Jeffrey could have been forgiven, it seems to me, for wondering what 'those first affections' and 'those shadowy recollections' refer to, especially when the poet glosses them as 'be they what they may'. Neither phrase has been used so far, so we have apparently referential terms with no obvious referent. Do they belong only to the infant in stanza V, still trailing his clouds of glory, or equally to the six-years child in stanza VIII engrossed in imitative games? And how do either affections or recollections (which appear to point in contrary directions—the human and natural world in one case, and the celestial home in the other) both constitute 'truths', let alone 'truths that wake | To perish never' (IX)?

Of all Wordsworth's poems this one seems to depend most upon ideas outside itself, and one's interpretation of its various cruces will differ considerably depending on whether one looks elsewhere in Wordsworth's work, or to Vaughan's very helpful and much briefer analogue, *The Retreat*, or to philosophers of Coleridge's persuasion—to Plato's the *Phaedo*, for instance, or the *Enneads* of Plotinus. There are many ways of looking 'through death' (X). The poignancy of 'To me the meanest flower that blows can give | Thoughts that do often lie to deep for tears' has no specific philosophical content. The poem may not persuade one that 'heaven lies about us in our infancy' other than in the *Prelude* sense of the infant's world being beautified by the mother, which surely pertinent sense is not explored in *Intimations*. While the premise that we come 'from God who is our home' is entirely compatible with Wordsworth's core pantheism, the notion that Nature is a prison-house and that our only light is otherworldly constitutes such a break with almost everything in the *oeuvre* prior to 1804, that it leads to an *impasse*. What does one do with the assurance in line 73 of the poem, that the Westward-bound youth 'still is Nature's Priest'? That 'still' also has no antecedent within this poem, so it effects a ruinously inconsistent bridge to the pantheistical close of *The Poem upon the Wye* where the poet overtly is 'a worshipper of Nature'. And interpretation of the mysterious lines 'High instincts before which our mortal Nature | Did tremble like a guilty Thing surprised', though not impossible, relies to an exceptional degree on guesswork—or an implied invitation to construct your own argument from desire.

Coleridge, of course, accepted that invitation. Needing to believe in immortality, and familiar with Kant's argument for innate ideas and 'postulates' of the moral life, he found the sense of the poem 'perfectly plain' (*BL* 2: 147). *The Friend* had already paraphrased *Intimations* IX quite succinctly as showing the 'elevation of the spirit *above the semblances of custom and the senses to a world of spirit*, this life in the idea, even in the supreme and godlike, which alone merits the name of life and without which our organic life is in a state of somnambulism' (*Friend* 1:524). In *Aids to Reflection*[1] Coleridge appears to reflect on Wordsworth's speculation cited above from the first of the *Essays upon Epitaphs* that the 'fore-feeling' of immortality is among Reason's 'earliest offspring'. Consider, for instance, this meditation on infancy, which appears to suggest, as does the ode, that the light of Reason, and 'those first affections' and 'those shadowy recollections' are tantamount to one and the same thing. Coleridge does not mention Wordsworth but he marries stanza 7 of the ode, and his own and Wordsworth's treatment of childhood, to his own sense of 'great First Truths':

> The great and fundamental truth and doctrines of religion, the existence and attributes of God, and the life after death, are in Christian countries taught so early, under such circumstances, and in such close and vital association with whatever makes or marks reality for our infant minds, that the words ever after represent sensations, feelings, vital assurances, sense of reality—rather than thoughts, or any distinct conception. Associated, I had almost said identified, with the parental voice, look, touch, with the living warmth and pressure of the Mother, [whose 'upraised eyes and brow are to the child, the Type and Symbol[2] of an Invisible Heaven!'] ... these great First Truths, ... in the preconformity to which our very humanity may be said to consist, are so infused,[3] that it were but a tame and inadequate expression to say, we all take them for granted. (*Aids*, 157)

Somewhat surprisingly, it is only in *Aids to Reflection*, twenty one years

1   With apologies to the Bollingen Coleridge editors, my quotations are from *Aids to Reflection and Confessions of an Inquiring Spirit* (Bell & Sons, 1913; repr. New York: Cosimo Classics, 2005).

2   Compare Wordsworth's 'The types and symbols of Eternity' in the (very Coleridgean) diction of the *Prelude* Book 6: 571 (the Simplon Pass).

3   'Infused' may suggest that Coleridge is correcting Wordsworth's error in 'blest the infant babe', *Prelude* 2:262ff: 'Along his infant veins are interfused | The gravitation and the filial bond | *Of nature* that connect him *with the world*' (my italics).

after *Intimations*, that Coleridge first speaks clearly of the 'pre-assurances' implied in that poem:

> I am persuaded, that as the belief of all mankind, of all tribes, and nations, and languages, in all ages, and in all states of social union, it [the belief in immortality] must be referred to far deeper grounds, common to man as man; and that its fibres are to be traced to the tap-root of humanity.

And the argument concludes, magisterially:

> No pre-assurance common to a whole species does in any instance prove delusive .... nature is found true to her word. (*Aids*, 237)

That may sound like a friendly nod to 'Nature never did betray | The heart that loved her', but much of *Aids to Reflection* is corrective of Wordsworth. Coleridge's climactic assault on the materialism of Priestley and his disciples backhandedly identifies *The Poem on the Wye* as responsible for misguided doctrines that it has become Coleridge's life-mission to contest. Wordsworth's poem exemplifies 'contagion', 'unhealthful influence', and a 'false and sickly taste' that has led some religiously constituted people to prefer 'A sense sublime | Of something far more deeply interfused' [Coleridge quotes six lines of the poem at this point], over 'the Jehovah of their Bible' (*Aids*, 270). And the uncited text which is his ally in this rooting out of the naturalistic heresy is of course *Intimations*. On the very next page after quoting Wordsworth's inadvert heresy, Coleridge's peroration quietly annexes *Intimations* once again, giving his précis of stanza IX a still more doctrinal inflection than he gave it in *The Friend*:

> Now I do not hesitate to assert, that it was one of the great purposes of Christianity, and included in the process of our Redemption, to rouse and emancipate the soul from this debasing slavery to the outward senses, to awaken the mind to the true criteria of reality.

There, at last, is the simple and direct expression of the redemptive argument that Wordsworth failed to prioritize in *The Prelude* and *The Excursion*.

For Coleridge 'that immortal sea | Which brought us hither' was, one supposes, the ocean of Platonic ideas, rather than the Darwinian one from which, for most intellectuals today, if not most people, all life emerged. As medicine for Coleridge—and the poem was, after all, initially conceived in that light—*Intimations* affects, or affects to affect, an argument of the kind to which the *Opus Maximum* and *The Recluse* were directed, an argument based upon eternal verities and a redemptive process. It is doubtful whether *Intimations* can ever be read in quite his way again. Without Coleridge's peculiar confidence in things unseen, the imagistic logic of the *Ode* seems no more concerned with a celestial afterlife than does the *Extempore Effusion*, in which the procession of poets passed in that gloomiest of valedictions, 'from sunshine to the *sunless* land'.[1] Along with the Calvinist baggage which Talfourd was pleased to have lost, Coleridge's Platonic baggage has gone missing also, and Emerson's new world optimisms are momentarily in abeyance. What Carlyle sardonically referred to as 'transcendental life-preservers' have been decommissioned. Without them, for all its rhetoric of compensations, the only heaven *Intimations* can truly envisage—and it is in this that its difference from Vaughan's *The Retreat* is most marked—is that of infancy. Compared with its argument for pre-existence—which is overt, emphatic and (we are told) no more than a poetic idea—its argument for immortality was never more than implied. Consequently, for a reader who lacks such instinctive pre-assurances, it is no longer there.

But it seems not to matter. Wordsworth's writing, I have argued in this volume, is designed to reconcile. Nowadays, for most readers, the poem's consolatory power may derive from nature and nature's continuities, just as Dorothy takes the place of the divine comforter in *The Poem upon the Wye*, and Charles and Mary do for each other in the lines for Lamb. This poet, after all, never lyeth because he nothing affirmeth. As an expression of an ability to take *disinterested* pleasure in the sound of 'mighty waters rolling evermore'—waters with all their Darwinian freight of quite another kind of pre-existence—the *Ode* somehow crosses the bar between comforting faith and stoic rigour. Neither those mighty waters nor 'the clouds that gather round the setting sun' have any bearing on personal immortality. Least of all does the poem's terminal *memento mori*, 'the meanest flower that blows'. But like Ted Hughes's post-Romantic harebell in the poem *Still Life*—a trembling harebell in whose delicate veins 'sleeps the maker of the sea'—such images movingly juxtapose the grand sources of life, water and sunlight, and all their fragile yet perpetal syntheses.

---

1   I am indebted to Graham Davidson for making me aware that an earlier version of this sentence (despite surviving two revisions!) made no sense.

That the poem takes refuge in musical enigma is not surprising. 'Points have we all of us within our souls | Where all stand single'. Wordsworth, it is now beginning to be understood, was his own man intellectually. The work of Bruce Graver, Adam Potkay and John Cole, in uncovering the intellectual foundations of Wordsworth's thought in his classical education at Hawkshead and Cambridge, and his self re-education at Racedown, has established that alongside his immense attraction to the Roman poets, Wordsworth was deeply invested in Stoic thought, both rhetorical and ethical.[1] Alan Richardson has confirmed much of H. W. Piper's thesis concerning his investment in enlightenment science. And Mark Bruhn is now establishing with unprecedented particularity, that the Wordsworth Coleridge reverenced as a philosopher in 1797 had indeed sufficient foundation in philosophic enlightenment to stand his ground, or to pursue currents of his own. Thanks to these scholars we may be on the cusp of understanding, at long last, the thinking that takes place in such poems as *An Evening Walk* and *The Poem upon the Wye*, and *The Prelude*. If seeing 'no line where Being ends', or sensing 'something far more deeply interfused', or drawing consolation from the 'ebb and flow' of spirit, and 'that immortal sea | Which brough us hither' sound as if they might be fusions of pantheism, stoicism, and the speculations of science upon our maritime origins that is probably because they are.

Stoicism is certainly writ large in Wordsworth's startling equanimity in the face of universal conflagration in *The Prelude*: if all life should perish, he assures himself, what he calls the 'living Presence' would yet exist, and life begin again.

> A thought is with me sometimes, and I say—
> Should the whole frame of earth by inward throes
> Be wrenched, or fire come down from far to scorch
> Her pleasant habitations, and dry up
> Old Ocean in his bed, left singed and bare,
> Yet would the living Presence still subsist
> Victorious; and composure would ensue,
> And kindlings like the morning—presage sure

1 Bruce Graver, 'The Oratorical Pedlar', in Don H. Bialostosky and Lawrence D. Needham (eds), *Rhetorical Traditions and British Romantic Literature* (Bloomington, IN: Indiana University Press, 1994), 94–10; Adam Potkay, *Wordswoth's Ethics*, (Baltimore, MD: Johns Hopkins University Press, 2012); John Cole, 'Wordsworth and Classical Humanism', *Oxford Handbook of William Wordworth* (OUP, 2015) 563–80.

> Of day returning, and of life revived.
>
> (*CWRT*, 3: 202; *Prelude*, 1850: 5: 29-37)

The notion that life is periodically consumed in fire and then reborn goes back to the very origins of Stoic thought in Zeno of Citium, whose ideas are reflected in Cicero and in Virgil. But a closer contemporary analogue to such a vision of extinction and renewal, in somewhat showier style, is to be found in Erasmus Darwin's *Economy of Vegetation* (1791), Canto 4: 384–92: there, even if all the constellations should 'Headlong, extinct, to one dark center fall' Nature would mount from her funeral pyre, 'Another and the same'. Darwin's poem, which Wordsworth read in 1798 (Wu, 45), helped to inspire the hymn to the 'one life' that concludes the two-part *Prelude*. Moreover, Darwin's *The Temple of Nature,* published posthumously in 1804—just in time to inform those 'children sporting on the shore' in *Intimations*—explains the reason for Darwin's and Wordsworth's confidence in 'Immortal Nature' and its powers of regeneration. 'Organic life beneath the shoreless waves | Was born', Darwin explains; first 'forms minute, unseen by spheric glass' from which there spring, after innumerable generations, 'countless groups of vegetation ... | And breathing realms of fin, and feet, and wing'.[1]

Or as Wordsworth rephrases Darwin's thought in his 'Ode—1817':

> Her procreant cradle Nature keeps
> Amid the unfathomable deeps
> And saves the changeful fields of earth
> From fear of emptiness or dearth.[2]

This Darwinian utterance seems quite as 'incautious' as his earlier confession of being 'a worshipper of nature' in *The Poem upon the Wye*, and it disappears after 1827. Speaking to Isabella Fenwick of this poem he said that it was 'composed to place in view the immortality of succession, where immortality is denied, as far as we know, to the individual creature' (*Fenwick Notes*, 68). Does 'the individual creature' include human ones? Miss Fenwick would have thought it did not. But the poet?

Faith in that 'procreant cradle' surely underlies Wordsworth's many equable benedictions: Margaret 'sleeps in the calm earth'; Lucy has no individual 'force', she 'neither hears nor sees', but she participates,

---

1   *The Temple of Nature*, 1. 295-7, 301–2. Online. Romantic Circles.
2   *CWRT*, 3: 114, lines 35–8. Composed 1817, included in *The River Duddon* (1820) 'Changeful fields' became 'peopled fields' in the 1827 version entitled 'Vernal Ode'.

and grandly, in the diurnal course of a living globe. Think too, of the strange impasse in 'We are Seven', where Wordsworth's young heroine seems already in full accordance with the author of the 'Lucy' poems, and with Zeno, and Cicero, and Spinoza, and Whitman, and even with the Wanderer's melodious and consoling thought, amid the passing generations,

> Of Life continuous, Being unimpaired;
> That hath been, is, and where it was and is
> There shall be,—seen, and heard, and felt, and known,
> And recognized,—
>
> (*Excursion* 4, 751–4)

My treatment in this chapter of Wordsworth's questioning of death and immortality has, I confess, been quite as wilfully enigmatic as Wordsworth's own. Perhaps Wordsworth believed in imperishability 'for some part of our nature', as he put it, because he could not bring himself to do otherwise; or perhaps it was because he had met the spirits of the fathers lingering by the roadside near Hawkshead, as Elysian presences are wont to do. Those classical archetypes allowed Wordsworth to write with a freedom that is not permitted to the apostles of faith. Perhaps he simply accepted that whatever is 'deeply interfused', must always 'ebb and flow'. Or perhaps he agreed with Hazlitt and Mill (as Adam Potkay has argued)[1] that it is the (relatively) immortal life of the kind that counts.

Wordsworth himself may have made do with thoughts of 'Life continuous, Being unimpaired', but he knew there were limits on what could be 'recommended to faith' (*FN*, 161), and it is, after all this poet's heart-easing business to console and reconcile. Whatever our structure of belief regarding what Whitman called 'the impenetrable mystery of the afterwards'—whether we await translation in some way to heaven (*FN*, 160), or embrace the thought of our 'dissolution', or welcome a return to 'breathless Nature's deep abyss'—we can all agree that

> The clouds that gather round the setting sun
> *Do* take a sober colouring from an eye
> That hath kept watch o'er man's mortality.

1 *Wordsworth's Ethics*, 173–8.

INDEX

Abercrombie, Lascelles 364
Abrams, M. H. 197, 199
Akenside 83, 100, 123
Alfred the Great, King of England 40, 64, 75, 88, 119, 321, 332, 342
American Revolution, The 63, 123, 125, 129, 184, 296, 330
Ammianus Marcellinus 46, 47, 51
Aneirin 18–20, 23, 29, 35, 64, 68, 70–4, 76, 77–8, 88, 116, 230, 337 *The Gododdin* 73, 77–8, 80, 267, 320
Arnold, Matthew 51, 71, 232, 261, 313, 392; *Study of Celtic Literature* 51, 66, 72
Arthur and Arthurianism 35, 68–74, 76, 77, 78, 85, 88, 115 6, 284–5, 291; *The Egyptian Maid*, 285–8
Asterix the Gaul 56
Averill, James 84

Bagehot, Walter 111
Bainbridge, Simon 259–60, 261
Ball, P. M. 364
Ballad of Chevy Chase, The 255, 271
Bannockburn, 76, 105
Barden Fell and Barden Hall, 267–8
Bards and Bardism, 18–21, 23, 25, 26–7, 35 nn, 36, 45, 46, 49, 51, 53, 59–63, 86–90, 116, 214, 254, 271, 29; survival into 18th century, 67; see also Aneirin, Dafydd ap Gwilym, Gay's *Bard*, Llywarch Hen, Myrddin, Taliesin.
Barker-Benfield, G. J., 261, 262
Barrell, John 194–5
Bateson, F. W. 234-5, 247
Baum, Joan 206
Beattie, James 67, 88, 92; *The Minstrel* 88–9, 99, 142

Beaumont, Lady 82, 163, 265, 319
Beaumont, Sir George 102, 266, 341, 373
Beaumont, Sir John, *Bosworth Field*, 269–71
Beaupuy, Michel 25, 127, 184, 189, 198, 217, 272, 345
Bede, the Venerable 75, 111, 116, 223; Wordsworth on, 117-8
Beer, John 12, 247
Bewell, Alan 11, 26, 186, 196, 208, 233, 345
Bialostosky, Don 146, 149, 154, 155, 212, 256, 293, 311
Blackwell, Thomas 214
Blackwood's 234, 263
Blair, Hugh *Critical Dissertation*, 87
Blake, William 54, 56, 60, 62, 63, 112, 113, 153, 154, 155, 161, 162, 166, 190, 241, 286, 317, 335, 338, 340, 369
Blencathra 50, 74, 118, 229
Booth, Mark 181
Borlase, William 44
Borrowdale 40, 52, 102-5, 110, 119
Bosworth Field, Battle of 69, 268-70
Boudicca 27; in *Resolution and Independence,* 27, 149
Bradley, A. C. 196
Bragg, Melvyn, 278
Brinkley, Robert A. 12, 226
British and Foreign Review 354, 355, 356, 357, 360
Bromwich, David 12, 178, 179, 259
Brooke, Stopford 107
Brooks, Cleanth, 103, 104
Brougham, Henry, Lord 325, 329, 340, 343-4
Browning, Robert 131, 144, 160, 359, 378–9
Bruhn, Mark 12, 125, 401
Buber, Martin 369
Burke, Edmund, 43, 157, 184, 196,

Wordsworth from Humanities-Ebooks

The Cornell Wordsworth: a Supplement, edited by Jared Curtis ††

The Fenwick Notes of William Wordsworth, edited by Jared Curtis, revised and corrected †

The Poems of William Wordsworth: Collected Reading Texts from the Cornell Wordsworth, edited by Jared Curtis, in 3 volumes †

The Prose Works of William Wordsworth, Volume 1, edited by W. J. B. Owen and Jane Worthington Smyser †

Wordsworth's Convention of Cintra, a Bicentennial Critical Edition, edited by W. J. B Owen, with a critical symposium by Simon Bainbridge, David Bromwich, Richard Gravil, Timothy Michael and Patrick Vincent †

Wordsworth's Political Writings, edited by W. J. B. Owen and Jane Worthington Smyser. †

Other Literary Titles

John Beer, *Coleridge the Visionary*

John Beer, *Blake's Humanism*

Richard Gravil, *Wordsworth and Helen Maria Williams; or, the Perils of Sensibility* †

Richard Gravil and Molly Lefebure, eds, *The Coleridge Connection: Essays for Thomas McFarland*

John K. Hale, *Milton as Multilingual*

Simon Hull, ed., *The British Periodical Text, 1796–1832*

W. J. B. Owen, *Understanding The Prelude*

Pamela Perkins, ed., *Francis Jeffrey: Unpublished Tours.*†

Keith Sagar, *D. H. Lawrence: Poet* †

Trudi Tate, *Modernism, History and the First World War* †

Irene Wiltshire, ed. *Letters of Mrs Gaskell's Daughters 1856–1914* †

† Also available in paperback, †† in hardback
http://www.humanities-ebooks.co.uk
all PDF ebooks available to libraries from Ebrary and EBSCO